The Ultimate Protest

THE ULTIMATE PROTEST

*Malcolm W. Browne,
Thich Quang Duc, and
the News Photograph
That Stunned the World*

RAY E. BOOMHOWER

HIGH ROAD BOOKS | ALBUQUERQUE

ISBN 978-0-8263-6570-5 (cloth)
ISBN 978-0-8263-6571-2 (ePub)

Library of Congress Control Number: 2023947997

Founded in 1889, the University of New Mexico sits on the
traditional homelands of the Pueblo of Sandia. The original
peoples of New Mexico—Pueblo, Navajo, and Apache—since time
immemorial have deep connections to the land and have made
significant contributions to the broader community statewide.
We honor the land itself and those who remain stewards of this
land throughout the generations and also acknowledge our
committed relationship to Indigenous peoples. We gratefully
recognize our history.

Cover photograph by Malcolm Browne (AP Photo)
Designed by Felicia Cedillos

Composed in Alegreya

As always, for Megan

"In a free society the duty of all newsmen is to tell all of the people all of the truth all of the time. The newsman is obliged to fight forces that interfere with this vital process. From there on, it is the job of the people themselves to make up their minds how they feel, and for what or for whom they will fight. But to decide wisely, the people must have the facts, and that is our job."

—MALCOLM W. BROWNE, APRIL 11, 1967

"You can't write the story if you're dead."

—STANLEY KARNOW

Contents

Prologue

THE SINGLE, SMALL-CALIBER BULLET ripped through the thin, aluminum skin of the Piasecki H-21 troop-carrying helicopter just two feet from where Malcolm W. Browne, the Saigon bureau chief for the Associated Press, sat near the chopper's rear door. The Viet Cong insurgent who fired the bullet at the helicopter, nicknamed Geisha Girl by its American crew from the 121st Aviation Company, had remarkable luck, as his projectile "tore through a pressure line and four engine control cables," Browne recalled, and bounced against other parts of the aircraft before exiting out the other side. The helicopter's engine stopped, and the correspondent could hear someone shout, "We're going in! Hang on!"[1]

It had been a busy day in early January 1964 for the Geisha Girl. The helicopter was involved in what Browne described as "a particularly dangerous kind of field operation" known as an "eagle flight." Such missions involved more than five helicopters packed with seasoned troops, often South Vietnamese rangers or marines, seeking out VC strongpoints that had been pinpointed by intelligence reports. Browne, who had been reporting about the conflict since his arrival in 1961, noted that the helicopters flew at low-enough altitudes to draw enemy fire, at which point the troops disembarked and engaged in sharp, bloody exchanges with the VC. "Often, the eagle troops racked up excellent successes against enemy units," he wrote, "and brought back weapons and severed heads as trophies."[2]

The Geisha Girl's pilot and copilot had prepared for their dangerous duty by donning bulky, bullet-resistant flak vests before slogging down a muddy path to the flight line at the airstrip near Ca Mau, South Vietnam. "Pilots climbed up into their plexiglass-surrounded cockpits and slipped on heavy, white flight helmets," Browne remembered. "Switches were flicked, and red instrument lights glowed from dashboards." Outside the chopper, its two gunners waited for the starting signal from the pilots. Nearby, Vietnamese soldiers stood up to adjust their field packs, which included cooking utensils, while, here and there, Browne saw, there "was a live duck hung by its feet from a soldier's pistol belt. The Vietnamese army, perhaps more than other armies, travels on its stomach." Finally, the reporter heard the order to depart. "Pilots adjusted themselves in their seats, changed their engine mixtures, and tuned up radios for communications checks," he reported. "Forward gunners took their positions at the open doors on the right side of the H21s, just behind the cockpit. They fed belts of ammunition into their guns and swung the gun mounts around into firing positions. Rear gunners gestured from their positions at open doors on the left side near the tail for the troops to come aboard." Those inside the helicopter had to sit or squat on the floor, as there were no seats. Browne could see the glow from cigarettes piercing the gloomy morning light as the chopper cruised down the runway, "much like conventional airplanes taking off. Hovering or taking off vertically puts too much load on the engine of a loaded H21."[3]

In addition to participating in eagle flights, the Geisha Girl delivered supplies to Nam Cam, a town that had been attacked and damaged by the VC the previous night, leaving behind seven dead, sixteen wounded, and seven missing South Vietnamese soldiers. The helicopter also made stops at "other dangerous places" in the area, including Cai Nuoc, Dam Doi, and Cha La, all of which had recently been overrun by the Communists, Browne wrote. With its day almost over, Geisha Girl was only two miles away from its home base. "Helicopters had been making the same approach to the air strip all day long without incident," he noted, "and the crew was almost ready to relax when the slug hit." As the gunners kept the enemy busy by blazing away at the ground below, Captain Joseph Campbell of Drexel Hill, Pennsylvania, threw the two rotors overhead into auto rotation, a technique used by chopper pilots that kept their crafts "from dropping like rocks when their engines quit," Browne said. If the helicopter had enough forward speed, the rotors continued to whirl, keeping the aircraft aloft enough so it could glide in for a safe landing. If a helicopter did not have enough speed, its pilot had to dive to make it happen. "He cannot do this if he is too near the ground," the newsman pointed out. "For this reason, slow-speed flight at an altitude lower than two hundred feet can be fatal in the event of engine failure."[4]

Luckily for Browne and the Geisha Girl crew, Campbell had just enough speed to survive. "The ground came up fast," Browne remembered. "Campbell skimmed the banana-shaped craft over a high dike, and then pulled the nose up sharply to flair the ship out on soft ground. It bumped down into a bramble patch, and everything was suddenly very silent." Both gunners, Private First Class Edward Weglarz of Haddonfield, New Jersey, and Private First Class David M. Sands of Gassaway, West Virginia, scrambled out the doors in just a few seconds. With their guns at the ready, the two men sought cover in the brambles, establishing a defensive perimeter against an expected enemy attack. "The Viet Cong has never shown mercy to downed helicopter men," Browne noted, "and has never taken one alive."[5]

According to established evacuation procedures for such incidents, the crew had to make sure to remove the chopper's guns and as much ammunition as they could carry. "If it looks as though the Viet Cong is certain to capture the aircraft," Browne wrote, "it must be destroyed. The guerrillas love to capture guns and radios from downed helicopters." The evacuation from the Geisha Girl went "smoothly, quickly and silently," he said, but no enemy appeared. "Apparently the guerrilla who shot us down was content with his one lucky shot," Browne concluded. Within a short time, a second H-21 had landed near the crash site. The correspondent and crew hastily scrambled through the brambles to climb aboard the rescue craft. Safe at the base, the survivors smoked cigarettes while a company of Vietnamese troops moved out to provide security at the downed Geisha Girl. "This sort of thing happens often in South Viet Nam," Brown informed his readers, "but even the most seasoned helicopter crew never gets accustomed to it. Sometimes everyone comes out without a scratch. Sometimes a few people are hurt. Sometimes everyone aboard is killed."[6]

Trying to relax after the ordeal, an impressed Weglarz told Browne that the VC gunner must have been pleased with the result of his day's work.

Weglarz pointed out that for the cost of only about seven cents, how much it cost to produce the bullet, the insurgent had been able to down an American helicopter costing thousands of dollars. Using such "cost-effective weaponry," Browne noted, had become a hallmark of the way the VC operated in its fight against the government of South Vietnam's president Ngo Dinh Diem. During an operation in the An Xuyen region, Browne and the Army of the Republic of Vietnam soldiers he accompanied came upon a hidden weapons factory that manufactured mortars and shotguns. "They made the shotgun ammunition from short lengths of brass tubing, to which they soldered old French ten-centime coins, the kind with a hole in the middle," Browne recalled. "The workers crimped percussion caps into these holes and loaded the finished cases with powder and shot."[7]

The crash sobered Geisha Girl's crew. One of the men told Browne that he and the other Americans engaged in such operations knew their jobs were not safe; as Browne reported, of the first hundred combat deaths in South Vietnam, forty-three had been in helicopters. "We just keep hoping from one day to the next that our luck won't run out," the crewman commented to the reporter. "But the job has to be done, and you can't keep worrying about it."[8]

Browne's day was far from over. Returning to Saigon, he went to the AP office on Rue Pasteur Street, rolled a sheet of paper into an old Underwood typewriter, and began writing an article to send over the wires about his perilous adventure. Still aching from the crash, however, Browne discovered that nothing he put on paper seemed to capture what he experienced. "It's astonishing how often war correspondents face writer's block after witnessing dangerous battles," he observed, "often falling back on stupid clichés just to finish some kind of dispatch."[9]

As he finished his piece, Browne received a telephone call from a diplomat he had always assumed also worked as an intelligence agent. The man called to invite the newsman to a black-tie cabaret show at the Caravelle Hotel that evening for which the other guests would include senior Vietnamese officials Browne had been trying to interview; he accepted the invitation. Years later, he could not remember the conversation he had with the officials that night, but knew that the featured performer was Juliette Greco, a well-known French singer and actress. "Her sultry songs were balm to her footsore listeners, and it crossed my mind, not for the first time, that Saigon was a city of astonishing contrasts," he recalled. Enraptured by Greco's voice, Browne glanced out the window overlooking the Saigon River and could see streams of red tracers "arching through the darkness beyond the river, and occasional yellow flashes marked the impacts of shells."[10]

Feeling restored, Browne returned to his apartment, located over his office, only to find, stuck under his door, three blue-and-white envelopes containing messages from his superiors at AP, reading: "Unipress [United Press International] has three choppers down but your crash has only one stop if correct need matcher sapest foreign." Translating the cable language, Browne knew he had to confirm if UPI's account was correct and, if so, produce a comparable story as quickly as he could. "I wearily picked up the phone and began trying to raise a U.S. military spokesman," Browne said.[11]

Despite the frustrations Browne faced when dealing with his superiors and those in authority who wished to tailor the news to fit their own needs, he persevered, believing that the free press would remain alive and vibrant. He took as his inspiration the example of the great Irish reporter William Howard Russell, who had been sent by the *Times of London* to cover the Crimean War. British authorities threw Russell out of its headquarters area, going as far as depriving him of food, shelter, and transport. The British commander, Lord Raglan, prohibited his officers from talking to the reporter. "Despite their hostility, Russell covered every major action of that war, in mortal danger most of the time," Browne noted.[12]

In his dispatches for the *Times*, Russell did more than just "root for the home team," Browne recalled. Although he had touted the bravery of British soldiers—the "thin red line tipped with steel"—Russell let his readers know that the commanders who had ordered the disastrous Charge of the Light Brigade into the deadly fire of Russian artillery had also mishandled every other aspect of the war. They had bungled the supply situation, leaving their men with inadequate stocks of blankets and uniforms, and British soldiers were "dying in large numbers of illnesses and infected wounds, for want of medical attention," Browne said. Russell's words mattered: "Parliament and the English public were electrified. The commanders were changed, Florence Nightingale went to the Crimea (incidentally founding the Red Cross) and the fat was pulled out of the fire." Because of his articles, Russell became known as "the man who saved an army." Browne always tried to remember that his idol had not earned that title by being "a brainless journalistic cheer leader."[13]

CHAPTER 1

Korea, 1956

THE US ARMY DEUCE-AND-A-HALF truck clattered and banged its way over a pockmarked road through Seoul, South Korea. The driver aimed his cargo toward its destination, the war-damaged village of Munsan-ni, located north of the Imjin River close to the dangerous demilitarized zone with Communist North Korea. Malcolm W. Browne, a native New Yorker, college graduate, and one of the approximately thirty American replacement soldiers aboard, peered through the back of the canvas-covered truck. He observed that three years of war had "obliterated the rice fields and villages, swept away the inhabitants and left a wasteland roamed by packs of ferocious wild dogs; to some of us on that truck, the broad, muddy Imjin seemed akin to the [river] Styx." A laboratory chemist for the Foster D. Snell company in civilian life, but trained as a tanker by the military, Browne had orders to stay for a few days at the headquarters of the Nineteenth Regiment, Twenty-Fourth Infantry Division, while awaiting his final assignment.[1]

Killing time before his next stop, Browne—wondering what he had gotten himself into for his two-year hitch in the service—got to know some of the regiment's men. The soldiers lived and worked in green Quonset huts and canvas tents scattered against a landscape dominated by high hills, barbed wire, and minefields. "As I sized up the place I discovered that its inhabitants were friendly, helpful and casual—very unlike regular army troops in domestic posts," Browne recalled. "It was then that I learned something about fighting men in general: the closer they are to enemy guns, the more they behave like human beings rather than cardboard soldiers." Curious, he wandered into a hut emblazoned with a sign reading "PIO," marking it as the home of the unit's Public Information Office. Inside were a half-dozen soldiers busy preparing the Nineteenth's weekly newspaper, as well as articles and images destined for the Pacific edition of *Stars and Stripes*, the US Armed Forces daily newspaper. While Browne talked with the men, one of them, Private First Class Mike Poust, mentioned that a member of the team was about to return home, leaving an opening in the outfit. Poust asked Browne if he had any interest in working for the PIO. "If you go out with an armored recon unit you'll spend your whole tour eating dust and seeing nothing but the DMZ," Browne quoted Poust as telling him. "Join us and you'll see the world—or at least the greater metropolitan Munsan-ni area."[2]

It took less than a minute for Browne to decide that he would do less damage to the American cause by working for the regiment's newspaper than by maneuvering an M48 Patton tank through the Korean countryside. He made his choice, although growing up he had never had much respect for journalists or even displayed any interest in following the news. "In fact, I was not a great newspaper reader as a kid, I read the papers every now and then, but I never took them seriously," he remembered. Instead, Browne displayed an early passion for science, especially chemistry. After attending Swarthmore College in Pennsylvania and New York University, he spent five years as a laboratory research chemist for Foster D. Snell Inc., a consulting company whose chemists and engineers supplied their expertise to firms wishing to improve their products. He eventually found himself spending less time in the laboratory and "more time writing reports and articles about the results of scientific research. I felt it was time for me to make a break."[3]

Poust cleared Browne's transfer with his commanding officer and the young recruit moved his barracks bag to a vacant bunk at the back of the PIO hut. The structure had electricity but lacked plumbing and depended upon a balky kerosene stove for heat during the frigid Korean winter. "On that day I became a journalist," he noted. Browne and his colleagues worked weekly to fill a dozen mimeographed pages with such items as training exercises, movie schedules, and soldiers' unusual hobbies, including raising eels from the Imjin River as pets. Browne wore on his shoulder a patch proclaiming him an "Official US Army Correspondent" and enjoyed special privileges. "We were never required to stand in unit formations, pick up cigarette butts or even submit to regular inspections," he remembered. "Best of all, we had access to a jeep and could travel throughout the regimental sector, which extended quite a distance."[4]

Browne's job also gave him the opportunity to visit the South Korean capital, Seoul, where he met and became friends with some university students. Through their interactions, he could feel "the seeds of rebellion sprouting" against the dictatorship of Syngman Rhee. Browne found himself falling in love with Asia and became "hooked on journalism—even the wretched version the army had taught me." Sometimes his duties were interrupted by feints from North Korean troops threatening another invasion, prompting the GI journalists to grab their "shovels, sleeping bags and carbines, and dive into open trenches, where we sometimes remained for several days." Browne found life stuck in slit trenches to be "excruciatingly dull," but at least it gave the opportunity to finish reading a Jane Austen novel he had with him. The army also provided Browne a bit of sartorial splendor that set him off from his contemporaries. As a soldier he grew to hate the olive-drab uniforms he had to wear while on duty. On the day he got out of the service, he came across a sale on red socks at an Eighth Army post exchange in Seoul; he bought them all and started wearing them daily. Browne believed that by "standardizing I could avoid the annoyance of losing socks in the wash when I got out of the Army, and I've worn them ever since."[5]

After fulfilling his military commitment in 1958, Browne left chemistry and threw himself into a new profession. "I wished I could tell you that I prepared for a career in journalism by the light of a candle in a log cabin" by reading the works of such luminaries of the profession as Ben Franklin, William Randolph Hearst, and others, he joked. "But no. As a matter of fact, I am an accidental journalist." Browne first worked for a small newspaper in Middletown, New York, the *Daily Record*. While there he gained experience as a foreign correspondent, traveling to Cuba to cover the chaotic early days of Fidel Castro's revolutionary government. "The assignment wasn't lucrative, but for me it was pure gold," Browne noted. After his time in Cuba, he left the *Daily Record* for a job with the country's leading news service, the Associated Press, serving in its bureau in Baltimore, Maryland. In 1961 AP general manager Frank Starzel, seeking a permanent correspondent to head the agency's bureau in Saigon, South Vietnam, selected Browne to replace John Griffin, the reporter then covering the region. "It is my belief that Asia is the fulcrum of contemporary history, and I want to have a part in reporting it," Browne told AP editors. While undergoing a week of training at the news agency's home office in New York, he remembered the thrill of preparing for overseas travel— picking up his ticket, preparing his passport and necessary visas, purchasing supplies (a map, flashlight, and Band-Aids), saying goodbye to his friends, and signing his will.[6]

Before he left the United States Browne received a warning from an AP editor that he should avoid producing any travelogue articles on what he saw in Southeast Asia, sticking instead to hard news from the war-torn region. After all, wire services such as the AP did not tolerate "agenda journalism," and Browne embraced his employer's "depersonalized, factual approach of wire service news coverage." He avoided, whenever possible, confrontation and tried "to keep personal views out of my reporting, because I was employed as a journalist, not a pamphleteer." A former French colony, Vietnam had been divided by terms of the 1954 Geneva Accords drafted by representatives from France, the United States, the Soviet Union, China, Great Britain, Vietnam, Laos, and Cambodia. The agreement led to the removal of French forces from Vietnam and temporarily, it was believed, split the country at the Seventeenth Parallel. Eventually, South Vietnam came under the direction of President Ngo Dinh Diem, a Catholic whose tightly controlled anti-Communist regime received American support. North Vietnam was led by Ho Chi Minh, whose Viet Minh forces had defeated the French at the Battle of Dien Bien Phu and had driven the colonial occupiers from the country. Browne, who could speak French, had resolved to treat his assignment "as a piece of observation that should be as accurate and as telling as possible, looking for the truth behind the truth." He anticipated being plunged into "an existence as alien as Mars," and wondered, as he wandered New York's streets before leaving for his overseas assignment, if he would "ever see New Yorkers in their native habitat again."[7]

The situation in Vietnam proved to be "unique in many respects," Browne said, because it lacked some of the key features of most wars in history. There existed no front "to march off to, camera and typewriter tucked into a rucksack," he learned. The front could be everything from a once-peaceful village bridge where he had stopped to buy pineapple one morning and where "the Viet Cong killed 20 militiamen in a little post last night." The front could also be a shady trail in the jungle on which a column of troops on a routine patrol was suddenly mowed down by hidden machine-guns and a mortar barrage. "It may be a bar in downtown Saigon that suddenly shatters into a heap of rubble and blood as a terrorist heaves a few pounds of plastic [explosive] concealed in a loaf of French bread through the door," Browne noted. But, most of all, he viewed the front as a remote hut late at night where villagers gathered to listen as an intelligent man dressed in a peasant's black attire recited from memory from the works of General Vo Nguyen Giap, the Vietnamese commander who proved years before at the Battle of Dien Bien Phu against the French that "a peasant militia with the proper indoctrination can defeat even a modern army," he added. He came to share the opinion held by many who became regulars covering the war that there were those who "either listened to other people as to what the war was all about and those who went out and got muddy boots. I preferred the muddy boots."[8]

Browne won the respect of his colleagues in Saigon for his professionalism, as well as high marks from US ambassador Frederick Nolting for his sensitivity to the "nuances of the Vietnamese situation," especially compared to other newsmen in the country. As his AP associate Peter Arnett later observed, Browne was not "one of the boys" when it came to the often lively "social life of those years" that he, AP photographer Horst Faas, and David Halberstam of the *New York Times* sometimes indulged in. "There was a comradery that existed beyond news competition, a sense of 'us against the world,'" Arnett recalled. "Mal Browne was an intellectual who could stand above it all." Fox Butterfield, who covered the fall of Saigon in 1975 with Browne for the *New York Times*, remembered his compatriot as possessing an encyclopedic knowledge of the country. Correspondents could be quite turf-conscious when it came to covering a major story, but Butterfield said that while Browne had a healthy ego, he was not driven by it and proved to be a generous colleague, letting him take some of the better stories. "He was a pleasure to work with all the time," Butterfield said of Browne. And while Browne had been born and raised in New York, Butterfield remembered his colleague as possessing more of a modest, Midwestern character.[9]

Those who spent time in Vietnam covering the conflict grew increasingly frustrated by urging from their superiors in New York and elsewhere to be more like the correspondents of World War II, especially beloved columnist Ernie Pyle of Dana, Indiana. Brown considered Pyle to be "a great and courageous reporter who made World War II come alive for Americans. But that was World War II, and this is Viet Nam, where I expect Pyle would feel utterly lost." Pyle's faith in the basic goodness of an American fighting man might have been "sorely tested," Browne observed, by "policies that compel this decent GI to shoot aging women (or be shot by them)." The Hoosier reporter, too, would also come to know that the cliches of the past war "just don't seem to apply here, and that's why explaining things to the folks back home (who basically rely on cliches) becomes so difficult," concluded Browne. Vietnam war correspondents did their best to pay attention to battle coverage and bring the war "to life for American spectators at home," but Browne believed that more so than in either World War II or the Korean War, reporters felt heavier responsibilities. "More subtle things are involved," he noted, "which must be reported and analyzed. For that matter, the general lines of American policy in the Far East themselves are no longer a sacred cow. Like everything else, the rationale of the war itself is a fit subject for the examination of journalists." By 1963 he had become convinced that "the United States had neither a legitimate nor sustainable role as a belligerent in Indochina." But as a "conscientious newsman," Browne set aside his "personal views when reporting events," trying instead to "emulate the detachment of a camera lens."[10]

Browne's time as a draftee in the US Army had not only given him a basic understanding of reporting, but it had also educated him in ways that proved useful during his time immersed in a war zone. He knew how to handle weapons and had insight into how soldiers thought, spoke, and acted. "In a world more often shaped by the sword than the pen," Browne emphasized, close familiarity with soldiers and how they performed their duties would be crucial for historians and journalists. History had shown, said Browne, that for as long as wars had been documented there was friction between military commanders and the newsmen who covered them. He remembered that the great Civil War Union general, William Tecumseh Sherman, had once threatened to hang a reporter he discovered trying to follow his march across Georgia, and Sherman had even written to his brother that "Napoleon himself would have been defeated with a free press." Some field commanders, however, liked to have journalists around to write about them, "even when it would have been better for the reporters to stay home in bed," Browne noted. He pointed out that General George Armstrong Custer saw to it that AP reporter Mark Kellogg had a mule issued to him so he could accompany the Seventh Cavalry as they rode into action at the Battle of the Little Bighorn. Kellogg died alongside Custer and his men.[11]

Another skill Browne learned while serving in South Korea that came in handy in Vietnam was photography. During his days with the Nineteenth Regiment, he had gone to the post exchange and purchased an inexpensive Japanese Ricoh single-lens-reflex camera that served him faithfully over the years. The other members of the PIO staff guided him through the process of taking and developing photographs, all done in less-than-ideal conditions, as the chemicals they used to develop pictures often froze at night in their poorly heated hut. Brown recalled their "daily darkroom routine including thawing out the chemicals while we melted snow for shaving." He discovered that having a camera handy compelled the person carrying it "into the heat of the action. If you're writing text, you can fake it. But if you're carrying a camera, there's nothing in the world you can do to fake it, and so you get your boots muddy; you become part of the scene, and that is absolutely vital to writing a text that's convincing and which contains the essence of whatever it is that's going on." As AP's bureau chief in Saigon, he made it his policy that all correspondents should take pictures whenever they could, and that all photographers should gather information to fashion into news dispatches. "To do otherwise would have spread our meager resources too thinly, and it was a formula that worked," he said. After all, reporters could always take the information supplied by a photographer and churn out a respectable story, and photographers could take a newsman's "technically lousy picture" and improve it enough so that it was publishable.[12]

Browne discovered that the one-room, ground-floor AP office at 158D/3 Rue Pasteur in Saigon offered the same challenges as the PIO accommodations in Korea, especially when it came to photojournalism. A frequent visitor to the office, Halberstam remembered that the space "felt more like a converted closet than anything else; if there were two people there at the same time then it seemed overcrowded." With space at a premium, the office's one bathroom became a rudimentary darkroom used to develop and print photographs for distribution to AP outlets around the world.[13]

Despite these challenges, Browne persevered and was ready in the spring of 1963 when South Vietnam was wracked by demonstrations from organized members of the Buddhist community. Using an inexpensive, Japanese-brand Petri 35mm camera, he captured on film the self-immolation of a senior Buddhist monk, Thich Quang Duc, while the monk sat calmly on a cushion in the traditional lotus position at the intersection of two busy streets in Saigon. "I think it was one of the worst things I've ever seen," Browne said years later. His stunning image of a man giving his life for his cause appeared on the front pages of American newspapers from Lawrence, Kansas, to Cumberland, Maryland; from Bluefield, West Virginia, to Colorado Spring, Colorado. "That picture put the Vietnam War on the front page more than anything else that happened before. That's where the story stayed for the next 10 years or more," noted Hal Buell, AP deputy photo editor in New York.[14]

Although Browne left Vietnam in 1966 for a reporting career that took him all over the world, from South America to Eastern Europe and even the frozen Antarctic, his legacy has always included his haunting photograph of Quang Duc in flames, often cited under the title "The Ultimate Protest." It became one of the iconic images of the Vietnam War, standing alongside two other indelible AP photographs that are now part of the collective American conscience—"Saigon Execution," Eddie Adams's February 1, 1968, graphic photograph of a suspected Viet Cong guerrilla (Nguyen Van Lem) being summarily executed at point-blank range by South Vietnamese general Nguyen Ngoc Loan; and "Terror of War," Nick Ut's dramatic shot of a naked nine-year-old girl, Phan Thi Kim Phuc, screaming as she runs down a road with her skin burned from a South Vietnamese napalm bomb that mistakenly hit her village. "We all—the soldiers and the journalists—poured water over her from canteens," said Ut, who loaded Kim Phuc into his van and took her to a hospital fifteen miles away. She survived and eventually became a Canadian citizen.[15]

Browne never quite escaped questions about what had happened that day in Saigon. He was often asked if he could have done anything to prevent Quang Duc from taking his life. At the time his main focus had been on getting his pictures taken and out of Vietnam "to the AP in one of its far flung octopus tentacles as soon as possible," especially given the tight censorship imposed by South Vietnamese officials. He had realized that it would have been fruitless to intervene, as the monks and nuns gathered for the protest were sure to have stopped him or anyone else who tried to interfere. Quang Duc's horrific sacrifice, however, weighed on him until Browne's death from complications from Parkinson's disease in 2012. "I don't think many journalists take pleasure from human suffering," he noted, but he did have to admit to "having sometimes profited from others' pain." Although by no means intentional on his part, that fact did not help. "Journalists inadvertently influence events they cover, and although the effects are sometimes for the good, they can also be tragic," Browne said. "Either way, when death is the outcome, psychic scars remain." There were other violent deaths he witnessed in Vietnam—losses that became mere "footnotes" in the history of the war compared to the "theater of the horrible" that Quang Duc's suicide represented for his cause. Browne never forgot them. He avoided indulging in anger or self-recrimination, as he realized that doing so would cause him to lose "the balance needed to ply his trade." Such tragedies, however, should make all journalists, he advised, "think twice about writing something that may leave blood on our hands."[16]

At the time and for years later, the Saigon correspondents were hounded by critics who blamed them for Diem's downfall and America's ultimate defeat and humiliation in Vietnam. The fault-finding followed Browne when he reported on the 1991 war in the Persian Gulf with detractors back home, who had not actually read what he had written, accusing him of harming the American cause in its fight against Iraq. "This is just silly, of course," Browne said. "To the extent that America newsmen 'took sides' in either Viet Nam or the Persian Gulf, it was on the side of the United States." Of course, he pointed out, that did not mean the journalists backed either the governments of South Vietnam or Saudi Arabia. For all societies at war, the important truth seemed to be the truth "that tells you 'we are the good guys and we are winning,' regardless of what team you're on," reflected Browne. As American involvement in Vietnam wound down, it no longer seemed possible "to believe in the goodness and rightness of our cause," he added. Instead of pointing fingers at the individuals who involved the country in the conflict, many in the United States decided to "blame the messengers—people like myself who had been sending back discouraging tidings of how bad things had been going," Browne said. What torpedoed the American effort in Southeast Asia was the sense that "it didn't seem to be going anywhere," he noted. The public had been regularly promised by its government that there was "a light at the end of the tunnel," yet victory never came. "There was no longer excitement," Browne explained. "The days when there were songs about the Green Berets were long past."[17]

Browne's important journalistic contributions regarding America's early days of involvement in Vietnam have been unfortunately overshadowed over the years as the fame of his Vietnam contemporaries outgrew his. Both Halberstam and Neil Sheehan of United Press International achieved spectacular late-career successes that eluded Browne. Halberstam left daily reporting for the life of a freelance author, producing such classic best-selling books on politics and sports as *The Best and The Brightest, The Powers That Be, The Breaks of the Game, Summer of '49,* and *The Teammates: A Portrait of a Friendship* before his death in an automobile accident on April 23, 2007, in California. Sheehan spent years painstakingly crafting what became one of the seminal books about the Vietnam War, *A Bright Shining Lie: John Paul Vann and America in Vietnam,* which won the Pulitzer Prize for general nonfiction and a National Book Award for nonfiction in 1988.

Examining Browne's dispatches from Saigon, however, offers an important window into how most newspaper readers in the United States received their information about what was going on in Southeast Asia. From Allentown, Pennsylvania, to Raleigh, North Carolina, from Birmingham, Alabama, to Del Rio, Texas, from Tucson, Arizona, to Tacoma, Washington, subscribers opened their daily newspapers and were greeted by Browne's regular reports from the AP—a place that he considered "the greatest news organization in the world." As an employee of this nonprofit cooperative with members all over the country, Browne knew that the publishers and editors of AP member organizations, many of whom supported America's involvement in Vietnam, exercised "a powerful influence on AP policies." Despite such pressures, Browne remained determined to provide his readers "a continuous, honest assessment of the situation" of what he called "a puzzling war," believing as well that officials in Vietnam—both Vietnamese and American—should try to do the same. After all, he noted, Vietnam had been too important to "look at through rose-colored glasses." Journalists, he acknowledged, were fallible, but he asked his readers to show some understanding. "When you really get into almost any subject it turns out to be much more complicated and confusing than you thought," he pointed out. "For journalists, life and work are a continuous learning process, and although we often get it wrong to start with, sometimes the second draft is better."[18]

Browne stands as one of the preeminent journalists of the Vietnam era. Few, if any, except for his AP colleague Arnett, could match his depth of knowledge about the conflict in Southeast Asia and his commitment to uncovering the truth in a country in which lies and obfuscation were the norm, when, in fact, as he pointed out, the war was fought by both sides with "lies and counterlies." He was there during the early days of American involvement in Vietnam, becoming the dean of the Saigon correspondents as the United States escalated its commitment and continuing to return as South Vietnam battled for its existence. Browne cared deeply about what happened to the Vietnamese people—a concern that only deepened after he met and married Huynh thi Le Lieu. In Vietnam the war was not only fought in the open on the battlefield but also behind the scenes among supposed allies. "Many a career was made or ruined in Viet Nam," Browne said. With the war finally ended, his reputation and self-respect remained intact.[19]

Although Browne realized he had missed the career he might have made for himself if he had become an editor rather than remaining as a reporter, he had no regrets, considering himself tremendously lucky to have the life he lived. He had fond memories of sharing roast potatoes with Sherpas in the Himalayas, bantering about territorial water rights with Masai warriors in Kenya, and attempting to fathom the intricacies of quantum electrodynamics over tea and fruit cake at the homes of Russian physicists. But in filling his passport with pages of visa stamps, he also had to endure trying to sooth angry diplomats whose sleep had been interrupted by his requests for emergency travel visas, airline flights canceled at the last minute just when he needed to be where news was breaking, and arrests and expulsions by border guards whose job it was to keep out nosy journalists from their totalitarian countries. He also had to contend with working in many parts of the world where the communication vital to gathering and transmitting news was hindered as much by technological shortcomings as by censorship. During his days in Brazil, for example, the telephones in his offices in Rio de Janeiro "more or less worked, but use of them entailed a half-hour wait just to get a dial tone." Browne soon came to expect inadequate communication systems in countries "where governments have a lot to hide." In the Soviet Union, the phones were dangerous because the Communist government could be counted upon to electronically surveil (bug) most communications, and "sensible people with politically sensitive matters to discuss talked to each other only in public parks or on noisy street corners." He recalled that a search of an apartment used by *Times* reporters in Moscow uncovered more than a dozen hidden microphones.[20]

Browne described journalism as always entertaining, enlightening, and even uplifting, but also realized that coming to terms with death and "endless suffering our cruel species inflicts upon itself" had been one of the "fringe benefits" from his long involvement in the profession. Reporters did not fear death less than others, he confessed, but they were "a little more familiar with it than some, and we realize that despite its sting, death had its points." Paradoxically, he had not seen much death during his time as a soldier in Korea. Instead, his familiarity with it came during his early harrowing days as a reporter in Middletown, New York, where his beat included "an endless parade of the dead: farmers mangled by disc harrows, highway victims smeared over the blacktop, suicides with heads turned inside out by shotguns, picnicking families electrocuted by lightning, drowned children, bludgeoned husbands and wives, ad nauseum." Each death he saw drained from Browne his reserves of "pity, grief, and horror," leaving behind the scar tissue that enabled such professionals as journalists, physicians, police officers, and morticians to get through their workdays. Browne viewed death as "more of a kindly friend than a malign predator." After all, he noted, even with the best medical care in the world, everyone succumbs to death, and "its face is sometimes more benign than people outside the news fraternity may realize."[21]

CHAPTER 2

From the Laboratory
to the Newsroom

THE YOUNG CHEMIST NEVER saw it coming. Strolling down Thirteenth
Street in New York City with his wife, Diana, Malcolm W. Browne casually
stepped on a heavy, steel subway-access hatch. Unfortunately, at the same
time, a subway worker underground decided to lift the hatch, tripping
Browne. As Browne started to fall, the worker below, realizing what was
happening, stopped what he was doing. The unlucky pedestrian hit the
ground and the hatch landed on one of his outflung appendages. "The
plate came down on the first two fingers of my right hand," Browne
recalled.

Browne's fingers remained where they should have been, but a few were
injured badly enough that he could not use a pencil to write the extensive
laboratory reports necessary for his job at Foster D. Snell. He had to switch
to a typewriter, a machine he had never used before. "At first my hunt-and-
peck typing was wretchedly slow," he said, "but with practice, I got faster.
Eventually one of my injured right-hand fingers mended enough to join the
two left-hand fingers I had been using, and a limping three-finger gait
became my typing style for life."[1]

Although Browne never learned to touch type, his three-finger method proved effective, and he was able to "pound out pages pretty fast." He had stumbled on one of the most important skills he would need in his future career as a reporter, working for such notable institutions as the Associated Press, the American Broadcasting Company, and the *New York Times*. Until his retirement in 2000, his three-finger tapping on typewriter and, eventually, computer keyboards could be heard in such far-flung locales as Cuba, South Vietnam, Laos, Cambodia, Pakistan, Argentina, Serbia, Spain, Portugal, France, Morocco, Kenya, Saudi Arabia, and Antarctica. Kicked out of several countries for asking too many pointed questions of government officials, Browne survived helicopter crashes, physical attacks from secret police, and Scud missiles dropping on him during the 1991 Gulf War as the oldest accredited correspondent covering the conflict. Browne "had no fear of sticking his nose where it wasn't wanted," one of his colleagues remembered. In dealing with a variety of dangers, Browne learned to "cope with the ugliest events of our times. Because of this, I can walk across a battlefield where men are dead and wounded and not fall apart. I can do this by concentrating on the mechanics of news coverage. I have the nightmares afterwards." Above all in his work, he tried to maintain what he called "the Feel," a term he had learned from Paul Gallico, a reporter and novelist who "believed deeply in the need for direct, personal experience as the way to rounded reporting," so much so, in fact, that Gallico even dared go into the ring to spar with heavyweight boxer Jack Dempsey; the champ knocked him out. "Life for him was a quest for the greatest possible range and depth of experience," Browne said of Gallico, "including physical sensations, of course, but much more. That's the way to do it. The Feel is the way to top-flight journalism."[2]

It always seemed to Browne that James Thurber's classic 1939 short story, "The Secret Life of Walter Mitty," could serve as an allegory for the field of journalism. Thurber's Mitty is a timid, introverted man who creates an imaginary existence as a brilliant surgeon, a brave pilot, and other glamorous professions. In a way, said Browne, journalists lead "a similarly vicarious existence. When we study and write about politicians or generals or actors or gangsters or chemists, we actually have a chance to get inside these characters and their lives for a while. We get to experience some of the things they do, at least in a small way." He did not mean to imply that journalists were as timid or introverted as Mitty, as most he came across could be classed as "assertive loudmouths with opinions about almost everything." Of course, journalism does have some "redeeming social qualities," Browne acknowledged. For him, however, the trade's biggest attraction was the variety of experiences it offered to those who practiced it. "Journalism, in other words, is fun," he said. "If it weren't, I know I wouldn't be doing it. . . . We journalists get to ride roller coasters and helicopters, we learn what it's like to be shot at, and we travel to the ends of the earth. We get to experience pain and fear and pleasure and sometimes deep satisfaction."[3]

It was quite a career for someone who remembered hearing as a child the clip-clop of horse-drawn wagons delivering milk in glass bottles at dawn to his family's apartment in New York City's bohemian Greenwich Village neighborhood and lived long enough to watch humans place their footprints on the moon's surface. As a child Browne loved his Erector set, a toy whose parts he could fit together in myriad ways. "I was never very creative myself, but I was always intrigued that you could put something together that would be greater than the sum of its parts," he recalled. Born on April 17, 1931, he was the eldest of four children raised by Douglas and Dorothy Wilde Browne. Misfortune had plagued Malcolm's family before his birth. His maternal grandmother, Florence, had a rich Dutch American businessman as a father who, for a time, held a seat on the New York Stock Exchange and owned a palatial mansion filled with servants to tend to the household's every need. "His many children were brought up to enjoy the fruit of educated leisure such as painting, composing music and reading poetry, none of which particularly prepared them to earn a living," Browne remembered. The family hosted parties that included such well-known names as Ignace Paderewski, the Polish pianist and statesman. Florence, called Donna by her grandchildren, passed along to them her memories of attending Buffalo Bill's Wild West shows, where she sat marveling at the marksmanship of Annie Oakley and also saw Sitting Bull, the Hunkpapa Lakota leader who had defeated George Armstrong Custer at the Battle of the Little Bighorn. Ill-timed speculation on the spice market, however, caused the family's finances to collapse. Fortunately, Browne's grandmother married well, becoming the wife of a physician, Doctor Harry

Wilde, who was part of a long line of medical professionals originating from Dublin, Ireland. The only stain on the family's reputation came from a controversial relative, Oscar Wilde, the poet and playwright whose reputation was ruined by his imprisonment in the 1890s for "gross indecency." For a time, until he was old enough to admire his kin's vast literary accomplishments, the young Malcolm tried to conceal from his schoolmates that his middle initial, W., stood for Wilde.[4]

Tragedy struck Florence when her thirty-five-year-old husband died from a pulmonary embolism one frigid morning while making house calls to his patients on Long Island. Undaunted by the blow to her family, the talented Florence, an accomplished sketcher and watercolorist, started offering art classes to make ends meet; she could also depend upon complimentary medical care for her family from her husband's medical friends. One of the students Florence attracted to her class was a young man, Douglas Granzow Browne, born in 1903 in a rural suburb of Detroit whose family later moved to Los Angeles. Although raised as a Roman Catholic, Douglas abandoned his family's Catholic faith and traveled to New York City to become an architect. Forced to quit his studies because of a lack of funds due to the Great Depression, he had enough money left to take some commercial art classes given by Florence. Those courses led to his meeting his teacher's daughter, Dorothy, called "Buddy" by her friends. The couple married and raised four children: Malcolm, Miriam, Timothy, and Christopher. Dorothy became a devoted Quaker, who, as her son noted, "opposed war and killing in every way, shape, or form. She was one of the few people during the late 1930s, when war was looming in Europe and when the Spanish Civil War was raging, who advocated no war." She also dreamed of becoming either a concert pianist or successful writer of detective or adventure novels, said Browne, who remembered hearing her clatter away at her typewriter until late in the evenings, producing stories that failed to find any takers.[5]

By the 1920s Florence's art classes had grown enough in popularity that she could afford to take out a mortgage to buy an old stone house built by Dutch settlers in the Catskill Mountains in southeastern New York. The ancient structure had practically no modern conveniences, lacking electricity and piped-in water. She used the property as a summer art school and, when students became scarce during World War II, switched to renting the property's rustic cabins to young vacationers looking for inexpensive accommodations. During the winter months, Florence spent her time teaching art at Rollins College in Florida.[6]

Browne described the Catskill property as situated on "sixteen hilly acres, mostly wooded, with a delightful tree-shaded creek whose frigid pools . . . enticed swimmers for three centuries." On cool nights he remembered lighting crackling blazes in its many fireplaces, with the flames casting "spooky shadows on the dimly lighted walls." When winds were high Browne could hear moans coming from the chimneys and imagined "the sounds as the lonely shades of former residents." During the depths of the Great Depression in the early 1930s, Florence came close to losing her land when the bank threatened to foreclose on her mortgage. She was saved thanks to President Franklin Roosevelt's New Deal programs, a boon that turned her into a lifelong supporter of the Democratic Party. The release of Walt Disney's *The Three Little Pigs* inspired Florence to send the bank that held her mortgage a small payment along with a note that read, "Who's Afraid of the Big Bad Wolf?"[7]

During the summer, while Browne's father struggled to earn a living during the week in New York at a variety of trades—architect, elevator operator, cabinetmaker, and designer of wooden squirrels used to decorate the city's parks—Browne, his mother, and his siblings retreated to their grandmother's stone house in the Catskills. The house and its rugged surroundings became Browne's tutor, teaching him needed survival skills. Water had to be hauled to the house in buckets, either drawn up by hand from a well or via an old-fashioned, gasoline-powered pump located a quarter mile away that Browne had to start "by cranking a heavy iron flywheel" that "could backfire and break an arm." While the engine ran, someone always had to be nearby to keep an eye on its balky pressure gauge. One day, when Browne was young, his father, who visited from the city on the weekends, fell asleep in some tall grass instead of watching the gauge; the pressure reached a critical level and the tank exploded "with a blast that we heard a mile away." Fortunately, Browne's father escaped injury.[8]

His family depended upon Browne to be the property's handyman, responsible for fixing machinery, repairing plumbing, painting walls, mowing the grass, hoeing and weeding the gardens, and digging trenches for the outhouse and garbage pit. "I loved the work," he remembered. Because the house lacked refrigeration, and his family did not own a car, he also had to pedal his bike daily for an hour to buy fresh milk, eggs, and butter. Browne's mother sometimes had to cook for more than twenty people at a time using a four-burner kerosene stove, had to heat water to wash dishes and clothes, and scrubbed laundry by hand using a washboard. "There were times late at night when I could hear her weeping, exhausted and depressed," Browne said of his mother. "Her lifelong bouts with depression, I suspect, had as much to do with her death at age fifty-seven as did her heavy smoking and genetically weak lungs—a curse of our family." To save money Browne's grandmother used to toast stale bread until it blackened almost into charcoal, grinding it up and steeping it in boiled water to produce an ersatz coffee that he preferred over the real thing. The adults in his life may have worried how they would make ends meet, but, for Browne, "the Depression was fun."[9]

For recreation Browne and his family often retreated during the heat of a summer day to the nearby creek to cool off. The creek provided him an introduction to science, as several rocks scattered on its banks "could be cracked apart to reveal fossils of fern leaves and other defunct organisms." His father also introduced him to the wonders of biology, showing him how to capture pollywogs and care for them until they grew into adult frogs. Cooler evenings often featured his grandmother preparing cocoa and entertaining her grandchildren by playing Frédéric Chopin etudes and waltzes on the piano, in addition to "her rousing rendition of a tune she had learned as a girl—[Scott] Joplin's 'Maple Leaf Rag.'" She also introduced Browne to Asian art, including the work of Japanese printmaker and painter Katsushika Hokusai. "The magic images of the place always fascinated me," said Browne. "When I got there, I was surprised that Asia looked like the Asia I always imagined."[10]

Because the stone house lacked a television and had limited radio reception, Browne depended upon books for entertainment. As a teenager he became interested in reading medieval romances, including *Sir Gawain and the Green Knight*, as well as novels from Russian authors. He also became fascinated with the works of German poet, playwright, and novelist Johann

Wolfgang von Goethe, so much so that he began learning German so he could read *Faust* in its original language. He learned the intricacies of the internal-combustion engine by examining a Model T Ford stored in the barn, which also contained a pair of old sleighs with crumbling leather accessories. "I sometimes sat in those sleighs," he recalled, "trying to imagine what a dash along a snow-crusted lane must have been like in my grandfather's day at the turn of the century." He could also pore over bushels of old magazines and newspapers, thrilling to news articles about the kidnapping of the Lindbergh baby, battles of the Spanish Civil War, and the rise of Fascist dictator Benito Mussolini in Italy. A lover of fireworks and the explosions they produced, Browne noted that the high point of every summer came at the Fourth of July, a holiday for which everyone—his parents, grandmother, and even the art students—purchased pyrotechnics to set off. "The best part came with night," he said, "when the pinwheels, sparklers, Roman candles and rockets were lighted up."[11]

During his childhood Browne also loved to build model airplanes and counted himself lucky when he received one as a present. He remembered that the kits he made "consisted of little more than plans, balsa wood, and silk paper. With a week or so of painstaking work, a boy could build one of these things into a fragile but very beautiful model airplane that would fly beautifully. I loved them—and I think I loved them especially because they were so difficult to make." Building these models led to a lifelong interest in both the Spanish Civil War and World War II, in particular the aircraft flown by pilots from Great Britain, Germany, and Japan. He drew upon the many books written by aircraft expert William Green to learn their paint schemes and logos. In addition to securing kits from around the world, Browne bought wood and other parts to craft his own designs. "In building them," he recalled, "I learned many interesting and surprising things about the science of aerodynamics." What appeared to him to be "perfect designs" failed to take to the air, and it took him many days trying to analyze the problem. "And when I discovered what it was, and when I had something that would fly with grace and beauty, I was proud and happy," he noted. One he was particularly proud of was a three-inch-long model, "perfect down to the last instrument," of a Russian-built Polikarpov I-16 fighter in the unit markings of the International Brigade from the Spanish

Republican Air Force. Later in life, when he came across aircraft, particularly smaller ones used by the military for observation or artillery spotting, something in Browne felt "very warm and very fine; somehow these little planes are familiar to me as my own body. I know every hinge and pin in them, and the beautiful but subtle simplicity that makes them fly." [12]

The inexpensive price ($150 for the summer) Florence charged for renting the cabins on her property attracted not only young people looking for a bargain but also those seeking peace and quiet from their haunting World War II experiences. One whom Browne remembered for the rest of his life was Maxim Schur, a Latvian native who had been wounded while serving with the US intelligence service and later became a naturalized American citizen. A talented concert pianist and teacher, Schur, who died in 1974, practiced for six to eight hours a day on the Browne family's battered, old upright piano, trying to master a variety of Mozart piano concertos. Whenever he was nearby, either working or reading, the music, which also included Schur taking on concertos and sonatas by Beethoven and Brahms, "seeped" into Browne's soul. "In time, I came to know the piano scores for these compositions by heart, and that gift . . . brightened the rest of my life," Browne remembered, particularly during his days covering the Vietnam War. [13]

Reinforcing Browne's self-improvement was a quality education provided by the school he attended from kindergarten through twelfth grade in Manhattan, the Friends Seminary, founded by the Religious Society of Friends (Quakers) in 1786. "For me it was wonderful," Browne said. "It happened that the school had marvelous teachers, and the only objection I had was that they got me so interested in everything that it took me a while to settle down on a career." The teachers helped him to begin "seeing the world as a kaleidoscope of many colors and shades of gray rather than a simple-minded game of good guys versus bad guys." He particularly remembered the instruction provided by Earle Hunter, who taught history and was a man "whose scholarship, wit, good humor and wisdom made him as immune to propaganda and cant as any human being I've known." The greatest lesson Hunter taught Browne was to be wary about trusting such established institutions as the government and the media. "He taught us to question anyone seeking to thrust an idea or factoid upon us without offering evidence," he said. Browne found such advice invaluable in a journalism career that ranged from the rice paddies of Vietnam to the deserts of Saudi Arabia. Another Browne favorite was Rose Wilcox, who taught English literature and composition and demanded that her students be familiar with the "thinkers of all nations and ages who have helped to shape the human condition," including William Shakespeare, Charles Dickens, William Blake, John Keats, and Fyodor Dostoyevsky.[14]

The sternest taskmaster Browne faced at his school was Walter Hinman, a World War I veteran whose lungs had been damaged by mustard gas late in the conflict. Hinman's chief responsibilities were general science and biology, but his mind ranged far afield to explore such matters with his students as physics, chemistry, and mathematics. Like most of the best teachers Browne knew, Hinman possessed a knack for grabbing his classroom's attention. Realizing that a lot of young people were interested in explosions and bright flashes, Hinman sometimes had his classes "prepare eutectic mixtures of oxygen and methane, and let us ignite them with a spark coil," said Browne. Hinman stimulated some to try "louder experiments, a few of which had destructive consequences." Trying to impress some girls at his school, Browne discovered how to produce and ignite nitroglycerine, mercuric fulminate, and other noisy compounds. By doing so, he realized, he risked earning the displeasure of adults. "Unsupervised chemistry experiments gave little joy either to the parents who tolerated them or the teachers who inspired them," Browne noted. "There were acid-stained fingers, scorch marks on floors and pyrotechnics." One of his experiments earned Browne a three-day suspension from school. It involved using liquid hydrogen and produced an impressive explosion "in a mid-Manhattan softball field; it harmed no one but broke some windows in a nearby building."[15]

Hinman's only intolerance in the classroom came for students "too lazy to work hard and give his or her best," Browne recalled. For his physics lessons, Hinman began class with a written quiz he graded while students worked on lab assignments. Hinman posted the results at the end of the class. "Woe befell the student whose grade was six or lower—his mark went up on the bulletin board marked in red," Browne said. Hinman also persuaded the students in his physics class to come early to school several days a week to tackle calculus. "With that and an arsenal of pedagogical tricks," Browne said, "he first showed us the edifice of classical physics built by Newton and his followers. Then, having hooked us on the comfortable assumptions of Newtonian determinism, he knocked out the props with blasts of relativity and quantum theory, leaving us jolted but fascinated. It was heady stuff for school kids." Browne had always been uneasy about his mother's "deep religious faith," viewing religion as merely a ritual "designed to celebrate some characters as manifestly implausible as Santa Claus and the tooth fairy." He thought there must be a better explanation for life than religion, and he found it in science—something that, despite its limitations, supplied his "spiritual needs" for the rest of his life. As an adolescent, Browne also differentiated himself from his mother's extreme pacifism. "For one thing," he later noted, "it seemed to me that there are times when you do have to fight, when the enemy is a clear and present danger and if you don't fight him you're just going to have to put up with the consequences."[16]

One world-shaking incident reinforced Browne's desire to immerse himself in science. It came on August 7, 1945, when he heard a staticky radio broadcast announcing the dropping of the atomic bomb on Hiroshima, Japan. Just a year before, a scientist visiting Browne's school had described for him and his classmates the 1939 discovery of uranium fission by Otto Hahn and Fritz Strassmann. "Furthermore, he told us, an equation that [Albert] Einstein had worked out meant that astonishing things were now possible," Browne remembered. "For instance, he said, it would be possible to build a nuclear engine that would drive the *Queen Mary* back and forth across the Atlantic [Ocean] scores of times on just a pound or so of fuel." Nothing had prepared Browne, however, for hearing that an entire city had been obliterated by the same small amount of nuclear material. "I hung on the radio for more details," he said. While other boys of his age might have dreamed of being a baseball player or fireman, he had picked a far different profession to pursue—nuclear physicist. He even had the opportunity to attend symposiums at New York's Cooper Union featuring J. Robert Oppenheimer, known as the "father of the atomic bomb" for his work with the Manhattan Project. Oppenheimer held his audience "spellbound with his portrayal of physics as the golden key for solving the great universal riddles," Browne said.[17]

Reflecting about his fascination with this new power source, Browne said that it pained him to admit that at the time he had not thought about the thousands of dead civilians that "the dawn of the nuclear age had left in Hiroshima." What he knew of the war had been learned from often inaccurate reports he watched in movie newsreels or read in newspapers and magazines, all the while cheered on by government propaganda to hate the enemy, especially the Japanese. "In movie theaters, images of flaming enemy suicide planes and smoking enemy cities prompted applause, not horror," he noted. Although the country's lust for vengeance during the war had been tempered by his family's pacifism, Browne said the mushroom cloud produced by the atomic bombs dropped on Hiroshima and Nagasaki appeared to him as symbols of "scientific genius and righteous victory over an evil foe." The atomic bomb's incredible power represented a Faustian bargain whereby human beings had sold a bit of their humanity "to gain the knowledge that made controlled nuclear fission possible." Rather late in life, he finally fully appreciated his mother's pacifism. "I came more and more to feel that all wars are evil, even the good ones," he said. "War is intrinsically evil and should be avoided at all costs."[18]

After graduating from Friends Seminary in 1948, Browne studied chemistry at Swarthmore College, a private liberal arts Quaker institution located in Swarthmore, Pennsylvania, from 1948 to 1950, and spent a year at New York University before marrying Diana Kirchwey on June 26, 1951; the couple had a daughter, Wendy, and eventually made their home in a small apartment in Brooklyn Heights. Needing a job, Browne worked as a chemical laboratory technician with Foster Snell in New York City. "It was one of those consulting outfits that help businesses operate profitably without doing much real science," Browne recalled. For example, in 1954 the Dwight Eisenhower administration, in a move some historians have called one of "the most reprehensible acts" in American history, overthrew the democratically elected government of President Jacobo Arbenz of Guatemala. A reformer, Arbenz was ousted in a coup engineered by the Central Intelligence Agency based on the false charge that the country was on the verge of falling into the hands of Communists but more likely because the threatened land was controlled by the American-owned United Fruit Company. The political instability in Guatemala, one of the leading suppliers of chicle, a key ingredient in chewing gum, threw manufacturers of the product into a panic. "Our lab was hired by a French chewing gum maker to quickly find a substitute for chicle and keeping Parisians happily chewing," noted Browne. In just a few weeks he managed to blend gums with "assorted polymers and plasticizers, and I saved the day," he said.[19]

Browne became what he described as "a virtuoso with food additives," including helping a company keep the wrapping on its blintzes from cracking when frozen. Other assignments, however, did not go as well, including one involving the maker of a well-known after-shave lotion. Browne and his colleagues were tasked with increasing the yield of benzaldehyde "from a rather tricky oxidation of toluene." He remembered that benzaldehyde had an aromatic almondy smell, but "when you oxidize toluene you can get into trouble if you let the temperature get out of hand." While Browne was away from the office ill with a cold, his lab partner risked pushing the benzaldehyde synthesis a bit too far and too fast, resulting in an explosion that smashed most of the laboratory's glassware and put him in the hospital for a few weeks. "Those were the days before safety glasses and blast guards, and he was pretty badly cut up," he said. "That was one explosion I wasn't sorry to miss."[20]

Following the outbreak of the Korean War on June 25, 1950, Browne had been expecting to be drafted into the US Army. Before that could happen, he volunteered for Officer Candidate School, hoping that he might join the military as an officer in an artillery or tank unit. Although his mother had wanted her son to file for conscientious-objector status, she need not have worried as the military seemed to have forgotten about Browne's existence during the war. The administrative "foul-up" probably saved his life, Browne reasoned, as life expectancies of "second lieutenants in Korea in 1951 and 1952 was appallingly short." The war on the Korean peninsula ended with the signing of an armistice on July 27, 1953, but Browne still had to seek permission from his local draft board when he and his wife wanted to leave the country for a European vacation in 1955. "Only then did officialdom seem to realize that I should have been in the army long since," he recalled, "and the board reluctantly agreed to our trip, provided I report for induction as soon as I got back."[21]

Inducted into the army in 1956 during the uneasy days of the attempted uprising by Hungarians against their Soviet-dominated government, Browne received his basic training at Fort Knox, Kentucky. Classified as a linguist because he spoke German and French, Browne and the other specialists in his unit, nonetheless, were sent to Fort Hood, Texas, to be trained on the American M48 Patton tank, as well as several Soviet models, something he enjoyed as tanks were fun to drive, except for during a war. "As we maneuvered our own tanks across the Texas desert we often coordinated our movements by radio in German, to the annoyance of our non-linguist sergeants," he remembered. "But we became good tankers; about half our group were Germans, and perhaps Panzer warfare is in the Teutonic blood." Never an athlete, Browne nonetheless found that he could handle himself well on the army's usual tests of its soldiers—training marches, obstacle courses, daily calisthenics, and firing a weapon (he had learned to shoot at age fourteen). "I could crawl under barbed wire, disarm mines and shoot well enough to win a marksmanship badge," he said. He also never forgot the savage skills unearthed during bayonet drills, with a sergeant leading his unit in its daily catechism of "Kill! Kill! Kill!" Although viewing the whole thing as a silly game, Browne realized that the army had been attempting to thicken its charges' "psychic callus, so that when the time came, real slaughter would seem almost part of the natural order of things."[22]

By the time Browne finished basic training, the Hungarian uprising had been crushed by the Soviets, and the army sent him to Fort Devens, Massachusetts, to train veteran soldiers in modern gunnery. Unfortunately, his company commander had been ordered to send two of his men to Korea, and the two draftees in the unit, Browne and another soldier, received the assignment, tearing him away from Diana. "The draft had its points, in that it democratized the army and salted it with educated men," he noted. "But it was a cruel institution that sometimes broke more hearts with forced separations than it did with bullets." Browne's marriage did not survive the separation, ending in divorce.[23]

Sent to Fort Lewis, Washington, Browne left the army post and endured a thirty-two-day journey across the Pacific on a dilapidated transport ship, all the while trying to avoid his seasick shipmates. After the ship landed at Inchon Harbor in central Korea, he expected to spend his service viewing the Korean countryside through the turret of a tank. Instead, Browne moved to a new specialty, journalism, joining the Public Information Office staff to write for a mimeographed weekly newspaper for the men of the Nineteenth Regiment, Twenty-Fourth Infantry Division. Some of the better stories Browne and his comrades produced were included in the division's weekly newspaper printed in Tokyo and also turned up from time to time in the military's daily *Stars and Stripes* and civilian papers in the United States. Articles covered such subjects as training exercises, who had earned Soldier of the Month honors, a column from the commanding officer, and the results from various sporting contests among the regiment. "Considering how little we did to keep the soldier informed about anything that really mattered, I found it hard to understand why the army tolerated our existence," he noted. It did, however, and Browne found his newfound job meant he never had to stand in formation or submit to daily inspections. "Best of all," he remembered, "we had access to a jeep and could travel throughout the regimental sector, which extended quite a distance."[24]

Browne's travels included trips to Seoul, still recovering from the war, as well as occasional visits to Japan to oversee printing jobs for his commanding officers. Inspired by the country's beauty, he studied the Japanese language, which, he said, slipped "from the tongue as gracefully as Italian." With his military service nearing an end, he plotted how he could find work in Japan. "I was enchanted with Asia the whole time I was in the army," he remembered. Browne made friends with some of the Americans who worked for news bureaus in Tokyo, but no job offers of any substance came his way, so he decided to return to the United States. After failing to find work with newspapers in New York City, Browne tried his luck with an employment agency for journalists. It worked; in August 1958 he got a job as a reporter for the *Middletown Daily Record*, a newspaper in New York's Orange County, located about an hour and a half northwest of New York City in the Hudson Valley.[25]

Beginning publication just two years before Browne started working there, the *Daily Record* was created by Jacob M. Kaplan, president of the Welch Grape Juice Company. Kaplan established a nonprofit company to fund the tabloid newspaper. The *Record* received national attention by being the first daily paper in the country to be produced by the offset printing method instead of the usual hot-metal typesetting process. "*The Record* boasted better typography and printing quality than its Middletown competitor [the *Times Herald*]," recalled Browne, "and it had a staff of young men and women recruited in various parts of the nation, all eager to win their spurs." He remembered that the newspaper's editor, Avrom "Al" Romm, gave all those looking for a job in his newsroom a test to judge an applicant's general knowledge and vocabulary, reasoning that most probably had little experience in the field. "One of his questions asked for the gestation period of an elephant, and my guess of two years was evidently close enough, for I was hired on the spot," Browne said. According to a later editorial in the newspaper, Browne had not done well on the test's vocabulary portion, misspelling such words as accommodate, judgment, occurrence, separate, all right, and sizable. But the "thin, blond, intense young man" possessed some "special qualities" that prompted the newspaper to hire him: "A great knowledge of the world around him and a keen desire to succeed in journalism." A former *Record* staffer described Browne as someone who owned a lot of books but was far from bookish. "He was a very hard-nosed guy who was tough about getting what he wanted," the newsman remembered.[26]

The *Record*'s management may have hired inexperienced journalists, but its editors had a knack for picking talented people for the newspaper's staff. In addition to Browne, who would go on to win numerous prizes for his work, including journalism's top award, the Pulitzer, the newspaper hired a young US Air Force veteran, Hunter S. Thompson, later an iconic writer for *Rolling Stone* magazine and a leading figure of the New Journalism movement of the 1960s and 1970s. Describing the *Record* as an "experimental newspaper," Thompson wrote to his mother after his hiring that only one person on the staff was more than thirty-five years old and "most of the boys are between 23 and 30," and they averaged approximately seventy-five miles a day on the road tracking down interesting stories. He went on to praise his associates as "young, smart as hell, from all over the country, and all on the way up. The *Record* is one of the best little papers in the country and one of the best opportunities there is."[27]

For the years he worked on the newspaper, Browne tackled a wide array of stories in its circulation area, which included Orange, Rockland, and Sullivan Counties. His pieces examined the escape of five cows from a group being hauled off by truck to a slaughterhouse, a hotel fire that rousted fifty guests from their sleep, a former Nazi ace teaching his wife how to be a glider pilot at an airfield in Middletown, tensions at the Chester Cable Company that led to the shooting death of a labor organizer by the firm's president, and life in a community (Monroe, New York) that had an ordinance outlawing the wearing of shorts. He remembered his coworkers—most earning low pay and expected to be ready to tackle any task assigned to them—as "a family of happy zealots, most of whom worked twelve-hour stints and produced more good copy per day than any comparable bunch I've known since." The skills Browne acquired in photography while in Korea were helpful in Middletown. Reporters were expected to not only meet their deadlines when it came to producing readable copy but also were supposed to provide photographs to illustrate their articles. "We typed our stories on cheap newsprint paper, and we edited using scissors, paste and pencils with the softest, dirtiest lead available," he remembered. Although reporters had regular beats (police, school boards, local politics), everyone, Browne noted, was "expected to pitch in on murders, fatal accidents, fires and other crises, and I found that big cities have no monopoly on mayhem."[28]

In the summer of 1959 Browne, who had hoped to be able to return to Asia as a foreign correspondent, had an opportunity to get some experience reporting from a different country. Earlier that year, the revolutionary July 16th Movement, led by Fidel Castro and promising radical social reform, overthrew the corrupt Fulgencio Batista government. The *Record* offered Browne, who had a shaky grasp of the Spanish language, time off and paid some of his expenses to travel to Cuba and report on what he observed about the revolution. "The assignment wasn't lucrative," he recalled, "but for me it was pure gold." When he arrived via air from Miami at Havana's José Martí Airport, he observed signs touting the revolution were displayed everywhere in the city, as well as photographs of Castro and other heroes, including one from Argentina, Ernesto "Che" Guevara. "A festive atmosphere prevailed, with crowds of boisterous strollers in the plazas and streets at all hours, packing the coffee stands and bars, and seeking entertainment," he remembered. Browne explored Havana and made connections with the new government, whose representatives appeared to be friendly and helpful. There were signs, however, that not all was well. Covering an outdoor rally speech by Castro before a crowd of sugar-cane workers bused in from the countryside, Browne tried to take a photograph of the gathering at a moment when those in the audience had "raised a salute to their leader, their right fists clenched in the classic communist style," he noted. Police suddenly appeared out of nowhere, grabbed Browne, and hustled him off to the local station. Fortunately, the authorities released him after a couple of hours and returned his camera, but without the film he shot. The police chief told the American newsman: "You'll understand that your readers might get an erroneous impression seeing pictures of our people saluting that way."[29]

During his time in Havana, Browne picked up stories about Americans who had fought on the revolution's behalf. US embassy officials told Browne that most of the American soldiers of fortune had left the country "like rats from a sinking ship" once they realized that the rewards they expected from the rebel government were not forthcoming. Intrigued, Browne tracked down three Americans—William Morgan (later shot as an antirevolutionary), Herman Frederick Marks, and Gerry Holthaus—and wrote about two of them for an article that became the first in the series from Cuba published by the *Record*. One of the most infamous Americans was a former merchant seaman from Wisconsin, Marks, who became feared as "the Yankee butcher" at the prison at the La Cabaña fortress, located across the harbor from Havana's downtown. Marks led the firing squads that executed approximately two hundred Batista supporters with the order: "Atención, Preparen, Aputen, Fuego!" ("Attention, Ready, Aim, Fire!") The American relished any chance he had to deliver the coup de grace to prisoners, shooting them in their heads with his .45 Colt pistol. "They were war criminals, and it was necessary to stamp them out," Marks explained to Browne. Although there seemed to be no comradeship between Marks and the Cubans he commanded, he said he was finished with the country of his birth. "I don't care about American citizenship one way or the other," said Marks, who had a long criminal record and sported a double-heart tattoo reading "Love, Nellie" on his left arm and a tattoo of a snake coiled over a dagger with the words "Death Before Dishonor" on his right arm. "America never gave me much of a break. I'm a Cuban now." Some members of the new Cuban government grew alarmed at the attention Marks received, with one privately telling Browne, "He's bad public relations for our government, at a time we need favorable opinion most."[30]

Browne's interview with another American, Holthaus from Decatur, Illinois, stood in stark contract with the one he had conducted with Marks, which had taken two hours of negotiations between the reporter and heavily armed Cuban soldiers. Browne met the twenty-three-year-old Holthaus, who had deserted from the Marine Corps while stationed at the American naval base at Guantánamo Bay, at a soda fountain, formerly a favorite spot for tourists. A believer in the revolution, Holthaus, a specialist in heavy weapons, had left the US base in a jeep loaded with arms on November 25, 1958. "A lot of Americans fought in the Cuban revolution to make money or gain power," Holthaus noted. "It wasn't that way with me. I just wanted to see the rebels win." He had been a real asset for Castro's rebels battling Batista's forces, turning a captured 20-millimeter cannon into a formidable weapon by using parts from a Ford Model T and assorted junk. "We mounted it on a truck," Holthaus told Browne. "It came in very handy one afternoon when we were pinned down by a Batista-held block house. We drove up the truck and prepared the gun. It only fired about six rounds before jamming, but it shattered the wall and killed three of the enemy. They hoisted the white flag immediately." The homesick Holthaus expressed a desire to leave Cuba if he could avoid a harsh sentence for his desertion. Later, Browne learned that Holthaus's plight had drawn the attention of photojournalist Dickey Chapelle, a friend of the Marine Corps from her coverage of the action on Iwo Jima and Okinawa during World War II. Chapelle helped to negotiate Holthaus's return in September 1959 to Guantánamo Bay to face charges. Although Chapelle testified on the marine's behalf, calling him "an idealist fighting for what he believed was a just cause," a navy court sentenced him to serve twenty-four months in prison.[31]

As part of his Cuban series, Browne pondered the revolution's future, trying to arrive at an answer to a question most Americans asked: Would Cuba become a Communist country, directly under the influence of the

Soviet Union? The officials Browne talked to issued strong denials that Castro had any personal ties to Communists, but a few expressed their worries to the American reporter. One thing he knew for certain was that confusion and immaturity dominated when it came to governing. One day, while waiting to meet with Osvaldo Dorticós Torrado, the minister of revolutionary law and minister of agriculture, Browne met another American who owned and managed a tomato farm he wanted to give to the Cuban government so it could be turned into a cooperative owned and managed by the workers. Officials rebuffed the American's offer, with Dorticós telling Browne that Cubans had "no need of gifts from the imperialist planters. We shall expropriate the land for ourselves at our own pace, and reorganize it according to socialist norms, not the wishes of its former Yankee owners." A member of Cuba's criminal class admitted to the reporter that he could kill anyone he wanted for $1,000, half of the total ahead of time and half after the kill, the same as he could under Batista, but "only now there's a tax on it for agrarian reform." Several people told Browne that the revolution could survive without turning to Communism, instead becoming "neutralist." During his time in the country, Browne thought that while Castro supported "sweeping social and political reforms, many of which parallel Communist aims, I think it is too soon to call the government Communist, however." He believed nobody could predict anything about Cuba with any certainty, and, in the end, it all came down to a "useless statement made by one of my friends: 'Cuba certainly bears watching.'"[32]

Returning to Middletown, Browne resumed his usual editorial duties for the newspaper. Having enjoyed a taste of the "nectar of foreign correspondence," he wanted more. In the summer of 1960 he decided to act, driving to New York City to apply for a position with "the world's largest employer of foreign correspondents," the Associated Press, at its offices at 50 Rockefeller Plaza. Founded in 1846 through a meeting of five New York City newspapers looking to share news transmitted via telegraph, the AP had expanded its reach by 1965 to include fifty-seven news bureaus outside the United States staffed by reporters dedicated to what became known as the holy grail: "Get the news; get it first, best and fairest; and God help anyone who got in the way." In the mid-1930s the service had developed wirephoto transmission of images for breaking news. Those lucky enough to earn a spot as an AP foreign correspondent were described in near-mythical terms by Ben Bassett, AP foreign editor, who noted that collectively, "He speaks 24 languages. He shivers in weather 40 below zero and sizzles in 100 above. He eats rice or sheep's eyes or caviar, as the occasion demands. He writes around 100,000 words every day and spends over a thousand dollars getting them to market." Those working for the AP were conditioned to long hours and the belief, Browne pointed out, that no matter what they produced it should have been done "quicker and better. Wire service people used to say there was a deadline every minute, and it was literally true."[33]

To test his newswriting ability, AP editors in New York gave Browne fictional information he had to shape into an article. He must have done well, as a month later he received an offer from the AP to work at its bureau in Baltimore, Maryland, under the tutelage of its news chief, Max Fullerton. Browne also had to write a letter to AP's personnel manager, Wes Gallagher, a veteran correspondent who had covered World War II, describing what he hoped to accomplish in the future. Browne remembered that he "put my heart into it," noting that he spoke French, German, and Spanish and asking for "a foreign post, preferably in a third-world country, Viet Nam if possible," because he believed that Indochina "was likely to be a fulcrum of news and history in the years to come." After all, the Vietnamese had defeated their colonial masters, the French, after winning a decisive victory at the Battle of Dien Bien Phu in the spring of 1954. Much still had to be decided in Indochina, and that meant plenty of opportunity for a young journalist such as Browne.[34]

Browne considered his year in Baltimore as "a low point" in his life, due in part to an ill-fated second marriage, but he did receive essential training in "filing the wires," a job he described as almost as tense as being an air-traffic controller at a busy airport. The nuts and bolts of his position meant that the copy he wrote had to be turned over to desk editors, who gave the finished text to "punchers" responsible for retyping the pieces onto machines that converted the letters and numbers into holes on paper type. "This tape could then be read by a device that translated the holes into electrical impulses sent over teletype wires," Browne recalled. AP-member newsrooms received the stories via large, metal teletype machines that printed out pieces at about sixty-six words per minute. Ringing bells on these machines marked important news—three bells for an Urgent, five bells for a Bulletin, and ten bells for a Flash, "a transcendent development—one likely to be a top story of the year," according to the AP stylebook. Browne learned that editors desired from their reporters, above all, speed to beat their competitors, especially the AP's chief rival, United Press International. "Accuracy is important, too," he noted, "but newsmen can't afford to spend so much time checking something that they end up beaten." AP bureau reporters dreaded receiving a "rocket," an urgent message from the home office rebuking him or her for missing a major story that a competing journalist had secured and demanding a response at the earliest moment. Usually that meant the correspondent had to call the person quoted by the competition, sometimes rousting them from sleep, to ask: "I know you've been through all this with my competitor, but I need some information, too."[35]

Although worried that he might spend the rest of his AP career in Baltimore, relegated to rewriting sports stories, Browne had his life changed in the fall of 1961 when he received a telephone call at his apartment from Fullerton. His boss's message was to the point: "You have three days to get up to New York for a week of indoctrination. The AP wants you in Saigon. Congratulations, and get going." Packing everything he owned in just one Samsonite suitcase, Browne set off for his new assignment as not only a foreign correspondent but a war correspondent as well. "I was overjoyed," he remembered. "Any consideration that I might have had about the overall galactic import of Cold War-ism escaped me completely. I was interested only in serving Gallagher, serving the Associated Press, and reporting everything as freely and completely as I could. Not with any idea of siding with any side." His dedication to his profession overshadowed his responsibilities as a husband and father, which caused him some regret later in life. "But it seemed to me that coverage of the war was more important than personal feelings," Browne reflected.[36]

Traditionally, Americans war news had the flavor of sports reporting, Browne believed. "Wars lend themselves very well both to the general game story with box score, and to the locker room sidebars featuring interviews with outstanding players," he said. "In both types of reporting, graphic images and strong, evocative verbs are mainstays." He learned that the war in Vietnam, by its nature, did not lend itself "as well to sports reporting as other wars," mainly because there existed "no line between friendly and enemy forces to follow on a map." Another overlooked reason, he added, was that in this war "personal allegiances count for more than bullets," and, Browne discovered over time, the United States had failed in its attempt to "win over" Vietnam to "its way of thinking." But at least in 1961 Saigon was still "a hotbed of public-relations lobbying," a majority of which, Browne realized, was aimed directly at the foreign press corps he had become part of.[37]

CHAPTER 3

"Welcome to Viet Nam, Mal"

BUILT AND LAUNCHED BY the Seattle-Tacoma Shipbuilding Corporation, the USS *Core*, a Bogue-class escort carrier, did yeoman service protecting Allied shipping from German U-boats in the Atlantic Ocean during World War II. Remaining in the US fleet after the war, the *Core* had transitioned into an aviation transport ship by the late 1950s. On December 11, 1961, the 7,800-ton ship, "her unmistakable deck cargo visible for miles," steamed past wooden sampans and junks plying the Saigon River before docking at the foot of downtown Tu Do Street at a pier in front of the Majestic Hotel in Saigon, South Vietnam. As one onlooker recalled, the *Core* "loomed menacingly over the low waterfront buildings of the Saigon quay, and a crowd gathered to gape at the vessel as its American crew and technicians worked the cranes and machinery." The ship had been assigned to deliver approximately thirty H-21 Shawnee helicopters (known as "flying bananas" for their distinctive shape), a handful of North American T-28 aircraft, and more than four hundred US soldiers.[1]

The distinctive ship, and the hundreds of "grinning, waving service men" crowding its deck, quickly caught the attention of reporters based in Saigon. They had come to the "Paris of the Orient" to report on the burgeoning fighting between Communist North Vietnam and President Ngo

Dinh Diem's anti-Communist, Catholic-dominated government of South Vietnam, supported by the United States under its new young leader, President John F. Kennedy. Malcolm Browne, the head of the Associated Press's bureau, at his new job for only a month, dutifully trooped with his fellow journalists to the riverfront to attempt to wrangle his way onto the *Core* or at least gain the attention of someone on the ship to come ashore to offer details about its mission. A military policeman, with "a twinkle in his eye," Browne recalled, told the assembled newsmen that there was nothing to see and if anyone wanted an official statement, they had talk to the staff at the US Information Service's downtown press office. The gathered newsmen took to their heels for the USIS office, where they were shown to the director's office. Confronted with questions about the ship's sudden appearance, the director responded: "Aircraft carrier? What aircraft carrier? I don't see any aircraft carrier." He reminded the journalists that he could not discuss matters relating to military movements, adding that US service members were in South Vietnam as advisers only and were not supposed "to engage in combat."[2]

It seemed laughable to avoid acknowledging the carrier's plain-as-day presence, but Browne saw the official intransigence as "merely a nuisance," as, after all, he and the other reporters could not be stopped from filing news articles and photographs detailing the *Core*'s delivery of supplies. They were scooped, however, by North Vietnamese spies, who reported over Radio Hanoi about the number and type of aircraft delivered and provided individual serial numbers. Browne's report, sent over the wires to newspapers around the world, identified the units involved—the Fifty-Seventh Light Helicopter Company of Fort Lewis, Washington, commanded by Major Robert J. Dillard, and the Eighth Light Helicopter Company of Fort Bragg, North Carolina, commanded by Major Charles M. Hardesty. The reporter also pointed out that while American and Vietnamese officials had declined to make any official comments about the material being delivered, because the ship "had to dock at rush hour at a pier on one of Saigon's busiest streets, real secrecy was impossible."[3]

The incident pointed to a larger problem for newsmen in South Vietnam: US government officials in Washington, DC, as well as those stationed in Saigon, appeared determined, Browne noted, to reveal as little as possible about the growing American involvement in the struggle—a situation he described as his country's "gray war." Any mention of the word "combat" in connection with anything Americans did in South Vietnam "is avoided by all officials at any cost," he reported. "Combat is a dirty word, despite the purple hearts awarded and 'combat hours' logged." Browne realized that everything the press was being told was "if not a total lie, at least a distortion of the truth." Secretary of State Dean Rusk had even cabled the American embassy in Saigon that officials should give only "routine cooperation" to reporters about American military activity in the country, nor should they admit that the 1954 Geneva Peace Accords were not being followed to the letter. Robert Manning, an assistant secretary of state in Kennedy's administration tasked with examining press relations, reported that the problem had been complicated by "the longstanding desire of the United States government to see the American involvement minimized, even represented as something less in reality than it is." Just eleven days after the *Core*'s arrival, serviceman James T. Davis of Livingston, Tennessee, became the first American combat fatality of the Vietnam War. He would not be the last. By the time the final helicopter lifted off from the US embassy grounds in April 1975, approximately fifty-eight thousand Americans had given their lives or were listed as missing in action in a war that tore the United States apart.[4]

In addition to facing stonewalling when it came to cooperation from US officials, and pressure by such senior military leaders as Admiral Harry Felt, commander of all US forces in the Pacific, to "get on the team" and support American policy in the region (a situation that never seemed to get better), reporters were confronted with outright hostility and sometimes violent reprisals from Diem's government, which had instituted tight controls over its own media and kept a close eye on what reporters from other countries had to say about its rule. "The Vietnamese government is against us," Browne quoted another correspondent in an AP dispatch. "They figure we are all spies or Communist propagandists." Government officials expected US journalists to support their fight against the Communists without question. "You all act as if you were just spectators here," Madame Ngo Dinh Nhu, Diem's powerful, fierce sister-in-law, said to members of the Western press. "Don't you realize you are with us and we need your support?" Some Diem family members even hinted that the government had prepared a list of foreign correspondents to be assassinated, hoping to intimidate the newsmen. Any articles that were overcritical or viewed as possible Communist propaganda were "delayed or stopped," Browne noted. Reporters who dared to be too independent were hauled before South Vietnam's director general of information for harsh reprimands; some were summarily expelled from the country. One of Browne's AP predecessors, Rene Inagaki, was kicked out of the country when one of his stories displeased Madame Nhu. Veteran reporter Homer Bigart of the *New York Times*, who had survived covering battles in World War II and Korea, came to view Vietnam, Browne noted, as "a snake pit, where nothing was as it seemed and no one told the truth." While the Saigon government regarded correspondents as "scabby sheep" and treated them accordingly, Browne recalled that the Vietnamese people were "friendly and agreeable," and reporters could cultivate private sources among them.[5]

One incident typified the South Vietnamese government's mendacity and the willingness of US officials to support such dishonesty. On May 1, 1962, the Viet Cong released two American soldiers after holding them for several weeks. The VC gave them several leaflets to distribute to their comrades urging the Americans not to participate in a "dirty imperialist war." Because such mercy from the Communists conflicted with South Vietnamese government propaganda, officials came up with a cover story, passed along to correspondents by the US military information office, that Vietnamese troops had raided an enemy camp and freed US prisoners Sergeant Francis Quinn of Niagara Falls, New York, and George E. Groom of Saint Joseph, Missouri. Browne believed that the official story "made the whole thing sound like a cowboy movie, in which the good guys wipe out the bad guys."[6]

Reporters were suspicious from the start, pointing out it seemed odd that the Americans had been freed on May 1, International Workers Day, a major holiday for the Communists. "It turned out later that the Viet Cong had not only released the two men," Browne said, "but had sent a squad of escorts with them to make sure they got into no further trouble on the way back to the nearest government guard post." Behind the scenes, an American military official also sought to keep the sergeants from telling the press about the leaflets they had received. John Mecklin, a public affairs officer for the US embassy, who had just started his job, argued against this suggestion, pointing out that Americans did not "take that kind of propaganda seriously, just as we all had laughed at Tokyo Rose and Axis Sally during World War II." The military ignored Mecklin's advice. One of the sergeants lied when asked if he had received any leaflets, and the press learned they had been lied to. Peter Kalischer of CBS television obtained a copy of one of the leaflets from the American soldiers. As Mecklin discovered, US officials viewed a reporter "as a natural adversary who was deliberately trying to sabotage the national interest, or as a child who would not understand and should not be asking about grown-up affairs."[7]

To overcome the obstacles placed in their path and present an accurate portrayal of the war, Browne advised, a reporter had to be aggressive, resourceful, and use, at times, clandestine methods "uncomfortably close to those used by professional intelligence units." Correspondents could expect only "very little help from most official sources, and news comes the hard way," he added. As officials learned, however, the new AP reporter, as one of his colleagues pointed out, "had no fear of sticking his nose where it wasn't wanted." Much later Browne realized that he had been guided in his thinking about the war from his previous experience as a chemist. "So when I got to Saigon," he remembered, "I was resolved not to treat this as journalism but as a piece of observation that should be as accurate and as telling as possible, looking for the truth behind the truth." During his years covering the war, he discovered that there were "no unalloyed good guys in Viet Nam. There were plenty of bad guys on all sides, and everyone sometimes stooped to savagery when it suited them." As Browne pointed out, liberal actress Jane Fonda was just as naïve in her idealistic views of North Vietnam's motives in the war as conservative actor John Wayne was in his idealized opinions about the US Special Forces, the Green Berets. "Neither of these extreme views corresponded to the shades-of-gray distinctions we newsmen saw," he concluded.[8]

Browne knew he would be facing unique challenges in his post when he arrived in the country on a Pan-American flight at Saigon's Tan Son Nhut Airport on November 11, 1961. He had not dressed for the climate; he wore a heavy wool suit and a topcoat in the oppressive ninety-six-degree heat that he attempted to deal with by smoking three packs of cigarettes a day, a habit he later quit. Although the heat caused him to sweat like a pig and feel miserable, at the same time, Browne recalled that he was "delighted to be there. . . . It was just a glorious place." After accepting greetings from his Chinese Vietnamese assistant, Bill Ha Van Tran, who said, "Welcome to Viet Nam, Mal," Browne headed toward the immigration counter to have his documentation checked. Two photographers were on hand to snap his photo. With his blond hair, blue eyes, and standing six feet one in height, he made an easy target. Tran told him that one of the photographers worked for a local English-language newspaper, the *Times of Vietnam*, while the other represented the government's secret police.[9]

Adapting to his new surroundings, Browne soon switched into clothing better suited for field assignments—khaki chino pants, a sports shirt, a canteen and belt (making sure to bring along on assignments a bottle of water-sterilizing tablets), and sneakerlike canvas shoes, the same as those worn by members of the Army of the Republic of Vietnam (shortened to ARVN in press reports). As the fighting grew more intense, he and other correspondents took to wearing "inconspicuous olive-green fatigues and boots with steel plates in their soles" to protect against the numerous booby traps scattered over the countryside. On any given day, Browne could arrive at his office "muddy and tired from a military operation in the country side, hit the typewriter for a 300 or 400 word lead, shower and change into dinner clothes for some diplomatic dinner, then duck out before dessert to file a new lead or check out a tip."[10]

Traveling from the airport to the AP's office on Rue Pasteur Street, Browne looked out the taxi's window and saw a couple of young men flying a small, noisy gasoline-powered airplane at a landscaped park that served as the home of a model-airplane club. He thought that the city must be luxuriating in a brief respite from its war, but later realized what he observed was normal. As his taxi driver dodged the crowded street vendors and their customers, Browne was perplexed for a bit, as the news from Vietnam he and other Americans had been receiving "conveyed a radically different impression from what someone actually on the scene saw." As he gained more and more experience in reporting about combat, he learned that war consisted of "long, relatively peaceful periods and a lot of waiting, interrupted by occasional battles and violence." The ground-floor office he occupied in a three-story apartment building had a court-yard that opened on Rue Pasteur Street. The frosted-glass windows obscured what would have been a splendid view, as just a few steps from the front door Browne could sample the pleasures of the landscaped grounds of the Gia Long Palace, which eventually served as the official residence of the country's ruling family, including President Diem; his brother, Ngo Dinh Nhu; and Nhu's wife, Madame Nhu. Because of its closeness to the palace, those who worked at the bureau became used to seeing white-uniformed policemen standing guard there and regular police patrols on nearby streets. During tense times in the capital, AP employees had to deal with military vehicles, including half-tracks sprouting anti-aircraft guns, parked near their office's front door.[11]

Saigon's sights and sounds entranced Browne from the start. He had been primed for his stay from his time in New York as a child when he caught "the first whiff of a spice from the bark of a tree called Saigon cassia—a close relative to the cinnamon. I'll always associate the name Saigon with that delicious smell." He was impressed by the tamarind trees that arched over the city's downtown streets, providing much-needed shade for the numerous pedestrians and bicyclists. People loved to stroll down Nguyen Hue, a wide boulevard that led from city hall to the river. Browne treasured each day's dusk, which he remembered usually occurred in Saigon at about 7:00 p.m. "That was the time when office workers and shop-keepers headed home on their bikes," he recalled, "permeating the town with the tinkle of bells—a gentler sound than the blasts of our Western car horns and electronic sirens." He became transfixed by the sight of the city's women pedaling their bicycles while clad in conical "palm-leaf hats, silk trousers and brilliantly colored *ao-dai* dresses, which billowed behind their bikes like the plumes of exotic birds." As the skies darkened, residents lit gasoline lanterns and Browne could catch a "symphony of food odors—the pungent smell of *nuoc-mam* fish sauce, the mouth-watering aroma of noodle soups, the reek of durian (sometimes called 'jack fruit') and the scent of curry spiced with Saigon cassia." Evening also brought "special sounds," including the wooden raps from the sticks of noodle vendors, croaks from geckos who had stuffed themselves on the abundant mosquitos, and the "tuneless music of Vietnamese folk opera weeping from a million portable radios slung from the hammocks and mosquito nets of Saigon's street people."[12]

The fighting, Browne discovered, had failed to disrupt a Vietnamese tradition—a midday siesta that saw soldiers laying down their arms, farmers putting aside their watering pots, and merchants locking their stores' doors. Browne came across an intelligence report on a unit of the 269th Viet Cong Company operating in the Mekong Delta indicating that the rebels turned in for a daily one-hour nap at 12:30 p.m. "Essential services in Saigon and the other big towns continue, of course," he wrote, "and fighting men never completely relax. But between noon and 3 p.m. most of the nation is in suspended animation." The national siesta flummoxed and annoyed many newly arrived foreigners, including military personnel, who complained that a "valuable part of the working day is wasted."[13]

Browne found lodging—an inexpensive room without windows—at the Hotel Catinat, whose best feature was its rooftop swimming pool. Later, he moved into more comfortable accommodations: a one-bedroom apartment located over the AP office that came equipped with "a bottle-gas stove on which I could cook simple meals, a functioning air conditioner and an electric water heater." Assisted in his duties by Tran and a "capable office boy named Huan," Browne became a member of a small community of foreign reporters tasked with explaining what was happening in a land few in the West knew much about. (AP opened its Saigon bureau in 1950.) "There weren't many of us around, back then," he recalled. Other correspondents living in Saigon during those days included Merton Perry, bureau chief for the United Press International, AP's main competition for breaking news; Peter Smart of Reuters, the international news service; John Stirling from the *Times of London*; Simon Michau and Jean Burfin of Agence France Presse; and Rakshat Puri of the *Hindustan Times*, an India-based English-language newspaper. Also on the scene were a handful of freelance reporters, nonresident correspondents based elsewhere in Asia, and a few who "used press credentials as a cover for conducting intelligence work and black propaganda," Browne noted.[14]

John Griffin, the AP reporter whom Browne had been picked to replace, kindly took him to a Vietnamese tailor, who offered to make Browne a new wardrobe, quoting him a price of thirty dollars for each tropical suit, including a tuxedo. "The tuxedo, John said, was likely to see nearly as much use as my field pants and shirt," Browne recalled. The diplomatic set in Saigon included such US officials as Frederick Nolting, ambassador, described by one reporter as not a great news source but "brilliant and a gentleman"; Lieutenant General Charles Timmes, US Military Assistance Advisory Group, Vietnam, commander; and William Colby, the Central Intelligence Agency's station chief. A resident correspondent could be invited to three to five cocktail parties every week, Browne noted. Most of these began at the inopportune time of 6:30 p.m., but he found it "wise to attend as many as possible. The faces and subjects of conversation don't change much, but the most influential people in town go to them. People you can't get to interview any other way you often can nail down at receptions." Different nationalities offered varying avenues for gathering information, with Browne noting that the higher the position an American official occupied, "the more vague he is likely to be." The British were usually closemouthed but had excellent information and were good sources on occasion. The French were poorly informed and were "deeply suspicious of the press, particularly American correspondents." The Germans proved to be good company at parties, sponsored some fine press dinners, were good sources on cultural developments, but were "worthless" when it came to hard news. Japanese and Korean officials were both well informed and sought friendly relations with the press. For news from Hanoi, the Canadians, Browne said, had good sources and would occasionally talk to the press. Although President Diem, Nhu, and Madame Nhu rarely attended anything but official celebrations, other South Vietnamese officials could be tracked down at receptions, especially Ngo Trong Hieu, the minister of social action. "He was mistrusted by some Vietnamese generals, who whispered that he had not entirely renounced his onetime Viet Minh afflictions," Browne recalled, "but such rumors merely added to his social luster."[15]

Although Colby and other American intelligence agents agreed to chat with Browne during social occasions, they refused to divulge any substantive information. Browne had better luck with foreign intelligence services, making friends with a British agent who offered a suggestion that led to a better understanding of the conflict. The agent told Browne he should read the writings of Vo Nguyen Giap, the commander of Communist North Vietnam's military forces and victor over the French at the crucial battle at Dien Bien Phu. Browne read Giap's best-known book, *People's War, People's Army*. Although put off by its sometimes "turgid Marxist-Leninist style," the American reporter was impressed by its practical good sense, and it seemed to him that "a lot of American officials were missing an important part of their education by neglecting it," as it represented a classic politico-military warfare textbook. In outlining the Communists' long-term strategy, Browne noted, prophetically, that, above all, Giap stressed patience: "All the conceptions born of impatience and aimed at obtaining speedy victory could only be gross errors. Only a long-term war could enable us to utilize to the maximum our political trump cards, to overcome our material handicap and to transform our weakness into strength. To maintain and increase our forces was the principal to which we adhered, contenting ourselves with attacking when success was certain, refusing to give battle likely to incur losses to us or to engage in hazardous action." Thanks to his British friend, and other contacts he made, Browne began to understand more about the "people's war" being conducted in Vietnam.[16]

The AP's Saigon office eventually came to look "more like a combat command post than a news agency office," Browne said. For one thing, it had no teleprinters, as the government banned private organizations from using radioteletype equipment. Instead, Browne had to rely on a single green, plastic telephone "strapped together with adhesive tape because of its many cracks" because new models were "almost impossible to get." Also, while trying to keep the interior tidy, Browne said that the "clutter of cameras, copy, bits of battle paraphernalia and so on is generally too much to cope with." The office opened daily, except Sunday, at 8:30 a.m. and closed at 7:00 p.m., although someone usually remained until much later in the evening. At the beginning of his time in Saigon, Browne could count on Tran and Huan to keep him from "suffocating in the avalanche of red tape that beset all foreign correspondents, and the three of us maintained a tight ship, paying our bills and stocking the news wire night and day." The staff monitored broadcasts made by Radio Hanoi (North Vietnam) and

Radio Phnom Penh (Cambodia). Browne bought a tape recorder to capture quotes verbatim from the broadcasts and allowed others in the office to use it when they monitored the radio. He warned his colleagues that the equipment was expensive, he owned it, and "if you break it, there'll be hell to pay." A messenger from the British Information Service brought a mimeographed bulletin listing important stories from the local press at noon, and Cambodia's official news agency, Agence Khmere de Presse, sent dispatches, in French, via mail from Phnom Penh once or twice a week. The AP had a mailbox at MAAG (later, the US Military Assistance Command, Vietnam) headquarters, in which news releases and mail from its "military friends" were left, and staff checked it daily. The Vietnamese Director of General Information held a daily military briefing Monday through Saturday in both Vietnamese and English. "An official reads the daily military communique published later in the day by Vietnam Press," Browne observed, "but we usually attend the 'briefing' anyway to benefit from the several-hour lead it has on the published report. No questions are answered at the briefings. In general, events up to one week late are reported, and information frequently is inaccurate."[17]

Communicating news from Vietnam to the outside world proved to be almost as difficult as gathering it, Browne learned. Without any radio equipment of its own, the AP had to send news dispatches by cable to Tokyo, Japan, through the government-operated Post, Telegraph and Telephone office, whose officials, he recalled, "did not make life easy for reporters." Two copies had to be made of each press cable and then had to be submitted to the PTT building that faced the Saigon Cathedral. The article had to be "verified and accepted before the message was placed at the bottom of a stack of other press cables (from competition), which were also awaiting transmission," Browne noted. How soon news reached the outside world directly depended upon how politically sensitive it was. Although Vietnamese officials did not formally censor news dispatches, every story was read by security officials before transmission. During his first month in Vietnam, Browne accidentally discovered that the "most important dispatches were circulated not only among key Vietnamese officials but also, secretly and illegally, among American officials." If American or Vietnamese authorities deemed a story to be "prejudicial to political or military interests," PTT employees would either make it disappear or delay its transmission until its news value was lost. To evade Vietnamese censors, Browne went as far as to wrap his copy in old newspapers and hang around the Saigon airport's lounge for hours hoping to convince an airline passenger to carry it out of the country for him—individuals referred to by newsmen as pigeons. "You have no idea how difficult it is to get an American traveler to carry a small package—even *after* you show him what it is," he said. "The military people are impossible, but business-men are just as bad. Not one in a thousand is willing to help."[18]

To help uncover interesting stories and images, Browne could turn to freelance reporters and photographers, known as "stringers" in the trade. He paid five dollars on acceptance for photos, five dollars for accurate tips on breaking news stories, and ten dollars for information on major battles or incidents in which there were multiple American casualties. "A tip is just what the word implies—the first fragmentary bit of information that something important has happened," he pointed out. Even if there were not a lot of details available, a tip could be valuable to the AP, Browne added, and its staff could usually fill in what was missing once they knew something had happened. The best way to make money as an AP stringer, Browne advised, was to be lucky enough to be at a village or outpost when an attack occurred and clever enough to find a way to send accurate details to Saigon. "Speed is vital on all tips and news stories," Browne informed freelancers. "The development that was news today may be worthless tomorrow. News gathering is a hotly competitive business in which speed is worth money." The AP allowed its stringers to work for other organiza-tions, except for its main competitors—UPI, Reuters, and Agence France Presse.[19]

Browne had arrived at his new assignment at a critical period in rela-tions between the United States and the Diem regime. In October General Maxwell Taylor, a top Kennedy military adviser, led a group that included Walt Rostow, the president's deputy national security adviser, on a fact-finding mission to South Vietnam. In a letter to Taylor before his trip, Ken-nedy stressed to him to keep in mind that ultimately the "responsibility for the effective maintenance of the independence of South Vietnam rests with the people and government of that country." Kennedy added that while the military aspect was important, the country's "political, social, and economic elements are equally significant, and I shall expect your appraisal and your recommendations to take full account of them." Taylor's assessment after the group's weeklong stay included the need for increased military aid and the development of a "limited partnership and working collaboration with the Vietnamese." Using recent flooding in the Mekong Delta as a possible pretext for providing relief aid, Taylor recommended sending six thousand to eight thousand American soldiers to South Vietnam, who would, of course, protect themselves if attacked. Taylor's report emphasized that South Vietnam faced major troubles ahead, the United States had a key stake in seeing the country succeed, and if the administration "promptly and energetically takes up the challenge, a victory can be had without a U.S. take-over of the war."[20]

There were some in the Kennedy administration, however, who spoke out forcefully against any major commitment of American forces to South Vietnam. George Ball, undersecretary of state, met with the president, warning him that shipping large numbers of American troops to South Vietnam "would be a tragic error," simply replicating the mistakes made by the French. "Once that process started . . . there would be no end to it. Within five years we will have three hundred thousand men in the paddies and jungles and never find them again," Ball told Kennedy. Although the president believed Ball's prediction of hundreds of thousands of US troops in Vietnam "crazier than hell," Kennedy eventually refused to send the large force Taylor recommended. The president believed that this influx would only lead to future requests for additional soldiers. "The troops will march in; the bands will play; the crowds will cheer," Kennedy said to Arthur Schlesinger Jr., the noted historian and a member of his administration, "and in four days everyone will have forgotten. Then we will be told we have to send in more troops. It's like taking a drink. The effect wears off, and you have to take another." Kennedy did acquiesce to a "limited partnership," dispatching more advisers and providing such vital equipment as American helicopters. The American commitment, however, seemed to grow despite Kennedy's best efforts. When Browne first arrived in South Vietnam, American advisers numbered approximately 3,200; by the end of 1962 that number had grown to more than 9,000. And while the

Kennedy administration tried to pressure Diem to make some reforms to his autocratic rule, it could find no alternative to him when the Vietnamese leader pushed back against the Americans. As Kennedy pointed out, "Diem is Diem and the best we got."[21]

Three days after his arrival in Saigon, Browne witnessed firsthand just how sensitive Americans in Vietnam were to any reports about the activities of US military personnel over and above their stated role as advisers to ARVN soldiers. Browne remembered that he had not come to Vietnam "harboring any opposition to America's role in the Vietnamese civil war," believing that since Kennedy's administration had allied itself with the Saigon government, it only seemed natural for American servicemen to fight back if fired upon. The AP reporter, however, did have concerns about the Kennedy administration's unwillingness "to fight openly, preferring instead to wage a shadow war," keeping news of it away from the US public. "If we Americans had nothing to be ashamed of, why not frankly acknowledge our role as belligerents?" Browne asked.[22]

To catch his first glimpse of the guerrilla-infested countryside and learn how deeply Americans were enmeshed in the fighting, Browne drove approximately thirty miles along the county's only four-lane, divided highway from Saigon to Bien Hoa, the site of the Vietnamese Air Force's main base, also home to a contingent from the US Air Force. He had heard reports that the newly arrived American pilots were not only flying missions against the enemy but also were "actually toggling the bomb-release triggers themselves—something mere advisers were not supposed to do." That November the North Vietnamese government had filed a complaint against the airfield with the three-nation International Control Commission, the agency responsible for supervising the haphazard truce that was supposed to be in effect since the 1954 peace accords. "I felt that I should investigate, for after all, if the United States was really at war, Americans deserved to know it," Browne said.[23]

As he drove on, Browne thought to himself how easy it would be for a Viet Cong, as the Communist insurgents in the South were usually described by reporters at that time, to ambush his car on the lonely road. No shots came and he continued his journey. He drove by peaceful, broad, rectangular rice fields bounded by high earthen dikes and large groves of banana and pineapple trees. "In some of the fields water buffaloes were grazing, often with small boys or birds riding on their backs," Browne noted. He later learned a key survival lesson—rice fields devoid of children, farmers, or water buffaloes marked danger ahead. "Seemingly empty fields were places where ambushes were likely to await the unwary," he recalled. When he arrived at the airfield's main gate, Browne found his way barred by a pair of Vietnamese military police, with a US MP looking on. Any VC insurgent who stood outside the barbed wire fence and guard posts that dominated the base, however, could plainly see "the looming shapes of [American] C124 Globemaster transports" and could watch "single engine reconnaissance planes landing and taking off," Browne wrote in an article about his visit.[24]

Strolling outside the perimeter fence, Browne had a clear view into the cockpits of two taxiing North American T-28 aircraft with Vietnamese Air Force markings; both were piloted by Caucasians. He also observed a Douglas Skyraider fully loaded with bombs ready for takeoff with an American at the controls. "Here, then, was visual proof that Americans were not simply placing themselves in harm's way; they were actively fighting, not just advising," Browne noted. Just moments after he began taking pictures of the scene, the reporter was set upon by Vietnamese and American MPs, who took his camera, tore out the film, and took him to the security office. The base's authorities were "extremely polite" after learning that Browne was an American news correspondent but warned him that if he returned to the area and dared try to take photographs, he would be prevented from doing so.[25]

Although his photographs had been destroyed, Browne managed to relay a full dispatch describing the base to the AP for distribution to member newspapers around the globe. In his article Browne pointed out that Vietnamese forces were hard at work protecting the countryside around Bien Hoa, as well as keeping the roads between it and Saigon clear. "Columns of troops can be seen fanning out in the rubber groves and fields at the sides of well-paved highways," Browne wrote. "Brick watch towers dot the countryside." Troops were also a known presence in the village near the airport, patrolling the streets. "Squat, black armored cars control the market place and key intersections," he said. "The rickety, one-lane bridges on the secondary road between Saigon and Bien Hoa are covered by machine-guns. Gunboats patrol the waterways to guard against sabotage to the bridges." During daylight hours the base appeared to be "one of the best protected airports in the world," but Browne noted that as darkness fell insurgents took over, creeping into the area to plant mines in the roads, assassinate village leaders, and clash with government soldiers. "Bien Hoa operates as an island of U.S. and South Vietnamese strength in the midst of an enemy that strikes in the night and will do all he can to strangle the installation," he concluded. To his astonishment, Browne's article about the air base caused little reaction. "I hadn't realized," he recalled, "that most Americans neither knew nor cared about Viet Nam in those days."[26]

In addition to facing indifference from Americans at home, Browne had to deal with an overabundance of rumors and a "growing atmosphere of uncertainty, secrecy and intrigue" in South Vietnam from a burgeoning community of intelligence operatives. Most of the rumors he heard from the various spies turned out to be nothing of substance, but they were repeated often enough that they dominated conversation for days at a time. "The available facts tend to be skimpy," Browne learned. "But there are enough hints, innuendos, veiled suggestions and wild rumors for all—much of them generated by the intelligence operatives themselves." In addition to professionals, the region teemed with informers paid by all sides, who contributed their own "rumors and counter-rumors. . . . Sometimes they work for intelligence agencies and sometimes just for various government factions trying to find out what's behind all the intrigue," he wrote. Because of the duplication of efforts and poor coordination among the various intelligence agencies friendly to the South Vietnamese government, confusion reigned. "The whole problem," one unnamed official told Browne, "is which spy do you listen to?"[27]

Unwilling to be swayed by the constant rumors or become tied to his desk, Browne continued to tour the countryside, hooking up with American advisers and ARVN forces in the field. "Correspondents in Viet Nam were always free to travel wherever they chose, provided they could find the means—private car, bus, train, Air Viet Nam, boat or whatever," he remembered. "Covering operations sometimes required military transportation, but correspondents rarely missed stories for lack of access to transportation to the places they needed to visit." In addition to finding the means to travel, Browne also had to deal with the red tape involved in gaining the necessary permissions from the proper authorities. When US advisers were involved, he could make arrangements with George Ortiz, a civilian adviser with the Vietnamese government who had been hired to publicize American military activity in the best light possible.[28]

For South Vietnamese operations, permission had to be sought from the Ministry of Information office on Le Loi Boulevard, where Browne met the assistant to the information minister, Huynh Thi Le Lieu. Her father, a provincial official during the days of French rule, had been killed by Communist Viet Minh guerrillas when she was just nine years old. Worried about Le Lieu's education, her mother sent her, along with her twin brothers, to France. "I had friends who leaned toward Socialism or Communism and they often spoke to me about North Vietnam," Le Lieu remembered. "In casual conversations they invited me to go live with them there. They said, 'You speak French and English. The North Vietnamese government badly needs people like you and you'll be received with open arms.'" She thought it a "preposterous idea," and returned to South Vietnam in 1959 "to serve my country under Diem. I had heard that the South was peaceful and free."[29]

While working for the Ministry of Information, Le Lieu had responsibility for "taking care of foreign correspondents' needs, issuing accreditation cards, and setting up interviews with the President or Mr. or Mme. Nhu, or other high-ranking officers." She provided transportation and accompanied the press and diplomatic corps on excursions outside Saigon. She also censored publications written in French and English. "Mostly I read novels to see if they had anything in them that was pro-Communist," Le Lieu noted. "If so, we'd cross off the names of those books from the list of titles submitted to the ministry prior to shipment." She remembered that Browne came into the information office to receive his accreditation and made a few requests, including the opportunity to interview Madame Nhu and participate in a military operation in the Mekong Delta with ARVN soldiers. "He was polite and respectful," Le Lieu recalled. "He spoke in [a] soft voice unlike most American journalists with their loud and condescending [voices]." Browne assured her that he was learning Vietnamese and proved it to her by speaking in her language, showing her he could at least direct a taxi driver to a destination. "I welcomed him in Vietnamese and expressed my pleasure of knowing someone who had made an effort to communicate with the natives," Le Lieu said. "Malcolm seemed at ease, friendly and communicative unlike most of his colleagues who were impatient, impertinent and business like." She told the newcomer she could make no promises as she had to submit his request to the Vietnamese Defense Department, but she would do her best and call him later if she heard anything. As Browne thanked her and turned to go, he stopped and asked her if she would like to have dinner with him some evening, starting a romance that led to Browne seeking a divorce from his wife in the United States so he could marry Le Lieu. "Oh, I liked her!" Browne later noted about their first meeting. "And although I knew she was on the other side of things that I stood for, I was so impressed by her kindness and generosity that I liked her right off the bat."[30]

The relationship between Browne and Le Lieu had plenty of bumps before the couple married in 1966. She had grown disillusioned with the Diem regime's "onerous mimicking of communist style" that included, recalled Browne, "weekly self-criticism meetings for officials, blue Personalist Party uniforms, secret-police surveillance and harsh suppression of political criticism—all copies from Ho Chi Minh's style of rule, but without the Marxist-Leninist component." Because her family was Buddhist, there seemed to be little opportunity for her to advance her career. "To be manager or director of my office I would have had to convert to Catholicism," she pointed out. "That was the rule." Le Lieu had gone so far as to leave the country, taking a job with the Australian Broadcasting Corporation for the Vietnamese-language version of its Voice of Australia international broadcast. As she noted in her memoirs, she took the position because of two threats "constantly looming" over her. "Malcolm's wife now had me as her rival and could concoct tales that could harm me if I were still a civil servant," she said. "Or I might be accused of collaborating with the foreign press, if ever Malcolm wrote something that displeased the regime." Le Lieu stayed in Australia for only three-and-a-half months, leaving in mid-September and returning to South Vietnam shortly before Christmas (during that time Browne wrote her about five letters per week). "Malcolm's letters kept me going," noted Le Lieu. "They were full of wit and information from home. He bared his soul and his sensitivity to humanity in these letters." As Browne explained to her in one of his letters, he believed that correspondents "hold a tremendous responsibility to be selfless, hard-working truth seekers. . . . Their lives are more interesting than those of most other people, but this is incidental. There are too many of them who might just as well be shoe salesmen. Weak, selfish people who want an agreeable adventure without accepting the responsibility that goes with it." Upon her return to Saigon, Le Lieu moved in with Browne in his apartment over the AP office and she began to live a life that she "had never even dreamt could be real." As for Browne, he was delighted to establish a "stable and satisfying" home life in Saigon with Le Lieu and with her "very sociable" family. The couple became "rather close to being a Vietnamese-American Ozzie and Harriet, when I wasn't busy at my job," he remembered.[31]

In early December Browne came face-to-face with the stakes involved in the war, including the dreadful toll on civilians, during his first trip to a South Vietnamese military operation in the Mekong Delta at a village called Ben Tre, located about fifty miles south of Saigon. Conditions were primitive in the field at that time, with few helicopters and poor communication, he reported. Browne did his best to "stay close to soldiers or officers who could speak French. Most of them could." Although securing the needed field gear in Saigon's flea markets proved to be difficult, he found and bought a used French Foreign Legion field pack, canteen, web belt, hat, and cans of food. "I was as happy as a kid getting ready for a camping trip," Browne said. His journey included speeding through the wide streets of Cholon in a black Citroën automobile loaded with Vietnamese officials and, outside the city's gates, passing every few miles stockades and checkpoints protected by barbed wire. "The farther south we traveled the more tropical the countryside began to look," he said. "Tall flamboyant trees lined stretches of the road, their great boughs and flaming red blossoms forming a majestic archway." The group broke up its journey by stopping at My Tho, the province's capital, whose streets were filled with busy open-air cafes serving their customers steaming cups of French coffee sweetened with condensed milk.[32]

Arriving at Ben Tre, Browne met the chief of Kien Hoa Province, Colonel Pham Ngoc Thao, who had worked with Ho Chi Minh and had led the Viet Minh's intelligence efforts in the fight against the French. Although lauded as a convert to the anti-Communist fight, and seeming to have Diem's support, Thao, Browne noted, had a habit of "switching sides a little too readily to suit even his ardent admirers," with some questioning just where his real loyalties lay. Before being visited by Browne, Thao had been lauded by another American journalist, Joseph Alsop, who wrote the nationally syndicated column Matter of Fact. Alsop had written a couple of columns outlining Thao's success against the Communists in the province, and he glowingly approved of the colonel's supposed motto, "We cannot win with arms, but we can win by dealing wisely and well with the people." Not surprisingly, Thao had a warm welcome for Browne, inviting him to go along on a mission with his Civil Guard provincial militia, although Thao stayed behind, and entertaining him the night before the operation at a theater in Ben Tre. "He said the show was part of his strategy for keeping the people happy and opposed to communism; bread and games, he called it," Browne noted.[33]

Early the next morning, Browne boarded one of the three landing crafts used by the raiding party, which numbered about three hundred troops, an "odd-looking bunch, a mixture of civil guards and self-defense corpsmen. Some were in neat fatigue uniforms with helmets, others in the loose, black garb of the Vietnamese peasant, topped with old French bush hats." Armed with machine guns and mortars, the irregular force was commanded by an officer trained by the French who sported several rows of combat ribbons on his uniform, said Browne. In the darkness it was hard to tell where the craft was heading through the tricky waterways with the only light coming from small boats moored along the river. "The landing craft chugged away into the inky night, the troops talking quietly or dozing on their field packs," Browne wrote in his account of the operation. "A clutter of light machineguns, rifles, carbines, submachine guns and automatic rifles obstructed all movement." The reporter's attempt to get some sleep was interrupted when the landing craft he was on rammed into a small wooden sampan with a family aboard that included six children. The impact knocked the family overboard. "The commander barked an order, the landing craft backed away from the wreckage, and we roared off at full speed," the correspondent wrote. "Horrified, I asked him if we couldn't try to help the people whose boat we had destroyed, but he shook his head gloomily and muttered something about the importance of our mission."[34]

Browne's landing craft reached shore at a mud flat, while the other two craft pressed on to land about a mile farther up the river. The plan was to seize two hamlets on the river front, thereby "trapping the reported Viet Cong battalion in the wide expanse of rice fields in between." Upon the party's landing Browne reported that the troops "stumbled through the marsh to a path running parallel to the water and fanned out. Units poured into the huts, looking for men." Mortars began lobbing shells "at random" into a nearby rice field and troops fired several bursts of automatic-rifle fire to announce their presence. As the firing stopped and the Civil Guards started searching the huts, a man dressed in a black shirt and pants burst out and ran into a nearby rice field. One of the troops fired at the man, striking him in the chest. Browne joined the rest of the soldiers who ran to examine the runaway and found the farmer lying on his back with blood streaming from his mouth. "Noticing a stout stick on the ground, one of them picked it up, jammed one end into the mud next to the wounded man's throat, and pressed the other end down, trying to strangle the dying man," he recalled. "I yelled and pushed the soldier, but his comrades pulled me back, and all I could do was photograph the atrocity."[35]

During the commotion, the dying man's wife appeared, "screaming hatred at us," and dropped to the ground to comfort her husband. "She cradled his head in her lap and chanted a kind of lullaby to him as tears streamed down her face, and the farmer gave her a faint smile just before he died," Browne remembered. With one of her hands over her husband's eyes, the woman looked at the troops gathered around until her gaze landed on the Westerner. "Her eyes fixed on me in an expression that still haunts me sometimes. She was not weeping, and her face showed neither grief nor fury; it was unfathomably blank," he wrote. Moving away, Browne tracked down the field commander and handed him a 500-piastre note (worth about five dollars) and asked him to give the money to the dead man's widow. "Monsieur Browne, please do not be sentimental," the commander reportedly told him. "That man undoubtedly was a Viet Cong agent, since these hamlets have been Viet Cong strongholds for years. This is war. However, I will give her the money, if you like."[36]

The group moved to join its comrades, making slow progress through the muddy terrain. "The soldiers filed along cautiously, checking for possible ambush points in the jungle growth and bayou on both sides of the path," wrote Browne. "Every few hundred feet, a barricade had been thrown up across the path, some made of palm branches, others of still-fresh adobe. The adobe barricades were equipped with gun slits. Women and the few old men in the area tore them down at gunpoint." The government soldiers found some propaganda leaflets, but no weapons. "Throughout the operation, women and children, dressed mostly in rags, huddled among their clay water pots and meager furnishings," Browne noted, "or tried to quiet their restless water buffaloes." All young men had disappeared. By noon the raiding party had finished its mission and returned to the landing craft for the voyage to Ben Tre. In the reporter's opinion, the excursion had been a "disgusting fiasco." Browne's experience, however, had made him understand, for the first time since his arrival in South Vietnam, that the war he had been sent to cover "was something quite different from the crusade Washington depicted."[37]

In addition to his time in the field, Browne had the opportunity to interview one of the most important individuals guiding the fight against the Communists in South Vietnam—Madame Nhu. Few people, Browne wrote, had "aroused such strong reactions in the press of various nations" as Madame Nhu, who served as the official hostess for President Diem, a bachelor, as first lady, and played a forceful and often contentious role in supporting her brother-in-law's rule, winning lavish praise from the local press and attacks by Western media as a real-life dragon lady. "Madame Nhu was as brave and cantankerous as she was colorful, and whether they admired or hated her, foreign newsmen never ignored her," Browne remembered. She actively denounced the Communists and organized a women's reserve military force she dubbed "my little darlings." In her interview with Browne, Madame Nhu reminded the American reporter that to keep the Communists down, "you must have a line and stick to it. Once you have this line, you must not allow critics to confuse you with their talk. The Communists look for confusion to make gains." She warned that if the United States wavered in South Vietnam, it faced having Communism sweep into power throughout Southeast Asia, echoing the "domino theory" espoused by many American politicians.[38]

Madame Nhu defended her brother-in-law's government, especially against any charges of corruption by outsiders. One of Diem's great failings, she noted, was that he was "terribly human and loyal to people." When the president learned of wrongdoing by one of his officials, he became "furious, demand[ing] that the official make restitution, but then allow[ing] the official to submit his resignation instead of exposing him publicly," she said. Faced with accusations that her country was not doing enough to achieve a Western-style democracy, Madame Nhu reminded Browne that South Vietnam had only been an independent country since 1954, while England, France, and the United States had representative government for much longer. "Some think new countries should go through a period of neutralism, but neutralism is the path to communism," she explained. "So the Communists are trying to swallow us, and the free world spits on us if we do not suddenly become a democracy. . . . An immediate jump into complete democracy would fail." His decision to present his talk with Madame Nhu in a straightforward way, mostly via a question-and-answer format, might have saved Browne some future trouble from her. As he later noted, his journalism often annoyed the ruling family, and his name appeared on a list of enemies, but he was able to stay in the country. Madame Nhu was straightforward with Browne, letting him know that she considered him a "foe of Viet Nam," though "I was fairer in my reporting than some of my colleagues," he recalled. Browne was not flattered, as a "compliment from her of even the backhanded variety could tarnish a newsman's career."[39]

Having received authorization to spend time with those Americans risking their lives in the field, Browne celebrated Christmas with fifteen US special forces troops, the Green Berets, at an advanced training base located about thirty miles north of Saigon at a tiny hamlet named Trung Lap ("neutrality"). Traveling in a jeep with three Green Beret escorts, Browne knew he might see some action. Even before they left the Saigon city limits, the soldiers loaded their submachine guns and "began looking warlike." Turning onto a rutted, unpaved road, the jeep's driver increased the vehicle's speed. "If Charlie [the Americans nickname for the Viet Cong] tries to zap us we'll lay down fire in all directions and go like hell," one of the men yelled to Browne. "We probably won't hit him, but it usually rattles him enough to get us through."[40]

The soldier's wariness was justified, as Browne learned that during the past week the VC had attempted to burn down two bridges that connected the camp to the outside world and sniper fire had resulted in casualties among a few of the five hundred Ranger trainees. These rookie troops were to begin field exercises the next week based on the "learn while you fight" principle, Browne learned. Sergeant Al Combs, a special forces veteran later killed in the war, expressed satisfaction with his new assignment, telling the reporter that because Trung Lap was situated next to a VC base he and his trainees "did not have to go far to get into a firefight. Our guys train on them, and they train on us. They have a bunch of tunnels around here and they're always popping up, popping [shooting] at us, and disappearing. It's kind of a subway war." Browne learned that the trainees were Khmer Krom, ethnic Cambodians. "Most of 'em speak English better than they do Vietnamese," an American officer told the reporter. "They're larger and tougher than the Vietnamese, they're loyal—at least to us—and they're the best killers in Asia." Although most of the Cambodian Rangers really had no interest in Christmas as a religious event, they did like parties. The trainees prepared a special yuletide dinner for their guest—a stew that included meat from a boa constrictor caught in a nearby rice field, crayfish, large blackbirds, and a basket of rats. "As a journalist I've often eaten figurative crow," Browne noted, "but the real thing was a new experience for me." He chased the stew with large helpings of watermelon and "an immoderate quantity" of Larue beer brewed in Vietnam.[41]

As the sun set and darkness fell on Christmas Eve, the Americans started a diesel generator and the lights flickered on in the new mess hall, complete with a decorated Christmas tree. Browne could hear traditional holiday carols issuing from a tape recorder belonging to Captain Linton C. Beasley, the camp's senior US adviser. When the generator failed, the men persevered, lighting candles and singing along with the carols. Moments before midnight, the base's gate swung open and the Vietnamese trainees escorted about twenty women and children from the area to celebrate Mass conducted by Reverend Dinh Tuan Ngan, who had crafted a makeshift altar and a confessional in a training hut. "The villagers were joined at the Mass by the Christian rangers and most of the Americans," Browne reported. "Firecrackers were exploded to scare off mosquitos, and the priest solemnly intoned the Roman Catholic rites." After the ceremony ended, the villagers returned to their homes, serenaded by an American mortarman who fired five flares into the sky, "casting a bright light over the rice fields. The shells exploded in the sky, forming the rough pattern of a star." As the troops cheered, Browne wrote that an unknown insurgent lurking beyond the camp's perimeter fired off a long tracer burst that was not aimed at his opponents but rose into the sky "where our dazzling flares were descending, and the guerrilla seemed to be trying to embellish our Christmas star. It was rather touching."[42]

On Christmas Day the Americans left camp to inspect the bridges and nearby village. Their presence attracted a flock of children, to whom the soldiers gave candy. The day also saw an army plane dropping a long-awaited treat—a box of mail. After a game of volleyball involving the US soldiers and their trainees, the group enjoyed a meal of turkey and all the trimmings prepared by Combs, a Brooklyn native. Browne discovered that, like all the other Green Berets based at Trung Lap, Combs could "cook, fire mortars, train Vietnamese rangers, perform minor surgery, fix communications equipment, demolish enemy emplacements, fight in any kind of terrain, make combat parachute jumps or hack paths through the jungle." At least for Christmas, however, Combs's biggest problem was how to prepare the cranberry sauce. The soldiers retired early as there had been reports that an enemy platoon armed with at least one automatic weapon had slipped into the area. They knew, Browne wrote, that "the war would continue tomorrow."[43]

Browne's article about the Christmas celebration received wide play in AP-member newspapers across the United States, including a spot in the *New York Times*. His superiors at the news agency were pleased with the work he had done. Ben Bassett, AP's foreign news editor, wrote Browne that he admired the "enthusiasm" with which he had begun his assignment. "This priceless ingredient, plus a demonstration of the merits of

good, old-fashioned reporting, places you high on the list of Foreign Service 'finds' for 1961," Bassett wrote. There was more fighting to cover, as
Browne began to accompany Vietnamese troops into action onboard
American helicopters. These missions meant rising at three in the morning
to dress, eat, and hail a taxi for the ride to Saigon's Tan Son Nhut airport.
Next came long, tedious briefings, most of which were "widely unrealistic
in their assessments of enemy positions and strength." Browne came to
hate those predawn gatherings, especially because the gasoline lanterns
used to illuminate maps always "attracted maddeningly dense cloud of
mosquitoes."[44]

Despite the many problems faced by the South Vietnamese government, including continuing infiltration by Communist forces into the
country's rural areas, Browne, by the beginning of 1962, wrote that American officials strongly believed they were on the right track due to the
increasing economic and military aid provided to the Diem regime. "It is
clear that the United States has committed itself to the support of South
Viet Nam as completely as it has in any of its Western allies," he reported.
Officials hoped that US economic aid would work to indirectly improve the
fighting strength of South Vietnam's forces by improving the living conditions and pay of regular soldiers, civil guards, and self-defense forces. "Pay
in all three groups has been low with reports some self defense units have
not received any salary for three months," wrote Browne. He tempered his
optimistic assessment by adding that "responsible officials" did not expect
to win the conflict overnight, comparing the Vietnam situation to the
long, and ultimately successful, campaign against Communist rebels in
Malaysia.[45]

CHAPTER 4

The Young Turks

ONE FALSE STEP WAS all it took for Malcolm Browne to almost lose his foot. It happened outside of Ca Mau in An Xuyen Province in the extreme south of Vietnam. The Associated Press reporter had decided to take advantage of the relative quiet following the Tet New Year celebrations in February 1962 to travel outside of Saigon to see how the war in the countryside was progressing for the Army of the Republic of Vietnam. It did not go well. The chief of the Dam Doi district was Captain Tran Van Kha, whom Browne described as "an ambitious young officer, spoiling for a fight with the guerrillas who ruled the murky jungle." The captain had received information, probably passed along to his mistress by an intelligence agent working for the enemy, that some Viet Cong propagandists were operating in a nearby hamlet. Hoping to surprise the enemy, Kha set out from Dam Doi Long with sixty militiamen. When nothing was heard from the captain's unit, a rescue force of Vietnamese marines, dressed in green-and-black camouflage fatigues and armed with machine guns and mortars, set out from Ca Mau on a ragtag flotilla of civilian ferryboats and former French gunboats to find out what happened. Browne went with them.[1]

The relief force left Ca Mau midday on Sunday, February 25. Most of the officers had received training at the US Marine Corps base at Quantico, Virginia. "Man, it's hot," Browne heard one of the officers say, "just like Quantico in summer." Although the VC had attacked and sunk several boats on the river using homemade rocket launchers, the marines did not seem worried, Browne recalled. "Rather than crouch tensely behind their rifle sights," he noted, "most of them went to sleep." On his previous trips into combat, Browne had donned the same canvas shoes worn by ARVN soldiers. Although the shoes were light and dried quickly when wet and muddy, they did not have the best grip or offer adequate protection, as Browne learned when he tried to cross a series of precarious log bridges scattered throughout the watery terrain. "It was an arduous hike for an ill-coordinated civilian," he remembered, "and because I was tired I became careless." Browne had learned to always watch his steps to avoid booby traps. This time, however, the reporter thoughtlessly stepped into a water-filled ditch in which the VC had implanted several sharp bamboo stakes. Immediately he felt "an excruciating pain," as one of the spikes "pierced the rubber sole of my shoe and deeply penetrated my foot." Hoping to avoid an infection, Browne ground up a handful of Halizone tablets, usually used to sterilize drinking water, and rubbed the powder into his wound; it worked. On subsequent combat operations, he went out clad in a pair of specially made leather boots equipped with steel plates in the soles.[2]

The news was not good for Kha's missing forces. Browne and the marines moved cautiously through the jungle about three miles from Dam Doi. As they marched, the marines occasionally fired bursts from their weapons at shadowy figures in the distance. "Pigs, water buffalo and poultry huddled around scattered huts, but the human occupants had fled," reported Browne, who had gamely trudged along despite the throbbing pain in his foot. At about noon on Monday, February 26, the marines found, scattered in the mud and wild grass, litter consisting of cartridge cases, grenade handles, and craters scooped out of the soil by mortar shells. "The smell of rotting human beings was almost overpowering, as we moved along, and a few marines tied pocket handkerchiefs over their noses," he wrote. "This does no good whatever, by the way." Browne and his companions found the "bloated corpses" of several militiamen arranged around a waterhole "like spokes in a wheel." The enemy had also left behind a large VC flag fluttering from a small, bamboo flagpole, which the guerillas had made sure to booby trap. The marines also discovered, scattered under trees and weeds, the bodies of other soldiers, including Kha's beheaded corpse. "The Viet Cong no doubt held a fine victory celebration before we arrived," Browne said, "with drill formation, salute to the colors, photographs of the war booty, and all the rest. But now they were gone."[3]

Browne suffered a greater shock when he returned to Cam Mau. He heard radio reports that two "discontented" South Vietnamese Air Force pilots, First Lieutenant Pham Phu Quoc and Second Lieutenant Nguyen Van Cu, flying American-built Skyraiders, had attacked the presidential palace on Tuesday, February 27, with napalm, bombs, rockets, and machine guns, hoping to assassinate President Ngo Dinh Diem. A stunned Browne realized he had to return to Saigon as fast as possible to keep up with his competition, including United Press International, Reuters, and Agence France Presse. Although he managed to secure a ride in a Buick sedan, his driver refused to travel through areas the VC controlled unless the American paid him triple his usual rate. Two truckloads of government troops accompanied Browne's car, which drove at "breakneck speed" until it reached the province's border. Less than ten minutes after the troops had turned back, six men, one of whom carried an AK-47 assault rifle, stepped out of the jungle and ordered Browne's car to halt. "The guerrillas inspected our car registration and questioned the driver for about five minutes," he remembered. "By turns, they stuck their heads through a window to look me over, and I felt the sweat starting from my brow." Finally, one of the men looked at him, smiled, and said: "Peace, American. You go." The driver theorized that the VC had allowed them to proceed because they believed Diem might have been killed in the palace attack and the war would soon be over. The Vietnamese president, however, survived unscathed and credited his escape to "divine protection."[4]

Browne might have been lucky with the guerillas, but he still had to face the music upon his return to AP's Saigon office. Piled on his desk were blue-and-white envelopes containing urgent messages from his bosses wondering where his stories about the attack on Diem were. "The last couple of cables plaintively wondered if I needed emergency assistance,"

Browne noted. "I knew I was really in trouble." Luckily for Browne, in just a few months he received reinforcements—two newsmen who provided invaluable service for the AP for many years to come in Vietnam, reporter Peter Arnett, born and raised in New Zealand, and photographer Horst Faas, survivor of a war-torn upbringing in Berlin, Germany, during World War II. The three men reported about the war for many years (Browne left the country in 1966, later to return; Faas stayed until 1973; and Arnett remained for North Vietnam's victory in 1975) and all would win Pulitzer Prizes for their work in Vietnam. "I was 27, a gadfly in the journalistic backwaters of Southeast Asia," noted Arnett, who worked for the *Bangkok World* newspaper in Thailand and Laos before joining the AP. He had already been kicked out of three countries in a region, Arnett noted, "where you have not really made the grade with Old China hands until you have been expelled from at least six." The newcomers soon learned, as Browne later pointed out, that the main issues in covering the war centered on the issue of "whether a reporter should merely observe the scene and pass on what is approved by the commanding officer, or whether he should get himself completely apart from the local authorities and stick his nose where it was not wanted. Particularly for the news service reporter who must present an accurate, fair and balanced report, the dilemma poses terrible problems."[5]

The two new AP newsmen arrived separately in Saigon on the same rainy day, June 26, 1962. Arnett had stuffed all his worldly possessions, including a Laotian, red-tasseled ceremonial tribal sword that he hung on the wall of his room at the Caravelle Hotel, inside of two scruffy suitcases. It was not the first time he had been to Saigon. Four years earlier, Arnett and his girlfriend, Myrtle, had visited the city as penniless tourists. He did not expect to stay in his new posting for long. "There was still a desperate quality about the country and its people that I remembered from my first visit and that had unfolded in newspaper headlines since that time: the attempted coups d'état against the dictatorial family regime, and the ferocious guerrilla insurgency that made the chaotic events I had witnessed in neighboring Thailand, Laos and Indonesia seem mild by comparison," he noted. To Arnett, Saigon seemed a much more "Americanized" city than others in Southeast Asia. He could see young men in crew cuts—US advisers on leave wearing civilian clothes—looking to grab drinks at bars and trying to find rooms in hotels. The families of the American diplomats, senior military officers, consultants, and civilian aid workers seemed to be prepared to stay in the country for a long time. Arnett picked up a pamphlet at the US embassy advising the "new arrivals to bring necessary items unavailable here, including 'card tables with additional round folding tops, seating six or nine, available at Sears, $6.95; ice cream freezer, hand operated, Sears, $10.97; playing cards forbidden to be sold here; picnic equipment with portable ice chests; folding aluminum tables; Thermos jugs; beach umbrella (two and one-half hours to beach),' along with other items."[6]

Arnett had heard disquieting comments from AP people based in Asia that Browne "was something of an intellectual bore," who "kept his own counsel" and appeared distant to those who had visited the Saigon bureau. While most AP stories were short, the news service's management allowed Browne to send over the wires long, two thousand– or three thousand–word pieces "about his adventures going out with Vietnamese troops, going to the highlands," Arnett recalled. Although Wes Gallagher, the man who hired Browne and the wire service's new general manager and chief executive, believed the longer dispatches added great value to what the agency offered its member newspapers, Arnett noted that the "regular AP guys are saying, 'What's a 3,000-word story doing on the wire?'"[7]

When Arnett presented himself for work at the AP's office the day after his arrival, Browne experienced some initial misgivings about his new associate, as the New Zealander seemed "a little bewildered." Noticing Arnett's small stature (about five feet, six inches tall), Browne worried that he might be someone who could be easily browbeaten by "all of the rotten stuff that went on in Vietnam those days, lying bureaucrats, lying military officers," as well as be too polite to stand up for himself. In about an hour, however, Browne's doubts had melted away as Arnett started "swearing like a trooper and bawling into the telephone and getting on his combat togs and going out and doing the Arnett thing." Later, one of his fellow newsmen noted that if someone had been asked to design the ideal reporter to cover the Vietnam War, Arnett would have met all the requirements. As for Arnett, he recognized, as some people had suggested, that he might have compensated for his small stature "with a pugnacious attitude," but he had learned during his years in the journalism profession that "a shrinking violet doesn't get the story."[8]

Arnett also changed his initial assessment about his bureau chief. He realized that Browne possessed an intensity and directness that made him stand apart from the "easygoing attitude of the American journalists I had met up to that time." The two men worked smoothly together, with Arnett enjoying Browne's intellect and how he held governmental officials accountable for their actions. "He was into the story," Arnett noted. "He gave me fascinating documents and books to read about the Viet Cong and the history of the war." Arnett became enamored with a twenty-four-page guide to news coverage in Vietnam Browne had prepared to help acclimate him to his new surroundings. Arnett had heard of the guide through the AP rumor mill, with most of the comments about it negative, especially from veteran newsmen "who figured they had nothing left to learn." Arnett, however, believed that Browne's pamphlet contained the finest journalism instruction he had ever received and added that if "the military had anything similar it would be classified!" Poring over the manual, he paid great attention to the pointers it offered for how to cover guerrilla warfare. Browne advised those who went out into the field the following:

> Try to keep in good physical condition so you can march or run for a reasonable distance. You might have to save your life doing this at some point. You should know how to swim. Canals and ditches often are above your head.

> If you hear a shot and think it's not from your own side, don't get up and look around to see where it came from. The second shot might get you. Lie prone under fire, and move only on your belly. Look for cover and move toward it.

> When moving with troops DO NOT stay close to the head of a column or the "point man" in a formation. Professional soldiers are paid to do this. DO NOT stand or march next to a radio man or an aid man. They are prime targets. Stick close to the commander, who is generally in

the safest position available. The whole idea of covering an operation is to GET THE NEWS AND PICTURES BACK, not to play soldier yourself.

When moving through enemy territory (a good part of Viet Nam is enemy territory) watch your feet. Spikes, mines, concealed pits and booby traps are everywhere. When possible, step in exactly the same places as the soldier ahead of you. If he wasn't blown up, you probably won't be.[9]

Years later, in his memoirs, Arnett remembered that after reading Browne's extraordinary document, he looked up to scan the items decorating the AP office's walls. What came next encapsulated the personalities of the two journalists. Arnett spied what he believed to be a twig hanging on one part of the wall. Upon another glance, however, he saw that it was a "blackened human hand," which he later learned had been discovered at a Viet Cong ambush and returned to the office by part-time AP photographer Le Minh. Another macabre souvenir Arnett recalled was a bamboo water container stained with a red liquid that office assistant Bill Ha Van Tran told him was human blood. Browne's memory had less-sensational details for the office's battlefield mementos. He admitted to having a photograph of a severed hand stuck to the wall, but not the real thing. "And yes," he noted, "there was a bamboo-log canteen . . . that I had brought back from an ambush, but it was stained with rotting sugar water, not blood."[10]

Born in Berlin, Germany, in 1933, the same year Adolf Hitler came to power, the husky Faas was familiar with the "dangers of war and the effects of war and bombing and shooting." Hired as a photographer by the AP in late 1955, he had been exposed to the hazards of combat in both the Republic of the Congo and Algeria, as well as the pressure of being a wire-service employee. "Working for the AP it was always that you worked in fear," Faas remembered, including fear about events that have not yet happened, and when they did they "invariably happened at three in the morning." The AP sent him to Saigon to bolster the quality of photography issued by the bureau. (Faas learned that a stringer cameraman had been reusing film he had shot on previous military operations and passing them off as new engagements.) Arnett had worked with the German in Laos and found him to be very competitive and single-minded about completing his assignments. Arnett recalled that Faas responded to a compliment from him about one of his photographs with what could have been his motto: "Great photographers are not born, they just get up earlier in the morning." Faas considered Browne to be quite different from any of the people he has come across working for the AP: "Very serious. Very studious. . . . And very good sources." Staffers sometimes had to vacate the office so that Browne could talk with his informants about sensitive matters in private, according to Faas.[11]

Despite his bulk, at more than two hundred pounds, Faas believed in pursuing a story no matter where it occurred. "If something is happening somewhere, get there—by foot, or bus, or boat," he advised. "If you're not fast you'll miss it all." Faas blanched at relying on Saigon photo shops to develop the bureau's film. He decided to commandeer the AP office's single bathroom, the only water source available, and turned it into his darkroom. He filled the cramped space with the equipment he needed, sometimes improvising, using, for example, large clay pots to hold the chemicals for developing film. Faas also convinced Pham Van Huan, the bureau's office boy, to assist him in the darkroom. Browne marveled at Faas's efficient operation, finding him to be a "delightful guy, very friendly and warm and a terrific sort of person, but still, he could be an awful kraut [German] sometimes." Faas also equipped himself for his work by visiting Saigon's black market to purchase army trousers and a jacket, replacing the insignias with a nametag that also emphasized his affiliation with the AP, as well as a jungle cap, backpack, hammock, and several water bottles. "This was when everything on the market was still old French or Vietnamese source, Vietnamese supplies; they didn't have all that fancy, fancy gear the Americans came with later on," Faas remembered. He always wanted to be properly equipped so he did not have to "depend in any way on troops in the field." Arnett recalled that Horst set himself off from other photojournalists, who had been transitioning from using the clumsy Speed Graphic cameras of the Korean War to the smaller Rolleiflex models. "Horst used the 35mm Leica series, small finely machined cameras that he hung around his neck like Hawaiian leis," Arnett said.[12]

Browne learned that Arnett and Faas were "absolutely fearless" when it came to visiting the most violent combat zones, complete with fire coming from all directions and "people dropping like flies." Although intrepid, Faas, who came to be considered one of the best photographers to document the war, proved to be prudent when it came to risking his life, believing that no picture was worth being wounded or killed. "If there is a good chance, an overwhelming chance that you are about to get hurt by doing something," he later explained, "don't do it." Faas made it a habit to always be the first person to exit a helicopter, as he believed that the excitement of the first encounter caused the enemy's aim to be inaccurate. He also tried to check the quality of the troops he accompanied into battle, avoiding those armed with poorly maintained weapons or displaying other signs of ineptitude or bad leadership. "I thought he was the smartest of us," recalled Richard Pyle, later Saigon bureau chief for the AP. "We would be thinking of what was going to happen and after that happened, what would happen next, but Horst was always thinking what would happen after *that*. He was always one or two steps ahead of the rest of us." Arnett and Faas developed into a superb team, so much so that Charley Mohr, who covered the Vietnam War for *Time* magazine and later the *New York Times*, lamented that if he heard about a big battle in the Central Highlands and managed to make his way to the area on a plane or helicopter he would inevitably "find that Peter and Horst had already been there and were back in Saigon filing [their story]."[13]

Everybody in the Saigon AP office did what was required to fill the agency's rapacious appetite for news. Luckily for Browne, the office in Saigon was different from other AP bureaus. While bureau chiefs in other locations had to sometimes spend more time on "member relations, contracts and so forth as on news," he did not have to deal with such bureaucratic tasks. "Things tend to run themselves," he said, "thanks to the very high caliber of our people here." Browne maintained a policy that "all correspondents should take pictures whenever possible, and all photographers should gather material for stories." On operations Faas snapped superb photographs with his Leica cameras and gathered material that, when he returned to the office, he would work on with Arnett to fashion into a story they could send out on the wires. Both Browne and Arnett took cameras with them and used them, bringing back images that, if fuzzy, underexposed, or overexposed, Faas could use his darkroom wizardry to produce a decent photograph. The photographer advised the reporters on the proper shutter speed and f-stop (aperture measurement) to use and told them: "Set the distance at six feet. Don't move the camera; don't focus. Just look through the viewfinder and—*click!* Click only when things are moving. Don't click when people are standing still and looking at you."[14]

Even with the added manpower, Browne realized that his bureau could not be everywhere, and he had to manage his resources with great care. "There is no single front anywhere in Viet Nam, but a hundred battlefields, where the war flickers on and off like summer lightning," he said. "Coverage means a seven-day week for everyone." Daily Browne could never tell where the next attack might come from, either from the ARVN or the VC. He had to "gamble constantly" when it came to picking areas to cover. In addition to hitching rides into battle on US Army helicopters, Browne and his staff had access to a battered, but "very serviceable," British Land Rover, one of his first purchases he made as bureau chief. The vehicle's off-road capability saved AP staffers' lives more than once, as they did not have to stick to the main road when encountering "a road block or some kind of nastiness up ahead, we could always sort of swivel off. Even through swamps if they weren't too mushy, we could get through them," Browne remembered.[15]

A not-so-dispassionate observer, David Halberstam of the *New York Times*, who arrived to cover the Vietnam conflict for the paper of record in September 1962, commented that Browne imparted an important tone to the bureau in two ways. First, he stood behind his staff when they were "challenged by the Saigon officialdom, something which was very important, and which greatly liberated those who worked for him to give their best work," Halberstam noted. Additionally, he recalled that Browne never "big-footed the story," which prevented any "pettiness and back-biting" among the staff. Browne was able to do this, Halberstam added, because he believed hogging the story was "morally wrong, and because his own philosophy which soon became the philosophy of Arnett and Faas as well, was that there was going to be enough here for everyone—plenty of war, plenty of heartbreak, plenty of stories."[16]

The action Browne, Arnett, Faas, and others reported on in Vietnam proved to be far different from what the previous generation of correspondents had experienced during World War II. In that conflict, Browne noted, amphibious landings involving enormous amounts of men and material, "battles for ridgelines, bridges and towns, 1,000-bomber raids, and territory won or lost were the things that counted." The fighting he reported on from Vietnam often involved one side or the other capturing "a town or strong point without making the slightest difference to the overall course of the war. There were no front lines." The newsmen in Saigon knew that what really mattered was if those living in a village or hamlet were willing to share information with South Vietnamese officials and ARVN soldiers about the VC's whereabouts. "Without intelligence provided by the ordinary people," Browne insisted, "efforts by Saigon and Washington to come to grips with the enemy were of no more avail than trying to sink a floating cork with a sledge-hammer."[17]

When the AP Saigon bureau's journalists returned from action with stories to tell, they faced other difficulties getting news to the public, as Arnett quickly learned. He had spent the first few weeks on the job handling the daily news output expected from the office, something that helped him to understand "the dominant forces at work in the country, and at the time it was not the Vietcong waging war in the countryside but the Ngo Dinh Diem government." Breaking free from the office, Arnett spent three days with the US Marine Corps's 163rd helicopter squadron in the Mekong Delta. The squadron ferried ARVN forces into battle against the VC sheltering in the area's mangrove swamps. Arnett wrote a four-page story to present for review to a South Vietnamese censor at Saigon's Post, Telegraph and Telephone office. Once there, he handed his piece over to a Vietnamese officer in uniform. "He takes up a fountain pen with a thick nib that bleeds black ink on the typewritten onionskin pages each time he strikes out a line," Arnett remembered. "He strikes out many lines, 18 of the 23 lines on the first page, 16 on page two, all of page three and 13 lines on page four." After completing his work, the officer stamped what was left with an official seal, signifying it could now be transmitted by a communications clerk. "My story is dead in the water," noted a frustrated Arnett, who supposed that his piece included too many details about the combat role played by American advisers and/or gave too much credit to the enemy's toughness. "Both American and Vietnamese officials prefer to downplay all these points," he said.[18]

Browne tried to get more details about America's intentions in the country as US servicemen and equipment flooded in. "The military buildup is obvious to any Saigon pedestrian," he reported, "yet the United States officially acknowledges the presence only of the small military mission it has had here for years." Browne profiled both Ambassador Frederick Nolting and General Paul D. Harkins, the top military officer at the US Military Assistance Command, Vietnam. Although they proved to be cagey about the increased involvement of American advisers in combat, Browne, in his articles, gave them opportunities to air their views about the war's progress. The newsman seemed aware of the difficult position Nolting found himself. The United States believed that Vietnam's crisis was not only military but also had to include social and economic reforms. "Nolting faces critics at home and abroad who contend reform in Viet Nam is not moving fast enough and that the United States should press for it harder," Browne wrote. And while a key part of the American's mission was to improve "liaison with the Vietnamese in all fields," the ambassador had to "see that there is never a suggestion that Americans are interfering in internal politics." Faced with these sticky problems, Nolting, who was fluent in French, carried out most of his duties "in secret," wrote Browne, offering only cautious statements to the press. "He's a terrible news source," Browne quoted another correspondent as saying about the ambassador. "But there's no doubt he's brilliant and a gentleman." Nolting had a reputation as being well-liked by Vietnamese officials, who respected him for his intelligence and calm manner. Letting his guard down for a moment, the ambassador told Browne during one conversation that for many years the Communists "have been working in the shadows out here. They control the press in their own areas, so they don't have to worry about their activities being publicized. For once, we're going to try to beat them at their own game." At least Nolting respected Browne's integrity, observing that in his estimation the AP bureau chief was "more sensitive to the nuances of the Vietnamese situation and therefore a more persuasive reporter" than the other journalists in Saigon.[19]

Harkins, who had taken over command of US forces in Vietnam in February, had an impressive record. A West Point graduate, World War II veteran, and former chief of staff of the Eighth Army during the Korean War, Harkins had a "ticklish job," reported Browne, who met with the general in the officer's modestly furnished office in Saigon with the clatter of typewriters banging away in the background. The reporter compared Harkins's position to being more like "a corporation executive than of a field marshal." Although he had five thousand American servicemen to command, Harkins had "no combat units to direct, no battles to engineer," but saw to it that US support and advice flowed "smoothly to Vietnamese forces doing the actual fighting." The general praised the ARVN soldiers' fighting ability, calling their training "some of the finest" he had ever witnessed. While Harkins expected the fighting in the country to remain at about the same level, he gave no long-term prediction to how long it might take to achieve victory. "I've only got half a crystal ball," he told Browne.[20]

Above all, as Browne learned upon his arrival in Vietnam, US officials in the country, Nolting and Harkins included, as well as members of the Kennedy administration in Washington, sought to downplay the growing role of American advisers in the conflict. "Depending on how words are used, the United States either does or does not have combat forces here, is or is not at war with the Viet Cong, and does or does not carry out combat missions," Browne pointed out in one of his articles, trying to explain a situation that would have flummoxed George Orwell. "The use by newsmen of such words as 'combat' and 'attack' has caused heated reaction in the Pentagon." According to the official view, termed as the "party line" by US advisers, America had no combat forces in South Vietnam, he wrote. "Its men are here purely in advisory or supporting roles, and shoot only to protect themselves," Browne said. "Confronted with rising American casualties and the fact that several thousand US field advisers trade shots almost daily with the Viet Cong, civilians are tempted to use the word 'combat.'" Also, there were US helicopter and fighter pilots flying missions to wipe out the enemy below, and, Browne noted, the VC were responding by shooting back, sometimes turning the aircraft into flaming wreckage. But according to the US Army dictionary of terms issued by the Defense Department, the Americans in Vietnam were not combat forces. Browne explained: "Under 'Combat Forces' in the dictionary is the entry: 'See Operating Forces.' 'Operating Forces' are defined as 'those forces whose primary missions are to participate in combat and the integral supporting elements thereof.' The primary mission of the Americans here is to help the Vietnamese government win the fight against the Viet Cong. They are classed as 'supporting elements' for the Vietnamese combat forces, because they are not under Vietnamese command."[21]

Gallagher sympathized with the roadblocks placed in front of Browne by military and civilian officials, both American and Vietnamese, and praised him for his "excellent work." Unlike some news executives, Gallagher, Browne noted, had risked his life as a war correspondent, covering the action in North Africa and Europe for AP. Because the AP was a nonprofit cooperative, with all its user publications and broadcasters as its members, Gallagher faced daily "pressure from conservative publishers and editors," Browne recalled. From his office in New York, Gallagher wrote Browne that during his own wartime duty he had to deal with censors who used to delete such phrases as "mud-splattered," because the use of such a term might indicate a vehicle had been at the front, or "fatigued" when describing nurses, because it might show weakness to the enemy. "You have handled yourself extremely well in difficult conditions in Saigon," Gallagher wrote Browne. "Just try to bear the irritations in stride." He added that the news agency was having its own troubles with the US government withholding information during its tense standoff with the Soviet Union during the Cuban Missile Crisis: "These, however, are hazards of the trade and the only solution is to avoid disputes to get personal on the local level and do your darndest to get everything out that you can."[22]

In addition to regular pieces from AP's Saigon bureau, reports about the Vietnam conflict had been appearing in the influential *Times*, which had sent a seasoned foreign correspondent, Homer Bigart, whose stutter belied his talent (two-time winner of the Pulitzer Prize). Bigart reported about the war from January to July 1962. As Pierre Salinger, Kennedy's press secretary, recalled, the president did not want the public to believe that there was a "widening war in Southeast Asia" due to newspaper stories outlining the activities of US forces. "President Kennedy was particularly sensitive about some of these articles," Salinger said. "It was my view at the time that we should be prepared to take the good stories with the bad in Vietnam, but the President pushed hard for us to tighten the rules there under which correspondents could observe field operations in person."[23]

When Nolting arrived in Vietnam to present his credentials in May 1961, he expected to enjoy cordial relations with the Western media reporting from Saigon. After all, he had often been responsible for press relations for the American delegation at the North Atlantic Treaty Organization in Paris and believed he had been "reasonably successful" doing so. In his memoirs Nolting expressed puzzlement about why relations between the press and the US mission "deteriorated as it did," so much so, in fact, that he believed the media "played a major role in undermining US confidence" in President Diem's government. Nolting wondered if "we did not accommodate the members of the media, socially and otherwise, as much as they expected." He noted that his office was open to them, and reporters did visit, but he and his staff had "much to do, and I for one found it difficult to spend hours sitting down, having a drink, and discussing matters with members of the press, some of whom wanted individual interviews to give them a separate story." What he failed to mention was that US officials in Saigon had received instructions from the Kennedy administration to offer only "routine cooperation to correspondents on coverage [of the] current military situation in Vietnam."[24]

Nolting reflected that he misjudged the antagonism between the fifty-four-year-old Bigart, who he believed disliked reporting from a "backwater assignment," and the South Vietnamese government. As a veteran war reporter, Bigart was respected by his peers and displayed little patience for anyone he suspected of playing fast and loose with the truth. Browne noted that Vietnam's hot, humid conditions were not easy for a man of Bigart's age, and the climate may have aggravated his usual curmudgeonly nature. "Homer hated Vietnam," Browne remembered. "He never made any bones about it. It was a country he despised because of the essential falsity of its protocol." Although always remaining skeptical when doing a story, Bigart, Browne believed, preferred to trust people if possible. Unfortunately, the *Times* reporter viewed both American and Vietnamese officials as engaging in "deceitful games that left no room for trust in anyone,"

Browne noted. Bigart found Vietnam to be a "most frustrating place to work." He believed that American and Vietnamese administrators viewed reporters with the "deepest suspicion," with the US Mission preferring to treat its involvement in Southeast Asia as a covert operation. "There is an absurd atmosphere of conspiracy," Bigart concluded. He remembered that early on in his assignment he discovered that a C-47 transport aircraft dropping propaganda leaflets on Communist-controlled territory had been shot down with eight Americans onboard. He only learned about the disaster a day after it happened and wondered why several details were kept secret, including what happened to the US military men and why, if the plane had South Vietnamese markings, it was piloted by Americans. Bigart had also heard that the United States was jamming the signal of Radio Hanoi, but that fact had been under wraps because "we always held jamming was immoral when the Russians did it." All of this "nonsense," Bigart said, was "too hypocritical for me."[25]

Realizing that the sniping between the media and US officials in Saigon had to be addressed, key members of the information officers in the Kennedy administration set out to craft a policy to ease tensions. Salinger remembers that those involved in the decision to do so included Bob Manning and Carl Rowan of the State Department, Edward Murrow and Don Wilson of the US Information Agency, and Arthur Sylvester of the Defense Department. Rowan, with the assistance of Sterling Cottrell, a State Department official, crafted a memorandum, later known as State Department Cable 1006, sent to the embassy in Vietnam on February 21, 1962. The cable established guidelines for dealing with the media. Salinger insisted that the document's "clear intention" was to improve the "situation for the press covering the war in Vietnam. The fact that certain paragraphs in the memo were later used to repress rather than give out information does not detract from the clear intent of the drafters of the memorandum to improve the situation."[26]

Cable 1006 had a promising start, with the State and Defense Departments as well as the US Information Agency agreeing that in the absence of strict censorship it was in the best interests of the United States to pursue a "policy of maximum feasible cooperation, guidance and appeal to good faith of correspondents," particularly because speculative stories by reporters were "more damaging than facts they might report." Unfortunately for journalists, the memorandum went on to include guidelines stating that it was not in the administration's best interest to "have stories indicating that Americans are leading and directing combat missions against the Viet Cong," and that accurate numbers of Americans involved in action, the equipment being provided, and the casualties incurred were to be avoided. One guideline alone would have especially infuriated any self-respecting combat reporter: "Correspondents should not be taken on missions whose nature such that undesirable dispatches would be highly probable." Although Cable 1006's purpose was to "liberalize" the information policy in Vietnam, its actual effect, noted John Mecklin, the former newsman who became the American embassy's public information officer in May 1962, became "little more than codification of the errors the Mission was already committing." Bigart noticed the hard line taken by the US Mission, describing its unwavering support for the Diem government as "sink-or-swim-with-Diem," noting that American officials who attempted to leak stories deemed unfavorable to the regime were "tracked down by the embassy and muzzled. Correspondents who send gloomy dispatches are apt to be upbraided for lack of patriotism." Browne also was troubled by what he saw. "It made life very difficult," he remembered, "to be facing spokesmen for your own nationality who are the truth suppressers. And it looks at times as if the world is only made up of journalists and truth suppressers, and it's an uncomfortable role for any American to play."[27]

According to Mecklin, who had worked as a reporter for the *Chicago Sun*, *New York Times*, and *Time* magazine before joining the diplomatic service, the basis of the problems between the media in Vietnam and the US Mission happened because American officials believed as true much of what the newsmen thought were lies and had reported them as facts to the Kennedy administration, which was eager to squelch any negative news reports for fear they might damage the president's political standing with the country. "Events were to prove that the Mission itself was unaware of how badly the war was going, operating in a world of illusion," Mecklin observed. "Our feud with the newsmen was an angry symptom of bureaucratic sickness." The explanation could just be simple incompetence on some occasions, he noted, as well as US inexperience with the warfare being waged in Vietnam. "We made the error of basing critical judgments of both the political and military situations on information provided mainly by the Vietnamese government," said Mecklin. The information often was "prettied up to keep the Americans happy," but mostly it "was plain wrong," as the Diem government never really "understood what was happening in the countryside." Thus, Mecklin concluded, the US policy supporting Diem "became an article of faith, and dissent became reprehensible." The reporters were not blameless, he pointed out. With a few exceptions, most were "so simon-pure that it was painful, always with basketball-size chips on their shoulders." Mecklin recalled that the journalists' "solemn, self-righteous, unceasing complaints, however justified, became boring."[28]

South Vietnamese officials, Mecklin believed, thought that the US government possessed the same authority it had to tightly control the media. Realizing that it could not win over Western newsmen to it side, the Diem regime, Mecklin recalled, "sought to control them. It tried to limit their movements around the country, to block their sources, and to keep them under surveillance." Any dispatches that displeased the regime led to protests to the US Mission, which, he pointed out, gave them a sympathetic hearing "in the understandable human hope that by doing so we could get on with other business." Unfortunately, this only encouraged the Vietnamese to make other complaints and connected "the Mission with the regime's hysterical attitude toward the press, including eventually even its physical reprisals against newsmen." Like several politicians before him, Diem believed that the press had it out for him. Meeting with Nolting after the failed assassination attempt by the rebel pilots in February, Diem insisted they had been swayed to attack him due to "derogatory articles in the press." The president did not see the bombing as a warning to him, but as something the newsmen should take to heart as "an indication of the danger of their irresponsibility." The press, as one Western journalist in Vietnam observed, was the "only thing in the society that they [the Diem government] couldn't control."[29]

Browne did all he could to convince US officials to mollify their restrictive policies but he failed. He wrote an impassioned letter to Harkins setting out the problems faced by the newsmen and called for a "general reassessment of press policies as they relate to the military." Browne told the general that military officers, both American and Vietnamese, who had been helpful in providing information in the past were now "unable to disclose even trivial details," and reporters were also prohibited from access to maps and briefings. "None of us expects the government of Vietnam to pay much attention to the press, except as a potential propaganda organ," he noted. "But we are not gathering news for Vietnam. Our primary concern is for Americans." Browne outlined for Harkins how, like soldiers, the press had its own traditions. The AP's reporters had been covering warfare for a century, Browne pointed out, and they had paid a price in blood on occasion. "Somehow or other, we have managed to keep the people accurately informed," Browne wrote. "And we are proud of this tradition." His complaints remained unanswered.[30]

Browne encountered firsthand how US information channels massaged news to present as rosy a picture as possible about what was occurring in Vietnam, especially when it came to American battle casualties. He had received information from US military authorities that an army enlisted man had "slightly injured his arm" on "a training exercise with Vietnamese troops, when he accidentally tripped over a wire." About a week later, Browne discovered that the injured soldier was a sergeant he knew, so he paid a visit to his hospital room. "It turned out that he'd been on patrol with Vietnamese troops, all right, and he tripped over a wire," Browne recalled. "He had tripped because the wire was connected to an electrically detonated Viet Cong land mine, which had blown away half his elbow." Correspondents could count on American authorities letting them know that US information channels were being "kept plugged" to keep diplomatic relations with the Vietnamese government smooth. "If they say one thing and we say another, where does that leave us?" Browne remembered a US spokesman telling him. "We can't offend our allies." Unfortunately, those kinds of official attitudes, combined with the journalists' keen senses, "led to a high degree of skepticism in the foreign press corps about all official statements," Browne concluded.[31]

Undeterred by the restrictions placed upon the media, Browne reported about the sometimes-tense relations between the South Vietnamese and American advisers in the field that sometimes imperiled the fight against the VC. In August 1962 he wrote that American Special Forces troops were being withdrawn from exposed outposts near the border with Laos "because of fear they will not have sufficient backing against Viet Cong onslaughts," and joint operations in some areas had bogged down due to a lack of cooperation. A high-ranking US officer told Browne that he had to deal with "a continuous ethnological clash here in Vietnam. There is tension between Vietnamese and American, between Vietnamese and tribesman, and among the various tribes themselves." The reporter also interviewed a Vietnamese official who blamed the trouble on the Americans' "inadvertently usurping national prerogatives." An antiguerrilla agent operating near Da Nung expressed a harsher opinion: "The Americans there give orders. They don't advise. They command in dictatorial tones, and have managed to offend a lot of people." An American official conceded that there were problems, noting, "One stupid American can do more damage to the free world and give more help to the Viet Cong than any Viet Cong could do himself."[32]

The tense relationship between the Diem government and the Western media came to a head in March 1962 when Diem told the US Mission that he wanted to expel two journalists—Bigart and Francois Sully of *Newsweek* magazine—because of their alleged negative dispatches. According to an account Bigart prepared for the *Times*, a South Vietnamese government official told him that he was being kicked out for spreading "false information which is considered to be tendentious and against the government and the people of Vietnam." Nolting worked successfully to convince Diem that such action would be disastrous for his government, particularly when it came to Bigart, a representative of America's leading newspaper. "This could do nothing but harm to our mutual efforts," Nolting remembered telling Diem. The ambassador met with Bigart, expecting some words of thanks for his efforts on the reporter's behalf. Instead, Bigart, who had grown "sick" of his assignment, expressed only annoyance. According to Nolting, Bigart, who had taken to blotting off days on the calendar until his return to America, told him he had wanted to leave Vietnam for some time and that the ambassador's intervention had only prolonged his stay in a country he wanted to be rid of, while "spoiling" a potential sensational story about his expulsion as well. "I suggested that perhaps he, too, would have to 'sink or swim with

Diem' a while longer," Nolting said. As for Sully, a few days before Diem's
order to leave the country, the ambassador had upbraided him for his pessimistic reporting. "Why, Monsieur Sully, do you always see the hole in the
doughnut?" Nolting asked. The reporter responded: "Because, Monsieur
l'Ambassadeu, there is a hole in the doughnut."[33]

Bigart may have been disenchanted with Vietnam, but he never let up
when it came to describing what was going on in the country, serving as
well as an early mentor to a young UPI reporter, the twenty-five-year-old
Neil Sheehan. A talented Harvard graduate, Sheehan arrived in Vietnam
in April 1962 after three years in the US Army. His employer sent Sheehan
to Saigon, he believed, because he was a bachelor and, due to his youth, he
probably would be "less likely to cause trouble, that is, by quitting for some
more money." He began his assignment feeling "scared as hell I would fall
down on the job," and fearful as well of the competition he faced from the
AP, something that "made me run like hell. I wanted desperately to succeed." Bigart served as a guide to Sheehan early on, especially when he
made some missteps. On one occasion Sheehan accepted as true an exaggerated casualty figure (three hundred enemies killed in action) from
South Vietnamese sources regarding an engagement with the VC near My
Tho, located about forty miles south of Saigon. Sheehan received a late-
night telephone call from Bigart: "Sheehan th-there better be 300 Viet
Cong bodies down there, Sheehan. Get out of bed. I'm hiring a car to go to
My Tho, and I'm coming over to pick you up." The reporters learned that
there had been some fighting, but only about a dozen VC had lost their
lives. Sheehan remembered feeling "almost suicidal" returning to Saigon,
aghast that he had made such an error on his first assignment. "And Bigart
said to me, he put his arm on my shoulder and he said, 'D-Don't worry
about it kid. I-I've done it too. Just don't let it happen again while I'm here,'"
Sheehan remembered. The two men later spent a couple of days together,
wandering through rice paddies with ARVN soldiers in the Mekong Delta
seeking out enemy units. When Sheehan complained about wasting their
time without coming up with a story to write, Bigart corrected him: "You
don't get it kid. They can't do it. *It doesn't work.*" The *Times* veteran had given
Sheehan a valuable lesson: "Take nothing for granted. Find the truth. Get
it if you can."[34]

Browne recognized that despite the young reporter's early mistake, Sheehan would be a formidable rival, describing him as "a bundle of nerves and about as competitive as you could get." The AP man realized his main duty was now to beat Sheehan "in terms of time, a few seconds earlier with the same event, or preferably, something exclusive." Because Saigon's time zone was twelve hours different from New York City, Browne found it "devilishly inconvenient" to have to deal with bosses eating their lunch while he was in bed, only to be wakened when the office received a "rocket," a wire-service cable that, in effect, he noted, thundered, "Your competition is beating the hell out of you. Where is yours please? Need soonest your side of things." Sheehan faced the same pressures from his superiors. He also had to deal with the fact that the AP had more resources to bring to bear on the story than he did. He expected little change in his situation, as his boss, UPI Tokyo bureau chief Earnie Hoberecht, was known for being parsimonious. The joke among UPI employees was that Hoberecht believed that any requests for an increase in salary would come directly out of his pocket. "We could hire more stringers," Browne noted. "We could bring in more correspondents. We had even better radios that extended a greater reach, but he made up for it certainly in the energy that he [Sheehan] poured into all of his work." UPI expected its staff to be on top of every detail. Sheehan noted that his agency never wanted to hear from him excuses for missing a story; it just wanted the story. Both men, Browne pointed out, had been through intense "wire service indoctrination," a process that worked to suppress "unequivocally" having personal opinions in their news dispatches. Sheehan recalled that when he came to Vietnam, he was like many young Americans who believed in the myths of the Cold War. "We thought this was the right war at the right time in the right place," he said. "You had to stop these communists . . . or they were gonna take over all of Southeast Asia. We'd end up fighting them in Honolulu or California." While Browne questioned the domino theory that all of Asia would come under Communist control if Vietnam fell, he did think, at the beginning, "there was some justification in trying to hold the line there."[35]

The media competition intensified when Halberstam, at the age of twenty-seven, arrived to take over the Vietnam assignment from Bigart. Halberstam had dreamed of reporting overseas for a great newspaper such as the *Times*. He did so, spending a little over a year reporting from the Belgian Congo, work for which he won an Overseas Press Club award and received a nomination for the Pulitzer Prize in international reporting. "I wanted a try at Vietnam," Halberstam remembered. "It sounded important; it sounded like a place where all these forces were going to be in conflict, and I thought, why not me?" Halberstam immediately noticed the tension between the press and the Diem government. The night he arrived in Vietnam he attended a going-away party for Sully. One of Sully's *Newsweek* articles had offended Madame Nhu and he had finally been ordered out of the country. "The expulsion of a colleague is a serious business for reporters," Halberstam said, "and in this case the arbitrariness and malice of the decision made it worse." Because Sully's exit was followed by that of Jim Robinson, NBC correspondent for Southeast Asia, and "since we all soon began to receive personal warnings of various kinds from agents of the government, we knew that the threat of expulsion hung over all of us," Halberstam noted. He also could see that the relations between reporters and the US Mission were unlike anything he had ever experienced. "We did not arrive with a built-in contempt for the high-level Americans we were to deal with," he said. Usually, there existed a "relationship of mutual respect" between diplomats and reporters in less-developed countries and, "if anything, reporters—and *New York Times* reporters in particular—may be treated too well," said Halberstam. An ambassador representing the United States in a smaller country could sometimes pass along information to a reporter, especially when things were quiet, thereby bypassing the normal State Department channels to "get his country and its problems to the White House" via articles in the journalist's newspaper. Halberstam could never have imagined that when he and other newsmen reported the truth, it "would make us the enemy of our own government."[36]

As a child of the Cold War, watching the Soviet Union control Eastern Europe after the end of World War II, Halberstam said he had a bias in favor of what America was doing for Vietnam. "I thought, there's America out there trying to help this country; I think it's an important thing and I want to cover it," he said. Halberstam knew he had to get out of Saigon and into the field to see what was going on. "So what I decided to do was to travel a great deal in general, but to reserve a couple of specific areas where

I would go back and go back repeatedly," Halberstam remembered. "I would systematically visit, revisit, revisit, so that finally the people would come to know me; they would, I hoped, trust me, and I would begin to be able to calibrate it." It worked. US military advisers "took a liking" to Halberstam, Sheehan said, eventually initiating him into its "Blackfoot Club," with membership limited to "those who spent enough time in the rice paddies so that the mud soaked through their boots and turned their feet black." Frustrated that pessimistic reports were being ignored by their superiors, military advisers, said Halberstam, turned to the press corps to get their opinions the attention they believed they deserved. "They were talking about the fact that the people they were advising would not listen to their advice, that they were deliberately telegraphing their attacks so that the other side could get away, that they were not acting upon intelligence as to where the VC units were, that they were refusing to take casualties because the palace in Saigon did not want casualties," he added.[37]

Halberstam enjoyed a honeymoon of sorts regarding his dealings with US officials in Vietnam that lasted only a few weeks. "I followed Homer [Bigart], and they were seemingly glad to see me because they were so angry at him," Halberstam pointed out. Nolting expected the new *Times* representative to be a considerable improvement over Bigart, initially describing Halberstam as "personable, eager, and energetic." Within a few weeks, however, relations between the two men soured. The ambassador believed that the *Times* reporter had begun to parrot the opinions of his predecessor and had even more actively tried to find reasons to criticize the Diem government. Halberstam rarely, if ever, Nolting complained, mentioned "the good things" the US Mission accomplished in Vietnam, viewing him as "the leader of the 'get Diem' press group in Saigon." Halberstam had previously enjoyed a good relationship with Ed Gullion, the US ambassador in the Congo, with whom he sometimes swapped information, because Halberstam "knew certain things about the country because I could get around readily and informally, as he could not." When he attempted to do the same thing with Nolting, it did not go well.[38]

Spending a week in the Mekong Delta, Halberstam "picked up nothing but pessimistic reports. The war was not being won, it was not even being fought." When he tried to talk to the ambassador about what he had uncovered, including unflattering comments about the ARVN's fighting abilities from a defecting VC colonel, saying they were unmotivated and poorly led, Nolting became angry, his face flushed. Getting up from his desk, Nolting, recalled Halberstam, berated him for his comments and for not attending the press conference with the defecting VC officer. "You come in here and challenge the word of our generals, but you don't even cover the most important press conference we have this year! Get out! Get out!" Nolting demanded, according to Halberstam's account. Later that day, when Mecklin called William Trueheart, the deputy chief of the US Mission, to ask how his day had gone, Trueheart responded: "Oh almost perfectly—other than the fact that the Ambassador of the United States of America threw the correspondent of the New York Times out of his office." Halberstam reflected that he left Nolting's office that day "significantly less innocent than I had begun it."[39]

Looking to establish a base for his sojourns into the Mekong Delta, the region he had decided to concentrate on, Halberstam first set his eyes on Browne's Saigon bureau. Halberstam knew Faas while both were in the Belgian Congo, and it seemed normal for him to visit the AP's office, perhaps using a typewriter to draft a story, making a call from the one cracked telephone, or accompanying Arnett and Faas on trips to battle zones. Browne believed that Halberstam had the idea that since the *Times* was a dues-paying member of the AP service, and had been involved in the organization's founding, it was not "completely out of place to assume that there is a special relationship between the *New York Times* and the wires." Realizing he was in Vietnam with no help, Halberstam, Browne theorized, "knew he had to link up with some news gathering vacuum cleaner to provide some of the grist for his mill." Halberstam asked Browne about the possibility of having a desk in the AP office. "And, as politely as I could, I told him, 'No.' This was out of the question," Browne recalled. The AP newsman never expressed any second thoughts about his decision. "It would have been highly improper for a news agency supported by its members and subscribers to grant special status to a correspondent of a single news organization—even of The New York Times," Browne noted. "All the other newspaper and broadcasting subscribers to the AP could rightly have charged us with discrimination [and] violating AP membership agreements."[40]

Reflecting on the situation with a fellow journalist, Browne acknowledged that whenever he was in a group, he preferred to "either control or [to] maintain my autonomy," a difficult thing to do if the forceful Halberstam was in the room. The tensions between the two men—Browne, the self-contained professional who thought prizes and awards could be harmful instead of helpful to a journalists' career, undermining "the very qualities they are supposed to reinforce," and Halberstam, a larger-than-life figure who strove always to lead the pack—remained, for the most part, a private matter. More than thirty years later, however, Browne, in his correspondence, disclosed his concerns about the *Times* reporter's "showmanship and confrontational style," wondering if such behavior might call into question "the credibility of much of what we 'young turks' were reporting."[41]

Rebuffed by Browne, Halberstam approached the competition—Sheehan. From Halberstam's arrival in Vietnam, Sheehan recalled, he and most of the other newsmen in Saigon were awed by his "appetite and stamina," noting that the *Times* journalist could "put away a lunch of soup, two filet mignons, french fries, salad, and pie a la mode, and then burn off extra calories in un-Kiplinesque activity through the heat of the tropical afternoons." Possessed with "long arms, big hands, and broad shoulders," the six-foot-two Halberstam, Sheehan added, resembled a boxer or football player. Later, Sheehan observed that his friend was someone who "saw the world in light and dark colors with little shading in between. A capacity for outrage at injustice and wrongdoing was one of his guiding motivations." Halberstam also pursued his passion for uncovering the truth that "infused his reporting with firm moral judgments about everybody and everything involved," Sheehan noted. Halberstam knew he could be an angry person, possessed as well with streak of anti-authority that suited him well for his profession. The anger, he explained to a fellow reporter, came mainly from handling the "bullshit" he had to deal with from officials. "It was the lies," Halberstam said. "It should make anyone angry."[42]

Sheehan remembered that one day in early January 1963 Halberstam, lugging a portable typewriter, showed up at the ground-floor apartment he rented that served as his home and office. "It was typical of the man that he did not ask, 'May I join you?'" Sheehan said. Assuming he would be welcome, Halberstam set his typewriter on the other side of the table Sheehan used as a desk. "We sat across the desk from each other typing," Sheehan said. "We enjoyed working together. We complimented each other in many ways. And it was a wonderful thing for me. And I think it worked out well for him. So, we became a team." Sheehan soon learned that Halberstam wrote incredibly fast, cranking out four thousand words in one morning. "There were no secrets between us," Sheehan said. When they were both in Saigon, and not in the countryside covering the fighting, Sheehan recalled that "we would fix on a story we sensed was ready to be told, set off separately to see our sources in order to limit their exposure and then share everything we gleaned." As for Halberstam, he considered Sheehan as the "younger brother that I never had," and the "best natural reporter I've ever seen. He had almost pure instincts. He saw things so clear." Although Halberstam and Sheehan both provided plenty of competition, Browne soldiered on: "I mean, it was certainly more comfortable to be independent and on your own or at least with your own organization without having to make deals of one sort or another."[43]

Browne bristled at charges from critics that the competing news organizations in Saigon colluded, meeting at the bar each night on the tenth floor of the Caravelle Hotel to decide what the "party line" was to be for the next day's stories. When it came down to news coverage, "we were all business and all hot competition," he pointed out. "We were friendly colleagues in the same spirit that a prosecutor and a defense lawyer may sit down after hours for a beer together." Browne believed that any reporter arriving in Vietnam in the middle 1960s who went into the field, talked to villagers, and saw what the VC had accomplished in the dark when nobody was looking "would be probably blind not to notice that the war was not going as advertised in Washington [DC]." Although critics used the Vietnam correspondents' youth against them, Browne saw such a fact as a positive. Young reporters, he pointed out, possessed the stamina "needed to fight through a pack of snarling colleagues, all out after the same story and all prepared to skewer each other for the sake of three seconds of TV tape or a paragraph of news copy." Browne and his team at AP needed all the resilience they could muster in the coming months, as a defeat on the battlefield at a small village named Ap Bac and a political crisis involving followers of Buddhism tested the resolve of both the Diem government and the US Mission.[44]

Figure 1. Malcom W. Browne at work in 1953 for the Foster D. Snell firm in New York City. Courtesy of Le Lieu Browne.

Figures 2a, b, and c. US Army Private Browne goes about his tasks for the Nineteenth Regiment, Twenty-Fourth Infantry Division's public information office while stationed in South Korea. Courtesy of Le Lieu Browne.

Figure 3. South Vietnamese troops run to board American-made Piasecki H-21 Shawnee helicopters for an airborne antiguerrilla operation in the jungles near Saigon, circa early 1960s. Everett Collection Historical / Alamy Stock Photo.

Figure 4. South Vietnam president Ngo Dinh Diem walks with Lady Bird Johnson as Vice President Lyndon Johnson follows with Madame Nhu during the vice president's tour of Asian countries in May 1961. Johnson described Diem as the "Churchill of Asia." Everett Collection, Inc. / Alamy Stock Photo.

Figure 5. A postage stamp issued to celebrate the Viet Cong's victory in the Battle of Ap Bac, including shooting down several US helicopters. Ivan Vdovin / Alamy Stock Photo.

Figure 6. From left to right: David Halberstam of the *New York Times*, Browne of the Associated Press, and Neil Sheehan of United Press International chat beside a helicopter during an operation in the Mekong Delta. Sheehan holds a map for the day's mission. Associated Press Photo / Horst Faas.

Figure 7. Browne (*left*), Horst Faas (*center*), and Peter Arnett at work in the AP Saigon bureau, March 23, 1964. AP Photo.

Figure 8. Browne jots downs notes as he listens to a taped interview at the AP Saigon bureau in South Vietnam, March 23, 1964. AP Photo / Horst Faas.

Figure 9. Journalists attend a briefing by military officers in Saigon, 1963. At the center foreground is Seymour Topping of the *New York Times*. Browne is immediately behind Topping (*right*), while Sheehan (*in glasses*) sits behind Topping (*left*). AP Photo.

Figure 10. Browne on patrol with South Vietnamese soldiers near Binh Hia, South Vietnam. As was his usual habit, Browne is equipped with a camera. AP Photo.

Figure 11. In this June 27, 1963, file photo, while Buddhist monks look on, Browne interviews Quang Lien, the leading spokesman for the Xa Loi Pagoda in Saigon. AP Photo.

Figure 12. Buddhist monks pray at the Xa Loi Pagoda, June 11, 1963, prior to staging a protest march against the South Vietnamese government of Ngo Dinh Diem. AP Photo / Malcolm Browne.

Figure 13. Buddhist monks march down Saigon streets on their way to witness the self-immolation of Thich Quang Duc. An Austin automobile carrying Quang Duc and other monks leads the way. AP Photo / Malcolm Browne.

Figure 14. A monk douses Quang Duc with gasoline in preparation for his sacrifice to the Buddhist cause in South Vietnam. AP Photo / Malcolm Browne.

Figure 15. Quang Duc on fire—the Browne photo that is most widely known today. AP Photo / Malcolm Browne.

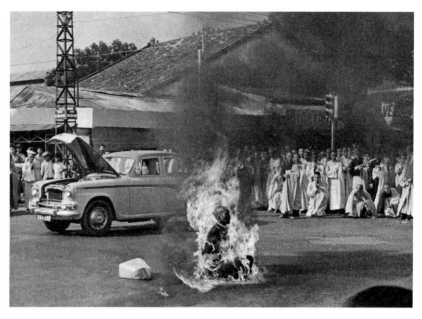

Figure 16. The photo of Quang Duc by Browne that was first published and widely used by newspapers around the world, often cropped to exclude most of its background and emphasizing the monk in flames. AP Photo / Malcolm Browne.

Figure 17. Buddhist monks take position under the wheels of fire trucks in Saigon, blocking their use as a fellow monk burns himself to death at a busy intersection in the capital city. AP Photo / Malcolm Browne.

Figure 18. A Buddhist monk kneels in prayer before the smoldering body of Quang Duc. AP Photo / Malcolm Browne.

Figure 19. *Times* reporter Halberstam (*center, in glasses*) rushes in to defend Arnett from attacks by plainclothes Saigon police agents, July 7, 1963. Browne had his camera smashed by the police, but his film, including this photo, survived. AP Photo / Malcolm Browne.

Figure 20. President John F. Kennedy (*in rocking chair*) meets with newly appointed US ambassador to South Vietnam, Henry Cabot Lodge. Oval Office, White House, August 15, 1963. Gibson Moss / Alamy Stock Photo.

Figure 21. Browne poses in front of his famous photograph of Quang Duc's self-immolation after his image was honored as the world's best news picture of the year at the Seventh World Press Photo Contest in The Hague, Netherlands, December 1963. AP Photo.

Figure 22. AP general manager Wes Gallagher meets with Browne during an inspection tour the senior newsman made of the wire service's news operations in Asia, March 20, 1964. AP Photo.

Figure 23. Home on leave in New York City in May 1964, Browne reads newspapers at a newsstand near his parents' residence following the announcement that he had received the Pulitzer Prize, along with Halberstam, for international reporting.

Figure 24. Browne does a "stand-upper" for ABC Television from an American airbase somewhere in South Vietnam, circa 1966. Courtesy of Le Lieu Browne.

Figure 25. Refugees from the defeated Republic of South Vietnam carry what belongings they could grab during their evacuation from their home country to the flight deck of an American aircraft carrier during Operation Frequent Wind, the evacuation of American civilians and "at-risk" Vietnamese from Saigon, April 29–30, 1975. CPA Media Pte Ltd. / Alamy Stock Photo.

Figure 26. A surplus helicopter is unceremoniously dumped over the side of the aircraft carrier USS *Okinawa* to make room for additional aircraft crammed with refugees during Operation Frequent Wind. CPA Media Pte Ltd. / Alamy Stock Photo.

Figure 27. A memorial in Ho Chi Minh City, Vietnam, commemorates Quang Duc's sacrifice during the Vietnam War. DPA Picture Alliance / Alamy Stock Photo.

CHAPTER 5

A Battle and a Crisis

THE FUTURE LOOKED BRIGHT for Captain Kenneth Good. His superiors had recommended the thirty-two-year-old West Point graduate to leave his role advising troops with the Army of the Republic of Vietnam to serve as an American representative on a guerrilla warfare team in Malaya. Once the popular Good had completed his duty in Asia, the road seemed clear for his future posting to the prestigious US Army Command and General Staff College at Fort Leavenworth, Kansas. "That man would have been a general one day," Lieutenant Colonel John Paul Vann, Good's commanding officer, predicted to Associated Press bureau chief Malcolm Browne. "He was one of the most competent, knowledgeable officers in the country." Good's position as senior adviser to the Second Battalion, Eleventh Regiment of the ARVN's Seventh Division, however, was the last he ever held. A bullet from a Viet Cong gunner struck Good in the shoulder during a fierce engagement near a small village named Bac—later cited as Ap (meaning "hamlet") Bac in newspaper accounts—in the Dinh Tuong Province, located approximately forty miles southwest of Saigon. Although he received immediate aid and joked with his comrades despite his wound, Good later died from loss of blood and shock.[1]

Good was one of three Americans killed in the January 2, 1963, battle that saw VC forces, cleverly concealed in well-dug foxholes and bunkers, shoot down five US helicopters and inflict casualties of approximately eighty killed and more than a hundred wounded on South Vietnamese forces under the command of Colonel Bui Dinh Dam. "Troops of nearly every description were involved on the government side; there were regular army troops, paratroopers, civil guards, self-defense corpsmen and others," Browne recalled. Also available to aid in the fighting were American-made M113 armored personnel carriers equipped with powerful .50-caliber Browning machine guns. Unfortunately, as Browne later learned, a M113 on the move made for a "very unstable platform" for the unfortunate soldier manning its top-mounted Browning. A gunner could fire a long burst and wind up missing his target at a range of only a hundred yards. The well-prepared enemy held their fire as the first few flights of US Army H-21 Shawnee helicopters ferried in troops to the designated landing zone. Then, a chopper crewman recalled, the tree line "seemed to explode with machine-gun fire. It was pure hell." The lumbering, banana-shaped H-21s made fine targets for the VC and were riddled with bullets. The ARVN troops they dropped off to fight had nowhere to hide. "When those poor Vietnamese came out of the choppers, it was just like shooting ducks for the Viet Cong," reported a US officer. Unprotected by any armor shielding, eight gunners on the M113s were cut down by well-aimed fusillades. Looking over the battlefield, an American adviser pointed out to a reporter that the enemy had selected its fighting positions with great care, so much so that it looked like a "school solution" from the infantry training school at Fort Benning on how a unit should prepare a defensive position. The VC units involved—more than three hundred men of the 514th Regional Battalion and the 261st Main Force Battalion—took their time, before leaving the battlefield, to collect their dead and wounded as well as grab expended brass shells to reload for later use.[2]

Peter Arnett of the Associated Press and David Halberstam of the *New York Times* had a bit of luck when it came to arranging transportation to the scene of the fighting. Steve Stibbens, a US Marine combat correspondent for the *Stars and Stripes* newspaper, had been visiting with Arnett in the cramped AP office in Saigon when Halberstam walked in. Tipped off to the fierce fighting, the two civilian reporters convinced Stibbens to change into his US Marine Corps uniform and drive them out of the capital to the battlefield in his Ford Falcon. "The uniform helped get us past roadblocks and checkpoints on the way to Tan Hiep airstrip, the staging point for the Ap-Bac action," Stibbens remembered. Arnett reported that the road became "jammed with long lines of cars and buses undergoing security checks at heavily guarded bridges and villages." Arriving at Tan Hiep, the trio came upon a chaotic scene, with jeeps, trucks, and helicopters jockeying for space on the small runway. For the first time in the war, Colonel Daniel Boone Porter told the reporters, the enemy forces "had stood their ground and fought back rather than hitting and melting away into the countryside."[3]

Inspecting the battlefield, Arnett recalled that he saw twenty-one holes in one of the downed US helicopters. "On its deck lay the open wallet of one of the dead Americans, a 21-year-old door gunner," he wrote. "There was a picture of his wife and child." Watching a procession of ARVN casualties limp off a medical-evacuation helicopter, veteran war correspondent Richard Tregaskis, who had flown to Tan Hiep on a Helio L-28 spotter aircraft, saw soldiers wrapped with "bandages across chests, wads of bandage on arms or legs, eyes covered with the bandage—the wretched cordwood of wounded men, their faces frozen with shock." A chopper pilot Tregaskis knew described Ap Bac as "about the worst engagement I was ever in." United Press International reporter Neil Sheehan asked Brigadier General Robert York, who had come to assess the situation, for his opinion. York gave a curt and honest answer: "What the hell's it looks like? They got away—that's what happened." As for Sheehan, who had to dodge friendly artillery rounds that fell short of their target, taking cover with York, he considered what had happened "the biggest story we had ever encountered in Vietnam." Although unnamed in press accounts, Vann, the senior American adviser to the Seventh Division, had lambasted the ARVN's lack of aggressiveness, describing what had occurred as "a miserable damn performance, just like it always is." He added that the South Vietnamese "won't listen—they make the same mistakes over and over again in the same way."[4]

What happened at Ap Bac degenerated into another war of words between the young Saigon reporters and top US military officials in

Vietnam, with the press considering the engagement a defeat for President Ngo Dinh Diem's government, while the top brass viewed Ap Bac as an ARVN victory. General Paul Harkins, who visited the battlefield the day after the initial fighting, confidently predicted to newsmen at the scene, "We've got them in a trap and we're going to spring it in half an hour." No trap sprung; the guerrillas slipped away into the countryside and the remaining ARVN soldiers appeared to be too discombobulated to track them down. Hearing the general's remark, Halberstam wondered, as he would on many other occasions in Vietnam, if "Harkins believed what he was saying, or whether he felt it should be said." In a later statement, the general defended the mettle of ARVN soldiers, indicating that anyone who criticized their fighting abilities was "doing a disservice to thousands of gallant and courageous men who are fighting so well in the defense of their country." Although US ambassador Frederick Nolting acknowledged there had been some "snafus" that were the fault of Vietnamese commanders, he downplayed the battle's significance, believing "it was blown out of all proportions by the American press." Nolting also criticized Vann for "spilling his guts to the American press and having it spread all over the headlines that the South Vietnamese Army, despite all that the Americans had done to train and supply them, were basically cowards and they couldn't win. I don't believe that." The ambassador added that Vann's comments to reporters were "emotional and not fair."[5]

Hoping to put a positive spin on the battle, Admiral Harry Felt, Harkins's superior due to his position as commander of the US Pacific Fleet, commented upon a visit to Saigon from his headquarters in Hawaii that he did not believe what he had been reading in the newspapers about Ap Bac. Felt insisted to reporters that South Vietnamese forces had won the battle. Spying Sheehan in the crowd, Felt told him: "So you're Sheehan. I didn't know who you were. You ought to talk to some of the people who've got the facts." A stubborn Sheehan was ready with an answer: "You're right Admiral, and that's why I went down there every day." Felt later told Secretary of State Dean Rusk that Sheehan's work typified the "bad news . . . filed immediately by young reporters without checking the facts." A top-secret report authorized by the joint chiefs of staff, the senior military leaders within the US Defense Department, said the journalist's reports were merely "ill-considered statements made at a time of high excitement and frustration by a few American officers."[6]

Veteran combat reporter Tregaskis, the author of the best-selling World War II book *Guadalcanal Diary* and a dedicated supporter of the American involvement in Vietnam, admitted that there probably were many mistakes made at Ap Bac, as "there always are in a battle." He protested that critical news stories produced by "younger and brasher correspondents" such as Sheehan could do a lot of harm with the American public. Tregaskis acknowledged that Ap Bac had been a setback to the South Vietnamese cause, but he also pointed out that the VC had suffered a similar defeat earlier at Phuoc Chau, where the ARVN crushed a guerrilla force, leaving behind 127 dead with very few casualties on its own side. "At Ap Bac, the VC, apparently a very well-disciplined and well-dug-in outfit did it to our side—but not quite as badly [as Phuoc Chau]," Tregaskis noted. "That's the way war goes, a bloody business any way you look at it." Of course, as Browne pointed out, the VC certainly regarded Ap Bac as a triumph. The 514th emblazoned the hamlet's name in gold letters on its battle flag and propaganda posters from the Communists, "professionally printed in four colors, bloomed throughout the [Mekong] delta, all glorifying the fighters at Ap Bac."[7]

A few weeks after the engagement, Browne wrote an analysis of the battle that offered US officials, who spoke to him with the understanding they would not be named, the opportunity to talk about their frustrations. "It's the same old story," one official told the AP bureau chief. "Americans don't know Asia exists until some Americans start getting killed." Most people Browne talked to believed that the negative political and public reaction to the "bloody clash" in the Mekong Delta came about through "a basic ignorance of the situation." A high-ranking official conceded that the conflict in Vietnam may have been presented to the American public in an "over-simplified form," with some believing that the war against the Communists had already been won. "On balance things are going well, but it's not that simple," the official told Browne. A military adviser made sure to point out that military leaders in Washington, DC, had been told several times that "this is not a simple war that you win in conventional ways. They see it in a thousand reports every day and they've learned the correct jargon about guerrilla warfare—how politics are important and all that. They think they understand, but they don't. The questions they ask show it." Browne acknowledged the anger felt by some Americans in Vietnam about the press coverage: "The setbacks are always on page one, but the victories—some of them less spectacular—see little print. This is going to be a long, hard struggle, and it's time people got used to the idea."[8]

As the bickering continued about what Ap Bac meant for the South Vietnamese government and the US efforts in the country, Browne set out to present to the American public the war's toll on those doing the fighting. In addition to chronicling Good's sacrifice, he wrote a dispatch detailing the dedicated service of a twenty-three-year-old American helicopter gunner, Private First Class John C. Dickerson, who survived the enemy's accurate and heavy fire at Ap Bac. "Your stomach turns over a little when you see them shooting at you," Dickerson, who grew up in Mapleton, Utah, and volunteered to serve overseas, told Browne. "Sometimes it's close enough you feel the burn of the passing bullet. It's not too pleasant. But you shoot back." Dickerson flew as a gunner with the Utility Tactical Transport Company onboard a Bell UH-1A escort helicopter, the beloved Huey that became synonymous with the Vietnam War. "His turbine-powered craft has been nicknamed 'Hotbox' in token of one of five hits it has taken from Viet Cong gunners," Browne wrote. "An enemy slug hit the rocket pod several weeks ago and started a dangerous fire. The pilot doused the flames by landing in an inundated rice field."[9]

During his three months in Vietnam, Dickerson flew about 120 combat missions, estimating that he had been shot at by the enemy on at least half of them as he skimmed over the flat, green battlefield of the Mekong Delta. According to Browne, the Huey's arsenal of "rockets and machine guns has brought a new dimension to guerrilla warfare, but it has to pay the price sometimes." One of Dickerson's comrades, an enlisted man who had the same job he had, was killed in action. Like the rest of the approximately twelve thousand US servicemen in Vietnam, Dickerson was under orders not to shoot at the enemy unless they shot first, something that really kept him alert. "It's a shame," he said. "Often we see Viet Cong sampans or units right under us, that we could knock out easily. But we're not allowed to shoot unless they do, and they know it, so a lot of them get away."

Dickerson credited the VC as clever opponents who seemed to know in advance when they were coming and were equipped with better weapons than they had been before. Asked about his recollections of the Ap Bac fighting, Dickerson told Browne that a VC bullet "ripped into the machine-gun ammunition box next to me, and there was a lot of metal flying around. A couple of pieces grazed me, but I was lucky." Dickerson shared his company commander's belief that the escort helicopters were doing a vital job but had no illusions about the dangers involved. "I'm going to fin-ish out 'my time in hell,' as we call it, and after that I'm not too anxious to come back," he said. Asked about his prediction for what might happen in the conflict, Dickerson noted: "We'll win this war but it's going to be a long, hard fight."[10]

To capture the South Vietnamese point of view and spotlight the ten-sions between US advisers and ARVN officers, Browne tracked down Brig-adier General Huynh Van Cao, a particular favorite of President Ngo Dinh Diem. Cao commanded the Seventh Division before his promotion to over-see the Vietnamese army's Fourth Corps, an area that included 43 percent of the nation's population. Although some Americans thought of Cao as a political appointee, rising to his position more for his loyalty to Diem than for having any keen battlefield skills, the general stood his ground when challenged, including reproaching US officers assigned to work with him. Browne quoted Cao as saying to the American: "You are courageous, but reckless. You are an American advisor, and as such, you are not authorized to set up an ambush on your own."[11]

Cao acknowledged to the AP reporter that he had been criticized many times for his apparent lack of aggressiveness when it came to tracking down and taking on VC units. The general pointed out to Browne that he had often told American advisers that when it came to guerrilla warfare, an officer needed to be prudent. "The Viet Cong fighters are using judo techniques," Cao said. "If we are too confident of our strength we will fall down." He also gave short shrift to charges from Americans that Diem had ordered ARVN officers to avoid attacking the enemy to keep their casual-ties low. "That is just not true," the general insisted. "The president always has told me to push my unit commanders to fight. He told me this: 'If you want to have an omelet you must break many eggs.'" During the past four months, Cao pointed out, his corps had suffered more than one thousand men either killed or wounded, while the "Viet Cong has suffered five or six times that number. I think those numbers speak for themselves."[12]

Despite the vulnerabilities they displayed at Ap Bac, helicopters became a vital part of the fight against the VC in South Vietnam, and Browne, fascinated by aviation, made sure to explore the machine's expanding role. Accompanying a mission meant Browne had to get up at three o'clock in the morning to dress and prepare for the day. He would take a taxi to the military gate at Saigon's Tan Son Nhut airport to meet the liaison officer responsible for guiding the newsmen. "Operation officers would generally let us listen as they briefed their crews and the commanders of the Vietnamese units we were carrying into battle," he recalled. During his time in the country, Browne was part of hundreds of these briefings, finding most of them "tedious, some of them uncomfortable and many of them wildly unrealistic in their assessments of enemy positions and strengths." Plans always seemed to include large sector maps with "plastic overlays, grease pencils in at least six different colors, and teams of staff officers to post the position of blocking forces, artillery positions and so forth." (Unfortunately, the enthusiastic discussions about planned operations were often picked up ahead of time by VC spies overhearing conversations in Saigon bars.)[13]

Browne discovered that the twin-rotor H-21 choppers were underpowered for their task of carrying a squad of soldiers armed with machine guns and light mortars to a landing zone. Halberstam remembered that one of his colleague's wives tried to prevent him from accompanying a mission on an H-21, tearfully warning him, "They're only put together with Elmer's glue." According to a pilot who regularly flew the craft into battle, everyone knew it was hard to fly. "It was eighty-seven feet long and could seat twenty people," recalled Richard Olsen, "but it didn't have enough power to fly 'em all up in the hot air so we only carried about nine or ten troops." The helicopter had to "make an airplane-type takeoff, charging down the runway until its forward speed was sufficient to get it off the ground," noted Browne. Pilots had to avoid making long takeoff runs in fog, he said, and too dense of a cover often halted missions before they could get started. Olsen pointed out that the H-21 had been designed in the late 1940s for service in the Arctic at a time when Americans believed the Soviet Union might invade over the North Pole. "We were stuck with the Banana in the tropics," he remembered.[14]

American pilots made sure to make their landings with the H-21's left side facing the opposition so the troops aboard could leap out the chopper's one door and fire at the enemy without taking valuable time dashing around the craft to get into position. On one mission, Browne scanned the "expressionless Vietnamese troops" crammed into the helicopter. As the US crew chief fired his carbine from the door "as fast as he could squeeze the trigger," Browne heard, above the whine of the chopper's engine, a "sharp clang" as an enemy round penetrated the H-21's thin aluminum skin. "The forward deck tilted up sharply as the pilot mushed the big craft in for a spot landing," he wrote. "Wheels banged hard against the brick-hard sod of the dry paddy." The troops jumped off, running toward a tree-lined canal. "One of them screamed and fell," Browne reported, "his face turned to red pulp by a Communist bullet." Meanwhile, escort helicopters peeled out of the formation to unleash bullets and rockets at the hidden enemy. He continued: "Flame and black smoke were rising now from buildings behind the trees, and brush fires were blazing everywhere. Men in black—peasants or Viet Cong—were running in all directions to escape the hail of fire." One memory burned into Browne's mind: A man armed with a rifle ran toward a hut and jumped through its door before the structure was "blown to bits" by a rocket fired by one of the escort helicopters.[15]

Browne recounted that none of the operations seemed to have a decisive effect on "this strange war." He compared the helicopter assaults to old-fashioned cavalry raids. "Win, lose or draw," Browne noted, "it's over quickly, and more will follow." It was a dangerous business, as during the time they had to sit on the ground to discharge their human cargo, the helicopters became sitting ducks for the enemy. Out of the approximately 150 helicopters then in South Vietnam, Browne estimated that most were struck by enemy fire at least once, with twenty forced down by VC gunners and nearly sixty downed due to mechanical failures. Still, without these aircraft, ARVN soldiers would not be able to "move fast enough to cope with the lightning hit and run tactics of highly mobile Viet Cong units," Browne wrote. And although technically American servicemen in South

Vietnam had been under orders not to shoot at the guerrillas unless the enemy shot first, new regulations gave them permission to fire, he noted, "if they felt themselves 'endangered,' without having to receive Communist fire."[16]

Browne admired the tenacity and skill displayed by the American units flying and servicing the choppers, adding that a real "esprit de corps has evolved among them" during their time under fire. They were able to maintain their morale despite operating inadequate machines such as the H-21, a craft that one pilot told Halberstam was "an accident looking for a place to happen." Because parts were scarce and repairs had to be completed with dispatch, Browne discovered that crews sometimes used simple masking tape to patch bullet holes. When a hit punched a hole in one helicopter's engine manifold, the AP reporter noted that its Marine Corps crew ingeniously fixed the problem by manufacturing a wooden plug from a tree branch and hammering it into the hole. "None of the helicopter men lead comfortable lives," Browne wrote. "Even those stationed in Saigon are billeted in scorching hot tents at Saigon Airport, miles from town. They work exhaustingly long hours, and have among the most dangerous jobs of an[y] Americans in Vietnam." Although nobody believed that the helicopters alone would win the war, he pointed out that without them the VC "might very well have won by now."[17]

While the US helicopters in Vietnam were mainly used to bring the war to the heart of the enemy, they proved highly useful in other ways. Before the choppers' arrival, many wounded men, both Vietnamese and American, died because it proved impossible to evacuate them for proper medical care. "Now they can be reasonably sure a helicopter will get them to a hospital in a few hours," Browne reported. In addition, lonely jungle outposts that before had to wait for weeks at a time for supplies could now count on regular deliveries of such crucial materials as food, medicine, and ammunition. A US Army officer confidently told Browne: "This is a running war and we're running faster and further than the enemy. We think the Viet Cong is losing breath." While the American military believed the helicopter operations frightened the enemy and kept them on the move, Browne, reflecting on the situation, agreed with the opinion held by Colonel "Coalbin Willie" Wilson, a senior US adviser to Vietnamese forces.

Wilson described the missions as "rattle-assing around the country" and believed they failed "to upset the enemy seriously, but merely exhausted friendly troops, helicopter crews and facilities."[18]

In April the men reporting from Vietnam for America's two leading news agencies—Sheehan of the UPI and Browne of the AP—returned to the United States to share what they had learned about the conflict at the annual meetings of each of their employers in New York. Sheehan expressed doubts about the support the Diem government had from its people. "It is ironic that the most vocal defenders of the Diem regime are Americans," Sheehan noted. "Very few Vietnamese, even those who work for it, privately support Diem's government." Sheehan also doubted that Diem would make the political and social reforms American officials asked him to implement. If South Vietnam's president wanted to achieve a "decisive victory over the Viet Cong," he needed to convince the majority of peasants in his country to actively support him. If Diem failed in this task, Sheehan predicted that "unknown years of struggle" would follow.[19]

Browne outlined for his AP-member audience the costs of what he called a "brutal little war," noting more than three hundred men, women, and children were dying weekly despite there being no major battles fought. "Twelve thousand American servicemen are now stationed there," he pointed out, "and the United States is sending more than $1 million a day to keep things going." Acknowledging that the issues involved in the war were "complicated and muddy," Browne did say that most people agreed on the big questions: Who's winning and how fast? How can the United States finish its commitment, bring its troops home, and reduce its spending? Browne shared a similarly pessimistic view about the future as Sheehan had, saying, "From where I sit, frankly, there's no end in sight. If present patterns continue, 10 more years of war seem entirely possible to me." Browne remembered that when he first arrived in Vietnam, US officials told him the war was going well, but the country needed American assistance. Before traveling to New York to give his speech, officials believed that the war was going well, but South Vietnam still required American aid to fight the VC.[20]

At the beginning of May 1963, Browne, in an AP article using a question-and-answer format, reflected on what he had learned about the war and the risks and rewards of American involvement in Vietnam. He explained that for the past few months "the war had been on a kind of plateau," with fighting and casualties continuing without either side gaining much ground. The most discouraging aspect Browne noticed was the VC's ability to recruit fighters "just as fast [as] it loses men in battle. In this pattern the war could go on indefinitely." Leaders in Saigon and Washington hoped, he noted, that the VC would realize it could not win and give up, while the guerrillas hoped "Washington will get tired of spending and bloodshed" and agree to a negotiated peace settlement along the lines of the one signed in Laos. Although Browne admired the courage displayed by most ARVN soldiers, he acknowledged that if they were not pushed by American advisers, they "insist on cooking lunch and having a long siesta, even when their units are in hot pursuit of the enemy." Also, because the South Vietnamese officer corps were organized based on their political reliability, many were reluctant to "initiate action that could backfire into a reprimand from the palace." As for the American military in Vietnam, Browne noted that field officers and soldiers were seasoned professionals doing "an impressive job."[21]

If the United States decided to withdraw its commitment to the Diem regime, Browne reported that most government officials in Saigon, as well as American diplomats and military officers, agreed that the Communists "would quickly take over. Without American support, President Ngo Dinh Diem's government could not stand." Browne saw at that time there seemed to be no choice but for the US government to continue backing Diem, despite the lack of progress toward a true democracy in the country. "President Diem rules by decree," he noted. "There is no habeas corpus. Secret police keep tabs on everything." Critics of the regime, Browne reported, believed that unless Saigon moved "faster toward giving the people a voice in their government, the Viet Cong will remain popular."[22]

Shortly after Browne wrote his evaluation about the situation in Vietnam, an incident in Hue involving an important religious group in the country, the Buddhists, set the stage for political turmoil that rocked the Diem government and continued the schisms among the press, American leadership in Saigon, and President John F. Kennedy's administration in Washington. The protests that hit Saigon and other cities in South

Vietnam by robed monks and their supporters stunned White House officials, including the president. "How could this have happened?" Kennedy
asked Michael V. Forrestal, a member of the senior staff of the National
Security Council. "Who are these people? Why didn't we know about them
before?" An American diplomat in Saigon admitted to Browne that the
Buddhists were "a complication we never expected to see. It certainly is a
very unfortunate development."[23]

Browne remembered that the rush-hour streets of the capital that
spring and summer started to include "clusters of angry monks, conspicu-
ous in their saffron robes and carrying flags and banners instead of their
traditional begging bowls." He decided to take on the crisis as his "personal
beat," using the knowledge he had gained about the country's society and
politics to cover what he believed was not only an important story but also
something that might just grow into a national revolution. "Relying mainly
on French to communicate, I could at least catch the drift of conversations
in Vietnamese," Browne pointed out. He possessed an advantage over his
colleagues, as he had many more close Vietnamese friends than they did.
Browne also had "tremendous help" from his wife-to-be, Le Lieu, a former
senior official in South Vietnam's Information Ministry, who possessed
"an unerring sense of the subtleties of Vietnamese power politics." He
found himself regularly spending up to four hours a day in pagodas "trying
to get a line on what was happening." Browne engaged in endless theo-
logical, philosophical, and political discussions with the monks that sometimes resulted in "a few hard facts that became the basis of news stories at
the time."[24]

The upheaval that led to Browne's being on the spot to shoot one of the
Vietnam War's iconic images, and weakened the Diem regime's grip on the
country, began in Hue, the old Imperial City straddling the Perfume River
close to the border between South and North Vietnam. Arnett had been in
Hue many times to visit the Imperial City, which was surrounded by "a
wide moat and high, thick brick walls constructed two hundred years earlier by a French engineer for a nervous emperor." He remembered that the
Perfume River flowed slowly from the hills above the city and seemed to
be a city itself "with houseboats for rent and sampans selling all you could
eat and drink and romance." The city was also Diem's hometown, and his

brothers were major figures—Ngo Dinh Thuc, who had been promoted by the Vatican as the Catholic archbishop of Hue, and Ngo Dinh Can, the region's political warlord.[25]

On May 8 Buddhists attempted to celebrate Vesak Day, marking the birth of Gautama Buddha with flags and banners. They were stymied, however, by a crackdown by the Diem government with a decree that prohibited the display of religious flags and banners, instead promoting the primacy of South Vietnam's flag. Tempers were inflamed because, just a few days earlier, Catholics had used religious flags to celebrate the anniversary of Thuc's elevation to bishop. A crowd numbering approximately three thousand in size marched in the city that day. When the Hue radio station's director that evening refused to broadcast a special Vesak Day program because it had not been cleared by censors, it seemed that some in the crowd might move against the station. ARVN soldiers and police under the command of Major Dang Si were called out to control the situation. Violence ensued, with explosions and gunshots scattering the crowd. Seven people died in the melee; two others later perished from their wounds and fourteen were injured. Government officials pointed to VC provocateurs as the culprits, but independent witnesses blamed the major's forces.[26]

Initial reports from Western journalists based in Saigon about the tragedy in Hue depended on information from officials in the Diem government and parroted its attempt to pin the blame on others. Browne's AP article said that the Buddhist demonstration that turned into a riot had been led by Communist agitators. Within a few days, Arnett remembered, eyewitnesses to the clash stopped by the bureau to provide far different details than those offered by the government. When word spread about the government's responsibility for the carnage, it refused to take any blame, further inflaming tensions. Charley Mohr, *Time* magazine's bureau chief in Hong Kong, noted, "It's the same old story. Diem can't admit he's wrong, and so the Government will pretend it didn't happen, and they'll lie and make a hell of a lot of people angry." Browne reported that critics saw Diem and his family as turning Roman Catholicism into "a state religion," making the Buddhists "especially resentful," as many of them believed that only Catholics "could hold the most important offices and jobs." As the

crisis deepened, various percentages were cited for the Vietnamese people's religious affiliations. Browne said that the Diem family always contended that "less than a tenth of the nation was Buddhist," with the US
Information Service estimating that approximately three-quarters of the
population "was at least nominally Buddhist, with large doses of ancestor
worship, animism, Confucianism and others thrown in." Still, Browne
thought from the beginning that the clash in Hue had "enormous propaganda significance," as the VC had repeatedly attempted "to make capital
on religious strife, charging that the Saigon government persecutes all
religions other than Catholics."[27]

Nolting bristled at charges that Diem's government represented a Catholic dictatorship. He pointed out that at the time of the Buddhist crisis,
"four of the seventeen cabinet ministers were Christians. Most of the others were Buddhists." One minister described himself to the ambassador as
"a confused Confucian." Nolting believed that Diem, as a politician, "was
not a creature of religion," instead calling him a Vietnamese nationalist
and "dedicated anti-Communist, but certainly not a religious bigot." Long
before the crisis in 1963, the American ambassador remembered that he
was with Diem when the president received a report that one of generals
had decided to convert to Catholicism, believing it would give him a better
chance for getting ahead. Nolting quoted Diem as commenting: "If these
fellows would only go ahead and be good men and stop trying for promotion by taking on a faith which they may or may not really believe in, it
would certainly help this country." Other critics also charged that the ranks
of the Buddhist leaders had been infiltrated by Communist agents from
North Vietnam—an accusation US embassy spokesman John Mecklin
doubted, noting "not a scrap of hard evidence of Communist penetration
of the Buddhists turned up during the 1963 crisis." Mecklin believed that
the upheaval was primarily just what it appeared to be, "an accidental flash
fire."[28]

William Trueheart, the deputy chief of mission, the number two man
at the US embassy in Saigon, remembered that Nolting, who was scheduled to go on vacation with his family in early May, approached Diem at
the beginning of the crisis urging him to "do what you would normally
think of doing: investigate, punish the guilty, recompense the injured."

Although Nolting believed it was possible that the Hue clash might "trigger long-lasting repercussions," the relative calm that prevailed the first few weeks after the incident convinced the ambassador that the crisis had passed, and he could safely leave the country on May 23 for his delayed vacation. Nolting pointed out that both Trueheart and the State Department in Washington, DC, had his schedule and he believed it was understood that Trueheart would get in touch with him through the US embassy in Athens, Greece, if there was an emergency. "I could not have made a worse mistake," Nolting later admitted about his decision. "I left my post on the eve of a storm—a storm that eventually destroyed nine years of constructive American help and support for South Vietnam's independence." The ambassador believed that the failure to inform him of what was happening in South Vietnam had been a deliberate ploy. "It seems obvious to me that those who wanted to let Diem hang himself didn't want me back in Saigon," Nolting charged. With Nolting absent, it was up to Trueheart to convince Diem to make some compromises to placate the Buddhists. American officials wanted the president to do something to "bring this matter under control because it was undermining our ability to support him," Trueheart recalled. Later, responding to charges of disloyalty from Nolting, Trueheart said, "I think he felt when he was away that I was responsible to him. I thought I was responsible to Washington." Mecklin thought that if Diem had followed Trueheart's advice from the start, he could have "stopped the upheaval before it got started." Such a move, however, seemed to be beyond the president's capability. "Instead he made token gestures," Mecklin said, "always too slowly, too little and done so grudgingly as to waste the psychological effect."[29]

Trying to educate American readers about the Vietnamese Buddhists, Browne traveled to Hue and other cities to interview monks (also known as *bonzes*) at their yellow-stucco-faced pagodas decorated with quaint bell towers, tile roofs with upturned corners, and statues of Buddha. He wrote that unlike the ornate and graceful pagodas of Thailand, Burma, and Cambodia, the buildings in Vietnam were "a disagreeable contrast." Most of them in Saigon and elsewhere in the country were plain with "almost no architectural adornments, and look a little like badly Orientalized versions of Spanish mission buildings." Despite the spartan surroundings, he enjoyed his talks with the monks. "I thought that they were often very clever, interesting people," Browne remembered. Monks arose at the first ringing of the temple bell at 4:30 a.m. and worked hard for the remainder of the day. "Their lives are austere and dedicated," he reported. "In the major sects, monks may not marry, and are forbidden to eat meat, fish or eggs. Their heads are shaved." Browne said that the monks were such adroit cooks that they could create "close imitations of pork chops and other meats out of bean curd and various spices." Senior monks prayed, meditated, and taught classes in theology, Vietnamese culture, and foreign languages—English was the favorite. Novices and junior monks had to prepare meals, clean the pagodas, and run errands. Changes and a new sense of identity, however, had occurred with "the problems of the 20th century," Browne noted. "Saigon monks, formerly forbidden to touch money, now carry small change to get around in buses and taxis. . . . Even the monks' practice of begging for rice and clothing from house to house largely has died out. Begging now is handled by lay business managers on a more efficient basis."[30]

While many monks were "barely literate sons of farming families," Browne wrote that contacts with foreigners had brought new ideas to Vietnamese Buddhism, and many monks decided to study abroad. Some monks had joined after spending much of their lives in other careers, including business, and these "holy men were politically sophisticated, despite their shaved heads and show of piety." A thirty-seven-year-old monk named Thich (a surname taken by monks to show their affinity with Buddha) Quang Lien, looked on with suspicion by US officials, had attended Yale University. Although he made no claims of sharing their religious or political beliefs, over time, Browne noted, the monks began to trust him. "As I made the rounds of the pagodas I picked up a lot of interesting news, as well as some delicious vegetarian meals served to the monks," he said.[31]

Tensions continued to grow as the Diem government refused demands from the Intersect Committee for the Defense of Buddhism, a new group formed to represent several Buddhist organizations in the country, for freedom from arbitrary arrest, the right to assemble in public, and ending the supposed Catholic bias in appointing government officials. Browne said that the temples, including Saigon's Xa Loi Pagoda, the headquarters of Buddhism in South Vietnam, remained peaceful places to visit. The droning chants, pinging of brass prayer gongs, smells of burning joss sticks, and the "stifling tropical heat could reduce even a visitor to an unwilling trance," he remembered. Arnett noted that newsmen were often briefed at Xa Loi by a monk named Thich Duc Nghiep, who spoke English and "served delicate Chinese tea in tiny cups in his upstairs office as he fed us snacks of philosophy and propaganda." An anonymous South Vietnamese government official made sure to tell Browne that outsiders should understand that Buddhist leaders in his country came in two categories: "There are the old monks, the true leaders of the faith, and then there are the young turks—young monks who have traveled abroad and who come back ready to make trouble."[32]

Early in the crisis, Buddhist leaders had promised a policy of nonviolence but also had warned that, if necessary, "we shall sacrifice ourselves to the last man for our cause." And while the movement was in no small way sparked by the perceived discrimination the Buddhists faced from the Diem government, it also sprang from a strong desire to revitalize Vietnamese Buddhism. Its fervent nationalism was typified by a remark from an older monk, Thich Quang Duc, someone who would become a martyr for the cause: "The spirit of Buddhism is bound together with the spirit of the nation. When Buddhism prospers, the nation prospers; when Buddhism declines, the nation declines. History has demonstrated this point clearly." Browne reported that the bonzes were aware of the "political implications" of the crisis. Quang Lien told the AP newsman that while the Buddhists believed in nonviolence, faith and political activity were not incompatible. "Traditionally in Southeast Asia there have been close relationships between Buddhist leaders and kings," Lien told Browne. "Buddhists believe that their kings must follow the path of righteousness—that is, the Buddhist way."[33]

The Buddhists arranged their demonstrations stealthily, with nearly military precision, Browne wrote. The monks arrived at an agreed-upon location from different locations and by a variety of methods, including buses, tricycle pedicabs, and the blue-and-cream Renault taxis common on Saigon's streets. Protests numbering three hundred or four hundred in size, Browne noted, seemed to "materialize from thin air, under the noses of security police." Tuesday became the favorite day for demonstrations "because the ascension of the spirits of the dead from the Hue incident was said to be marked by seven-day intervals, and the victims had died on a Tuesday." Within just a month of the violence in Hue, Browne believed that the Buddhists had been able to create a movement into "something almost resembling a political party." It served as a rallying point for all those wishing to do something to rattle the government, a remarkable achievement given Diem's past ability to stifle any political opposition (except for the Communists). "Rooms in pagodas have become command posts, where young monks rush messages, mimeograph machines grind out communiques, and the sounds of telephones and typewriters blend with the boom of temple bells," Browne wrote. One monk told him that his group had been fighting for "freedom of religion and social justice in South Vietnam. We will fight until we win—not violently, of course."[34]

The Buddhists were aware, Browne pointed out, that one of Diem's major strengths came from his ability to control his country's press, keeping any less-than-flattering aspects about his regime out of the spotlight. If the government wanted its views known, it could always depend on the support of most Vietnamese newspapers, especially the *Times of Vietnam*, which was operated by an American couple, Gene and Ann Gregory, who were closely tied to Ngo Dinh Nhu and Madame Nhu. The Buddhists were also frustrated with the lack of support from US officials, who, Browne noted, "tacitly approved of Diem's system of press control," believing, with some justification, that publicizing the current controversy "could only divert energy from winning the war against the Viet Cong." Mecklin remembered that those in the US Mission were not supposed to have any contact with Buddhist leaders, except through secret channels, due to fears that the news would get back to the Diem government.[35]

Resolved to get around the press blackout, the Buddhists had logically turned to Western journalists to get their message out to the world. "In a land where almost everyone had been against them," Mecklin said, "the newsmen suddenly found themselves being treated like heroes at pagodas all over the country. Occasionally they were even applauded in the streets by Buddhist demonstrators." At a time when General Paul Harkins headquarters did everything it could to keep tight control of any tips about military operations, Mecklin added, the Buddhists trusted the journalists enough to let them know in advance about demonstrations and public statements. "Harkins refused the minuscule risk that advance tips might somehow get back to the Viet Cong," he recalled. "The Buddhists accepted the large risk that tips on their plans would leak to the palace, with disastrous results from Diem's police—arrests, beatings and worse. They were not betrayed." Arnett remembered that during one demonstration a Vietnamese family had invited AP photographer Horst Faas into its home so he could take photographs of the crowd from an upstairs balcony. "He didn't stay long," noted Arnett. "The crowd below was ruining most of his shots by cheering wildly every time he clicked the shutter."[36]

While covering the Buddhist crisis, Browne's staff found itself in an increasingly messy situation for a variety of reasons, he informed his superiors. As he explained in a letter to Robert Eunson, head of AP's bureau in Tokyo, communications between Saigon and Hue, the two main areas of the struggle, were awful. "One cable sent by Ha Van Tran from Hue to Saigon was stopped by Hue censors, and finally arrived here four days later," wrote Browne. "Other cables have been similarly delayed." Both telephone channels—one controlled by the government's telecommunications system and one by the US military—between the two cities were by radio and both were unreliable. Browne noted that the government's system was open for only a half hour daily and, he expected, was monitored and recorded by authorities. "The second channel is almost ruled out, because most American field advisors don't want their phones used for anything as touchy as Buddhism," he wrote. The only method Browne could be sure to count on to obtain information for Hue was to keep Ha Van Tran "shuttling back and forth (at considerable expense and waste of time) between Hue and here." Browne also made sure to keep Eunson aware of how the Buddhists had decided to rely on the foreign press "as their only shield against destruction by government authorities. This means (and they have given every evidence of it) that they mean to use us as much as possible." Browne pointed out that when the Buddhists attempted to send messages to U Thant, secretary-general of the United Nations, and President Kennedy, the government cable office refused to send them. Instead, the Buddhists had the messages sent to the Western news agencies in Saigon, who passed them along in their dispatches.[37]

In early June it seemed as if Diem and the Buddhists had reached an understanding that might end the crisis, only to see it derailed by a group under the control of Madame Nhu, the Women's Solidarity Movement. The group issued a resolution that blasted the Buddhists for daring to question "the legitimate precedence of the national flag" and also chided the Diem regime for backing down to the protestors. The resolution also recommended expelling "all foreign agitators, whether they wear monks' robes or not." Earlier, in late May, Browne had learned "a piece of blood-chilling intelligence" from a source at the An Quang Pagoda. The English-speaking informant said that two monks had told Buddhist leaders that they were willing to kill themselves in public—one by disembowelment and another by burning himself—to show their support for the cause. Although the Buddhist leaders had not yet authorized such drastic actions, they were considering them, Browne recalled. "All correspondents in Saigon knew of the suicide plans at about the same time," he noted, "and none of us had any advance information about dates, circumstances or anything else. Buddhist security was tightly maintained."[38]

For a couple of weeks, newsmen made sure to cover the Buddhists' demonstrations. Halberstam recalled that one day during the crisis the correspondents were all gathered at the Xa Loi Pagoda on a tip that something had been planned by the Buddhists. He noted that Thich Duc Nghiep, the official press spokesman for the Buddhists, informed the newsmen: "There will be no human sacrifice today, gentlemen." Just thirty minutes after the reporters had left, demonstrators left the pagoda to protest in front of Nolting's residence. According to Halberstam, when asked why he had sent the newsmen away, Duc Nghiep responded: "Ah, because when you left, the secret police left too, and when they were gone we could leave the pagoda and demonstrate." Not surprisingly, most of the journalists relaxed their guard when it came to covering the demonstrations, except for Browne, who was convinced that "the monks would eventually make good [on] their threat." Obviously, he reasoned, it was a moment when only the most drastic measure "could have any effect against a regime flanked with tanks, a modern army, and a huge secret police apparatus." The Buddhists required "the eyes of the world in support of their cause," and sought what Browne described as "an appropriate eye-catcher."[39]

The Buddhists made good on their promise. During a meeting of the Intersect Committee at Xa Loi on the evening of June 10, Buddhist leaders decided to accept an offer from Quang Duc, who just a few weeks before had volunteered to immolate himself in public. Asked by a fellow monk if he was still willing to take such drastic action, Quang Duc responded: "I am prepared to burn myself as an offering to Buddha and for the purpose of persuading the government to fulfill the five demands." Later that evening, at his apartment over the AP office, Browne received a telephone call from Duc Nghiep, who informed him, "Mr. Browne, I strongly advise you to come. I expect something very important will happen, but I cannot tell you what." The monk delivered a similar message to all the foreign correspondents in Saigon, advising them to be at a small pagoda off Phan Dinh Phung Street; his counsel was ignored by most. As a wire-service reporter, Browne, however, could not take any chances at being scooped by his competitors on what could be a major news story. Also, Duc Nghiep's previous tips to him to him had all been good. "They [the Buddhists] were perfectly serious about doing something pretty violent," he recalled. "In another civilization it might have taken the form of a bomb or something like that." Browne realized that any "ghastly human sacrifice" by the Buddhists would be futile unless "the Western press—the only free press in the country—carried the word to the outside world." He would be the only Western newsman on the scene equipped with a camera, a cheap, 35-millimeter Japanese-made Petri, that he used to capture on film one of the most dramatic moments in the Vietnam conflict—one that had critical ramifications for the Diem and American governments, placed Browne squarely in the spotlight, and introduced him to a new kind of horror.[40]

CHAPTER 6

The Ultimate Protest

RITUALLY BURNED AT HOLY sites and homes in South Vietnam, long, brown joss sticks produced what Malcolm Browne remembered as "a pleasing fragrance said to find favor with ghosts" of one's ancestors. After what he encountered on June 11, 1963, at the intersection of Phan Dinh Phung and Le Van Duyet Streets in Saigon, however, the aroma of the strong incense became forever associated to Browne's senses with another, far more gruesome odor—the gasoline-soaked, burning flesh of a septuagenarian Buddhist monk, Thich Quang Duc. Also echoing through his mind for years were the chants of the ritual ancient prayer *Na Mo A Di Da Phat*, with each word "equally accented on the same monotonous note," as well as the screams of horror from the monks and nuns gathered to witness what Browne described as "one of the worst things I've ever seen."[1]

Browne set out before dawn on this hot and stifling day (still June 10 in the United States) accompanied by his Associated Press colleague Bill Ha Van Tran for the Tu Nghiem Pagoda, a small, nondescript building located about seven blocks east of the city's main pagoda, Xa Loi. The previous evening Browne had been directed to visit Tu Nghiem by his monk informant, Thich Duc Nghiep. Browne made sure to bring along an important item—a camera. The AP men arrived at the pagoda at exactly 7:50 a.m.;

services were to begin at 8:00 a.m. and, as Browne noted, the Buddhists were known for being extremely punctual. "The concrete pagoda building was set in about thirty yards from the street with a muddy alleyway as an entrance," Browne recalled. "In the rear was a small courtyard, jammed with yellow-robed monks and gray-robed nuns. Loudspeakers nailed to trees and corners of the pagoda building were blaring in rapid Vietnamese." There were additional monks gathered, standing, in the pagoda's main room, which also had been equipped with a blaring loudspeaker. The monks had set up a few chairs inside the pagoda for the newsmen who, in addition to Browne and Tran, included Simon Michau of Agence France Presse and Nguyen Ngoc Rao, a Vietnamese working for United Press International. "Tran and I had the only cameras," Browne pointed out. Looking around the room, Browne recognized a number of faces he had seen at the Xa Loi and An Quang Pagodas. "There were about six lay women Buddhists in the white dress of mourning," he reported. "Some were in tears as they served tea." It seemed clear to the newsman that he had come upon "a very somber moment." Spotting Browne, Duc Nghiep came over and said to him: "Be sure to wait until the end of the service. I think something very important may happen."[2]

At eight o'clock the murmuring of Vietnamese issuing from the loud-speakers stopped, replaced by a monk chanting the ritual prayer, accompanied by another keeping time by pounding on a gourd. "It was a sad chant, really a chant of the dead," Browne recalled. The nuns and monks all joined in, "quietly at first, then with rising, hammering volume, as the verses were repeated over and over, the tempo speeding up slightly." The smoke from the burning joss sticks scattered throughout the pagoda grew so thick that Browne struggled to breathe. Scanning the crowd, he could see that the eyes of the monks and nuns "were fixed straight ahead, almost glazed in the absorption of fervor." At nine o'clock the chanting stopped and the approximately 350 monks and nuns, as if they had practiced the maneuver beforehand, began to leave. They lined up in the alleyway and proceeded onto the street, walking down it while arranged in three or four rows. "It was by far the biggest Buddhist procession in Saigon up to that point," Browne noted. Some of the marchers unfurled banners with slogans printed in Vietnamese and English that beseeched President Ngo

Dinh Diem to honor Buddhists' demands. A gray Austin sedan with three to four monks inside led the march, an innovation for such demonstrations, Browne said. "It seemed strange to me at the time that the monks were now riding instead of walking," he recalled.[3]

While government crackdowns on such protests were happening throughout the rest of the country, the Saigon police had grown accustomed to such marches. They spent their time keeping traffic and curious onlookers away from the demonstration, treating the whole spectacle as "mere traffic nuisances." Browne remembered that a white police car stayed about a half block ahead of the Austin. "People leaned from shop-windows along Phan Dinh Phung, and children stared at the passing procession," he reported. The city's inhabitants "were accustomed to seeing columns of yellow-robed monks with nothing much happening," Browne pointed out. After walking for nearly a half hour, the Buddhist marchers stopped when they reached the intersection with Le Van Duyet Street, which Browne called one of the most important thoroughfares in the city, always crowded with traffic. The time was 9:17 a.m. The Cambodian consulate occupied one corner of the intersection, with an apartment building and an Esso service station on the other corners. "At precisely the center of the intersection, the Buddhist car stopped, apparently stalled," he said, adding that the police car, unaware that the marchers had halted, kept moving, traveling about halfway down the next block. "The marchers began to move past the car, and then abruptly turned left into Le Van Duyet, quickly forming a circle about thirty feet in diameter, of which the car formed a link," Browne recalled. "It was now nearly 9:20 a.m."[4]

The monks who had been in the Austin got out; one of them opened the car's hood and pulled out a five-gallon gasoline can made of translucent plastic and filled, it appeared to Browne, with a pink liquid: an equal-parts mixture of gasoline and—reports differ—either a mix of diesel and kerosene or jet fuel. Two younger monks accompanied an older member of their order, who Browne later learned was Thich Quang Duc. He did not know if the monk had been among the crowd at the Tu Nghiem Pagoda earlier that day and could not have known because he had never seen him before or heard his name. "He [Quang Duc] was resting his hands on their arms, and going over to the center of this circle," Browne said. Sweat broke out on the reporter's brow as he got his camera ready, anticipating that "a horror show was at hand." A monk placed a small, brown cushion on the pavement, and Quang Duc positioned himself on it, crossing his legs in the traditional lotus position. From his location—about twenty feet to the right and a little in front of Quang Duc, who kept his head slightly bowed—Browne watched as the monks assisting Quang Duc emptied all but about one liter of the liquid over the old man, "soaking his face, body, robes and cushion." The monks stepped away from Quang Duc, leaving behind the container, which still had some liquid inside.[5]

At 9:22 a.m. Browne could see Quang Duc's hands move a bit in his lap as he struck a match. The newsman called out to Tran, who stood in a different part of the crowd, about twenty seconds before this happened. At the moment Quang Duc lit the match, Tran appeared at Browne's elbow. Recalling the incident, Browne said: "In a flash, he [Quang Duc] was sitting in the center of a column of flame, which engulfed his entire body. A wail of horror rose from the monks and nuns, many of whom prostrated themselves in the direction of the flames." Browne spotted Michau running away from the circle and learned that the French correspondent had gotten into the Cambodian embassy. "He should have had a good general view, but he could have been no closer to Quang Duc than 150 feet." Rao had already left the intersection at a run, probably, Browne reasoned, to notify other UPI staff. While the flames engulfed Quang Duc, two monks brought out a cloth banner with the words, in English: "A Buddhist Priest Burns for Buddhist Demands." A slight breeze sometimes blew the flames from Quang Duc's face enough so that the reporter could see that his eyes were closed and "his features were contorted with agony." Despite the pain, the monk, Browne noted, kept his upright position, his eyes closed, his hands folded in his lap, uttering no sound as the flesh melted from his body. "The reek of gasoline smoke and burning flesh hung over the intersection like a pall," the newsman said.[6]

Browne found himself "numb with shock" at the horrible scene. Witnessing anyone commit suicide or suffer a violent death "is always a hard experience," he later noted. "You can get used to it in war, but there was something special about this. It was kind of a horror." Despite the grisly scene, Browne acted almost automatically, shooting several rolls of 35-mm, black-and-white Tri-X film. "The one thing that sort of keeps you going in war, or in times of crisis like that, is having something to do," he pointed out. Trying to keep his mind off the ghastly sight, Browne kept thinking: "'The sun is bright and the subject is self-illuminated, so f16 at 125th of a second should be right.' But I couldn't close out the smell." Although police had finally arrived, they appeared as stunned by what they were seeing as Browne had been, "running around aimlessly outside the circle of Buddhists." Three or four fire trucks arrived, accompanied by riot police equipped with helmets and fixed bayonets. "The riot police charged down the street in a wave," he reported, "but stopped short in confusion a few yards from the circle." As the fire trucks started to move down the street, several of the monks blocked them by throwing themselves in front of their front and rear wheels "so that the truck could advance only by rolling over them," Browne recalled. The monks ignored the blasting of the horn and siren of one of the trucks as its driver vainly tried to get them to move out of the way. One of the younger monks in the crowd used a portable, battery-operated loudspeaker to repeatedly proclaim, in Vietnamese and English: "A Buddhist priest burns himself to death. A Buddhist priest becomes a martyr." Later, when questions swirled about whether the monk had been drugged, Browne recounted that while he could not swear there was nothing wrong with the monk, "he didn't stagger as he walked to his place. He appeared calm, and exchanged a few words with the two monks with him, just before they poured the gasoline."[7]

As Browne captured the scene on film, other Western correspondents arrived to bear their own witness to the horrible spectacle, including David Halberstam of the *New York Times* and Ray Herndon, who came to Saigon to provide help to Neil Sheehan's United Press International bureau. (Sheehan had left Saigon that day to cover an operation in the countryside.) To save money, Herndon had been staying at a villa occupied by Halberstam. They had overslept on the morning of June 11 after a long night on the town. Halberstam was jarred awake by a frantic telephone call from Rao. All Halberstam could understand from the conversation was that he and Herndon needed to get to the intersection of Le Van Duyet and Phan Dinh Phung Streets, located about six blocks from the villa, as fast as they could. Along the way, Herndon suddenly remembered that he had forgotten some important items—his Leica cameras—but decided to press ahead, a decision he later regretted. Arriving at the intersection, all Halberstam could initially see was a crowd of chanting Buddhist monks. "Just another demonstration, I thought; we had become so used to these by then that I silently cursed Rao for waking me up," he remembered. "But at that moment I looked into the center of the circle and saw a man burning himself to death." The sight so astonished the *Times* reporter that he remembered not being able to cry, take notes, or ask questions, becoming "too bewildered to even think." Herndon, too, appeared flummoxed by what he observed, even more so when he spotted Browne, already on the scene and equipped with his camera and wearing, perhaps, a small smile on his face when he spied his competition. "Oh shit," Herndon thought, "I just lost the Pulitzer [Prize]."[8]

Both Browne and Halberstam struggled to come to grips with their responsibilities as journalists and humans that morning. Halberstam stated that he had conflicting emotions. One part of him wanted to extinguish the flames taking the monk's life, but another thought cautioned him that he "had no right to interfere, another told me that it was too late, another asked whether I was a reporter or a human being." With his practical nature, Browne, when later asked why he had not interfered, pointed out that he probably could not have done anything to stop Quang Duc's self-immolation, as the "monks and nuns had clearly rehearsed their roles for the ceremony many times, and had prepared methods for blocking interference," as they showed when they used their bodies to keep the fire trucks from moving. He divulged, however, that trying to stop the dreadful spectacle had not entered his mind. "I have always felt that a newsman's duty is to observe and report the news, not to try to change it," Browne stated. He believed it was his job as a journalist to take the pictures and get them and his story about the event to AP's wire service as quickly and efficiently as he could. "It is difficult to conceive of any newsman acting otherwise," Browne believed.[9]

After about ten minutes from the time the fire had started ("it seemed like an eternity," Browne remembered), Quang Duc fell over backward with his "blackened legs kicking convulsively for a minute or so. Then he was still, and the flames gradually subsided." A big, black delivery truck decorated with Buddhist flags along its sides arrived and some monks unloaded a wooden coffin from it. Although the monks tried to place Quang Duc's charred body in the coffin, his rigid arms and legs prevented them from doing so. About seven monks took off their robes and used them to carry the old monk's body and place it on top of the coffin. Some of the monks, inspired by the sacrifice, ran toward the police, yelling "Da Dao! (Down with the Regime)," but they were held back by others in the crowd. "The circle broke and formed into a procession once again, the body at its head," Browne remembered. "Marching a few blocks more, the group arrived at Xa Loi Pagoda, where a bell was tolling mournfully from the concrete tower. It was 10 a.m. sharp, and the demonstration was finished."[10]

Eventually, Quang Duc's body underwent cremation at the Buddhist cemetery just outside of Saigon. According to Browne, the monks in charge of cremating the body insisted that Quang Duc's heart refused to burn. "A single piece of meat purporting to be the heart," he noted, "was preserved in a glass chalice, becoming an object of worship." Buddhist leaders distributed the martyr's ashes to pagodas throughout the country. The yellow robes the monks had used to carry his body were cut into pieces for distribution to Buddhist adherents. "Pinned to shirts and dresses," Browne reported, "these bits of cloth were thought to have miraculous healing properties, and also were symbols of the Buddhist uprising against the government." While some monks who watched Quang Duc's suicide claimed "they saw the holy lotus throne flower in the flames," such miraculous happenings were downplayed by Thich Quang Lien, one of the Buddhist leaders, who told Browne that the suicide was an act of great personal courage and more of an inspiration than a miracle. "Thich Quang Duc was a courageous and intelligent old man, and an adept at yoga," Quang Lien noted to the reporter. "It was yoga and prayer that freed him of pain in his final minutes. His act has given Vietnamese Buddhism tremendous moral strength—a strength that will be able to stand even the test of bayonets and machine guns."[11]

With the appalling ceremony completed, Browne knew that he had to get his photographs out of the country as soon as possible. He realized that doing so "was a very difficult thing to do in Saigon on short notice."

What mattered to him was to get the raw film shipped by air freight or some other way to the closest transmission point, the AP's bureau in Manila in the Philippines, since the image would not be subject to censorship at that point. Thinking fast, he sent Tran to the AP office with the film and instructed him to arrange for an airfreight shipment and schedule a telephone call to the news agency's Tokyo bureau, in that order. Tran was able to find a "pigeon," a passenger on a regular commercial flight from Saigon, to carry the film to the Manila AP office, which had the facilities to send it via radio circuit to San Francisco, and from there to the news agency's headquarters in New York for publication by its clients all over the world.[12]

Browne returned briefly to his apartment over his office and told Le Lieu about what he had witnessed. He hugged her tightly and went to the bathroom to clean up. "He looked like an old man, his back bent and he was on the verge of crying," Le Lieu recalled. "I followed him to the bathroom wrongly thinking all the time that the monk was burnt on the stake as punishment by the secret police. He washed his face in slow motion. He told me the story in such a despairing tone that my tears began to run down my cheeks." She remembered that he took off his clothing, smelled it, handed it to her, and remarked that he would never forget for the rest of his life the smell of Quang Duc's burning flesh. While he changed his clothes, Browne looked at Le Lieu and somberly predicted that there would be "hell to pay very soon."[13]

Tran sent the first urgent cable about Quang Duc's dramatic death over the wires. His dispatch read: "aye yellow robed buddhist monk committed suicide burning himself with gasoline in street intersection near Cambodian representation building tuesday morning para several thousand people including monks etnuns watched the scene stop monks etnuns present at place sat down in street making prayers for suicided monk whos carbonized moment later paramere havantran." Arriving at the office, Browne sat down and constructed his own short piece to send via the South Vietnamese–controlled cable office (he later called the AP Tokyo office and dictated the rest of the story for relay to New York). The truncated cable read:

URGENT
ASSOCIATED PRESS

Browne 11145 firstlead buddhist 11/6 . . . an aging monk surrounded by
more than three hundred fellow monks calmly put aye match to his . . .
gasoline drenched robes in aye main intersection her monday comma
etburned to death before eyes of horrified crowd para victim comma
the reverend quang duc comma was moren seventy years old stop banners carried by circle of monks around him read quote aye buddhist
priest for five requests unquote para grizzly demonstration was latest
in wave of clashes between Buddhists etsaigon government authorities stop buddhists charge the government with persecuting them
comma etdemand guarantee of freedom of religion etsocial justice
stop government denies it ever . . .[14]

For Browne's images to appear in newspapers around the world they
had to make, the AP estimated, a fifteen-hour, approximately nine thousand–mile journey over the news agency's wirephoto system. The image
used by most newspapers was a tightly cropped one showing Quang Duc
engulfed in flames with the Austin and a small number of the monks in
attendance in the background. Later, Browne's full sequence, including an
expanded view of the self-immolation, described by AP's editors as "The
Ultimate Protest," became available for publication. The initial burning-
monk image competed for space on front pages of US newspapers with
news stories and photographs of Alabama governor George Wallace blocking the entry of two Black students—Vivian Malone and James Hood—
into the University of Alabama. Those newspapers worried about their
readers' reaction to the burning monk sometimes used Browne's photo
showing the Buddhist monks blocking a fire truck with their bodies. This
was the image the *Times* used to accompany Halberstam's page-three article that quoted President Diem appealing for calm following the monk's
death. Browne theorized that editors at the *Times* probably believed that
his photo of Quang Duc in flames "was too grisly a picture that wasn't
suitable for a breakfast newspaper." Casey Jones, editor of newspapers in

Syracuse, New York, scoffed at the squeamish attitude shown by those who refused to publish the upsetting image, noting, "An editor who didn't run that picture wouldn't have run a story on the Crucifixion."[15]

One of the newspapers that featured Browne's photo at the top of its front page, above the fold—the most sought-after space in any newspaper—was the *Tucson* (AZ) *Citizen* in its June 11, 1963, issue. The photo and story from Vietnam shared space on page one with an image and article about Wallace blocking the two Black students in Alabama. The prominent display of such a graphic image prompted an exchange of views that reflected the opinions of most of the country. In a letter to the editor, *Citizen* subscriber Lee H. Brown questioned whether it was appropriate to publish such a photo. "Surely there is some sensible person in your offices who has sufficient humanitarian feelings to know that this is not fit material to come into the home," Brown wrote. "I suggest that you select such a person and consult him when something of this nature comes up in the future." He believed that the picture "could appeal to no reader's interest apart from the morbid." Later, responding to Brown's letter, Mitchell A. Tuchman wrote that while he did not support the "voluntary or involuntary burning of Buddhist monks in public," he also did not "advocate the selective censorship of news or news photos in deference to reader pleasures and healthy appetites." Tuchman went on to say that it did nobody "any harm to feel uncomfortable even if this feeling is caused by a photograph of a distressing situation."[16]

If leaders of the Buddhist protest hoped to win some attention for their cause among American officials in Washington, DC, they succeeded. Robert F. Kennedy, the US attorney general, was talking with his brother, President John F. Kennedy, on the telephone about what was happening with Wallace in Alabama early in the morning on June 11 when he heard him exclaim: "Jesus Christ!" The president's expletive had been prompted by seeing on the front pages of newspapers scattered on his bedstand the photo of Quang Duc's suicide. President Kennedy met later with Secretary of State Dean Rusk, who told him that the State Department had sent a message to William Trueheart at the embassy in Saigon that read: "FYI—If Diem does not take prompt and effective steps to re-establish Buddhist confidence in him we will have to re-examine our entire relationship with his regime." The cable also suggested that Trueheart, in secret, let South

Vietnam's vice president, Nguyen Ngoc Tho, know that "in event situation arises due to internal political circumstances (in which US would play no part) where Diem definitely unable to act as president and only in this situation we would want to back Tho as constitutional successor."[17]

When Kennedy later called upon Henry Cabot Lodge Jr. to meet with him to discuss becoming the new US ambassador to South Vietnam, replacing Frederick Nolting, he had on his Oval Office desk a copy of Browne's burning monk photograph. "I suppose that no news picture in recent history had generated as much emotion around the world as that one had," Lodge recalled. "President Kennedy referred to that picture, to the overall importance of Vietnam, and to what was going on in Saigon—to the fact that apparently the Diem government was entering a terminal phase. He also mentioned the extremely bad relations that the U.S. Embassy in Saigon had with the press. He said, 'I suppose that these are the worst press relations to be found in the world today, and I wish you, personally, would take charge of press relations.'" According to Browne, Lodge also later informed him that when he met with Kennedy the president had informed his new ambassador, "We're going to have to do something about that regime."[18]

Meeting with Lodge before the new ambassador left the country to take up his post, Kennedy seemed resigned that a coup would remove Diem from office. "I don't know how well prepared you are for that out there, or who we would sort of support, or who we would—and—I think that's going to be the key—your key problem this year," the president warned Lodge. According to Lodge's assessment, Kennedy's policy was not to overthrow the Diem government, as the "Vietnamese were doing that for themselves and didn't need any outside help." Instead, Lodge continued: "What he was trying to do, and what I was trying to do as his representative, was to get them to change their policies, change some of their personnel, and try to rehabilitate themselves so that they could function as a government as long as they remained in power." Before leaving Washington, DC, a prominent Vietnamese shared with Lodge that he believed unless Diem and his family, including his brother Ngo Dinh Nhu and sister-in-law Madame Nhu, left the country, there existed "no power on earth" to prevent their assassination. Lodge's confidant pointed out that "the oppressive acts of the regime—the arbitrary arrests, imprisonments and executions, and the general reign of terror that was going on—would make assassination inevitable in any country."[19]

While the sensational photo found its way to outlets around the world, Browne and his staff were unaware of the splash the image had made. He compared the situation to something like "shooting into a black hole." Browne added that the staff learned his photo had made it to AP headquarters only after starting to receive complimentary cables for capturing such an intense shot. One of the messages came from Wes Gallagher, AP general manager, who wrote: "Congratulations to you and your colleagues for the excellent coverage news and photo under difficult conditions which is greatly appreciated." The messages to Sheehan from his bosses at UPI were not as complimentary, as they were aghast that its Saigon bureau had not been able to document Quang Duc's death with photos of its own. Earnest Hoberecht, UPI's vice president and general manager for Asia, cabled from Tokyo to complain that the wire service had taken a real beating because "the AP news man there kept his head, remained cool, took pictures and got them out." Hoberecht also sent to Sheehan a copy of an angry letter he had received from Frank Tremaine, who handled UPI's Pacific coverage. The letter lambasted Herndon for failing to take a camera with him to the demonstration, cuttingly adding that he hoped the reporter had remembered to at least take along a pencil. "I suppose this [AP] picture has hurt us more worldwide than any other single picture has hurt either service in recent months," Tremaine wrote Hoberecht, adding that an important client in South America had threatened to switch to AP. Later, Hoberecht let Sheehan know that one of UPI's clients in Sydney, Australia, lost out on five thousand extra street sales to an opposition newspaper, which had the burning monk image "splashed all over the entire front page," while some of the news service's clients in Europe were reportedly refusing to pay their bills because UPI did not have its own photos of the macabre event. "Saigon's failure on this picture has really, really hurt us," wrote Hoberecht. Sheehan finally had enough, exploding with a string of expletives during a telephone call with his boss, saying he would no longer take such abuse; Hoberecht finally backed off.[20]

Although millions of words had been written about the Buddhist crisis,

Browne pointed out that his photos "carried an incomparable impact," both upon its initial publication and afterward. Vietnamese Buddhists took his photo, had artists colorize it, and carried it with them at the head of their protest marches. "Men and women, tears streaming from their eyes, bowed in reverent prayer before the photograph," he recalled. Letters came from friends and others letting him know that copies of his photo were being peddled on the streets by back-alley merchants of "feelthy pictures" from Lisbon, Portugal, to Dar es Salaam, Tanzania. Communist China also tried to take advantage of the image's notoriety, printing numerous copies to distribute throughout Southeast Asia with captions blaming the monk's suicide on "the U.S. imperialist aggressors and their Diemist lackeys." A group of ministers in the United States, banding together as the Ministers' Vietnam Committee, used the burning monk photo for full-page advertisements in the *New York Times* and *Washington Post* over the words: "We, Too, Protest." The clergymen railed against America's military aid to the government that denied Quang Duc his religious freedom; the spraying of crop-destroying chemicals; moving South Vietnamese from their traditional villages into strategic hamlets (described by them as "concentration camps"); the loss of American lives and the expenditure of billions of dollars of taxpayer money to support "a regime universally regarded as unjust, undemocratic, and unstable"; and "the fiction that this is 'fighting for freedom.'" The advertisement urged Americans to write President Kennedy and their congressmen and discuss the problem with their ministers, and also asked for contributions for the committee to help spread its message.[21]

Diem's initial reaction to Quang Duc's suicide had been to take to the airwaves to give a radio broadcast urging peace. The South Vietnamese leader blamed propaganda that had spread doubt about his government's goodwill, leading to "an undeserved death that made me very sorry." Diem said no "scheme" existed to crush Buddhism in the country and declared that "behind the Buddhists in this country there is still the Constitution, that is, I myself." Behind the scenes, however, Diem could not shake his suspicions about the resident journalists, asking Nolting, who had returned to South Vietnam from his vacation on July 11, if it was true that Browne "had bribed the Buddhist monks to murder one of their number by fire for the purpose of getting a good picture." Hearing about Diem's question, Browne was dumbfounded but believed such a wild idea might have made sense to the president. "The question, absurd though it was, may have been sincere," he noted. "It was an indication of the suspicion and hostility Diem entertained for the foreign press in general." Browne suspected that the idea had been planted in Diem's mind by his brother, Nhu, who "certainly knew better, but he hoped to discredit both the Buddhists and the foreign press." It seemed characteristic of Diem during those days that he had so little contact with what was going on with his "exploding nation and the war," as "he tended to accept as fact anything told to him by his ruthless brother, the 'political counsellor,'" said Browne. As he reported in a dispatch he sent to his bosses at AP, the South Vietnamese government was a "master at the nazi and communist techniques of smearing the innocent to conceal its own rottenness." Browne also reported that there "is not the slightest doubt quang duc died of his own free will."[22]

Trying to cover the Buddhist crisis after the suicide proved increasingly difficult, as many Saigon streets had been barricaded. Browne, Arnett, Faas, Van Tran, and Roy Essoyan, who before coming to South Vietnam had reported from the Soviet Union, used every trick they could muster "just to move from one pagoda to another," noted Browne. Although a planned Sunday, June 16, funeral for Quang Duc had been called off at the last minute, Browne expected that there would be some sort of clash. "There had been crowds in various parts of the city, some of them in an ugly mood," he reported. "At 6 a.m. that Sunday, Saigon was quiet, but there was an air of trouble. We took up our posts around the city." Browne stayed at the office to receive incoming reports. The first call came from Arnett, who told him, "It's begun, Mal. They're throwing rocks." Arnett's graphic account of the incident was out on the AP wire within fifteen minutes, Browne recalled.[23]

Essoyan and Faas moved through the crowds, "dodging rocks and billy clubs," Browne noted, while Arnett received a dose of tear gas tossed at the demonstrators by the police. Fortunately, the newsman received help from Buddhist nuns, who wiped his face with wet towels. The thousands of demonstrators cheered whenever they saw a foreign newsman with a camera, some yelling in English, "The world must know." Browne reported that an angry plainclothes policeman demanded that Faas hand over the film he had shot. Thinking fast, the photographer handed over "several rolls of unexposed film, but managed to hang onto his fine documentary of the violence." The street violence ended quickly and talks between Buddhist leaders and the Diem government continued. "A truce went into effect," Browne recalled. "But the odds were the truce would not last."[24]

South Vietnam's government finally had an opportunity to crack down hard on the foreign media on July 7 during a Buddhist march from the Chantaransay Pagoda at the northern edge of Saigon. Browne, carrying a Canon 35-mm camera, and Arnett were on the scene with about ten other foreign newsmen to photograph and report on a Buddhist memorial service but were attacked by a group of about twenty plainclothes policemen, some armed with rocks, while approximately sixty uniformed policemen and a squad of riot police stood by and did nothing. According to a news report from Halberstam, the secret policemen first tried to grab a camera belonging to Joseph Masraf, a Columbia Broadcasting System photographer. At about 9:00 a.m. two Vietnamese men in civilian clothes tried to prevent Arnett from taking pictures by "grabbing at my camera and pushing at my hands," he recalled. A few minutes later, Arnett, after being told by a uniformed policeman "no pictures," had stopped and held his camera down near his waist. He later testified to what happened next:

> About several seconds later, a Vietnamese man in civilian clothes shoved me very hard, knocked the camera I was carrying to the ground with his closed fist, and kicked at it. As he turned to run away I grabbed him at the shoulder in an attempt to apprehend him. At that point two or three other Vietnamese men in civilian clothes jumped on me, made me fall to the ground, and beat me. I tried to stand up and they hit me in the ribs, and used their knees and elbows on my head.[25]

As Arnett struggled to fend off the blows, the burly Halberstam rushed in and placed himself between the AP reporter and his assailants. "He pulls me to my feet and turns to my much smaller attackers and says loudly, 'You want him? Then get through me,'" Arnett remembered. Although he doubted the security men understood English, Arnett said they recognized they were overmatched, "raised their hands in submission and slipped away." Always committed to getting his story, Browne evaded the police by climbing up a power pole to snap photos of the clash, capturing shots of his colleague, Arnett, his face bloodied. "The fight ended as quickly as it began," Browne recalled, "but one of the cops, noticing that I had been taking pictures, approached me from behind and brought a brick crashing down on top of my camera, shattering its lens and parts but happily leaving the film intact." When the journalists tried to detain the Vietnamese responsible for the attack, they were prevented from doing so by the uniformed police. Eyewitnesses at the scene, reported Essoyan, agreed that none of the correspondents had assaulted any of the plainclothes police.[26]

Recalling the attack, Arnett said he applauded Browne's initiative in hoisting himself up the power pole to capture images of a demonstration that had turned into a melee. Arnett also expressed his gratitude to Halberstam for rushing to his defense. "Had Halberstam not rescued me from continuing pain and had Mal just continued taking pictures, then my reaction might have been different," he noted. At that time, Arnett pointed out, there existed no protocol for how newsmen "were expected to react when violently attacked by the police of a regime" that accepted millions of dollars in American aid and depended upon US military advisers to protect it from being overcome by the Viet Cong. No such protocol ever emerged during his time in Vietnam, Arnett added, because the journalists there learned to "'make ourselves scarce' when future danger threatened."[27]

Standing next to Michel Renard, a CBS cameraman shooting the scene, Browne heard a loud noise and felt rock splinters fly into his eyes. As he turned to see that a large rock had struck Renard's camera, he also noticed an arm and hand holding a large rock swing around his body and down in front of his chest, smashing the camera that had hung around his neck and causing it to crash to the ground. "Fortunately, my hands were not on the camera, since otherwise my hands would have been injured," Browne reported. "I had a glimpse of the Vietnamese man who had done this, as he ran away into the crowd." The same man attempted to stop Faas from filming the event, damaging the film-transport system on his Leica camera and his wristwatch.[28]

Before Browne and Arnett could file any dispatches about the incident, police took them from the AP office and interrogated them for several hours at the third district police headquarters. Authorities threatened them with arrest for allegedly assaulting two Vietnamese men at the protest. An official from the British embassy, present at the interrogation, could not believe that the police were considering charges against the journalists, pointing to some large plainclothesmen police present and exploding: "You don't mean to tell me that these two correspondents assaulted those fellows!" The AP men asked that the plainclothesmen be charged with assault, sought thirty thousand piastres (approximately $430) for their damaged equipment, and asked for a pledge that no correspondents would be subjected to such unprovoked acts by police agents in the future. Seeking assistance from the US embassy, the journalists were initially rebuffed. Trueheart told newsmen at a meeting that he had decided not to make a formal protest about the attack to the Diem government, telling them, "I don't feel I have enough basis for making one. I can't conclude that it was a planned attack." Trueheart later cabled the State Department and recommended against making any formal protest, pointing out that given the "extreme emotional involvement of correspondents these days," which amounted to an "intense hatred" of the Diem regime, he would "not feel sure about refuting police." Vietnamese officials blamed the assaults on one or two of the secret policemen, who, they argued, had "lost their heads."[29]

Frustrated by the embassy response, Browne, Halberstam, Sheehan, and Peter Kalischer of CBS sent a telegram to President Kennedy. The telegram read:

mister president this sunday morning at the entrance to chantaransay pagoda in saigon nine representatives of american news organizations were subjected to a swift unprovoked and violent attack by government plain clothes police while covering an otherwise peaceful buddhist religious ceremony stop one correspondent was knocked down and kicked stop other newsmen were shoved comma jostled and struck by rocks thrown by the plainclothesmen dash all in full sight of forty to sixty uniformed metropolitan policemen and a squad of riot police stop in the course of the attack one camera was smashed and several damaged paragraph the uniform police did not offer any protection to the newsmen and in fact did everything to prevent the correspondents from apprehending the men who were attacking them para the inescapable conclusion is that the government of south vietnam comma a country to which the united states is heavily committed comma has begun a campaign of open hysterical intimidation to prevent the covering of news which we feel americans have aye right to know para previously foreign correspondents have been expelled from south vietnam stop this is the first time they have been assaulted by representatives of the government stop we believe a precedent has been set for increasing obstruction and violence stop since the united states embassy here does not deem this incident serious enough to make a formal protest comma we respectfully request that you mister president protest against this attack and obtain assurances that it will not be repeated.[30]

The tense relationship between the US Mission and the press only got worse following the July 7 clash. John Mecklin, the embassy's public affairs officer, remembered a particularly stormy meeting in his office with a delegation of reporters the evening of the day Browne and Arnett had been grilled. The newsmen, according to Mecklin, had "demanded to be told what, if anything, the Mission was doing." After his initial reluctance to act, Trueheart had decided to make a direct appeal to Nguyen Dinh Thuan, South Vietnam's secretary of state for the presidency and undersecretary for national defense, asking him to drop the charges against Browne and Arnett. Trueheart told Mecklin not to discuss these negotiations with anyone else. Receiving no satisfaction from Mecklin, the delegation, he reported, "exploded in such a tumult of four-letter invective on the theme of American 'gutlessness' that an officer next door came in to see if I needed physical protection." In addition to the pressure he received from the journalists, Mecklin also had to deal with news that Nolting would soon be replaced by Lodge. "There was no explanation of what this was all about," Mecklin recalled, "but there was immediate speculation in Saigon that it meant a change, at long last, in U.S. policy."[31]

Arnett and Browne received support from some journalism organizations in the United States. Herbert Brucker, editor of the *Hartford* (CT) *Courant* and president of the American Society of Newspaper Editors, sent a letter to Kennedy expressing the ASNE's concerns that South Vietnam's government was putting impediments in place to keep American reporters from doing their jobs. "What does concern many of us is the right to report without intimidation or obstacles tending in the direction of censorship," Brucker wrote. Although American officials in Saigon and the Pentagon in Washington, DC, might be tempted to slant their stories in favor of the South Vietnamese government or deter inquiries into the extent of US participation in the guerrilla warfare going on there, the basis of "the American system is an informed public." The struggle going on in South Vietnam, he continued, involved "public understanding as well as military action. It is a struggle that can be won only in an atmosphere of freedom." Although Brucker praised the Kennedy administration for its moves to address the situation involving the two AP newsmen, he added that he was unsure that all possible efforts were being made "to prevent further deliberate obstacles to free reporting." He believed that the American public needed to have "the fullest possible factual information from South Vietnam, no matter what anyone may think is right or wrong about the situation."[32]

The decision by Browne, Halberstam, and Sheehan to send the telegram to Kennedy did not sit well with their superiors. UPI officials warned Sheehan that he should not be attempting to make policy for the news service, as "Unipress must be neutral, neither pro-Diem or pro-Communist." Emmanuel R. Freedman, the *Times*'s foreign editor, warned Halberstam that the newspaper's correspondents should refrain from "firing off cables to the President of the United States without our authorization." In a private letter to Robert C. Eunson, AP Tokyo Bureau Chief Gallagher praised Browne for his "fine job of persistent news coverage" and agreed with Eunson's opinion that the Saigon bureau chief "is an outstanding prospect." But Gallagher also wrote that he believed Browne had "become emotionally involved in Viet Nam (which is perfectly natural considering his long stay there, just as you and I got emotionally involved in many war situations) and I believe he needs a respite."[33]

Gallagher went on to say that he did not want Browne or any AP correspondent "firing off protests to Washington, the President, or involving themselves in the news. Our job is to cover it, not make it." In Gallagher's opinion, the resident reporters in Vietnam had been making too much news themselves. While he indicated he understood just how such a situation happened, Gallagher thought it best to "play it a bit more on the cool side." He asked Eunson to "diplomatically" discuss the matter with Browne by telephone, but not to do it "in any critical way because I don't want to upset him." Gallagher wanted Browne to take a month's vacation with AP paying for his transportation, "whether he wants it or not. I specifically suggest that you get him up to Tokyo and park him in a geisha house for a month and try to relax him a bit and restore a little better perspective. I would specifically want him to go back." Although Essoyan recently left Saigon for AP's Hong Kong office, Gallagher wrote that after two or three weeks there, perhaps Essoyan "would not mind going back [to Saigon] and taking over for a month." Although Browne did take a vacation from his responsibilities, it occurred, luckily for the AP, *after* another major crisis involving the South Vietnamese government and *before* matters came to a violent conclusion for Diem and his brother.[34]

The looming threat of being arrested and hauled off for a crime he had not committed failed to halt Browne from trying to get the truth out about the violence the newsmen had confronted. The film he took of Arnett's ordeal survived, but South Vietnamese officials clamped down hard, blocking the transmission of any material deemed harmful to the government. The restrictions had made it difficult for Western journalists to find the "pigeons" they had previously depended on for carrying film or dispatches out of the country. "A helpful traveler faced possible arrest by Saigon police in that summer of 1963, and the supply of pigeons fell to almost zero," Browne remembered. Luckily for Browne, the new US ambassador to India, Chester Bowles, was in South Vietnam for several days on his way to his new post. Upon his arrival, Bowles had discovered that the US embassy "was at odds with the American military, and both were at odds with the American press. It was not a reassuring spectacle." Bowles endured a meeting with Diem, who rambled on for nearly four hours, leaving the American diplomat deeply concerned. Bowles later sent a private cable to the White House that noted: "President Diem is living in a world of his own and seems to be completely out of touch with the real situation. Any attractive South Vietnamese brigadier general with a little courage and organization could, I believe, take this place over in twenty-four hours."[35]

After Browne talked to Bowles, the ambassador immediately accepted the journalist's request to shepherd the film out of South Vietnam. "I think that helped to save our skin," Browne remembered. With Bowles's assistance, Browne's photos reached both his AP editors and the Kennedy administration. One image showed a bloodied Arnett in a crowd of people with the tall Halberstam, wearing sunglasses, standing in front of his fellow journalist to shield him from further beatings by the police "goons," as Browne described them. Kennedy reacted by sending Robert J. Manning, a former reporter and the assistant secretary of state for public affairs, to Saigon in mid-July with instructions, Manning believed, to "examine the situation and do what I could to mend relations between the American press and the American establishment." He also had been asked by Kennedy to try to explain to Diem "in the most diplomatic way possible that his government's mistreatment of American correspondents and the bad press his government was engendering in the United States could undermine American public support for him and, worse, for South Vietnam's struggle." Manning's trip seemed especially timely, as Browne began hearing rumors circulating throughout Saigon that several newsmen, including himself, Arnett, Halberstam, and Sheehan, were on "an assassination hit list the secret police had supposedly prepared. I assumed the rumors were merely intended to scare us, and ignored them." Sheehan and Halberstam were more cautious, making sure to continue their habit of always taking the second taxi in line, not the first one, to elude anyone who might be following them.[36]

The government's secret police, however, were not done with Browne. They decided to hit at someone he loved, Le Lieu, his wife to be, who was living with the correspondent. She had already angered the Diem regime by leaving her post at its information ministry and eventually taking a job at the US Information Service. At that time, Browne noted, the American government "was no more popular with the Saigon government than Ho Chi Minh himself." At about two o'clock in the morning one day, Browne heard a loud hammering on his apartment's front door. Peering through the door's frosted glass, he could see men waiting outside clothed in white uniforms, signifying they were policemen. In his dealings with Special Forces alumni, mercenaries, and spies, Browne had secured for his protection a World War II–era German Schmeisser submachine gun. "With the machine gun slung over my arm, I opened the door and bade the cops good evening," he recalled. Although they demanded to be allowed to enter and search the apartment for Le Lieu, they hesitated and became nervous when they saw that Browne had a weapon that easily overmatched the pistols they carried. "I politely told them that I was the only occupant of the apartment, and that it would be better for all of us not to insist on a search," he said. After a whispered consultation, the policemen departed, disappearing in the darkness.[37]

During his time in Saigon, Manning did all he could to repair the rifts between the US Mission and the press, as well as try to soothe tensions between newsmen and the Diem government. In reviewing the situation, he discovered that embassy officials had been mishandling press relations for a long time. For example, when veteran newsmen like Homer Bigart of the *New York Times* had been covering the war, the American officials in South Vietnam had discounted any negative reports, claiming, "Well, you guys have been covering these old-fashioned wars, and this is different," Manning noted. As the veterans were gradually replaced by young journalists such as Browne and Halberstam, the official story began to change. Embassy officials now pointed out that because of their youth "they didn't know how to cover this sort of thing." While Manning agreed that the journalists were "young and impressionable," they were also "good reporters and quite courageous," and the US Mission had an opportunity to make their case to them about the war, but instead handled it as, "Gee, another enemy is foisted on us."[38]

Manning finally realized that relations with the press in Vietnam could never be "ideal because we were trying to be involved there above and beyond what we publicly admitted was our involvement." He was surprised to discover that for the most part the correspondents at that time did not oppose the war or the American involvement in it, believing it was "a necessary free world policy." The reporters, however, as Manning wrote in a report Kennedy shared with Lodge, expressed a "bitterness toward, and contempt for the Diem government. They unanimously maintain that our Vietnam policy cannot succeed unless the Diem regime (*cum* family) is replaced; this conviction, though it does not always appear in their copy, underlies all the reports and analyses of the correspondents."[39]

Officials Manning talked to at the US embassy, however, viewed the press as, at best, "rude, insulting and insufferable (all adjectives which I am sure were sometimes deserved) and at worst, deliberate opponents of their own government." He wrote in his notebook that instead of treating them with candor and attempting to cultivate them as potential allies, they viewed the newsmen as nuisances and inconveniences (he cited Mecklin as an important exception). Although Manning expressed some sympathy for the officials' wary attitudes about the journalists, the result had "been the complete destruction of the Embassy's credibility." He was stunned to learn that it had been a year since "anybody in the embassy had any news-papermen to lunch or had invited a couple of correspondents to one of their thirty-person dinners or to their hundred-and-fifty-person cocktail par-ties." Manning noted that these simple favors were not aimed at buying the reporters' loyalties but rather at establishing personal relationships impor-tant in such situations overseas.[40]

Accompanied by Mecklin, Manning also met with Diem and Nhu for several hours each. Manning explained to South Vietnam's president that the Kennedy administration had been disturbed by the attempts to scare the newsmen and warned such efforts might harm relations between the two countries. Mecklin remembered that the visiting diplomat empha-sized to Diem that "free, critical news reporting, even if not always friendly, was better than no coverage at all of such a difficult situation because it reassured the American people that they were not being deceived about the commitment in Vietnam." According to Manning, Diem, how-ever, believed that the US correspondents were determined to see him ousted from office, "whatever the consequences for South Vietnam and the American national interest. They [the newsmen] had been given every opportunity to see the truth but persisted in ignoring it and in giving aid and comfort to the enemy." Manning did get the brothers to agree to readmit to South Vietnam a journalist they had previously kicked out of the country, James Robinson of the National Broadcasting Company. Although both Diem and Nhu would not admit that the police had done anything wrong, Manning recalled that they agreed to "urge the police to use all sorts of discretion" in the future when dealing with the foreign press. Diem did tell Manning that he would also consider dropping assault charges against Browne and Arnett. On July 24 Nolting announced that the

South Vietnamese government had decided not to charge the newsmen with any crimes. Mecklin considered Manning's visit to be "a limited success," believing that not much more could have been done short of "replacing not only Nolting, but also [General Paul] Harkins, the Ngo Dinh family, and the newsmen—all of whom were hopelessly incompatible."[41]

Manning, too, appeared less than satisfied with his visit. He became particularly frustrated when he had wrangled a concession from Diem that he would make himself available for interviews with some of the resident correspondents, something the president had mainly only done before for such visiting journalists as the *New York Herald Tribune*'s Marguerite Higgins, who was known to be sympathetic to his government. Believing he had won a concession from the prickly politician, Manning recalled that he informed the journalists of this new opportunity. "By this time they were so resentful they said, in effect, 'To hell with it. If we just go to him, he'll tell us lies and we'll have to print them,'" Manning noted. "So I found myself throwing up my hands and becoming quite impatient with the correspondents." Fortunately, Manning said, a new ambassador, Lodge, was preparing to travel to Saigon to replace Nolting, and the change in personnel represented a unique opportunity "for mending relationships with correspondents." The press issue, Manning realized, could not be resolved through public relations. "The basic problem will be removed as a critical factor," he reported, "only by time *and* decisive GVN [Government of Vietnam] victory over the Viet-Cong."[42]

For his part, Diem, frustrated by the unrest in his country, believed that he had done everything "within his power to placate these Buddhists." He told Higgins that the Buddhist movement had been overtaken by extremists and the Viet Cong had infiltrated the pagodas. Both were seeking "an excuse to continue agitation against this government. . . . How can I, in the middle of a war, allow these disorders in the streets to go on?" If he did nothing, Diem predicted that there would be more monk suicides and "more headlines around the world portraying me as some kind of a devil. The more passive we are, the more the demonstrators will be emboldened." The triumph over the enemy the president sought seemed to be more about the disorderly monks, not the guerrillas roaming about the countryside. The battles would now turn to the pagodas.[43]

CHAPTER 7

The Raids

"MR. BROWNE, THE POLICE have come. They're shooting, tell the American embassy quickly."

Malcolm Browne heard the high-pitched voice of a Buddhist monk over the telephone at his Saigon apartment at about twenty minutes past midnight on August 21, 1963. The call came from a trusted source, Thich Duc Nghiep. Just an hour earlier, the monk had rung Browne to inform him of a report "from a devout and important Buddhist" alleging that police had orders to mass around Xa Loi Pagoda. A few minutes after the monk's panicked midnight call, several hundred heavily armed South Vietnamese Special Forces troops and National Police blasted through the pagoda's iron gate and stormed inside, methodically tracking down their quarry. "Key pagodas in Saigon all were hit," reported Browne. "Bedding, furniture and doors were smashed and ripped with bayonets. Monks and nuns were handcuffed and beaten before being loaded into vans."[1]

Seven minutes after the assault began, Browne arrived at Xa Loi. On his previous visits, the pagoda had been a "cheerful looking place at night," with the Buddhist emblem, a blue, neon swastika, glowing at the central building's pinnacle and colorful lights strung along its stone archway into its courtyard. The temple's usual illumination, however, had been replaced by the harsh glare of police floodlights. "A wild din of gongs, drums and yelling was punctuated by heavy caliber shots, as troops ran to and fro," wrote Browne. "Police chased newsmen from the immediate area at pistol point."[2]

At the nearby headquarters of the US Agency for International Development, Browne saw marine guards armed with riot guns ready to "make a stand if necessary." As government forces surged through Xa Loi, two monks climbed the concrete wall separating the pagoda from the AID building and dropped into its parking lot. "They told the Americans they had seen at least one monk shot and killed but were not sure which one. Many were wounded, they said," Browne noted. Watching the raid from the third floor of the AID structure, Neil Sheehan of United Press International could hear the sharp retort of pistol shots from inside the pagoda, interspaced with the popping of exploding tear-gas cannisters. "Several shots rang in the street outside the parking lot," he reported. "One stray shot cracked a window in the U.S. Aid Mission." Although the government closed Saigon's Post, Telephone and Telegraph office, cutting off news dispatches, Sheehan skillfully shepherded his report about the assault out of the country to UPI for distribution around the world, scooping his competition during the first twenty-four hours. Browne admitted that Sheehan had "wiped me out."[3]

The gunfire Browne heard at the pagoda subsided after about fifteen minutes. He observed ambulances and police trucks loaded with prisoners speeding away from the scene. By 1:30 a.m. the raid had ended. Browne noticed that the troops involved started to leave while others "yanked cartridges out of their weapons and lighted cigarettes. The pagoda was reported completely sacked and all its several hundred monks and nuns taken off, except the two who escaped over the wall." Also at the scene, the New York Times's David Halberstam remembered the raid as "a horror spectacle." Had the government wanted to detain the Buddhist leaders, he added, it could have done so "efficiently in a few moments, but these troops were enacting a passion play of revenge and terror." Halberstam felt chills at one sight—a squad from the Special Forces, each troop carrying a submachine gun, entering the pagoda. Resembling a "football team coming up to the line of scrimmage, the mark of American instruction was all over them, and the endless clanging of that gong seemed to me to signal the end of a foreign policy."[4]

Forces loyal to South Vietnamese president Ngo Dinh Diem fanned out across the city to take over the telecommunications center and other key installations. Early in the morning, twenty-nine truckloads of troops arrived in Saigon from their post at Bien Hoa. Browne noticed that posters began appearing on buildings throughout the city denouncing the "Buddhist traitors." At 6:30 a.m. the national radio station broadcast a recorded message from Diem, who said he had declared martial law to safeguard the nation's security. "For the interim, there would be tough curfews [from 9:00 p.m. to 5:00 a.m.], rigid press censorship, a crackdown on black marketeers, and other restrictions," wrote Browne. "For most of Saigon's residents, the speech was the first news that anything happened during the night." Walking the streets, he saw a few tanks and cars guarding key intersections, while soldiers, fixed bayonets at the ready, stood nearby. The government prohibited gatherings of more than three people and roving patrols had orders to shoot curfew violators on sight, Browne recalled, which only added to the nightmare the nation now endured.[5]

The government conducted similar attacks throughout the country, including at two Buddhist pagodas in the provincial capital of Hue. At the Dieu De Pagoda, the Buddhists fought off government forces for nearly eight hours, aided by the city's residents, who streamed into the streets to protest. "While loudspeakers inside the pagoda urged the people to resist the attack, about 1,500 people, fighting with sticks and fists, fought for control of a bridge over the Perfume River leading to the pagoda. They ripped down barbed wire barricades bare handed," wrote Browne, who received reports about the fighting in Hue from AP photographer Horst Faas, detained by police for trying to get close to the action. Other dispatches from the city noted that protestors had picked up the tear-gas canisters thrown by the government troops and hurled them back at the attackers. Newsmen estimated that one monk had been killed and thirty monks and nuns wounded at Xa Loi, while the casualties in Hue included hundreds wounded and several people killed; approximately 1,400 Buddhists were arrested. For its part, the *Times of Vietnam*, the official mouthpiece for the Diem government, said none of the forces involved in the operation had fired their weapons and they were "shocked to be accosted by knife-wielding bonzes at Xa Loi, the nerve center for the campaign to overthrow the government." Government officials alleged that the Buddhists, described as "yellow-robed Reds," used the pagodas to stockpile weapons and communications equipment provided by the Viet Cong. Later, although the government displayed weapons and ammunition it claimed came from the Xa Loi and An Quang Pagodas, US intelligence sources indicated to Browne they were "certain that some evidence was planted."[6]

The raids had been masterminded by Ngo Dinh Nhu, who controlled the secret police and tried to pin blame for the Buddhist crackdown on the army, even fooling the US government for a time. An American embassy official confided to Browne that while Diem still ruled the country, it was "on the general's insistence the present crackdown and martial law were initiated." The *New York Times* went as far as to print on its front page competing stories about who was responsible for the attacks; Tad Szulc's article blamed the army, while Halberstam quoted "highly reliable sources" that the decision to storm the pagodas and declare martial law had been "planned and executed by Ngo Dinh Nhu, the President's brother, without the knowledge of the army." To keep Americans in Saigon in the dark and unable to interfere with the raids, Diem's regime had blocked telephone communications at the US embassy and at the homes of senior American officials in the city. The only exception, "in deference perhaps to the fact that there was still a war on with the Viet Cong," noted embassy spokesman John Mecklin, was the line from General Paul Harkins's headquarters. "For the next forty-eight hours this was the Embassy's sole means of telephone communication with the rest of Saigon," said Mecklin, who described the raids as an act of "political bankruptcy" and a "confession of a catastrophic failure of leadership" by South Vietnam's government.[7]

At a dinner with American and Vietnamese officials just a few weeks before, Nhu had been particularly indiscrete. Talking at the dinner, Nhu described foreign journalists as "disgusting" and accused his brother of being incompetent and weak for attempting to reach a compromise with the Buddhists, threatening to resign if Diem failed to adopt tougher measures against their opponents, Mecklin recalled. "If the Buddhists wish to have another barbeque I will be glad to supply the gasoline and match," Nhu said as he left. His comments parroted previous remarks made by his wife, Madame Nhu, who had deliberately called for more monk "barbeques," realizing the shock value using such a term held. She also said to a journalist: "Let them burn and we shall clap our hands." She explained that it was "necessary somehow to shock the world out of this trance in which it looks at Viet Nam with utterly false vision about religious persecution which does not exist."[8]

The Buddhists had been aware that the government might soon strike. In August several monks followed Thich Quang Duc's example, sacrificing their lives while engulfed in flames. According to Browne, the top monks at Xa Loi prepared for the expected assault by stringing barbed wire around the temple's walls. Nuns armed themselves with insecticide sprayers filled with a mixture of vinegar and pepper. As the press liaison for the monks, Duc Nghiep called correspondents "at all hours of night, saying he expected an imminent attack against Xa Loi, and that newsmen should be ready with cameras," Browne remembered. As their fears mounted, the monks went so far as to seek permission from US Aid officials to knock an escape hole in the wall that separated the pagoda from the Americans' building in case they needed asylum. "The request was politely turned down," Browne recalled, "on grounds that diplomatic immunity should not be abused."[9]

On the day of the government raid, monks at Xa Loi told the AP's Browne and Peter Arnett that they were concerned about the delay in the arrival of the new American ambassador, Henry Cabot Lodge Jr.—Frederick Nolting had departed South Vietnam on August 15—expecting serious trouble from the government during the interregnum. As young monks dragged wooden benches across the pagoda's staircases to act as barricades, Duc Nghiep informed Browne that he and other leading monks feared that the government might try to fake an assassination of Lodge and blame it on the Buddhists, or perhaps stage an army takeover and use it as an excuse to crush its opposition. Although American officials scoffed at such rumors, Browne pointed out that the last two US ambassadors to South Vietnam had survived attempts on their lives.[10]

Early in August, Nolting had angered the Buddhists when the *Times of*

Vietnam quoted him as saying that during his two-and-a-half years in South Vietnam he had "never seen any evidence of religious persecution." A Buddhist spokesman described the ambassador's statement as Nolting's "departing gift to Ngo Dinh Diem." Browne believed that the decision to raid the pagodas may have been sparked by an August 18 incident in Da Nang, a coastal city located about three hundred miles northeast of Saigon. According to American eyewitnesses, about three thousand to four thousand residents took to the streets. Although they had permission to gather from local authorities, troops still surrounded the area. The demonstration remained peaceful until Captain Vo Thanh Xuan and his driver drove their jeep into the crowd. Alarmed at being surrounded, the driver opened fire. Furious demonstrators, Browne reported, hauled the men out of their vehicle and beat Xuan. "Buddhist boy scouts fought their way through the crowd, and reportedly finally dragged the officer to safety," he added. South Vietnamese officials in Diem's cabinet confidentially told Browne that the Da Nang incident proved to be "the final straw for the palace. It was at that point that Diem and Nhu decided to apply all-out force to crush the Buddhist leaders, political opponents and American meddlers all at once." Halberstam had been puzzled why Buddhist leaders did not flee to secret hiding places before the raid, only to be told by one monk: "We had done nothing wrong; therefore we could not flee. If we had, it would have been an admission that we were guilty." Halberstam wondered if the Buddhists might not have wanted some martyrs for their cause, as well as seriously underestimated the extent of the government's crackdown.[11]

Americans in South Vietnam were shocked by the raids. A civilian official complained to Browne that once again "the United States has been kicked in the teeth by this regime." General Ton That Dinh, one of the few army officials involved in the raids, had even boasted to a reporter that he was a "great national hero. I have defeated the American Cabot Lodge. He was on his way here to pull a coup d'état, but I, Dinh, the hero, have foiled him." Although he had been stopped by authorities from going anywhere near the Buddhist pagoda at Nha Trang, Arnett had been able to talk to US military advisers stationed in the city about what had happened with the Buddhists. "In one night he [Diem] lost all the good will that we had helped to build up here in the past 18 months," an American captain told the reporter. An officer who had just returned after spending forty-four days on patrol in the Central Highlands complained to Arnett at Francois's Restaurant that the Americans were trying to "win people to the Saigon government in the mountains but we are losing them in the cities."[12]

American advisers had been warned by their superiors not to get involved in the crisis, but they were aware of the tensions existing between the government and the Buddhists. While some South Vietnamese officers told US advisers that it was necessary to rein in the monks because they had been influenced by the Communists, one American pointed out that from what he had seen nearly all the people in the country were Buddhists. "If they are Communists, what are we Americans doing here at all?" he wondered. Returning to Saigon, Arnett tracked down some US soldiers, who expressed scorn at the Vietnamese forces standing guard at street intersections to enforce the government's curfew. According to Arnett's account, one of the young Americans yelled: "They have their bayonets ready to shoot girls, monks and nuns. Why don't they try shooting up some Viet Cong [guerrillas] for a change?" Not understanding English, the Vietnamese soldiers, Arnett added, "just waved at him and laughed."[13]

President John F. Kennedy's administration condemned the raids, releasing a message that they had been a "direct violation by the Vietnamese Government of assurances that it was pursuing a policy of reconciliation with the Buddhists." In the final days of his ambassadorship, Nolting had followed instructions from the White House to do all he could to persuade Diem to issue a public statement about compromising with the Buddhists. Rather obliquely, the South Vietnamese president did relate to a friendly journalist, Marguerite Higgins, the following: "My policy of non-discrimination on religious grounds is irreversible." Stopping in Honolulu, Hawaii, on August 19, Nolting consulted about the situation in South Vietnam with Lodge and other US officials, including Admiral Harry Felt, William Colby of the Central Intelligence Agency, and Assistant Secretary of State for Far Eastern Affairs Roger Hilsman. Nolting said he and the other officials were "amazed and angered" when they heard the news about the raids. Nolting sent a personal telegram to Diem that read: "This is the first time that you've ever gone back on your word to me." The ambassador later said he regretted sending the message.[14]

Lodge flew out of Hawaii on August 20 and arrived in Tokyo the next day. While there he received a message from Kennedy about the raids and urging him to get to Saigon as soon as possible. Lodge believed that the attacks on the pagodas "marked the beginning of the end of the Diem regime. They had ceased to exercise the effective powers of government since April of that year, but when the troops went in and fired at people who were worshipping, it was just a matter of time before they would be through." Stanley Karnow, who covered Asia for the *Saturday Evening Post*, tracked down a South Vietnamese general now seemingly willing to move against Diem and the Nhus, whom he had known for years. Asked by Karnow how he could kill his friends in cold blood, the officer shrugged, responding sadly: "We must choose between a few people and a nation."[15]

The government next moved against South Vietnamese teachers and students, who had taken to the streets to protest the crackdown against the Buddhists. The Diem regime reacted by closing the country's two universities, in Hue and Saigon. Police grabbed students off their bicycles, scooters, and motorcycles and tossed them into trucks. News reports had shared that more than thirty truckloads of students were hauled off during a one-hour period. Browne estimated that approximately three thousand university students were arrested. When secondary and grade-school children also demonstrated, the government closed their schools and threw the youngsters in jail. The grim determination by the students was highlighted by one fourteen year old, who had asked his classmates, "What will you say 10 years from now when someone asks you what you did in 1963? Do something now so you can look him in the face and tell him."[16]

One of the most poignant memories Mecklin had of this chaotic time in Saigon was the sight of "hundreds of bicycles abandoned in neat array outside a shut-down school near my house where the boys and girls had stacked them that morning. They were there for several days, repeatedly drenched and rusting in rainy season downpours." Arnett had seared in his mind the memory of students attending a private girls academy who had been rounded up by the police on their way to school. "By late afternoon desperate parents were searching for their daughters' bicycles and swapping terrified stories of alleged torture and other atrocities," Arnett reported. "Among the tight-faced adults at the tearful scene were

high-ranking uniformed military men and well-dressed midlevel government officials and I wondered at the stupidity of this crude attempt at
intimidation by the regime."[17]

Newsmen feared that the Diem government might next fix its sights on
them. Arnett recalled that he and Browne discussed the possibility of moving out of their apartments over the AP office for the relative safety of rooms
at the Caravelle Hotel. An Australian correspondent, Dennis Warner, even
warned Arnett: "Peter, you're the top of the hit list now because of your Nha
Trang trip." Sheehan and Halberstam also feared for their safety. They took
the drastic step of seeking sanctuary with an embassy official—Mecklin,
who remembered being sought out by the journalists at his office at around
4:00 a.m. the day of the raids. "They said they were afraid of arrest or worse
by Diem's police and asked if they could move into my house, which was US
Government property and therefore relatively secure," Mecklin recalled.
"This was before it was clear what kind of madness the regime was up to, and
there certainly was no doubt that the palace regarded the newsmen as enemies." With Deputy Chief of Mission William Trueheart's permission,
Mecklin gave the journalists sanctuary for the next three weeks. Mecklin's
kindness might have been prompted by the memory of his friend Gene
Symonds, a reporter who had been beaten to death by a mob in Singapore in
1955, "simply because he was white and carrying a camera."[18]

The censorship clamped down by the Diem government on foreign
newsmen proved to be particularly severe. Arnett estimated that censors
often cut 90 percent from dispatches, while on other occasions entire articles were trashed. "They even cut out descriptions of President Diem as a
Roman Catholic," Arnett recalled. Returning after trying to get his story
approved, one frustrated reporter noted: "If they had taken out one more
sentence, all I would have had left is the address and my signature." Journalists never knew what was permissible to send and what might be forbidden. For example, censors cleared sending two radiophotos to Paris,
but military authorities refused to let them be transmitted. Even reports
from the Viet Nam Press, an agency responsible for official government
reports, had its messages stopped. In a censored dispatch sent to AP's
Tokyo office about how Saigon had settled down to living under martial
law, here is how the government altered Browne's copy:

Superficially streets looked about the same as they had before Wednesday morning when police and troops (four words deleted by censor) Buddhist pagodas and imposed martial law throughout the nation.

A few tanks and cars stood at key intersections. Soldiers were scattered around with fixed bayonets (eights words deleted).

A rigid curfew went into effect Wednesday night and there were orders to roving patrols to shoot violators on sight (nine words deleted).[19]

Despite the censorship, described by one newsman as worse than anything he had seen in Communist countries, and fears about their safety, Browne and his AP colleagues continued to do their best to inform readers about the tense situation. Arnett remembered sending carbon copies of his stories and extra photo prints, sometimes wrapped in old newspapers, via Westerners flying out of Saigon to Singapore, Bangkok, Hong Kong, and Manila. Browne waited for hours in the airport's transit lounge "trying to persuade airline passengers" to carry the precious material in their briefcases and pockets. The packages were labeled "Bundles for Bassett," as they were headed to AP foreign editor Ben Bassett. "They usually got delivered, though some packages didn't make it," Arnett noted. "It was like throwing a sealed bottle into the South China Sea and hoping for the best." Although Arnett believed that the authorities knew about the airport handoffs, they did nothing to stop them, perhaps because "they wanted to avoid disorderly confrontations." Browne believed that the police knew what the newsmen were doing, but "winked at the smuggling operation as long as we were discreet."[20]

Browne discovered a clever way of getting around the censors when some members of the government turned against Diem. Not only did the country's ambassador to the United States, Tran Van Chuong, and his wife, South Vietnam's observer at the United Nations, the parents of Madame Nhu, resign to protest the raids, Vu Van Mau, the foreign minister, also quit, shaved his head in solidarity with the Buddhists, and announced that he wanted to leave the country to embark on a religious pilgrimage to India. "This was the first sign that the government itself was falling apart, and was clearly a major story," Browne recalled. He devised an ingenious solution for slipping news of Mau's resignation past the censors. Authorities had permitted sending some photographs via a radiophoto transmitter located at the government radio station. The transmitter had a rotating drum on which black-and-white photographs were attached. "As the drum rotated, a light beam in the instrument scanned the photograph, and the reflected beam hit a photocell, which translated the variations in light intensity into electrical impulses that could be broadcast," Browne explained. It took about ten minutes to transmit a single photo to AP's Paris office.[21]

Hoping to get news about Mau's resignation out of the country, Browne walked to the telecommunications post carrying with him an innocuous photograph he knew would have no trouble being approved by the censor. He also took along a piece of paper with an adhesive backing on which he had written a short article about Mau's decision and the political implications of such news. After Browne had put the approved photograph in the transmitter and its drum started rotating, he saw the censor turn away momentarily. He seized on the moment and stuck his story on the revolving photograph. "Standing with my back to the radiophoto machine," he remembered, "I managed to block the censor's view until the transmission was complete, at which point I removed the paper and slipped it into my pocket." Although his ploy worked, it did not remain secret for long. According to Browne, the next morning the *New York Herald Tribune* published his Mau story on its front page, exactly as he had sent it, making it easy for Saigon's censors to find out about his subterfuge regarding the photograph, and making it harder to trick them in the future.[22]

The atmosphere for the newsmen, at least regarding their relations with the US embassy, brightened with Lodge's arrival in South Vietnam. With Kennedy's blessing, Lodge was determined to be the key figure when it came to handling media matters for the US embassy, and everything else for that matter, acting, as a journalist noted, not like a regular ambassador but more like a proconsul. "He said he was his own spokesman," noted Frederick W. Flott, Lodge's special assistant. "He wanted to deal with the press: he'd had a lot of experience with the press in his various political campaigns and as a senator and at the UN, and he was very skilled at dealing with them." Lodge, who had cut short his stopover in Tokyo, arrived at Saigon's Tan Son Nhut Airport on a US Air Force turboprop Lockheed Constellation aircraft at 9:30 p.m. on August 22. One of the first things the new ambassador did, after shaking hands with Trueheart and General Paul Harkins, was to ask, "Where are the gentlemen of the press?" Although he declined to answer questions about the current crisis, he did tell the approximately forty broadcasters and reporters who had been bused out to the airport under an armed police escort, "I don't have to tell you that I have arrived here in rather special circumstances and my time for declarations has not yet arrived." Mecklin remembered that Lodge also talked for several minutes about the key role the press played in America's democracy and "how much he welcomed any opportunity to help the newsmen do their jobs." The ambassador's comments, Mecklin noted, represented the "nicest thing anyone except the Buddhists had said to them in a long while and the newsmen were pleased." In another good sign for the resident correspondents, Lodge, a former reporter himself, had allowed four journalists to accompany him on his flight from Tachikawa Air Force Base. One of the journalists on the flight with Lodge, Robert Eunson, AP's chief executive in Asia, took aside Arnett and told him, "The ambassador's on our side."[23]

Possessed with impeccable Republican credentials and known for standing up to the Russians while US ambassador to the UN, Lodge seemed to be insulated from attacks that by putting pressure on Diem he was pursuing too liberal a policy and, therefore, was "soft on Communism," Halberstam pointed out. Lodge signaled that he was going to be different from his predecessor almost immediately after he arrived in Saigon. He visited the monks who had taken refuge in the US Aid building and later offered sanctuary in the embassy to a group of Buddhists, including a leading monk, Thich Tri Quang, providing them their required vegetarian meals. "He was a very sharp, clever, determined, energetic man," Lodge said of Tri Quang. "And he detested what Diem was doing." Such familiarity was sure to enrage the Diem government, which considered Tri Quang to be at best a Communist sympathizer and at worst a Communist agent; the monk insisted he strongly believed in the need to defeat the Viet Cong. Browne reported that according to secret police files kept on the monk he had two brothers in North Vietnam, one of whom worked as an agent for the guerrillas. "He [Tri Quang] is suspected by the central Vietnamese security services of being in relations with the rebels," wrote Browne. The reporter noted that a similar case could be made against many members of Diem's government, who fought as members of the Viet Minh against the French. While Tri Quang sheltered inside the US embassy, a platoon of plainclothes police took up positions on nearby streets, Browne noticed, keeping tabs on all who came and went. "I haven't figured out whether Viet Nam is a friendly enemy or a hostile friend," a US Army officer told Browne.[24]

Another effort Lodge undertook during his early days as ambassador was to improve the embassy's quarrelsome relationship with the resident correspondents. He had one-on-one, private lunches, also attended by Lodge's wife, Emily, with the three newsmen who had taken the most flack for their reporting—Browne, Halberstam, and Sheehan—to question them about their opinions about the crisis and the war's progress. "I liked him immediately," Browne said. "Unlike his predecessors and most of the other Americans guiding Viet Nam policy, Lodge spoke bluntly and honestly, and newsmen rarely if ever felt they were being misled by him." Sheehan, too, was impressed by the ambassador during their luncheon, in which Lodge sought the reporter's advice about the Diem regime, the Buddhist crisis, and the war. He noted that Lodge's face betrayed nothing, remaining "blandly uncommunicative," as he criticized Diem and Nhu for being "incapable of governing," while the VC gained more and more support in the countryside. Sheehan flatly stated that if the Diem family continued to hold power in South Vietnam, "the war was certain to be lost." Although Sheehan could not give any guarantees that a military regime would do any better, there at least existed a hope that it could. The newsmen had been advised by embassy officials that Lodge would be asking questions, not answering them, but Sheehan could not help himself and asked before leaving about the ambassador's impression of the situation. Lodge, sitting on the couch alongside his wife, smiled and responded: "About the same as yours." It appeared that the US policy for South Vietnam had switched from "Sink or Swim with Ngo Dinh Diem" to "No Nhus would be good news" or "No Ngos—that is, the whole family—would be good news."[25]

John Michael Dunn, who served as the ambassador's special assistant, believed that Lodge was able to convert what had been "a very hostile press" during Nolting's days into "basically a press very supportive of his [Lodge's] personal efforts and his personality in very short order." In addition to Lodge being accessible to journalists, Dunn, who had the office next to the ambassador, made sure to keep in touch with them as well. "They were fascinating people, all of them," Dunn recalled, describing them as "very, very useful people to talk to." There were times when Flott might be called upon by Lodge to talk to a reporter who was visiting the embassy if he were called away for an emergency, or if he had direct instructions from Lodge to discuss something that was "appropriately of my competence," Flott noted. In the long run, however, Flott did not believe that Lodge "would have wanted anyone other than himself being the spokesman." As in all the other ways he approached his duties as ambassador and his service to President Kennedy, Lodge "did it with the style of a senator or a very political ambassador in a very political place, like the UN," Flott observed.[26]

According to Mecklin, Lodge never became an "exceptionally good news source," but he had the ability to talk to reporters in a way that made them happy, perhaps because he did not try to debate them as Nolting and Harkins had done. "Instead he invited their ideas, confided enough information to make a story, and treated them as equals—tried and true devices that should have been used much sooner in Saigon," Mecklin concluded. The ambassador also knew the power of working behind the scenes, not out in the open. "The leak is the prerogative of the ambassador," Lodge reminded Mecklin.[27]

Browne, Sheehan, and Halberstam were under no illusions about what Lodge, the consummate politician, was trying to do with his charm offensive. The ambassador hoped to gain their trust, thereby, as Sheehan noted, gaining "as good a press as possible for himself." Halberstam pointed out that in journalism and government, "everyone is using everyone." He remembered talking to one of his key military sources, American adviser John Paul Vann, when the officer left South Vietnam. Halberstam walked to the airplane with him and told him that he had always been worried that in using the information Vann provided he might harm the officer's military career. "And he looked at me and he gave me a very flinty look and he said, 'You never hurt me any more than I wanted to be hurt.' Which meant that he'd been calibrating it to the edge. A very tight kind of careful thing." Something similar happened with Lodge, with the ambassador skillfully using the newsmen, and the journalists trying to do the same to the diplomat. Sheehan, a Massachusetts native like Lodge, later told Halberstam: "Lodge is what my Irish mother would call a crafty Yankee." While the ambassador did not always agree with the newsmen's assessments about the war, he saw their differences not as disloyal to the American cause but as honest disagreements. As Lodge later noted, while some reporters might say there was a "distinct possibility that this war may be lost," he preferred to believe there was "a distinct possibility that this war may be won."[28]

From the beginning of Lodge's time leading the US Mission, and probably before he even arrived in South Vietnam, the ambassador, the reporters sensed, believed the Diem government had to be replaced, as Browne said, "with a government more acceptable to the South Vietnamese people, most of whom were Buddhist." Lodge himself, Halberstam noted, had little expectation that Diem would be flexible in any negotiations, including any attempts to remove from authority the president's troublesome brother. "And the fact that Diem had cracked down on the Buddhists even while Lodge was flying over there, I think he regarded as an act of betrayal and an act of bad faith," Halberstam recalled. Day by day the US ambassador put pressure on Diem to reform his regime, while at the same time, as Browne recalled, Lodge gave backdoor encouragement to rebellious Army of the Republic of Vietnam generals to move against the government, keeping in touch with the conspirators through a Central Intelligence Agency contact, Lucien Conein. The ambassador believed that there was "no possibility . . . that the war can be won under a Diem administration." America's several years supporting the regime "gives us a responsibility that we cannot avoid," Lodge insisted.[29]

The ambassador had support to pursue such a course from some members of the Kennedy administration, including Undersecretary of State Averell Harriman and Assistant Secretary of State for Far Eastern Affairs Roger Hilsman. "Something had to give, as far as I was concerned," Hilsman recalled. "And I thought that we could not sit still and be the puppets of Diem's anti-Buddhist policies, you know. To make the United States of America be an instrument for this, to me, was unacceptable. So I felt that we had to do something." At a minimum, he added, the Diem regime had to adopt a "pro-Buddhist rather than anti-Buddhist policy," and Nhu had to be sent out of the country. Talking with another member of the administration, Mike Forrestall, a member of the senior staff of the National Security Council, Hilsman predicted at the time that there was a 40 percent chance that Diem would "send Nhu to Paris, and fall into line," a 40 percent chance that Diem would do nothing and the generals would move to oust him from power, and a 20 percent chance "that nothing will happen at all."[30]

Although the newsmen and the ambassador seemed to be on the same page when it came to changes in South Vietnam's government, the relationship did not always go smoothly. Lodge, Browne pointed out, kept his attempts to squeeze concessions from Diem out of public sight, but the ambassador "sometimes signaled his intentions in diplomatic ways." Browne had learned that since August 21 the US government had stopped, at least partly, its commercial-import program whereby it donated surplus agricultural products to friendly governments that could sell them to their people and use the resulting cash to fund such things as fighting a war. "The program represents about half the total economic aid the United States pours into South Viet Nam," Browne wrote in an AP dispatch. "Indirectly it pays about 70 per cent of the defense budget." Suspending the program, he added, was a way to coerce the Diem government to reform. Vietnamese opposition leaders had indicated that if American authorities would curtail aid to the regime, military leaders "would carry out a coup and set up a new government." An American official admitted to Browne that the United States was locked in "a dangerous poker game with the Diem government," with both sides holding "high cards, and the pot is full. The danger for all of us is that the Viet Cong may hold the fifth ace." Unfortunately for Browne, he did not realize that Lodge believed that he had given him the information about the economic squeeze play off the record. The ambassador was furious when Browne's article appeared, accusing the reporter of putting "sensitive diplomatic strategy in jeopardy by publicly proclaiming its purpose." A contrite Browne apologized for his mistake, and Lodge "forgave my unintended breach."[31]

While Saigon remained a city ready to blow at any moment, Browne did not neglect to track the war's progress, traveling to southern South Vietnam, a region he had reported from in February 1962, when guerrillas had cut off the head of a district chief there. Nearly a year later, the jungle town of Dam Doi had suffered a bloodbath that government officials termed a victory. "Perhaps it was," Browne wrote. "But it is not the kind of victory this shattered town can endure very often." Although Vietnamese marines had recaptured the town, killing more than a hundred of the enemy in the process, it reeked of death, with the bodies of women and children lying "rotting on corrugated iron litters, waiting for the burial squads," said Browne. "The few buildings still standing have been turned into morgues." Casualties included more than a hundred government soldiers and civilians killed, while probably another hundred had been carried off by the retreating VC, he added.[32]

Located about seventy miles south of Saigon, Dam Doi had been attacked by approximately five hundred "battle-hardened Viet Cong regulars" armed with recoilless rifles, machine guns, and mortars. The enemy had advanced on the town at night and overwhelmed its flimsy barricades, reported Browne. A few months before, an American adviser in Ca Mau, the province capital located twenty-five miles north of the village, had warned that if the VC ever made a big push, there were more than a dozen places in the An Xuyen Province that might fall. "We just don't have the strength to occupy an enemy zone," the officer said, "and this whole province is an enemy zone." A frustrated US adviser had gone so far as to shoot himself in the head with a pistol. "No one knows why," wrote Browne. "But the jungle closes in on people down here." The government had tried to clear the area, unleashing tanks, planes, helicopters, armored river boats, and up to five thousand men on two big operations. Although both operations were described as successful, recalled Browne, over time the VC had returned, as strong as ever. "If and when we win this war," the newsman quoted a mud-splattered American as commenting, "the last place we're going to win is down here."[33]

Browne's reporting seemed to buttress a Halberstam article from nearly a month earlier. Halberstam had determined, based on his talks with South Vietnamese officials and American civilian and military authorities, that the situation in the Mekong Delta had worsened over the past year with the VC "making a sizable military offensive in the most populous regions of the delta." Although Halberstam's article pointed out that there were "encouraging signs" elsewhere in South Vietnam, in the Delta the Communists appeared to be "moving free in unusually large units. Where a year ago they would group up to 250 men, they are now grouping 600 and even 1,000." These forces were confident, he wrote, eager to engage regular South Vietnamese troops instead of just attacking poorly trained and armed civil guards. Another source informed the *Times* reporter that the enemy planned to unleash "fast, hard-hitting mobile warfare" in battalion strength and as well-equipped as their opponent. VC units had armed themselves by capturing weapons from small outposts that the Americans described as "death traps." Also, military officials expressed their concern to Halberstam that the government's strategic hamlet program had not been able to stop VC movement in the region.[34]

The pessimistic reports from South Vietnam, especially Halberstam's August 15 Delta article, meant, as Sheehan pointed out, to be "a mine of facts . . . to compel the administration to face the reality that it was losing," were not highly regarded by Kennedy. The president went as far as to task his secretary of defense, Robert McNamara, to refute Halberstam's work, and Harkins staff also picked apart the article, offering a far rosier picture. "Goddamit," Kennedy had complained to his staff at one meeting, "I don't want you reading those stories in the *Times*. We're not going to let the policy be run by some twenty-eight-year-old kid." Later, at a lunch meeting with Arthur Ochs Sulzberger, the new publisher of the *Times*, the president tried to have Sulzberger do something about his man in South Vietnam. "I wish like hell that you'd get Halberstam out of there," Kennedy told the publisher, who had been at his post for only a few months. Sulzberger said he would investigate, later seeking input from his editors, including James "Scotty" Reston, the newspaper's Washington, DC, bureau chief, and the man responsible for bringing Halberstam to the *Times*. Although Halberstam indicated he had been scheduled for a two-week vacation, the *Times* told him to stay put; other reports had him set to be replaced by Hedrick

Smith. "We can't buckle in [to] that kind of stuff," Reston told Sulzberger. Halberstam stayed put. Later, he profanely dismissed the president's attempt to oust him from Vietnam. "The Kennedy thing never bothered me," said Halberstam. "I heard the story later and I thought, 'Well, fuck you.' What the Kennedys thought of our work didn't mean a shit."[35]

All kinds of strains were being placed upon the newsmen in South Vietnam, including severe pushback from people involved in their profession, such as Marguerite Higgins of the *New York Herald Tribune*, who had received a Pulitzer Prize in 1951 for her frontline reports from Korea, and Joseph Alsop, a nationally known political columnist for the *Washington Post*. Browne recalled that Saigon had been a regular stop for visits from those he called "nonresident" American newsmen, some of whom had made names for themselves by covering previous conflicts. "They back Diem's government not merely because of their conservative political views but because they saw Viet Nam as fundamentally similar to World War II and Korea," noted Browne. "Viet Nam, for them, was another conventional conflict pitting the home team against the bad guys, and provided Americans would quit whining and buckle down, our side would win." Consequently, these journalists viewed their younger colleagues—Halberstam, Sheehan, and Browne—as "wrongheaded purveyors of political rumor and baseless forecasts." Sheehan believed that by the late summer of 1963, the claim that the resident correspondents were "inventing bad news" was "ludicrous," as most of the established newsmen in Asia paying regular trips to South Vietnam shared their views about the war. The reporters he cited included Peter Kalischer and Bernard Kalb of CBS, James Robinson of NBC, Stanley Karnow of the *Saturday Evening Post*, Pepper Martin of *U.S. News & World Report*, and Charles Mohr of *Time* magazine. "These men were not the sort to be hoodwinked by a bunch of cubs," Sheehan noted.[36]

Although Mohr had quoted Higgins as commenting during a dinner at the Admiral Restaurant in Saigon that the foreign press in South Vietnam "would like to see us lose the war to prove they're right," she said she never made "so calloused and harsh a remark," believing there were no Americans who wanted "us to lose the war in Vietnam or any other place." Higgins believed, however, that the newsmen in Saigon were too engrossed by far in reporting on the Diem regime's deficiencies in the war and had failed to give equal weight to its successes. She expressed her puzzlement and anger about the emphasis of Halberstam's article on the failures in the Delta while she had often heard from American advisers that overall gains were being made against the VC. In his column, Alsop compared the journalists in Saigon with the reporters who had paved the way for the fall of Chiang Kai-shek's government to the Communists in China. Alsop wrote that it was time to ask "whether American crusades to reform foreign governments really are a good idea at any time." He went on to blame the "high-minded crusaders" in Saigon for presenting a "dark, indignant picture," easy to do, he noted, even without departing from the fact, if "you ignore the majority of Americans who admire the Vietnamese as fighters and seek out the one U.S. officer in 10 who inevitably thinks all foreigners fight badly." Confirming that the Diem government's press relations had "always been inadequate," Alsop blamed the correspondents' constant pressure on the regime for transforming Diem "from a courageous, quite viable national leader, into a man afflicted with galloping persecution mania," wanting them to spend less time in Saigon and more on the "fighting front."[37]

Browne recalled that when Alsop visited South Vietnam the columnist's usual routine involved stopping at the news agency offices in Saigon to be briefed. The columnist would then head off to "make the rounds of his high-level acquaintances," including a South Vietnamese colonel later revealed to be an agent for the Communists. "Joe would then return to the United States and inform his readers that the resident correspondents in Saigon were maliciously misrepresenting the war," Browne said, "and that in reality, the Saigon-Washington alliance was winning." Reflecting on Alsop, Reston described his fellow journalist as someone "who seldom allowed the facts to interfere with his prejudices."[38]

Higgins had engaged in a bitter battle with fellow journalist Homer Bigart during the Korean War, but Browne said that he hated to be involved in such feuds. After all, he noted, the "lives of reporters are tough enough without our rubbing salt into each other's wounds." Later, while Higgins and Browne were reporting from Phnom Penh, Cambodia, Browne decided it would "be nice if we could bury a hatchet or two," and invited her to dinner at the Lotus d'Or, a "floating dockside restaurant renowned for its delicious noodle soups." Browne tried to keep their conversation away from news coverage about the Vietnam War, but Higgins kept steering the conversation back to what she considered to be "the lack of experience and patriotism in most of the Saigon press corps." She leveled most of her attacks against Halberstam, who she seemed to believe was a "reincarnation of her archnemesis," Bigart, Browne remembered.[39]

One article infuriated the younger correspondents. It appeared in the September 20, 1963, issue of *Time* magazine, the flagship publication of Henry Luce's media empire, under the title "Foreign Correspondents: The View from Saigon." Originally, Mohr had written a flattering piece about the correspondents' work in Vietnam and had also filed long pieces about how the war was being lost. In the *Time* system, stories sent in by its reporters were often rewritten by the magazine's editors. In this case, managing editor Otto Fuerbringer spiked Mohr's reporting and instead used nearly a full page to vilify the journalism coming from the Saigon press corps, accusing them of covering "a complex situation from only one angle, as if their own conclusions offered all the necessary illumination." The article echoed critical comments from those who believed that the correspondents, as Browne recalled, "spent their days and nights at the Caravelle bar, picking up false rumors with which to defame the regime." Fuerbringer's article charged that many of the journalists were "reluctant to give splash treatment to anything that smacks of military victory in the ugly war against the Communists," and if they did, such good news had to be tempered with bad news. As an example, the article cited an AP dispatch that gave government forces credit for a significant victory against the Communists but went on to note that there had been "renewed civilian opposition" to the Diem regime. And while the correspondents viewed Diem as inevitably "stubborn and stupid, dominated by his brother and sister-in-law," they regularly assigned "justice and sympathy to the Buddhists, who are well aware of their favored position."[40]

A despondent Mohr resigned from *Time*, along with the magazine's dedicated Saigon stringer, Merton Perry. Mohr eventually return to Vietnam for the *New York Times* and received a Bronze Star from the military for carrying a severely wounded US soldier to safety. Browne, who wanted to sue the magazine for libel, believed that Fuerbringer had decided to start a "campaign to ridicule and discredit the American resident correspondents in Saigon, using whatever ammunition came to hand, regardless of its accuracy." Unfortunately, Browne noted, American officials, believing what had they had read in *Time*, arrived in Vietnam assuming that the press corps were "enemy agents," and it took some time to "disabuse them of such nonsense."[41]

A few weeks after its initial article, *Time* revisited the situation, this time grudgingly giving the newsmen some credit for their work, noting that what they had written about the Diem regime's decline had been correct and praising them for their "strong sense of mission." The piece also quoted Lodge as saying: "The regular press here is appealing, brave, tremendously hard-working." Other defenders chimed in with their opinions. After spending several weeks in South Vietnam, Milburn P. Akers, *Chicago Sun-Times* editor, returned with the belief that as a group the US correspondents in Saigon presented "as nearly an accurate picture of that which has taken place in South Viet Nam as is possible," especially when faced with opposition from some American officials preferring that their mistakes be buried from public view. Akers described the reporters, including Browne, Arnett, Sheehan, and Halberstam, as "a group of capable youngsters whom almost any editor, if he were acquainted with them, would be happy to have working for him."[42]

Reflecting on his time as the AP bureau chief in Saigon, Browne always credited his boss, Wes Gallagher, as one of the "real heroes" of the Vietnam War for trusting his employees "implicitly until and unless the trust was betrayed." Browne pointed out that Gallagher had to field complaints from AP member newspapers, several of which were run by conservative publishers and editors. On his trip to the United States the previous year, Browne had attended a luncheon where he sat next to Gallagher and William Knowland, a conservative former US senator and then publisher of the *Oakland Tribune*. Browne remembered Knowland expressed his displeasure with the "overly liberal" reporting coming out of the Saigon bureau. Perhaps to quiet such critics, in October AP officials told Browne to "take a month off to cool down," according to a *Time* report. Sheehan, too, was ordered by his bosses at UPI to take time off in Tokyo. Both men were certain that a military coup could happen at any moment. Before leaving the country at the end of October, Sheehan had worked out with

one of his sources to alert Halberstam or Ray Herndon, Sheehan's UPI colleague, to send him a coded signal that a coup was imminent: "Please Buy
Blue Lotus Two Geisha Dolls, Kyoto Style." Sheehan made sure to let the
staff at UPI's Tokyo office know to call him if such a message came in.
Tipped off by a source that a military move against Diem appeared to be
imminent, Halberstam fired off the agreed-upon cable to Sheehan. When
the message arrived at the UPI office in Tokyo, a clerk placed it among the
other messages and did not alert Sheehan about its arrival.[43]

Luckily for Browne, he had returned to Saigon before Sheehan left on
his forced vacation, cruelly shut out of what could have been one of the
biggest stories of his career. Browne's instincts told him that something
might be stirring. He had noticed that whenever South Vietnamese officials screwed up the courage to call the AP office, police swooped in to
arrest them. Trying to help any would-be whistleblowers, he started
answering the bureau's phone by announcing: "Associated Press, this line
is being monitored by public officials. Go ahead please." Arnett remembered that Browne became so worried about police raiding the office he
sent some private files to the US embassy to keep them safe. Police arrested
and hauled off for questioning chauffeurs who worked for Western correspondents, and the government ordered desk clerks at Saigon hotels "to
furnish reporters only with cars with government drivers," Arnett added.
Mecklin blamed Nhu for the "war of news against his own people, the correspondents, and the US Mission," driven either by anger or his belief he
could "scare" American officials enough they would alter their policies.
Several Americans who had close Vietnamese friends saw them "perse-
cuted uselessly" for those relationships, Mecklin added. As rumors about
pro-Diem mobs attacking the US Information Agency grew, Mecklin and
his staff took precautions, including designating those responsible for
closing the building's steel antimob gates, reading instructions on how to
use special chemicals to burn classified materials, and outlining possible
escape routes if a mob broke through the barriers.[44]

Browne recalled that he could not openly let his employers know a coup
might be imminent because of censorship and government monitoring.
"But there had been several false alarms before, and we had worked out a
signal," Browne noted. During one incident of street violence in the city, Le

Lieu, his wife-to-be, had taken cover in the bureau's bathroom-photography lab. Edwin Q. White, AP's Tokyo news editor, was in Saigon at that time and knew that, in case of a looming coup, Browne would send him a simple message: "Le Lieu's in the john." Browne sent the coded message in the last week of October, and White flew to Saigon "with some other AP recruits to help out with the crisis." Unfortunately, two of Browne's best men, Arnett and photographer Horst Faas, were away from Saigon on assignment; Arnett in Vientiane, Laos, and Faas on patrol in Ca Mau, a place, he noted, "as far away as you could be in the Delta."[45]

Not every newsman believed the rumors swirling around regarding a strike against the government. Keyes Beech, a former US Marine Corps combat correspondent during World War II, who reported on Asian affairs for the *Chicago Daily News*, had written an article, published in several American newspapers, under the headline, "Why U.S. Didn't Oust Diem," in late October. In his article Beech pointed out that while Americans could "produce more autos, more bathtubs, more telephones, more wheat and more corn . . . than any other people in the world," they were not very good at overthrowing governments. The lesson, Beech wrote, was to never attempt to unseat a foreign government "unless you are sure you can bring it off. Failure leaves a bad taste in everyone's mouth, especially the people you have tried to overthrow."[46]

On November 1, after attending a meeting between Diem and Admiral Felt, visiting from his Honolulu headquarters, Lodge and Diem talked. The Vietnamese leader, noting Lodge was scheduled to leave the country for consultations in Washington, DC, reminded him that there was an old saying in South Vietnam that "every time the American ambassador leaves there is a coup against the government." Diem had also given the ambassador a message to pass along to the American leader: "Please tell President Kennedy that I am a good and a frank ally, that I would rather be frank and settle questions now than talk about them after we have lost everything. Tell President Kennedy that I take all his suggestions very seriously and wish to carry them out but it is a question of timing." Lodge returned to his residence with General Harkins to have lunch. They had just started to eat at about 1:30 p.m. when Lodge heard the rattle of automatic-weapon fire and planes roaring overhead. The coup had begun.[47]

CHAPTER 8

The Coup

THE FIRST SIGN OF trouble came on a clear Friday afternoon, November 1, 1963. Saigon had been "empty and silent" for the traditional noon siesta when Malcolm Browne received a tip from a source at the US embassy. He learned that rebellious Army of the Republic of Vietnam troops had surrounded the central police station and the country's naval headquarters on the riverfront was also under siege. The Associated Press bureau chief drove his office's Land Rover at "breakneck speed" to the navy compound. He ignored the base's security guard, traveling past him for a half block until he heard yelling and the unmistakable sound of someone "chambering a round in his carbine." Uncertainty reigned, however, until 3:00 p.m., when Browne and his staff heard planes roaring over their office. With the AP office located only a short distance from the Gia Long Palace, the official residence for President Ngo Dinh Diem, "the combined sound of the strafing and heavy antiaircraft guns was shattering," Browne remembered. An incoming shell came close to hitting the journalist as he tried to get a better view of the action, but a guard loyal to Diem saved Browne's life by pulling him through a hole in a wall to safety.[1]

Edwin Q. White, who had come from the AP's Tokyo bureau to bolster the staff, dispatched the first bulletin describing the heavy gunfire at the presidential palace and reports about ARVN troops in full battle gear deployed throughout the city. In his article, delivered out of the country with the assistance of the American and South Korean embassies, White predicted that the firing could well signal the start of a military coup against Diem's government. "Marines in battle dress with heavy weapons and artillery surrounded national police director headquarters about 1350 [1:50 p.m.]," he wrote. "Other police headquarters throughout city were taken over by marines, apparently without resistance." White also received news that a firefight had occurred at Tan Son Nhut Airport, antiaircraft guns had opened fire at planes flying over naval headquarters, and approximately a hundred trucks carrying troops had been seen heading into the city from the north. As White remained at the office, Browne, Roy Essoyan (from AP's Hong Kong bureau), and Bill Ha Van Tran set out to discover what was happening. "We did a lot of walking, running and crawling, machinegun fire and shrapnel snapping just overhead," Browne recalled. "There was action everywhere, and no telling where the fire was going to come from next."[2]

The gunfire grew more intense as the sun set. Browne and his colleagues were able to identify where the hotspots were and which units "were clearly on the offensive against government troops and which ones were trying to counterattack. So, it was pretty confusing. The whole city was divided up into a patchwork of different loyalties and different uniforms and plenty of shooting." The bureau's "indefatigable" messenger, Dan Van Huan, sidestepped numerous firefights, said Browne, risking his life to keep messages flowing to White at the AP office. "We all think it will be nice to get back to the relative peace and safety of the normal war operations against the Vietcong," joked Browne.[3]

Rumors, plots, and heralds from above absorbed the attention of Saigon residents in the days leading up to the coup and even afterward. Conspirators seemed to be everywhere, scheming away in each other's homes, in nightclubs, and in the countryside. "Everybody knew that something was coming," Browne remembered. He even wrote an article, sent over the AP wires, about a rumor that the Vietnamese expected the sun to start revolving strangely in the sky. Large crowds of office workers, shoppers, and strollers jammed into the city's central markets, only to be scattered by the police. He reported that the sun's abnormal motion was supposed to be the sign of a Buddhist miracle. Officials were suspicious about the rumor, believing it had been spread "as a test, to see how fast crowds could be assembled at key places in the city," he added. AP reporter Peter Arnett pointed out that tensions were so fraught that after a *Newsweek* photographer asked a South Vietnamese high school student, Ly Thi Lien, who had been out cycling, to pose with Henry Cabot Lodge for a photograph, a plain-clothes policeman later arrested the girl, who then underwent questioning about what she and the ambassador had talked about. After indignant protests from the US embassy, the police released her, and she returned safely home. Buddhists in Da Nang were convinced that a large carp swimming in a local pond was a reincarnated disciple of Buddha, drawing large groups of pilgrims to the area. Angry Diem supporters did all they could to kill the fish, using grenades and machine guns, but it survived.[4]

David Halberstam of the *New York Times* received a tip that the coup was set for October 24. He and some of his colleagues ate lunch that day at a Chinese restaurant located a few blocks from the palace. Every five minutes, one of them, Halberstam remembered, "would get up and make a quick tour of the block. But nothing happened—which was just as well; when the real coup came a week later, that particular restaurant was badly shot up in the first hour of fighting." A top US embassy official, John Michael Dunn, whose family had joined him in the country on the day the coup began, noted that more than one reporter told him they had heard that his family's arrival had been the agreed-upon signal for the rebellion to start. "If you get people that nonsensical, what can you say?" Dunn recalled. "But the general aura of intrigue there would have to be seen and experienced to be believed. There was no one who believed anyone else was entirely what he seemed to be."[5]

Diem's regime and the administration of US President John F. Kennedy both flirted with making a final break in their relations. Using French and Polish diplomats as intermediaries, Diem and his brother, Ngo Dinh Nhu, floated the idea of a reunified and neutral Vietnam with Communist leaders in North Vietnam, who considered the imperialist Americans as the real enemies, realizing they could always deal with Diem and Nhu later. "Why do the Communists attack us so ferociously?" Diem questioned a reporter. "After all, our two systems are not so much different. We're both for the welfare of the people." Nhu, seemingly forewarned about a coup and ready with counterstrokes of his own, told a group of US newsmen that he had "lost faith in America." A government official recalled that Nhu had also lost all touch with reality, believing "only in what he wanted to believe and fitted all facts to his concepts. If we tried to tell him what the situation actually was . . . he simply told us we were fools and defeatists." South Vietnamese generals, however, waffled about moving against Diem that summer, waiting to gather additional forces to their side and secure firmer pledges of support from the Americans. "Perhaps they're afraid to die, like everyone else," Ambassador Lodge pointed out when coup plans fizzled out in August. Some high officials in the Kennedy administration, including the president's brother, Attorney General Robert Kennedy, believed that it might be time for the United States "to get out of Vietnam entirely."[6]

There were others who were in favor of such radical action, including Paul M. Kattenburg, who had served as a Vietnam desk officer and director of Vietnam affairs for the State Department. Kattenburg appeared at an August 31 meeting of the executive committee of the National Security Council, invited there by Assistant Secretary of State Roger Hilsman. Kattenburg had just returned from a brief visit to South Vietnam. While there, he talked to Lodge and some old friends in Saigon and met with Diem. "He struck me as a man in very dire straits already," noted Kattenburg. From these conversations he had concluded that "our leadership, from the top down, was almost entirely uncomprehending of the nature of the struggle in Vietnam and particularly of the enormous sociopolitical pulling power that the Viet Cong adversary possessed in an area still so recently colonial and sociostructurally so little modified by the nine years of the Diem regime." With top administration officials in attendance, including Vice President Lyndon Johnson and Secretary of State Dean Rusk, Kattenburg recommended that the United States consider "withdrawal with honor," an idea met with "cavalier dismissals" by Johnson and Rusk. Such reactions, Kattenburg said, were indicative of "what I felt: that these men were leading themselves down a garden path to tragedy."[7]

Looking for answers to the Vietnam problem, Kennedy, in September, decided at a meeting of the National Security Council to send a two-person, fact-finding mission to South Vietnam. The team included Marine General Victor Krulak, nicknamed "Brute" for his tough nature and small stature, and State Department official Joseph Mendenhall, who had previous experience in the country. The two men went their separate ways after their arrival in Saigon, with Krulak visiting and speaking with General Paul Harkins and US and South Vietnamese military officials throughout the country. "I knew that Krulak would come back here and say, 'Well, I have been in x many number of provinces. I know the situation on the ground and the war is going excellently,'" Mendenhall recalled. "So I knew I had to get out in the countryside in order to counter balance his view and I got up to Hue and Da Nang." He also visited Saigon, where he spoke to some old Vietnamese friends whose views he trusted and who risked possible arrest for daring to meet with an American official, an indication to Mendenhall that the Vietnamese were "living under a reign of terror."[8]

During the short time they were in South Vietnam—arriving on a Friday afternoon and returning to Washington early Tuesday morning—Krulak and Mendenhall came to opposite opinions about what news to deliver to the president. The marine general remained confident that the "shooting war is still going ahead at an impressive pace. It has been affected adversely by the political crisis, but the impact is not great." Mendenhall presented a far gloomier picture, with Diem's government falling apart, growing civilian unrest, and "the possibility of a religious war or a large-scale movement to the Viet Cong." A perplexed Kennedy asked: "Are you sure you two gentlemen visited the same country?" For his part, Krulak believed he had the answer, commenting that Mendenhall had given the president "an urban or metropolitan viewpoint. And the two views may be quite opposed, but I will only say I'll stick with mine, because the countryside is where the war is." The general's optimistic report came under fire by Rufus C. Phillips, the chief American adviser on South Vietnam's strategic hamlet program. "I am sorry to tell you Mr. President, but we are not winning the war, particularly in the Delta," Phillips said. His statement created an uproar, with an ensuing verbal exchange with Krulak, who accused Phillips of knowing nothing about military matters. "This is a political war and we are losing it," Phillips responded.[9]

Still seeking answers about the military and political situation in South Vietnam, Kennedy, in late September, sent out another mission, this one a ten-day tour led by Secretary of Defense Robert McNamara and Chairman of the Joint Chiefs of Staff Maxwell Taylor. They received encouraging reports that the "military campaign had made and was making considerable progress," Taylor noted, so much so, in fact, that a thousand US advisers could leave by the end of the year, with most of the American force withdrawn by 1965. Kennedy insisted that the decision to remove the troops not be "raised formally with Diem," but instead be done "routinely as part of our general posture of withdrawing people when they are no longer needed." The political situation, however, did not appear as rosy. Meeting with Diem, McNamara expressed the Americans' concerns about South Vietnam's political unrest, but the president remained intractable, displaying no interest in making any changes and blasting the "vicious attacks of the American press on his government, his family and himself" as one of the leading causes for the misunderstandings about the true situation in his country. Taylor left the meeting depressed, as Diem did not seem to understand "the realities which threatened to overwhelm him, his family, and his country." Taylor and McNamara reported to Kennedy that the South Vietnamese government had been growing more and more unpopular with its people and predicted that future repressive acts by the regime "could change the present favorable military trends." To push Diem to change his ways, they advised placing "selective pressures" against his government, including removing funding for special forces unless they operated outside of Saigon against the Viet Cong and freezing millions of dollars in aid to the Vietnamese government from a program that subsidized imports of such US products as condensed milk and cotton. According to one of the coup plotters, the "aid cuts erased all our doubts" about moving against Diem and Nhu.[10]

When mutinous ARVN units finally struck on November 1, plots and counterplots continually rose and fell. Rebel officers sometimes lied to their men about the true purpose of their movement into the capital. A colonel admitted to newsman Stanley Karnow of the *Saturday Evening Post* that he told his platoon leaders the police "were plotting to overthrow Diem and we were going to save him." A mystified paratrooper asked his commander who they were supposed to fight and received the answer: "Anyone who opposes us is the enemy." Confusion also marked attempts by rebel forces to convince government supporters to join their cause. Browne uncovered the story of Captain Ho Tan Quyen, Diem's naval commander, whose schedule that day was supposed to include an official dinner commemorating his birthday. Early Friday Quyen had been summoned to report to general staff headquarters by Major General Duong Van Minh, one of the key coup leaders. "Quyen drove to the headquarters near Saigon airport, where he undoubtedly met military commanders who were to lead the successful coup later in the day," Browne reported. Declining to join the rebellion, Quyen sped from the scene in his car toward Bien Hoa, hoping to rally loyalist forces. "Several jeeps and a civilian car were seen following Quyen outside the city," wrote Browne. "The pursuit continued for eight miles outside city limits, and ended when a burst of submachine gun fire riddled Quyen's vehicle. His body was laid out in the road and then taken away in a civilian car." That afternoon Quyen's staff learned of his death from a revolutionary naval officer, who called upon his colleagues to surrender. Fighter aircraft attacked ships docked nearby, and the craft responded by blazing away at the airplanes with their deck guns, downing one plane, Browne reported. "But about 15 minutes later," he added, "the naval command staff agreed to give in, and signed a document pledging loyalty to the revolutionaries."[11]

Diem had approved a complicated plan by Nhu to stage a phony coup, Operation Bravo, led by troops loyal to the government, drawing the traitors out in the open to be crushed. When a panicked police official called Nhu to let him know that troops were attacking his station, Nhu gave a blasé answer: "It's all right. I know all about it." The brothers seemed secure at Gia Long, ringed as it was, as Browne noted, with everything from anti-aircraft emplacements, machine guns, tanks, and "every other possible safeguard." Diem had also seen to it that the palace included several bunkers and an elaborate tunnel system, built at an estimated cost of $200,000, to serve as a possible escape route in times of trouble. A revolutionary general later told Browne that the palace had been "fortified like the Maginot Line." Gia Long's defenses were manned inside the palace grounds by about 150 members of an elite palace guard. "Because of their snappy white

dress uniforms, black berets, tough fighting qualities and dedicated loy-
alty to their leader, they sometimes were called 'Diem's angels,'" reported
Browne. The ARVN rebels, however, took the precaution to lay siege to the
Presidential Guard barracks located about five blocks from the palace.
"Later, when this garrison still resisted," he wrote, "rebel tanks lined up
fender to fender [and] blasted it to dust."[12]

Late Friday afternoon, Minh took to the airwaves to announce over
Radio Saigon: "During the past nine years, we have lived under a cruel
family dictatorship. . . . The army has decided to do away with the Diem
regime." According to Browne, the city's radio stations that had fallen to
the anti-Diem forces appealed to the president to surrender and become a
private citizen, adding a warning that he "would be held responsible for
any further bloodshed." Perhaps in answer, a loudspeaker inside the palace
that could be heard for blocks played a tape-recorded message from Diem
announcing that his generals had been "lured to a luncheon party given at
general staff headquarters, and forced to join the coup." Diem called on the
army to renounce the coup and rally to him. An unnamed US official later
told Browne the Ngo brothers' "greatest strength and greatest weakness
was that they never realized when they were beaten."[13]

Unable to find the needed troops to save his government, or to convince
the rebel generals to come to the palace to negotiate, a tactic that had saved
his administration during a failed coup three years before, Diem, at
4:30 p.m., called Lodge at the ambassador's residence to tell him that it
appeared as if some army units were rebelling and to ask the Americans'
attitude about the situation. "I do not feel well enough informed to be able
to tell you," Lodge responded. "I have heard the shooting, but am not
acquainted with all the facts. Also it is 4:30 a.m. in Washington and the
U.S. government possibly cannot have a view." Diem, speaking so loudly
that Lodge had to hold the phone away from his ear, continued to ask for
guidance from the American. "After all," Diem said, "I am chief of state. I
have tried to do my duty. I want to do now what duty and good sense
require. I believe in duty above all."[14]

Lodge acknowledged all that Diem had accomplished on behalf of his
country and expressed his concern for the president's safety. According to
Frederick Flott, Lodge's special assistant, who listened in on the call, the

ambassador had been prepared to send Flott in the embassy's limousine, an old, large Checker cab flying American flags, to pick Diem up and escort him out of the palace. Flott believed there was a "good chance" the coup leaders would have allowed such a scheme to take place. "If Diem had accepted our good offices to assure his escape to security," Flott later noted, "Lodge was prepared to assist and was prepared to have me up in the front seat of his automobile while doing so." Flott believed that to Diem, the coup was merely a "tempest in a teapot; it's a couple of hotheaded generals who don't speak for the army, and I know that the real troops are loyal to me and will soon have this all straightened out." Before the call ended, Lodge reiterated his offer to do all he could to ensure Diem's "physical safety." Diem's answer: "I am trying to reestablish order." One of the president's bodyguards later related a harsher response from Diem, who supposedly shouted over the telephone: "Mr. Ambassador, do you realize who you are talking to? I would like you to know that you are talking to a president of an independent and sovereign nation. I will only leave this country if it is the wish of my people. I will never leave according to the request of a group of rebellious generals or of an American ambassador. The U.S. government must take full responsibility before the world in this miserable matter." [15]

According to John Michael Dunn, Diem had a second telephone conversation with Lodge early in the morning on Saturday, in which the ambassador offered Diem asylum. Fearing that the rebel generals might kill the brothers, Dunn offered to escort them to safety, but Lodge rebuffed his offer. "We can't," Dunn quoted Lodge as saying. "We just can't get that involved." From the first reports about the coup, the Kennedy administration had attempted to place itself at arm's length from any direct involvement with the military uprising. A State Department spokesman released a statement to reporters that read: "I can categorically state that the U.S. Government was not involved in any way." Behind the scenes, however, Kennedy had approved instructions to be sent to Lodge that the rebellious leaders, if successful, should be sure to "develop strongly and publicly the conclusion reported in one of their broadcasts that Nhu was dickering with Communists to betray anti-Communist cause. High value of this argument should be emphasized to them at earliest opportunity." [16]

As Browne rallied his AP staff to cover the coup, two of his top men, Arnett and Horst Faas, both away from Saigon, did all they could to get to the capital. Returning to South Vietnam after a trip to Cambodia on an Air Vietnam passenger jet, Arnett recalled that the plane had flown into Vietnamese airspace at 3:00 p.m. when he felt it starting to veer away from its destination. "I banged on the pilot's cabin door and my fears were confirmed by the captain, who was talking with an air traffic controller; a coup d'état was in progress; bombers were in the air over Saigon, blasting the Presidential Palace," Arnett remembered. "I would miss the biggest story of my life because Tan Son Nhut Airport was closed to all traffic." Thinking fast, he argued with the pilot, pointing out that the aircraft "had a right to land on its own soil" and raising terrible fears about the fate of the crew's families amid the chaos. Arnett's arguments worked, and the plane's captain guided his craft to a safe landing. An airline bus took Arnett most of the way to the AP office before its driver lost his nerve and made his passenger disembark. "Gunfire roared and ricocheted around me," Arnett recalled. "I could see soldiers firing from upper-story windows at the Gia Long Palace. Our three-story office and apartment building had been turned into a fort with soldiers firing their weapons at the palace across the street, protecting themselves behind makeshift sandbagged emplacements in the parking lot and the first-floor balcony outside my apartment door." Bursting into the office, Arnett saw White, known by his colleagues as "unflappable Ed," calmly puffing away on a cigar while typing; the rest of the staff had left. "The others are at the Caravelle [Hotel] and I'm holding the fort, which is something I've said plenty of times in the past but for once is true," White told Arnett, who took advantage of a lull in the fighting to make his way to the Caravelle. White remained at his post until 6:30 p.m. when, as Browne noted, "he decided things were getting a little too hot." Later that night, a shell hit an M48 tank parked in front of the AP's office, igniting the tank's ammunition and causing it to burn throughout the night.[17]

When he arrived at the Caravelle, Arnett discovered Browne and Essoyan on the hotel's upper floors, where they had a spectacular view of the fighting going on at Gia Long and the barracks housing its guards. "The rumors and the speculation of months past were coming true before my eyes and I watched it all with a glass of Johnnie Walker Red Label Scotch in one hand and a cigarette in the other," Arnett remembered. As it grew dark, Browne saw tracers and shells streak through Saigon's skies, with many hitting the palace, while others fell short, bringing down power and telephone lines. Leaving the hotel as the battle continued to rage, Arnett came upon children running around collecting spent cartridges from the sidewalks, two US soldiers who stopped him to ask directions to the nearest bar, and two drunk Americans walking near the National Assembly building, one of them loudly complaining, "Tell them to knock that off, they're scaring everybody." Walking to the Rex Hotel, which housed American troops, he found its officers mess crowded with soldiers, who had been warned by authorities to stay off the streets. "They were whiling away the time rolling dice or playing the slot machines," he noted. Later, on a suggestion from Browne, Arnett made his way to the US military mission, where he stayed for the rest of evening. He even received a briefing about the coup from an American intelligence officer, "a rare display of generosity toward the media," Arnett recalled. The official had been impressed by what he had seen from the anti-Diem forces, telling Arnett that it showed that the Vietnamese could "run a pretty good war if political considerations are removed."[18]

While Browne and Arnett tried to stay safe in the embattled city, Faas was in Ca Mau, on patrol with South Vietnamese Rangers. A US adviser accompanying the Rangers heard a report on his radio telling him to prepare to pull his forces from the field, as a coup had broken out. "Oh shit," Faas remembered saying, "I'm two hundred miles away from Saigon and that's the story that's developing and I'm down here in Ca Mau. Get me out of here as quickly as possible." Faas hooked up with Steve Stibbens, a marine photographer for *Stars and Stripes*, and they were able to get tickets for a flight to Saigon. Unable to land there because of the fighting, the plane diverted its flight to the port city of Vung Tao, located about sixty miles southeast of Saigon. Faas and Stibbens commandeered a jeep from the Vietnamese and drove as fast as possible to the capital, getting there after the newly established 7:00 p.m. curfew. Dressed as he was, in a helmet and makeshift uniform, Faas discovered he had little trouble passing through roadblocks or driving around rebel units scattered throughout the city. Finding the AP office empty, he recalled feeling guilty about being late for such a momentous story.[19]

Shortly after midnight, Saigon "became still and dead as a city under the plague," Browne reported. A few hours earlier, he had placed a call to a palace operator, asking to speak to Nhu. A long silence ensued. Finally, the operator responded: "Mr. Nhu cannot come to the telephone." Downtown streets seemed deserted, and the guns fell silent. The lull allowed a dinner-jacketed headwaiter at a leading hotel, White wrote, to calmly seat a few guests, laughingly explaining to them that "service might be [a] little slow because some restaurant help had left." A dog's loud barking betrayed "stealthy movement in the shadows," Browne observed. "No lights showed from inside the waiting palace." Shortly after 3:00 a.m., intense gunfire broke out, with large shells from distant artillery hitting a building behind the telecommunications center. Browne could also see tanks moving through the streets, slipping "across the main boulevards from the west and from the riverfront, taking up positions just outside the palace walls." The final assault on the palace began at 4:00 a.m. "The blast of cannon, machineguns and rapid-fire pieces blended into a continuous roar," he reported. "The dark shapes in the streets spat clouds of green, yellow and blue fire, and great blobs of red flame marked the exploding shells. Buildings near the palace became infernos, and answering fire from the palace set two armored vehicles afire." Finally, at 6:37 a.m., Browne recorded, the drained, grimy palace guards surrendered, hoisting a white flag, which was greeted with "a thunderous cheer" by the rebel forces. "Marines, paratroopers and soldiers swarmed into the building. But the prizes of battle, Diem and Nhu, were gone," wrote Browne. He noted that a black sedan had long since driven away with the brothers inside.[20]

Watching the fighting from the roof of the US embassy with other Americans, John Mecklin found the fighting's din to be even greater than what he had experienced as a soldier in World War II. Although a few ricochets streaked by the embassy, causing everyone on the roof to seek cover, Mecklin recalled feeling that he was in no danger. He described the scene:

> As the frightful spectacle wore on, and indeed became a sort of tor-
> tured normalcy, the trance waned among the watchers. "I wish we

could get them to fight that way against the Viet Cong," said a voice in the darkness during a moment of relative quiet. "You know who's paying for all that ammo, don't you?" said another. "It's the good old American taxpayer." A third voice, evidently a military man, remarked: "This must be the first time all those tanks have ever been worth anything. They sure aren't any damn good against guerrillas." Said a fourth: "Do we have a course for teaching them how to shoot up a palace?" There was no response. Mostly the faces illuminated in the fitful glare from the battle were fixed and expressionless.[21]

Faas followed as Vietnamese marines stormed into the palace, smashing chandeliers, tearing down Diem's portraits, and firing their weapons, though there was no need to do so as the opposition had collapsed. By 9:00 a.m. Faas decided he had taken enough photographs and turned his attention to finding a place to develop his film. With the AP office's darkroom out of action as the power and telephone lines were out, he went to a local photo shop, scaring the store's staff when he burst through the front door in his makeshift uniform. He used the store's equipment to develop approximately twelve photographs. With the photos in hand, he walked to the Post, Telegraph and Telephone office to transmit his work with the assistance of an employee he knew, Madame Binh. Talking to her, Faas learned that he was the first photographer to arrive, beating his colleagues. "They had mistakenly believed that the post office, because it was occupied by troops, had been closed; it hadn't been closed. The troops went through it," he recalled. "The coup troops made a few propaganda broadcasts, occupied it with their people, but the personnel continued as normal." By 4:00 p.m. a line opened and Faas was able to send his photographs to the outside world. "I happened to be a hero when I thought I would be almost fired," he remembered. Later, Faas reconnected with the AP staff. They watched as delirious crowds tore down statues honoring the Diem regime and ransacked businesses connected in any way with the president's family. According to Arnett, Faas had been knocked down by a group of cheering Vietnamese. Helped to his feet, the photographer discovered that "someone had removed his wallet which contained two hundred dollars." Jubilant Vietnamese told their American friends that if an election had been held for the country's new leader, Lodge would have won by a land-slide.[22]

Halberstam, Roy Herndon of United Press International, and Peter Kalischer of CBS Television also made their way to the palace to record their impressions about the government's fall. The three men had to hit the dirt when they came under some stray rounds from the palace's last-ditch defenders but were able to press forward. In the streets around the complex, Halberstam saw groups of students cautiously approaching the area. "When they saw that the Palace had surrendered they crowded around the tanks, hailing the soldiers, lifting them on their shoulders, handing them food and taking pictures of them. Young girls offered bouquets of flowers," he noted. The soldiers accepted the accolades but appeared uneasy about all the attention. An officer expressed his shock at the outpouring of affection from his countrymen, pointing out to Halberstam that in the past "the people had always been afraid of the soldiers." The Vietnamese marines who had stormed the palace emerged with a few trophies, including Madame Nhu's negligees and bottles of whiskey from Nhu's private stock. Crowds of young people also roamed the capital's streets, ransacking the offices of several pro-Diem newspapers and burning copies of the English-language *Times of Vietnam* owned by an American couple, Gene and Ann Gregory, who supported the government. During the coup, Ann Gregory took refuge at the US embassy, Browne reported. She left the country a few days later, joining her husband in Hong Kong. "I am planning to do nothing but rest for about one month," Ann Gregory commented to reporters upon her departure.[23]

While the Gregorys had to abandon South Vietnam, Mecklin, driving around Saigon postcoup with a colleague, noticed a new "sense of friendliness" for Americans. "Where there once had been impassive courtesy, we now encountered smiles and even a few waves and hand clapping," he recalled. Mecklin, however, could not escape the fighting's human cost. Turning into a side street, he noticed lying on the ground a blood-spattered Vespa. "Next to it was a sandal with a human foot still in it," he remembered.[24]

As his fellow reporters scrambled to cover one of the biggest international stories of the year, Neil Sheehan, UPI's Saigon bureau chief who had been so sure a coup was imminent, tried to enjoy his forced vacation in Tokyo. While eating dinner at the Foreign Correspondents Club, Sheehan received a telephone call urging him to get to the UPI Tokyo bureau as soon as possible. Upon his arrival, the newsman checked the wires and read reports coming out of South Korea, relayed by its embassy in South Vietnam, that fighting had broken out in Saigon. The anguished Sheehan searched through the office's messages and found the one he had arranged with Halberstam to send signaling the coup's start. It had been sitting there for nineteen hours. Sick to his stomach, Sheehan could not believe what had happened. Questioned by someone in the office about what the message meant, Sheehan did not hold back, shouting: "It means a coup, you goddamned fool! It means the goddamned government is being overthrown in Saigon and I'm in fucking Tokyo!"[25]

Diem and Nhu's fates remained uncertain as the battle raged. In a censored dispatch, Browne noted that the new military junta told the press that both men had "slipped through their hands during a ceasefire" at a time when casualties were being removed from the palace grounds. Rumors swirled that the brothers had killed themselves, had been shot by the revolutionary troops while resisting arrest, or had escaped. The brothers had fled the palace long before the final attack, driving away from the scene in a black Citroën auto to Cholon, Saigon's Chinese suburb. They first stayed at the villa of a wealthy regime supporter, Ma Tuyen. "When the president arrived around 8 o'clock he was very tired and nervous," Tuyen recalled. "He kept pacing the floor and chain-smoking cigarettes. I took him and his brother . . . upstairs and served them tea. They were too agitated to eat." Diem made numerous telephone calls from his room and by morning had decided to surrender to the rebels. Tuyen allowed the brothers to use his car for the journey to Saint Francis Xavier Church, where they had arranged to turn themselves over. "The church is small," wrote Browne. "In it, there are two French priests and two Chinese priests. The time was shortly after 8 a.m., and parishioners were attending one of the masses of the morning. . . . Diem was said to have looked grave." Father Fernand Billaud could not believe it was really Diem himself at the church. He only knew it was the president when a former palace servant attending the mass, commemorating All Soul's Day, ran up and embraced Diem.

"President Diem, the servant cried, I want to live or die with you," Billaud recalled. "Diem only replied, 'Have courage, we face difficult times.'"[26]

Sometime after 9 a.m., reported Browne, a military convoy arrived at the church. The convoy included an M113 armored personnel carrier, there to supposedly protect the brothers from extremists. "Diem and Nhu met the rebels outside the church, and talked for some minutes with the officers," he wrote. "The parlay ended about 9:45, and the Ngo brothers stepped into the hatch of a tracked armored personnel carrier. It was the last time either was seen alive." When the convoy stopped at a railroad crossing, a rebel soldier, Captain Nguyen Van Nhung, murdered both men, shooting and stabbing them. "Neither Diem nor Nhu ever defended themselves," remembered Captain Duong Huu Nhgia, another officer in the M113. "Their hands were tied." The bodies were eventually taken from the rebellious generals' headquarters to Saint Paul's Hospital in downtown Saigon, where a few Vietnamese journalists viewed them but were prohibited from taking any photographs. "The nine-year drama of the Ngo era was over," Browne wrote, "and a new drama had begun in South Viet Nam—a new drama, as full of hope, danger and uncertainty as the old."[27]

The deaths of Diem and Nhu shocked Kennedy, who had been sending messages to Lodge that the administration could only support a coup if there was a guarantee that it would succeed. "We could lose our entire position in Southeast Asia overnight," Kennedy feared. At a meeting with his advisers the day of the coup, Kennedy received a message from Michael Forrestal of the National Security Council informing the president that Diem and Nhu were dead, with initial reports indicating they had killed themselves. According to Taylor's recollection, Kennedy jumped to his feet and left the room in a hurry "with a look of shock and dismay on his face which I had never seen before." Taylor pointed out that the president had "been led to believe or had persuaded himself that a change in government could be carried out without bloodshed." Later, reflecting on the situation, Kennedy expressed his dismay at Diem's death, noting that he had been able to hold "his country together, maintained its independence under very adverse conditions. The way he was killed made it particularly abhorrent." The president wondered whether the generals could hold the country together and maintain "a stable government or whether Saigon will begin—whether public opinion in Saigon, the intellectuals, students etc.—will turn on this government as repressive and undemocratic in the not too distant future." He believed his administration still had an obligation to "help this new government to be effective in every way that we can." Others in the administration who supported removing Diem appeared hard-hearted about the coup's bloody conclusion, especially to those who supported keeping South Vietnam's government intact. Hoping to help Madame Nhu, worried about the safety of her children still in the country while she had been touring the United States, reporter Marguerite Higgins called Roger Hilsman early one morning. She recalled the conversation: "'Congratulations, Roger,' I said. 'How does it feel to have blood on your hands?'" Hilsman responded: "Oh, come on now Maggie. Revolutions are rough. People get hurt." Hilsman did tell Higgins that the president would do all he could to keep Madame Nhu's children safe, a promise that was kept.[28]

With the Diem regime gone, thousands of Vietnamese who had been imprisoned, many of them tortured for their political beliefs, were released from incarceration, and Browne was able to learn details about their experiences. "Scores of students of both sexes say they were forced to drink quarts of soapy water until their intestines were pouring blood," Browne wrote of a torture known today as waterboarding. He found a young girl praying with a "jubilant crowd" gathered at the Xa Loi Pagoda. The girl told him that the secret police had attached electrodes from the generator of a field radio to her breasts. "Many U.S. military advisers and foreign newsmen have seen variations of this torture applied to Viet Cong suspects in the field," he pointed out. Vu Hoang Linh, who worked for the US aid mission, said she had been held at the Le Van Quyeh camp in a cramped cell exposed to the blazing sun that held forty-six prisoners. "Many became unconscious," she remembered. The police beat students with truncheons, chopped off their fingers, and blinded others, Browne reported. Some students expressed bitterness toward the Americans, believing they had to "share some responsibility for these things," as one told Browne. "You must have known about them for a long time, but you closed your eyes and went on training and equipping the police."[29]

Arrests of those seen as threats to Diem's government continued up until only a few hours before the coup. A typist for the British embassy, Hoant Thi Dong, a former refugee from North Vietnam, was picked up by the secret police at the home she shared with her aunt early in the morning on November 1. "There were five of them," she told Browne. "They searched the house with a flashlight, checked my identification, then led me to a jeep outside and blindfolded me. There was another girl in the jeep also arrested." Taken to Rach Cat, a forested spot located about twelve miles from Saigon, Dong found herself in a room that she later learned included six men and seven girls, including herself. Led to an office, she heard from a policeman that she was being charged with giving Buddhist documents to the British embassy, to foreign journalists, to the United Nations fact-finding mission, and to the US Information Agency. "I denied this, and said the correspondents were using other sources to get their information," Dong recalled. The policeman also asked if she knew a monk named Thich Thanh Nhan and knew where he was. She admitted she had seen the monk before the August 21 pagoda raids but did not let slip that she and her aunt had given him refuge in their home for several nights after the raids. "Then he charged that I was a Communist," Dong said. "He said I would be tortured if I would not admit all these things and tell them where the monk was. I refused."[30]

Upon Dong's refusal to cooperate, two additional police came into the office, stripped off her clothes, and tied her to a bench. They then put a cloth over her nose and mouth and poured dirty water from a can over the cloth until she felt herself drowning. "One of the men struck his fists into my sides, and another slapped my cheeks," Dong remembered. "I screamed when they released the cloth for a moment. One jumped on me to force the water out of my mouth, and another beat my legs with a club. I became unconscious." Before being taken away, the police warned her that she would be tortured again that afternoon. The guards looking over the prisoners, however, left the room and Dong heard jeeps and motorbikes fleeing as planes roared overhead. "We heard shooting all night long, and prayed that the government forces would lose, because otherwise we were sure we would die," she said. At 5:00 p.m. on Saturday a car drove up with four men, including the two police officers who arrested her. They told the prisoners that there had been a coup and Diem and Nhu were dead. "You can imagine the cheer we let out," Dong told Browne. "It was like heaven on earth." On Sunday the police took the prisoners back to Saigon in a closed truck and they were finally released later in the day. The police even honored their request to be taken to Xa Loi before going home, driving them there in a truck. One of the student prisoners who joined Dong at the pagoda offered a final comment to Browne: "May Buddha grant that Viet Nam is now on the road to salvation."[31]

The student's prayer was not answered. On November 22, 1963, an assassin gunned down Kennedy in Dallas, Texas; Johnson took over as the nation's thirty-sixth president. From his first few days in office, Johnson expressed his determination to win the war, telling his national security advisers, "I am not going to lose Vietnam. I am not going to be the President who saw Southeast Asia go the way China went." The revolutionary junta that had ousted Diem, however, did not last long, falling to another military coup in January 1964. Political instability continued in South Vietnam, ending only when North Vietnamese tanks rolled into Saigon on May 1, 1975. The seemingly never-ending parade of regimes made it sometimes difficult for Browne and his staff to keep track of developments. Browne wired AP officials during one attempted coup that if some of their copy appeared to be "confusing or contradictory, we are just reflecting the confusion and uncertainty of the government itself." He pointed out that the newsmen could not define such terms as "president, chief of state, premier, etc., because officials themselves do not know. Our dispatches try to boil down what is an incredibly complicated politico-military byplay."[32]

Breaking news still mattered for the AP, and Browne and his staff in Saigon continued to run themselves ragged trying to beat the competition. In September 1964 dissident ARVN generals tried, but failed, to unseat the ruling military junta led by General Nguyen Khanh. Browne had been aware that the government might be in trouble after Khanh fired several top officials, including many who still commanded troops. At about 8:00 a.m. on Sunday, September 13, 1964, rebel forces overran a police checkpoint on the main highway near Saigon. "The police in it had the presence of mind before giving up to telephone another police post inside the city limits," Browne reported. "This post telephoned city police headquarters, a source inside which telephoned us. We were off and running."[33]

While Faas and other AP staffers left the office to check on the possible coup, Browne stayed close by the phone. Faas later called Browne to let him know that he had run into the rebels and had a brief conversation with General Lam Van Phat, who said, "This is nothing to worry about. Just a little operation to clean up some politicians." Faas's report, coupled with dozens of other items he received from several sources, was enough for Browne to decide to try to book a telephone call to get the information out to the world. Unfortunately, on Sundays all normal international communications out of South Vietnam were unavailable. But as a service to American soldiers, the government's communications center opened to allow GIs to make calls to the United States. The men booked these calls weeks ahead of time and had to hang around for hours waiting for an available circuit to open. "I tried to persuade the station director by phone to let me have a few minutes time to the states," Browne recalled. "He refused, saying the American servicemen had booked his line solid." Because AP's Land Rover had a flat tire that morning, the AP bureau chief had to grab a cab to make a run for the communications building. "Seventh Division troops and armor already were beginning to arrive in the city and I knew it would be a close thing if I made it at all," Browne noted.[34]

Arriving at the communications center, Browne discovered that its doors had been locked. He found a way in but had to climb five sets of stairs because the building's elevator was out of service. Browne still could not convince the center's Vietnamese director to let him place a call. "But there's a coup d'etat and I have to let America know," the newsman exclaimed. The director remained unmoved: "Mr. Browne, we have coups all the time here and we can't make exceptions every time. No circuit." The director did finally agree to let Browne trade places with one of the servicemen if he could find one willing to give up his call. "I looked over the waiting list and started with the first GI—a U.S. Army military policeman," Browne reported. "The whole room full of Americans was in a surly mood and ready to throw me out bodily. I cajoled, dickered and bargained with this MP. In the end, he agreed to give me his time in exchange for $50 in cash on the spot. It seemed worth it and I paid him." In a few minutes Browne had a crystal-clear line, unusual for calls from Vietnam, to AP's cable desk in New York. He told the editors there: "This is Mal Browne and

I have exactly 10 minutes to dictate." After Browne finished dictating his story, he noted that no more than one or two servicemen were able to make their calls before rebel troops seized the center and all lines, even local ones, were cut. With their phone out of action, the AP staffers spent the next thirty-six hours steering the office Land Rover and two rented cars between besieged loyalist forces at the airport and rebel units at points in and around Saigon. Before the coup came to a bloodless end the next day, Browne had to sweat out government planes targeting his red-painted Land Rover before finally breaking off without firing. "I thought the end had come," he remembered.[35]

Browne shared his frustrations about the chaos in South Vietnam in private correspondence with Ben Bassett, the AP's foreign editor. In his opinion, Browne believed that success in the country could not depend upon the efforts of officials in Washington, DC. While there were "excellent U.S. intelligence men in Viet Nam," the top officials in Saigon and Washington did not seem to know how to use them. "They don't know the value of the information they get (and which we, incidentally, get from some of them too). Second, they don't have a riceroots feel for things here, and they don't have that intangible sense of what Vietnamese are really thinking," wrote Browne. He also pointed out that US official communication systems were only a little better than those used by the AP, which, he said, "are ridiculously poor." Despite all the counterinsurgency schools and training they received, "Americans just don't come out here ready for Viet Nam. They don't think in the twisted, devious, illogical ways Vietnamese think, and therefore they can't really understand them. The Viet Cong, and for that matter, the Chinese, do understand. Therein lies the tragedy." Browne did not want Bassett to think that he stood for any individual or policy as opposed to another. "I'm against everything," he noted. "And deeply depressed—not as a newsman, but as an American."[36]

Wes Gallagher, AP general manager, who had also received a copy of Browne's letter, thanked him for what he had written, particularly his emphasis on not being for any one individual or policy. A former war correspondent, Gallagher noted that over the years the US government had diplomats and officials who had badly handled matters overseas. "This has not been confined to the American Government—all governments seem to have the same trouble," Gallagher pointed out. "Such bungling seems inevitable in government relationships, and it is doubtful that any newsman who had the job of making the decisions would do any better." The AP executive, who later cited his news agency's goal as providing a "clear, cool, impartial voice in a world which has become increasingly strident, irritable and irrational," praised Browne for doing a fine job and being able to "keep your perspective in a very difficult situation." Gallagher asked Browne to continue to keep himself and Bassett up to date on what was going on in South Vietnam, as such letters would give him the opportunity to write more freely about sensitive matters than he could in a news story.[37]

Gallagher had received a firsthand look at the confusing situation in Vietnam during a visit he made in early 1964. The AP executive had a personal connection with General William C. Westmoreland, the new deputy commander of the Military Assistance Command, Vietnam, who took over as MACV commander in June from General Paul Harkins. During World War II in North Africa, Gallagher had been severely wounded, fracturing his spine when his jeep overturned and caught on fire; Westmoreland dragged him to safety. "Wes not only cut his teeth on World War II but had a special reason for listening to his friend and lifesaver, General Westmoreland," Browne noted. During Gallagher's visit, Browne arranged for him to see Westmoreland and other senior American and Vietnamese officials. Browne also took his boss on a tour of the Mekong Delta, as he "suspected that what he really wanted was a chance to get out and see for himself something of the war and its setting." As he traveled through the countryside with Browne, Gallagher learned from farmers, militia members, and village officials "how the Viet Cong ruled by night, and how informers against the guerrillas were brutally slain." Despite the "rosy reports" of success Washington received about pacified hamlets and high losses by the Viet Cong, Gallagher witnessed how badly the war was going for the South Vietnamese. "Never a man to allow preconceived ideas to color direct observation," Browne pointed out, "the gruff-voiced Gallagher changed his perspective. From then on he backed his AP Indochina correspondents more than ever, despite threats by the Pentagon, State Department, and President Johnson himself."[38]

In addition to Browne's tour, Gallagher received another indication of the war's growing intensity when Faas returned from four days in the field with photographs Arnett found to be the most disturbing he had seen since Browne's shots of Thich Quang Duc's self-immolation. Accompanying the South Vietnamese Seventh Division on an operation near the border with Cambodia, Faas witnessed a napalm air strike on a village guerrillas had moved through while attempting to flee the scene; the bombing had been ordered by an American military adviser. As ARVN troops pursued the VC, Faas stayed behind. "It was the first time he'd been in a village immediately after an air strike," said Arnett, "and he was shocked by the carnage that lay before him." One of the riveting, tragic images captured on film by Faas showed a villager holding a limp, wounded child in his arms and looking up for help from soldiers on an armored personnel carrier. According to Arnett, Gallagher predicted that every "picture editor in America . . . would want to know how such a thing could happen when American servicemen were involved." Gallagher also pointed out that to avoid any charges of bias from officials in Washington, the AP had to note that the VC had committed "similarly disturbing actions," Arnett recalled. With Gallagher's guidance in mind, Arnett and Faas produced an article to accompany the heartbreaking images, quoting an American officer as saying, "The moral dilemma we face here is what we faced in Korea and every other war we got in. We don't want to see the civilians killed and yet they are killed because this is a horrible byproduct of war." The article pointed out that Communist guerrillas would "burn a village to the ground rather than let people side with the government."[39]

Browne later sketched out for his readers the persistent theme of terror in the war, used by both sides for propaganda, punishment, and revenge, and coming in many forms. ARVN Rangers experienced it when a VC unit hidden in a Buddhist pagoda fired upon the advancing troops, killing sixteen, including a US adviser. Seeking revenge, the Rangers returned to the pagoda a few days later, finding only three "likely looking suspects, all of them Vietnamese of Cambodian extraction." The Rangers subjected their captives to the water torture, Browne reported, including using an innovation whereby one of the prisoners "was lowered head first into a waterpot with his hands bound." Eventually, the Rangers transported their captives to their command post by helicopter for further questioning. "They were lucky," Browne wrote. "Chances of surviving field interrogation are often extremely poor. Death can come for prisoners under the tracks of armored vehicles, by decapitation or by bleeding to death after both hands have been chopped off, or by a bullet to the head. It is all part of the war in South Viet Nam."[40]

Upon his return to the United States, Gallagher expressed his concerns about what he had seen. While he did not foresee the Americans forsaking their commitment, believing that doing so would lead to a quick victory by the Communists, he urged the South Vietnamese government to make sure that honest officials were put in office in villages. "The problem is to get the people in the villages to stand up against the Viet Cong," he noted. Later, reflecting on the American failure in Indochina, he believed the answer was not as complicated as people made it out to be. "The failure basically was that the people of South Vietnam were not motivated to fight for the country against the invader," he said. "No government could motivate them. And we couldn't do the fighting for them. And that's where the failure was." Gallagher's overall assessment mirrored that of many critics of the war: "It was a real first class mess."[41]

Gallagher remembered hearing that President Johnson had been telling newspaper editors that AP's coverage from South Vietnam had been "terrible," complaining about the reporting of a foreigner, Arnett. Gallagher, who brought with him a briefcase full of material, and Paul Miller, AP board chairman, had lunch with Johnson at the White House. After eating, Gallagher got down to business, saying: "Mr. President, I understand that you are dissatisfied with the Associated Press coverage." Johnson demurred, telling Gallagher that the AP had been doing a great job and slapping him on the back. "I knew the day before he had told these editors that because there were AP member editors and they came and told me about it," Gallagher recalled. "Well, you can't call the President of the United States a liar at lunch! So, I just packed up my little briefcase and went on my way."[42]

Browne had the satisfaction of seeing his work from South Vietnam honored in two highly respected journalism competitions. In December 1963 his photo of Thich Quang Duc's self-immolation won first place in the news section and first overall out of 2,100 pictures from fifty-three countries in the annual World Press Photo Contest. Browne used the $1,665 he received from the contest, which has been sponsored by the Netherlands since 1955, to buy an engagement ring to give to Le Lieu. A few months later, in May 1964, Browne received word that he and Halberstam had shared the Pulitzer Prize for international reporting for their "reporting of the Viet Nam war and the overthrow of the Diem regime." Halberstam, who left Vietnam late in 1963, said that he was "delighted on behalf of all that small band of reporters (in Viet Nam) who worked so hard under such difficult conditions." Browne, the nineteenth person to win a Pulitzer while working for the AP, noted that an overseas reporter's greatest satisfaction came from knowing that "an unfamiliar country, 12,000 miles from his home base, is attracting the interest of the American people at last, in part through his writing." The issues America and the rest of the free world faced in Vietnam, he added, were the issues the United States would confront for "years to come throughout the underdeveloped parts of Asia, Africa and Latin America."[43]

Winning a Pulitzer, one of journalism's highest honors, inadvertently led to Browne leaving the "most wonderful, exciting and rewarding job of my life" at the AP for "something new, untried, and potentially disastrous for me." Returning to the United States to give a series of lectures about his Vietnam experiences at universities and meetings of publishers and broadcasters, Browne traveled to New York to speak at a luncheon. Among those in the crowd were several executives from the American Broadcasting Company, including Jesse Zousmer, the vice president of the network's news division and a former producer for famed broadcaster Edward R. Murrow. Zousmer must have liked what he heard because several weeks later, while Browne was in London to speak at an international meeting of news organizations, the ABC executive called him to ask him to become a Saigon correspondent for the network.[44]

Returning to Saigon to consider Zousmer's offer, Browne, who had grown up without television and had never even owned a television set, had not been impressed by the occasional glimpses of programs he had seen in bars and hotel rooms. He described television as a toy to divert the attention of a child but could not "provide sustenance to an adult of average intelligence." While working for the AP, however, Browne had been interviewed for television reports and had also provided radio reports for ABC. "Correspondents sometimes get letters from our readers," he noted, but he got four or five times more correspondence from people responding to his radio broadcasts. This surprised him, as his news stories for the AP were read daily by millions of readers. "If letters are any indication of impact, this seems to me pretty significant," Browne wrote Zousmer. "It certainly gave me food for thought." Browne also started to believe that the written word was being supplanted as the chief way people got their news. "The fact is that people have begun to rely on television to inform themselves," he pointed out. "I think this tendency will prevail as television gets better and newspapers get worse or stand still." Browne was also under growing pressure by the AP to take on more executive duties, something he was not interested in doing. He did warn Zousmer that if he took the job, he could not hope to compete for spot news with the AP or UPI, nor would his face on a television screen "bring in an avalanche of teenage fan mail." But as far as "bringing home the Viet Nam story to American listeners and viewers, however, I feel I could give anyone else a run for his money," Browne wrote.[45]

Browne made the leap. He resigned from the AP in June 1965. In his resignation letter, Browne wrote that he felt like "a traitor" to Gallagher and the AP for leaving and fully expected to "probably louse it up and completely regret this decision the rest of my life, but somehow I just feel I'll never know if I don't try it." Arnett remembered that Browne had expressed to him his frustration that their reporting had little effect on American policy. "He said the country was marching into war regardless of the daily truths that he believed showed military involvement would be long and bloody and ultimately unsuccessful," Arnett recalled. He described Browne as "irreplaceable; his intellectual courage and reporting skills were unmatched in the war theater and his dedication to the craft of journalism was unflagging."[46]

Gallagher did all he could to persuade Browne to stay with the AP, telling him he had a bright future in the organization. The executive argued that there were "good gambles and bad gambles" in a person's life, and he considered that going to ABC would be a bad gamble for Browne. "They are the third network and the gap is nowhere wider with the other two than it is on news," Gallagher wrote. "They do not—despite a great deal of talk—allocate the resources that CBS and NBC do to cover the news. . . . The result is that they are not able to reach the quality that the other two networks constantly produce." He also prophetically warned Browne that television news was really "half news ability and the other half entertaining or performing ability. There is a large element of strictly show business and this is inevitable because the correspondent must project his personality to the audience," and those who failed in the personality portion were doomed to become "secondary performers." In the print-media world, Gallagher pointed out that Browne stood out as "a top performer, a Pulitzer Prize winner, and you do not have to take any 'secondary' role." Gallagher was also not afraid to play upon Browne's sense of loyalty to the AP, writing that the situation in Vietnam seemed to be reaching a climax and he wanted his star journalist to "stay on the job until it is decided one way or another." Gallagher left no stone unturned in trying to entice Browne to stay with the AP, ending his letter by offering to increase the reporter's yearly salary to $14,000. Gallagher's arguments and financial inducements, however, failed to sway Browne's mind.[47]

For his first trip as an ABC employee, Browne traveled to Mexico City, where the network held its annual meeting for its stockholders, executives, and affiliate radio and television stations. The network used the occasion to introduce actor Adam West as the star of its new *Batman* series, which one executive predicted would be an instant hit "with sophisticated young adults—those who like pop art, go to discotheques and buy Tiffany lamps." Browne found himself, in "a much more modest way," launched as ABC's new man on the Indochina beat. "From my very first contact with the medium I knew that I had a lot of learning to do," Browne recalled.[48]

The "Stand-Upper"

ON AUGUST 3, 1965, Company D of the First Battalion, Ninth Marines, climbed aboard armored personnel carriers and headed toward Cam Ne, a collection of huts near Da Nang, South Vietnam. Morley Safer, a television correspondent for the Columbia Broadcasting System, rode along with the Americans hoping to have a story for his network's nightly half-hour news program. On the way to the target, a marine officer told the reporter that his unit had been ordered to "take out" the village complex, but Safer believed the officer must have been exaggerating. "This will hardly be a surprise attack," remembered Safer, who had previously covered combat in the Middle East, Cyprus, and Algeria. "The marines are joking, smoking; one man is playing music on a tape recorder fixed to his helmet. . . . No matter, for the clanking and groaning of the amtracks give a good mile's warning that the Yanks are coming."[1]

What Safer captured on film at Cam Ne stunned US television viewers, who, as the reporter pointed out, saw their servicemen "acting in a way people had never seen American troops act before, and couldn't imagine." An outraged President Lyndon Johnson called his friend Frank Stanton, CBS president, to accuse the network of defecating on the American flag. Johnson also warned Stanton that he had in his possession reports from

CHAPTER 9

law enforcement agencies that Safer was a Communist. Later informed by his aides that Safer was a Canadian, not a Communist, the president replied, "Well, I knew he wasn't an American." The newsman had sparked Johnson's ire by daring to film the marines responding to automatic-weapon fire from suspected Viet Cong guerrillas withdrawing from the area by using flamethrowers, matches, and Zippo cigarette lighters to set fire to thatched-roofed homes containing old men, women, and children; the Americans burned down 150 houses, Safer estimated. As he said in the conclusion to his report for the *CBS Evening News*: "Today's operation is the frustration of Vietnam in miniature. There's little doubt that American firepower can win a military victory here. But to a Vietnamese peasant whose home means a lifetime of backbreaking labor, it will take more than presidential promises to convince him that we are on his side." As for the marines, one of their commanders pointed out that in several cases destroying the Vietnamese homes "was the only way to ensure that the house would not become an active military installation after the troops had passed." Military authorities reported there had been thirty to a hundred enemies based out of Cam Ne and the marines had uncovered an extensive system of booby traps.[2]

Safer's controversial news segment showed the power television possessed to bring the war in Southeast Asia into living rooms in the United States on a nightly basis. Television's ability to do so had been one of the main reasons Malcolm Browne left his secure job at the Associated Press in the summer of 1965 to become the full-time Saigon correspondent for the American Broadcasting Company, starting his assignment on August 16, 1965. Browne realized that there were many Americans in the 1960s "already glued to their light boxes, photosynthesizing their views and biases from the TV images that passed for news." He was tempted "by the lure of instant fame or at least instant access to the very public that I had failed to reach with my wire dispatches."[3]

It also was a fertile time for news from South Vietnam, as Johnson escalated the American presence in the country. Browne marked the turning point in the war as occurring on February 7, 1965, the day VC commandos destroyed a US Army officer's billet and an air base called Camp Hollaway at Pleiku in the Central Highlands. "We have kept our guns over the mantel and our shells in the cupboard for a long time now. I can't ask our American soldiers out there to continue to fight with one hand behind their backs," said Johnson, whose administration ordered long-term aerial assaults against North Vietnam, Operation Rolling Thunder. The day before the Pleiku attack, the United States had 23,500 servicemen in South Vietnam, Browne noted, "none of whom technically was a combatant." After February 7, however, American fighting men could "start firefights on their own, hunt for the enemy, and act as if Viet Nam were an American war, which, of course, it was," reported Browne. By the end of the year, there were 181,000 US servicemen in the country. By 1967 that number had soared to nearly half a million.[4]

Despite America's escalating involvement in the conflict, US officials continued to stonewall newsmen, leading to some tense exchanges. On July 17, 1965, a group of journalists gathered at the US embassy in Saigon to meet with Barry Zorthian, the mission's chief public affairs officer, the "information czar" in the country, and Arthur Sylvester, assistant secretary of defense for public affairs. Sylvester had raised the hackles of many reporters when, during the Cuban missile crisis, he supposedly insisted that the government had an inherent right to lie to protect its vital interests, particularly when "it's going into nuclear war. This seems to me basic." Later, Sylvester testified at a congressional committee that "no government information program can be based on lies; it must always be based on truthful facts. But when any nation is faced with nuclear disaster, you do not tell all the facts to the enemy." The Saigon meeting turned contentious; Safer described it as "the most disheartening meetings between reporters and news managers ever held." Sylvester reportedly lost his temper, complaining about what reporters had written about the war and recommending they distribute only information that made the American cause look good. Questioned about the Johnson administration's credibility problem with the press, Sylvester told the questioner, according to Safer's account: "Look, if you think any American official is going to tell you the truth, then you're stupid.[5]

At the time of the Sylvester meeting, Browne was still working for the AP and had just returned from a trip to the field. Instead of attending the embassy meeting, he sent the man who replaced him as Saigon bureau chief, Edwin White. The following day White gave Browne a memorandum outlining what he remembered being discussed at what was supposed to be a social gathering, which he described as often turning "bitter and personal." White recalled that Sylvester engaged in "name calling wrangles" with specific newsmen, twice calling Jack Langguth of the *New York Times* stupid. "At one point Sylvester actually made statement he thought press should be 'handmaiden' of government," wrote White. "Later tried to retrieve that one by passing it off as joke. But his many serious face statements included such things as 'don't you guys know men are dying out there?' It was a long disagreeable night." Reflecting on the relationship between the media and government years after the end of the Vietnam War, Browne noted that whether Sylvester was correct in his assessments or not, it was a fact that "governments do lie when they feel it is necessary, which is rather often. It is equally a fact that reporters in a free society are paid to penetrate and expose official lies."[6]

The differences between print and broadcast journalism became apparent to Browne early on during his time with ABC. In a conversation with Elmer Lower, president of ABC's news division, he had learned that the three main networks (ABC, CBS, and NBC) had a "gentlemen's agreement" to air their prime-time news programs concurrently, and "never to run a movie when competitors were broadcasting news. Otherwise, he [Lower] said, the movie would steal the ratings." The strong connection between television news and the entertainment industry came more into focus when his new colleague, Lou Cioffi, a veteran television newsman, advised Browne about such matters as how to apply pancake makeup, the correct way to style his hair, what clothes to wear, and how to craft visually interesting news stories. "We stopped short of buying me a pistol belt," Browne joked. Cioffi pointed out to Browne that each "half-minute 'stand-upper' (the correspondent's on-camera spiel) filmed at a battle (or wherever) must first be typed out and them memorized, rehearsed and performed—perhaps four or five times. Only when the cameraman, soundman, producer and correspondent agreed that a take was satisfactory could the team move on to other things, such as finding a ride out of the jungle after the last chopper has left." ABC executives also informed Browne that in his segments he should always strive "for conversational instead of literary speech."[7]

There were times when Browne did not have the opportunity to write his scripts before doing his "stand-upper," particularly when he and his crew were reporting on stories in the countryside, where he had only a few minutes to give his comments before moving on to the next location, forcing him to often ad-lib. Browne also discovered that he could not always have visuals for some of the stories he wanted to tell. For a report on the thriving black market in Saigon selling such hard-to-find items as jungle boots and replacement fatigue uniforms, for example, Browne noted that he could not have his cameraman, Ron Headford, an Australian with the "endurance of an Olympic marathoner" and someone he considered the "best in the business," accompany him and use his Auricon sound camera to capture the segment on film. Doing so would have resulted in both being shot. For other assignments, Browne and Headford each had to carry more than a hundred pounds of equipment in Vietnam's heat and humidity. "This does not permit us to carry a typewriter, for one thing, which makes script preparation slightly more difficult," Browne said. Cameramen such as Headford were the "real heroes of the TV news industry," Browne remembered, as they had to carry "killing loads under appalling conditions, and must produce exciting 'actualities' even at the risk of their own lives." He found it to be close to impossible to hitch a ride on a river-assault boat or helicopter when there was a crew of three men "linked together by wires and cumbersome equipment."[8]

Browne did have opportunities for solo adventures, including gaining permission to fly into combat aboard the first US Air Force plane to be able to reach supersonic speed in level flight—the F-100 Super Sabre jet fighter. With the American buildup in Vietnam, however, the F-100 often flew strike missions against enemy targets on the ground instead of engaging in air-to-air dogfights. One such mission occurred on October 15, 1965, with a flight of five F-100s from the 481st Tactical Squadron taking off from Bien Hoa Air Base to bomb a hamlet in the Mekong River Delta that intelligence reports indicated housed two hundred VC combatants. For this sortie, the flight also included a two-seat F-100F dubbed *Lillian*, piloted by First Lieutenant Rod Dorr with Browne as his passenger. While he thrilled to the memories of dramatic World War I dogfights and the high stakes of the Battle of Britain during World War II, Browne pointed out that although still dangerous for US pilots, the air war in Vietnam more often consisted of mere routine rather than dramatic aerial engagements, and "nothing decisive seems to come of it, despite the great hopes America has pinned to it."[9]

For the mission, Browne donned a white helmet, a g-suit, and a parachute before climbing into the F-100F. The tightly fitting g-suit helped to prevent pilots from blacking out due to high centrifugal forces when making high-angle dive-bombing runs and steep turns. The pilots from the 481st carefully examined their planes before taking off. "With difficulty, each man climbed the ladder hooked into the side of his plane and swung his legs over into the cockpit," Browne remembered. "The idea is to stand on the seat first and then slide in." Once inside the aircraft, Browne had to spend time buckling himself in, including not only the usual seat belt but also dealing with a shoulder harness, straps around each calf (to secure his legs in case of an emergency ejection), and various fastenings to the ejection seat. "There also is a compressed air coupling for the G suit to hook up to, a communications cable to hook into the helmet for earphones and microphone, and the oxygen tube for the face mask," he wrote.[10]

Strapped securely into place, Browne said that he felt about "as free and comfortable as a condemned man in the electric chair. Besides the discomfort of confinement, the heat in the cockpit of a fighter waiting to take off from a Vietnamese airfield is nearly unbearable." One of the pilots confided to the newsman that he regularly lost two pounds every mission due to excessive sweating. Clad in a helmet and earphones, Browne discovered that sound from outside the aircraft was blotted out, especially once the canopy was lowered and locked into place. While the air outside the plane could be rent with "the shattering hypersonic blasts of an after-burning jet engine," the pilot and his passenger heard none of that. "In the earphones there is almost constant technical chatter between planes, ground control and forward air observers," Browne wrote. "Besides that, there is an eerie moaning sound in the earphones, produced by the complicated electronic gear in the plane." He also reported:

> To hear only the moaning sound, like the sighing of wind around
> the corner of a house when bomb blasts are erupting and huts

disintegrating just below, or when napalm splashes so close below as
to scorch the plane's paint, is a phenomenon pilots call "cockpit isola-
tion." Outside there is the din and horror of jet-age war; inside there
is the calm and quiet of a computer room. The pilots are glad to be
spared the sounds they create. I have sometimes wondered whether it
might not be better for some Air Force officers to be better acquainted
with the ugly cacophony of warfare.[11]

Dorr and Browne had to wait about ten minutes to take off, as a long
line of transport planes and aircraft were ahead of them. When their turn
came, each man pulled a set of safety pins from his ejection seat, arming
them. Browne learned from his talks with the American pilots that they
regarded their ejection seats with "a mixture of gratitude and fear." While
being shot out of a disabled jet might save their lives, it could also "break
one's back, or at least result in permanent injury as the result of severe
spinal compression," he said. Once airborne, the five planes on the mission
grouped themselves into a loose formation in the crystal-clear sky with the
Mekong Delta spread out below them. Reaching 15,000 feet, Dorr and the
other pilots were in communication with "Beaver 79," a L19 light plane far
below serving as a forward air controller spotting the target. "Beaver 79
had found our hamlet and told us he would indicate it with a smoke rocket,"
Browne recalled, "one of several he had on racks under his wings. We
broke into a wide circle and watched Beaver 79 sail along a canal firing a
puff of smoke into a cluster of thatched huts. From where I was sitting I
could see no sign of life. Pilots tell me they rarely see people on the
ground."[12]

The first US fighter broke out of the formation and started his bombing
run, announcing to the group, "I bomb." One after the other, the planes
made their attacks. "The dive down seems vertical," Browne noted, "and at
one point the ground actually seems to rotate over one's head." The reporter
could see flames coming from the tiny objects on the ground as Dorr prepared to make a strafing run. "While we still were what seemed to be a long
distance above the ground, our cannon began to fire," Browne reported.
"Actually, I heard very little but the moaning in the earphones, but the
whole plane vibrated from the firing, like an electric massager." He could

see streams of shells rip into the huts below, as well as flashes of light as the shells exploded. Dorr repeated his firing passes several times and Browne observed that the target "looked properly battered." In his official report about the mission, Beaver 79 indicated that the F-100s had destroyed eight structures, damaged six others, and destroyed 30 percent of the target area.[13]

On the return flight to Bien Hoa, Dorr let Browne take the controls for a bit. The journalist was surprised by the "lightness and responsiveness of the stick. Lighting the engine's afterburner in level flight produced an exhilarating thrust forward, and I could imagine that the F100 must be very pleasant to fly, or, rather, 'drive,' as its pilots insist on saying." Upon hitting the runway, *Lillian* deployed tail parachutes to help slow his plane down. Taxiing to the flight line, Dorr and Browne climbed out of the cockpit, both drenched in sweat. As yellow tractors hooked up to the F-100s to haul them off to a hangar for refueling, rearming, and servicing, the pilots unloaded their gear, reported to their superiors about the mission's results, and showered at their billeting area. "In the evening after chow at the officers' mess there would be time for a movie, a few beers and perhaps a letter home," said Browne. Miles to the south of the air base, Browne pointed out that the embers of a Vietnamese community were "still smoldering and the blood was still fresh from the death that had struck from the sky that afternoon." Pilots, however, rarely thought or talked much about the results of their work, he noted, except in terms of the military targets hit. "Sometimes these raids kill enemy guerrillas. Sometimes they merely kill women and children cringing in improvised shelters," reported Browne. "Pilots have no way of telling which, and they are at the mercy of forward observers and men sitting at desks who take coffee breaks and make human mistakes."[14]

Browne recalled that the worst mistakes happened because of incorrect map coordinates. On military maps, square sections of land were designated by two letters (e.g., WR). "A mention of the two designator letters roughly locates an area," he said. "Following these two letters are six numbers, three each for coordinates reading across vertically. A complete coordinate, consisting of two letters and six numbers (i.e., WR825439) locates any spot in the world to within a few hundred feet." When a pilot was ordered to bomb a coordinate, he assumed that the location was accurate and represented a valid military target. Unfortunately, said Browne, some-times the same "slovenly work attitudes that prevail in the United States extend to the American military, even in war theaters." If care was not taken, two or more numbers in a map coordinate could be accidentally transposed, which could lead to a pilot being off by a few miles.[15]

Such inaccuracy could lead to tragedy. Browne noted that on one mis-sion such a transposition happened, and US planes swooped down on the village of Lang Vei on the evening of March 2, 1967. Located approximately four hundred miles north of Saigon, Lang Vei was "a hard-working little community considered friendly to the Saigon government," he noted. When relief workers arrived at the village after the bombing raid, they discovered 80 dead and 120 wounded civilians. "America promptly apolo-gized to the South Vietnamese government and sent blankets and rice for the survivors of Lang Vei," Browne reported. Government officials in Washington, DC, often touted the "surgical precision" of bombing and strafing attacks made by the air force, navy, and marine corps in North and South Vietnam, but from what Browne observed of the air war, such claims were "grossly exaggerated."[16]

Switching from print to broadcast journalism did not help when it came to getting Browne's stories out of the country. Competition among the three networks was as fierce as the rivalry between the AP and United Press International. As with the print media, gaining an advantage over a competitor in the television industry often depended upon quickly getting film to the United States. In the days before portable satellite technology made it easy to operate almost anywhere in the world, television corre-spondents had to ship their undeveloped film via a chartered aircraft or on a commercial air-freight flight. "If only one charter plane was available and all three networks wanted it, success sometimes hinged on treachery, bribery or some other low trick," recalled Browne, "and anger sometimes accelerated to blows." Once securely aboard a flight, the film traveled from Vietnam to Tokyo, where, he said, a "customs expediter" would take it to a laboratory for developing, then on to a satellite-transmission station. "One's lead over a competitor could usually be measured in seconds or minutes," Browne said, "and the shipping of film from some battlefield was always a nerve-wracking procedure."[17]

Browne never felt comfortable working in television. He thought what he said on the air could never compete with the pictures being shown on the screen. For a complicated report exploring America's harmful effect on the Vietnamese economy, Browne's voiceover was accompanied by film showing artillery pieces firing in the background. "I'm certain that fascinated viewers paid not the slightest heed to what I was saying," he recalled, "so intent must they have been on watching the flash and smoke of the guns." Browne feared that when he appeared on television he was not "doing much more than performing as a circus barker." Even his factually accurate pieces did not relay the full story because "at root, they always smelled of greasepaint."[18]

A frustrated Browne resigned from ABC on January 15, 1966, telling Lower that he had "reluctantly decided the broadcast business is not for me." There were a couple of reasons for Browne's decision. He had been upset about the network's New York office's denial of an expense claim he had made for twenty-five dollars for a new pair of boots; his old ones had been destroyed by barbed wire while covering a combat operation. While the amount involved seemed trivial, the issue was a serious one. "It boils down to this: a correspondent has two alternatives with an expense account—he can make honest claims, running the risk that some will be disallowed, or he can pad the thing to such an extent that it doesn't matter if a few items are shaved off," he wrote Lower. "I have always chosen the former, and I think a check will show my expense accounts as smaller than any other correspondent, by a wide margin." Browne added that he always regarded the items he put on his expense account as "legitimately reimbursable," and he would rather quit than waste his time haggling with accountants. He also pointed out that such items disallowed by ABC would not have been questioned at all by the AP "or any other news organization out here, as far as I know." Another irritation involved ABC's decision not to buy a company vehicle, but to depend on renting them when needed because of tax reasons. This led to major inconveniences for the network's reporters and probably cost ABC "a fortune," Browne argued. While these reasons may have seemed minor to some, he pointed out that nothing "can bug a correspondent more than lack of administrative attention to housekeeping details. I am not referring here to office administration in the field but to taking care of the troops. ABC has a long way to go in this field."[19]

The main reason Browne cited for his resignation came from a personality clash between himself and Charles Klensch, ABC News Saigon bureau chief. Browne found it galling that Klensch, a relative newcomer to South Vietnam, had the authority to pick what assignments he tackled. Browne believed that the decision on whether to cover a combat operation should "depend on the best guess as to whether the action will be significant or not." After more than four years in the country, he thought he could predict "what operations are likely to be mere routine—possibly dangerous routine, but routine all the same." Consequently, newsmen and cameramen in the war zone would only accept direction from their peers—people who knew the jungle as well as they did. "Klensch has not met this requirement," wrote Browne. The breaking point came when Klensch sent Browne, cameraman Bob Jennings, and soundman Maasaki Shiihara to follow a mission in dense jungle that produced "little in the way of news at a relatively enormous cost in exertion and danger." By the day's end Jennings had collapsed from exhaustion, and the ABC crew barely avoided being blown to shreds by a landmine. Browne added:

> I am willing to face danger as much as the next correspondent, and I have been present at some of the bloodiest fights in this war. I will continue to cover important fights. But I have been here too long to want to see the odds against me build up unnecessarily, and I think most seasoned men here feel the same way. For the future, we see not a fixed number of campaigns and battles, but an indefinite and continuous war. It's a war which goes nowhere. The battles fought today are about the same as the battles fought four years ago, except that there are more Americans now. In short, correspondents don't like feeding the gaping Viet Nam news hole just to stuff material into it. . . .
>
> For the past year I have made no real contribution to American understanding of this damned country and the tragedy it represents. I thought I could accomplish something with television, but that didn't work out. . . .
>
> As a parting shot, I would say this: I don't really think there's much

of a need for TV correspondents here, as such. Cameramen are the sine qua non. After that, producers are necessary to stage manage the show. After that, correspondents are little more than narrators, whose job is to stand in front of the camera in a number of appropriate settings, reading their scripts as convincingly as possible. There is no challenge to gathering the news for TV; the job consists 90 per cent in appropriately staging the obvious. This is necessary and proper work, and when done well produces an incomparable public impact. But it is not my kind of work.[20]

Browne never changed his mind about the problems facing the network news business. He found television unbeatable when it came to live coverage of such events as press conferences, space missions, and what he described as "war actualities," including artillery firing, soldiers dying, and women and children wailing in fear. "And in this sense," Browne added, "war has become much more real for Americans than ever in history. Or so the argument goes." In truth, however, Browne believed that television's coverage of battles had the same effect on viewers as such fictional military programs as *Combat* and *Rat Patrol*. "It's all taken as a matter of course, and when the marine dies on camera, it's only an actor bleeding ketchup blood," he noted. Because of what they saw on their screens in their living rooms in the United States, the real war came as a "brutal, ghastly shock to the fresh, 20-year-old recruit arriving in Viet Nam, for which television did nothing to prepare him." Browne contended that almost all the other media did a more meaningful job covering the war than did television, giving high marks to non-American networks, especially the British Broadcasting Company. "The [American] TV men are the overpaid, pampered darlings of a thriving commercial industry—not reporters worthy of the name," Browne insisted. "If they nevertheless manage to become good reporters, it's in spite of television, not because of it." Consistent readers of such magazines as the *Saturday Evening Post*, the *New Yorker*, *National Geographic*, *Look*, and *Foreign Affairs* enjoyed a more comprehensive and accurate view about the war than the average television viewer. Local newspapers had only the time, money, and space to print a fraction of the news copy provided by such services as the AP and UPI. "Unfortunately, it is always the best part that's thrown away—the lengthy analytical pieces, the well-written, leisurely pieces that try to tell the reader in an interesting and entertaining way what it's all about," he added. "The part that's left is the bald headline and a couple of paragraphs of skeletal details."[21]

Although Browne never regretted his decision to leave television news, it incidentally led to tragedy. The ABC executive who had recruited him, Jesse Zousmer, flew from New York to Saigon to try to change Browne's mind. The two men talked over the matter, and Browne convinced Zousmer that he had "deeper reasons for quitting than a mere temper tantrum." Zousmer persuaded the journalist to do some freelance work for the network, including television documentaries and a regular series of radio broadcasts from Vietnam. Unfortunately, Zousmer, accompanied by his wife, perished when their aircraft crashed trying to land in Tokyo, killing everyone aboard. "The Zousmers were wonderful, intelligent people, and I wondered whether they might have lived if I hadn't resigned from ABC," Browne reflected. It was a dark time for the journalist, as just a few months before, his mother, at the age of fifty-seven, died from a heart attack caused by her emphysema, a condition that she endured for several years and had been worsened by her heavy smoking habit. "On the whole, it has been a rather bad year for me," Browne related to a friend. "Some 20 of my friends have been killed in battle here, and a number of others have died in recent accidental plane crashes."[22]

In his correspondence, Browne wrote that he had come to believe there was no longer any reason for being a newsman in Vietnam. "A historian, yes, but not a newsman," he mused. "The satisfaction of being a newsman is in the possibility of influencing opinions and thereby events, to a degree, with the objective rules of the game." In Vietnam, however, he believed that historic forces "have been set in motion now that are beyond the reaches of public opinion and therefore (at least to me) uninteresting." He set out to work on a novel, tentatively titled "Follow the Flag," about the American tragedy in Vietnam; the book remained unpublished. To pay the bills, Browne had been lucky enough, before leaving ABC, to secure a steady source of income by establishing himself as a freelance writer, bolstered, in large part, through the critical success of his book, *The New Face of War*, published in 1965 by the Bobbs-Merrill Company of Indianapolis and dedicated to his fiancée, Le Lieu. Browne noted that he wrote the book not as a as an "ax-grinding opus, nor is it intended as a historical work." Instead, he built his story through vignettes and his "own body of personal experience in the field" as the dean of correspondents in Saigon. Browne attempted to "try to heighten general understanding of what I conceive to be 'the new face of war' by painting its sights, sounds and people." The new kind of war he wrote about included fighting not merely by weapons but through politics, diplomatic blackmail, propaganda, and terror—methods that had unsavory connotations in the minds of Americans, who were not used to involvement in a conflict in which "nice guys finish last." Browne pointed out that the "experiences of most of America's military tradition" seemed to be inapplicable for what soldiers faced in Vietnam, including ambushes, sniping, and boobytraps. "The only glory anyone is likely to get out of it is the satisfaction of carrying a bundle of human enemy heads, suspended by wires stuck through their ears," Browne concluded. "There will never be the handing over of a sword by a beaten general to his victor. If there is victory, the fighting will merely die down to a few isolated incidents."[23]

The New Face of War shared the stage in 1965 with another book written by a reporter who had been embedded deeply in the conflict, David Halberstam, who produced *The Making of a Quagmire*. The two books were often reviewed together, and reviewers, particularly those who were journalists themselves, pointed out how the two newsmen became unpopular with US officials by digging up material that contradicted the optimistic view the government was trying to present to the public about the war's progress. Not surprisingly, opposing viewpoints appeared, especially regarding Halberstam's effort. Veteran war correspondent Richard Tregaskis, who had spent time in Vietnam for his own book, *Vietnam Diary* (1963), complained in a review for the *Chicago Tribune* that Halberstam's fundamental attitude in covering the war seemed to be "that something must be wrong rather than right with it." Tregaskis also included a much harsher quote from an unnamed embassy official calling Halberstam a "young punk who'd never seen a war before and thought it should always go well. He just didn't know about wars. It didn't seem to occur to him that in all our American wars in the past, we had to run a little short of absolute complete democracy for the sake of winning." Instead of Halberstam's book, Tregaskis recommended Browne's work as "a more temperate example of the new books on Viet Nam."[24]

Browne's book played a role in his next writing assignment, producing a monthly Report from Vietnam feature for *True, The Man's Magazine*, based out of New York City. *True* had been the first periodical to jump on the chance to excerpt Browne's book, paying $5,000 for the privilege. Browne had been impressed by the magazine's condensation, noting it had been "effectively handled," and believed that regular articles by him from Vietnam could go a "great deal farther in conveying the real flavor of this war than can be accomplished either by the press or electronic media." Working closely with the magazine's managing editor, Howard Cohn, Browne received $750 for each 1,500- to 2,000-word article (an amount that *True* later raised to $1,200). "Magazine stories are more satisfying than news stories in some ways," Browne wrote a friend. "You can say exactly what you mean."[25]

In securing Browne as a contributor, Cohn had emphasized that he wanted him to cover and report "on the subjects that you, as a veteran and thoughtful reporter, want to write about to give the flavor and meaning of this war which suddenly and perhaps belatedly has come to have a deep significance for us all." Cohn and his fellow editors had hit upon the idea of the Report from Vietnam approach to provide a "continuity of coverage on a big and continuing story," while also giving Browne the chance to "put down on paper quickly stories you want to write that have been missed by other media." Browne remembered that the fiction and nonfiction articles that appeared in *True* did not always exemplify "hairy-chested machismo," but they did have to be "accurate, exciting, smoothly written and not about gardening, marriage, romantic scandal or other 'feminine' subjects."[26]

The subjects Browne wrote about for the magazine included how he had celebrated his first Christmas in Vietnam ("Ghosts of Christmas Past"), what slang US servicemen had developed during the war ("'Sorry About That'"), the combat experiences of men in the First Cavalry Division in the Central Highlands ("Hell in the Highlands"), how an air-rescue squadron operated behind enemy lines to save downed American airmen ("To Fly

Again Another Day"), and the tension felt by soldiers during their last week of their year-long tour of duty in the country ("The Last Week is the Longest"). Although Cohn had been unenthusiastic about a piece Browne proposed about women fighters of the VC ("Daughters of the Dragon Lady"), the magazine did publish it, thereafter discovering that his articles in *True* "were being read by women as well as men, especially the wives and daughters of American servicemen missing in action." They later inundated him with letters after publication of his article about how US prisoners were being treated by the enemy ("A Better Brand of Brainwashing"), seeking answers about their loved ones. (At the time he wrote his article, there were 160 Americans missing in both North and South Vietnam, including 77 from the US Air Force.) "I answered the best I could," recalled Browne, "trying to include anything I knew that might be comforting." Cohn expressed his appreciation to Browne for his work, noting with pride that *True* was the only monthly periodical he knew of that gave regular coverage "to this terrible and confusing war."[27]

The connection with *True* allowed Browne to continue to be accredited as a correspondent with the Military Assistance Command, Vietnam. There did come a time in the summer of 1966 when Browne had been angry enough with the "idiots" at MACV that he felt like burning his identification card. The military public information officers he dealt with on a regular basis always seemed to be "the castoffs, lacking both the guts and intelligence to become line officers," he complained to Cohn. "And the same goes for the likes of Art Sylvester who never could really make it as [a] professional newspaperman and thus had [to] turn fink." Browne's frustration deepened when he learned about a Stanford University poll indicating that 71 percent of Americans nationwide did not know who the Viet Cong were, with a majority believing they were actually US allies. "Maybe this poll is not accurate, but if even 10 percent of Americans are this ill informed . . . we have not done our job; we have just not got across," he wrote Cohn. "And . . . if we can't even get the most rudimentary things across, how the hell do we expect to maintain a democracy in the States? Only an informed people stays free for long." Browne also had to deal with difficulties in getting his stories out of the country in a timely manner and corrupt bureaucrats that could not be trusted by their own government.

For example, to pay car registration fees in South Vietnam, a person had to deposit payment in a commercial bank and then take a receipt to the government office in the form of a letter of credit. Otherwise, Browne recalled, bureaucrats embezzled payments for themselves.[28]

Browne's fortunes brightened in the spring of 1966 when he learned he had been awarded the Council on Foreign Relations first Edward R. Murrow Press Fellowship, which had been created the previous year thanks to a $300,000 grant from the Columbia Broadcasting System. "I will spend about nine months doing some academic battery charging," Browne wrote his former boss Wes Gallagher. "It's a very free fellowship with no fixed requirements, paying both a salary and tuition costs." (*Newsweek* reporter Bill Touey took over his spot reporting for *True*.) Browne had also cleared the way so he could marry Le Lieu; the couple wed at the Saigon City Hall on July 18, 1966. The newlyweds left South Vietnam for the United States, sending their dog, Nif-Naf, a Japanese spaniel, ahead to Browne's father's apartment in New York while they visited Greece, Italy, and Germany. They finally sailed to America aboard the *Queen Elizabeth*, arriving in mid-September. Living in New York in a small apartment in Greenwich Village, Le Lieu later noted, proved to be more dangerous than living in wartime Saigon. "We were burglarized, threatened by homeless bums, and pickpocketed at Macy's," she remembered. On the advice of the police, Browne bought a shotgun for Le Lieu to use to defend herself, if need be, against intruders. Coming naked out the shower one morning, she heard a noise and could see the doorknob turning. "I yelled out that I had a rifle in my hands," Le Lieu recalled. "I heard the foot noise receding down the staircase." Le Lieu did take advantage of the city's educational offerings, studying Spanish and taking writing courses at New York University.[29]

During his fellowship year, Browne had an office at the Council's mansion at 58 East 68th Street—the former home of oil tycoon Harold Pratt—and took courses at Columbia University on Middle Eastern and African politics, while also studying Mandarin Chinese. While such classes did not seem, at first, to be helpful for his subsequent days as a Latin American correspondent, Browne believed that his fellowship year had been "absolutely invaluable" for his subsequent journalism career and, if he a chance to do it all over, he would not have changed a thing. "We correspondents, for the most part, are a roving breed," he pointed out. "It's increasingly necessary to develop expertise in specific areas, but we all must be prepared to serve anywhere." With that in mind, he later recommended to Council officials that learning foreign languages was vital to both reporters and diplomats. "Virtually any other discipline can be acquired in the field," Browne believed, "given initial mastery of a language. In any case, no correspondent ever has enough languages, no matter how many he knows."[30]

Browne attended weekly black-tie dinners at the Council featuring "celebrity guests, often banana republic dictators, African potentates and others the State Department considered worth courting." He also got to know US government movers and shakers, "who think they know a great deal about the world, and who actually know almost nothing worth knowing." Browne did enjoy his time with Allen Dulles, the retired director of the Central Intelligence Agency, whom he described as "a down-to-earth, folksy sort of fellow." Dulles shared a fascinating idea he had in which the United States would make a deal with the Chinese government allowing it to send fifty of its spies to America. "We would take them to Langley [CIA headquarters], give them intensive training in American history, politics, sociology, military structure, the English language, intelligence tradecraft, the works," Dulles reportedly told Browne. "Then we'd give them three-year visas and turn them loose." Asked by Browne what such a deal might accomplish, Dulles pointed out that no government really trusted anyone but its own spies. "By giving China the best spies money could buy and giving them the freedom to look at America in its entirety," Dulles noted, "Peking would begin learning the realities of this country. From there, the Chinese could formulate realistic diplomatic and military policies, which for us would be easier to cope with than the nonsense we now confront."[31]

Discussing the "very interesting" atmosphere then in the country in a letter to Peter Arnett, still reporting from Saigon for the AP, Browne recalled that at the subway station he used to get to Columbia he saw a crowd gathered around a speaker on a soapbox with a giant VC flag, "singing the praises of the [National] Liberation Front." Arriving at Columbia, Browne accepted several pamphlets concerning the war being distributed by students. "Stands are set up all over the campus, handing out propaganda of various kinds," he wrote. "Then a big, howling rally begins, with a couple of hundred people chanting, 'CIA, Stay Away.' Seems a CIA recruiting officer was on campus, trying to recruit students into the agency. A fracas breaks out. My Chinese teacher shakes his head and says it was just like that in Peking before 1948 before the communists took over." Clashes about the war continued when Browne went to his office at the Council, as members with opposing views almost came to blows. "Load of laughs," Browne told Arnett. "And nearly nobody knows what he's talking about."[32]

While Browne worked on his Council fellowship, he also made regular speaking engagements at universities to discuss the Vietnam War. On many occasions, he had been impressed by the "sober intelligence of audiences all over America . . . who really seemed to be concerned with issues rather than invective." He often appeared on panels that tried to balance his gloomy views with those who saw America's involvement in Vietnam as a positive, including Sylvester and S. L. A. Marshall, a former journalist, army veteran, and military historian. Browne never felt comfortable with the polarizing terms "hawk" and "dove" then being used to describe how a person felt about the war. Such terms, he pointed out, were "completely at odds with the reality of Viet Nam, a war in which there were no good guys and very few good causes." He believed there were not enough people willing to "tell the whole truth, and too many let their prejudices color their conclusions." By 1967 Browne considered himself an "isolationist" when it came to Vietnam and Southeast Asia in general. In a letter outlining his beliefs to former ambassador Henry Cabot Lodge Jr., Browne explained: "I think all nations concerned, including the United States, would benefit by a complete American withdrawal from the area, leaving the Vietnamese and others to settle their own wretched fate. Brutal and suppressive though the forces of Hanoi and the Viet Cong are, I can hardly see that the United States has brought anything better to South Viet Nam at this point, nor is it likely to do so." Because Browne questioned the glowing statistics being promoted by MACV and the Johnson administration ("We were winning the war, as well as the hearts and minds of the people"), antiwar activists looked at him as an ally; Pentagon officials viewed him as a foe.[33]

Although his mentor Gallagher had advised him to "never get in a pissing match with a skunk," Browne could not help himself when antagonists such as Sylvester and Marshall impugned the integrity of what they considered were the "young and inexperienced" journalists being duped by the Communists overseas. Marshall believed that out of the hundreds of correspondents who covered the war, only about seventeen were truly qualified to tackle such an assignment. "Most of our correspondents over there are more callow than new police reporters," he said. "They know nothing about war, nothing about the services. They're not interested in the nature of war." In an article for the *New Leader* magazine, Marshall accused US reporters of being derelict in covering the battles in Vietnam, claiming they ignored individual engagements in which the American military and their allies had triumphed because "the majority of U.S. correspondents in Saigon don't give a damn about them. . . . Today's average correspondent prefers a piece that will make people on the home front squirm and agonize." Marshall went on to describe young reporters as "too lazy to gather the facts themselves," instead preferring to "sit around and sneer at all that is said." Too often, the journalists' attention was diverted from the front lines by political demonstrations, terrorist incidents, friendly fire incidents, and civilian casualties. "The war is being covered primarily for all bleeding hearts and for Senator [J. William] Fullbright, who casts about for a way to stop it by frightening and shocking the citizenry," wrote Marshall. "It is not being reported for simple souls who would like to know how it is being fought and how good are the chances that the South Vietnamese and American forces and their allies can bring off a military victory." Even when military public-information officers were able to convince reporters to "get off their duffs" to do some reporting in the field, Marshall viewed the reporters as "freeloaders," claiming some of them dared to bring with them large trunks to hold their belongings for short stays at the front.[34]

Responding to what he described as Marshall's "disgusting polemic," Browne argued that the article had insulted those reporters who had had their "eyes blown out, hands permanently crippled (and for a cameraman, this is the end of a career), feet lamed by spike traps, ligaments and tendons wrecked by grenade and shell fragments, and many, many bullet wounds." For the rest of their days these newsmen would carry with them brutal memories from such datelines as Song Be, Binh Gia, Ap Bac, Dong Xoai, Cai Lai, Bong Son, and hundreds of others, noted Browne. At the time, each of these engagements seemed important to the reporters and their editors. "Now, with the war still rolling on like the Mekong River, one begins to wonder," he said. "Did any of these battles secure any vital piece of real estate for one side or the other? Did any of them result in a breakthrough? Did any of them permanently eliminate a major belligerent unit?" Of course, Browne believed the answer was no because Vietnam was not a war for real estate, as were World War II and Korea, and there was no front. "There are hundreds of highly mobile hostile and friendly units engaged in endless maneuver, always seeking an advantage in one way or another," Browne observed. "When a hill or ridgeline or hamlet becomes an objective for one side or the other, it is important for a few hours or days." Usually, when the fight has ended, the "winner just abandons the objective." Answering Marshall's charge that journalists in Vietnam were freeloaders, Browne pointed out that for most reporters lodging cost a dollar a night; cases of C rations cost $12 apiece; fatigues, helmets, and other jungle gear had to be purchased at inflated black-market prices; it cost $44 a day for wounded newsmen to be treated at the navy hospital in Saigon; and it cost $140 (and other expenses) for the loan of an aluminum casket to transport those who lost their lives on flight to Travis Air Force Base in California. Browne concluded:

> The hard core of newsmen in Viet Nam grow weary of the endless ranting from their detractors. From the Pentagon or White House it is predictable. From journalistic colleagues it's professional backstabbing, as contemptible in a newsman as it is in any other profession!
>
> It would be good to see a truce, in which each writer on Viet Nam began tending his own garden and sticking to the business at hand— covering Viet Nam. Despite Marshall . . . and Assistant Secretary of Defense Arthur Sylvester and TIME magazine and some others, that is what the hard core of Viet Nam press corps has been doing all along. Fortunately for America, this hard core is the leader in coverage; let the others keep pace if they can.[35]

As his fellowship year at the Council neared its end in spring 1967,

Browne looked to his future. While he had been eminently satisfied with his experience as a freelancer, "both from the standpoint of freedom of expression and income," Browne had developed an "urge to return to the mainstream of journalism." In April he wrote Seymour Topping, *New York Times* foreign editor, seeking a job. "In practice, the only organizations that interest me are my alma mater, The AP, and The Times," Browne wrote. He admitted that the pull to AP was "very strong," as he remained good friends with Gallagher and "working for him was wonderful." But during most of his time at the AP in Vietnam Browne recalled that he never really believed that his reporting "was reaching people to the same degree that it would have through The Times. And to me, that consideration is the most important." Browne ultimately turned down an offer from Gallagher to return to the AP as a traveling correspondent in the Middle East and Africa, instead deciding to join the *Times*. Browne spent his first few months on the job reporting on New York stories before packing his bags and heading at the beginning of 1968, with Le Lieu and Nif-Naf at his side, to Buenos Aires, Argentina, as the newspaper's bureau chief with responsibilities for coverage of most of South America. After landing at Ezeiza Airport, the couple claimed their luggage and headed to the customs inspection area, where Nif-Naf, "having restrained himself in the flight bag in which we always carried him, copiously relieved himself," Browne remembered.[36]

For nearly a decade, Browne, accompanied by Le Lieu, traveled the world as a foreign correspondent for the *Times*. He endured bombing raids by Indian aircraft while reporting from Pakistan, hiked in the Himalayas, underwent an intensive interrogation by Bulgarian soldiers who believed he might be a CIA agent, witnessed the beginning of Yugoslavia's implosion as a country, hunted for Attila the Hun's tomb, endured being stalked by secret police in Czechoslovakia, eluded KGB snoops to interview dissidents in the Soviet Union, and survived an earthquake that knocked him out of his bed in Italy. While the Brownes sometimes were able to arrange long-term stays in an apartment overseas, they spent several years jumping from hotel room to hotel room in far-flung locales, leaving behind most of their possessions in a New York warehouse in which items had a habit of disappearing. "Since a war correspondent cannot lug along more than a suitcase or two even on an indefinite assignment," he noted, "pack rats like my wife and me have lost a lot of things over the years." Browne discovered that foreign correspondents who lived without real homes craved surrogates for their old lives, collecting "odd bits of furniture, antique firearms, pottery" that were probably better off "in museums than in hotel rooms or warehouses." Although he and Le Lieu suffered pilfering of their belongings from thieves all over the world, they never quit their habit of buying such knickknacks.[37]

Browne's determination to obtain accurate information for the stories he covered continued to get him in trouble with authoritarian governments. In September 1970 the Republic of Chile prohibited Browne and Le Lieu from entering the country to cover national elections that resulted in Salvador Allende of the Socialist Party becoming president. When the Brownes arrived at the Pudahuel Airport in Santiago, a policeman asked the American reporter what newspaper he worked for. "When I told him, he asked me to wait for a minute," Browne cabled the *Times*. "Shortly thereafter police took us to a detention room, where we were eventually told we could not enter Chile." The police gave no reason for the decision, telling the newsman they were just carrying out their orders, but Browne believed a couple of articles he had written about political issues might have been the catalyst for denying him entry. Both the Christian Democrats and Marxists in Chile had been berating Browne "as a Yankee imperialist in their press." The country's interior minister, Patricio Rojas, later claimed that Browne had been barred "because he has attacked Chile in his articles published in The New York Times." Browne pointed out that US journalists in Latin America, and all over the world, "never seem able to convince people that they are simply journalists, not spies or provocateurs. Of course, spies and journalists are both in the business of collecting information, but while the spy conceals his harvest, the journalist publishes his." The harassment continued at Browne's hotel in Lima, Peru, where he received some threatening calls warning him to be careful about what he wrote about Chile. Although he had been receiving such nasty calls and letters most of his career, and usually discounted them, he had been "more concerned this time because there are a lot of serious meanies in the countries I cover, both of the far left and far right, as well as the garden variety nuts." By

December, however, the Chilean government, under pressure from the *Times*'s executives, had agreed to reinstate Browne's right of entry into its country.[38]

A few years after his Chilean difficulties, Browne established himself in the Balkans, using the *Times* bureau in Belgrade as a base for assignments to Portugal, Spain, Egypt, and Kenya. One morning in March 1975 he was filling up the gasoline tank of the bureau's Opel for a trip to Budapest, Hungary, when he received an emergency message from James Greenfield, foreign editor for the *Times*. Greenfield informed Browne the newspaper needed him to get to Saigon as soon as possible. "The situation in Viet Nam had begun to fall apart and he wanted an old hand there to help out," Browne recalled. The end had come for the seemingly never-ending conflict, as North Vietnamese troops raced to capture Saigon. In South Vietnam's final spasm as a country, Browne was there to witness great acts of heroism, compassion, and loyalty, as well as guilt, greed, betrayal, and bitterness. For Vietnamese and Americans alike, the overwhelming memories they retained were full of "sorrow and betrayal and grief," with tears clouding scenes that resembled hell on earth. He never forgot the last remarks of a Vietnamese friend who tried to comfort the departing Americans: "You may hear after you leave that some here have died, perhaps even at their own hand. You must not spend the rest of your lives with that guilt. It is just a part of Vietnam's black fate, in which you, all of you, became ensnared for a time. Fate is changeless and guiltless."[39]

CHAPTER 10

Saigon, 1975

COMMISSIONED BY THE US Navy on September 20, 1969, the USS *Mobile*, a Charleston-class amphibious cargo ship, had over its lifetime been deployed several times to aid American forces in South Vietnam. The ship's more than six hundred–man crew, however, could not have imagined the hundreds of refugees who frantically sought sanctuary on their ship as part of the last-ditch helicopter evacuation—code-named Operation Frequent Wind—of Americans and their at-risk Vietnamese allies. Two of the thirty-three news-men who eventually found shelter on the *Mobile* were from the *New York Times*, Fox Butterfield and Malcolm Browne, who had recently celebrated his forty-fourth birthday. "It was almost like abandoning a dying friend," recalled Browne, who left Saigon on April 29, 1975, aboard a US helicopter for a rendezvous with the ships of Task Force 76, on station approximately eigh-teen miles offshore in the South China Sea. "In the end," he remembered about the evacuation, "it was hard to decide who had behaved worse on bal-ance—Vietnamese or Americans. The savagery and bitterness of the final weeks turned normally enlightened, fine people into mad dogs, robbing corpses, cutting throats to improve their own chances of survival." But Browne also witnessed "blazing sparks of real nobility, often in people from whom one would have least expected in normal times."[1]

After years of bloodshed, the end had come for South Vietnam. American combat forces left the country as the result of a peace accord signed in Paris on January 27, 1973. Taking advantage of the agreement, the North Vietnamese government resupplied its army and launched a major offensive at the beginning of 1975. That March, five North Vietnamese divisions, supported by tanks and artillery, struck the Central Highlands. South Vietnam's president, Nguyen Van Thieu, made a disastrous decision to withdraw Army of the Republic of Vietnam forces from the northern two-thirds of the country to establish a defensive line to protect the Mekong Delta, Saigon, and the southern coastal cities. As ARVN units withdrew, panic ensued. Traveling on buses, trucks, ox carts, motorcycles, bicycles, and by foot, retreating soldiers and their families clogged the roads. Military sources informed Western newsmen that nearly 400,000 people were using Route 7 to escape from Pleiku, with the column stretching all the way to the coastal city of Tuy Hoa. Hue fell on March 25 and by Easter Da Nang had been taken by the advancing Communist forces, who embarked on an ambitious campaign to capture Saigon before the expected May rains.[2]

Refugees not only had to endure enemy artillery and gunfire but also neglect from their own government. A barge filled to overflowing with thousands of civilians reached a hoped-for sanctuary at a seaside resort north of Saigon, but authorities refused to let them disembark. Greedy civilians took advantage of the chaos to enrich themselves when they could. A young woman in Saigon whose parents lived in Da Lat, taken by the Communists, cried with joy to learn that some refugees to the capital had brought along a letter from her parents. "Then they asked me how much I was willing to pay for the letter," she said. A *Washington Post* reporter covering the fighting wrote that as discipline collapsed some ARVN soldiers used their weapons to gain space on evacuation flights, looting and killing in the process. Civilians fled from their homes due to fear and simply because "everyone else was running." Sickened by the piles of dead women and children he saw, Browne later wrote friends that his experiences made him understand "the ugly stories of how inmates of the Nazi concentration camps savaged each other in the face of death at the hands of a common enemy."[3]

Browne was there to witness South Vietnam's final agony despite being blacklisted by its government for articles he had written a few years before. The *Times* called on him to return to Saigon to write about North Vietnam's April 1972 Easter Offensive. "We are determined and will throw everything we have into this effort," proclaimed North Vietnamese officials, who had committed twelve divisions to the operation. "The enemy also knows that this offensive will be decisive in determining the outcome of the war." President Richard Nixon, running for a second term in office in 1972 and seeking rapprochement with the Soviet Union and China, reacted forcefully to the threat against South Vietnam. "The bastards have never been bombed like they're going to be bombed this time," Nixon vowed, unleashing devastating bombing raids, known as Operation Linebacker, against North Vietnam that eventually halted the Communist offensive.[4]

Browne left his post in Pakistan and reported to the *Times*'s Saigon bureau chief, Craig Whitney, who remembered being "eager to accept anyone they [his editors] could send who knew their way around. Mal really knew his stuff, probably better than anybody. He had seen everything." Browne used Hue as a base to cover the fighting in the north, including the pitched battle for Quang Tri, finally recaptured by ARVN soldiers in September. Because cars were in great demand, Browne decided to save on expenses by sharing a vehicle—a "creaky old Citroën"—with Alex Shimkin from *Newsweek* magazine. He described his traveling companion as a "tall, rangy kid with thick glasses, a ready wit and a wonderfully sardonic sense of humor. He was good company." Using a car to get to the battlefront "was always tricky; if you go too far you may find yourself trapped in cross fire," recalled Browne, "and if you don't go far enough, you may miss everything of importance."[5]

The newsmen had driven up Route 1 to about four miles from Quang Tri until they had to stop because of nearby artillery and air strikes. Coming across a clearing in which South Vietnamese 105-mm howitzers were firing at the enemy, they stopped to ask an ARVN officer how things were going. "We win whenever you Americans stay out of our way," the bad-tempered first lieutenant responded. Put off by his brusk manner, Browne and Shimkin sought directions to a forward airborne command post that included a couple of American advisers. The officer told them that the command post had moved, but that if they drove north on Route 1 for about a mile, they would come across it, recalled Browne. Smelling a rat, the reporters stopped their car after going only a few hundred yards. "The road was straight as an arrow without any sign of life all along it," Browne noted, "and the thunder of the howitzers had abruptly stopped." They got out to reconnoiter the area on foot. They discovered that if they had followed the artillery officer's suggestion, they would have wandered into North Vietnamese territory "being raked by machine-gun fire, by rockets and by antitank guns," Browne noted. Because the artillery commander had been supporting the airborne troops, "he obviously knew where it was and knew that it had not moved. Other newsmen say they have been given similar potentially lethal advice a number of times in recent weeks," he wrote.[6]

The potentially deadly encounter with the artilleryman pointed to a worsening situation between the media and the South Vietnamese military, as well as friction between Vietnamese officers and their American advisers. An ARVN captain explained to Browne he and others in the military were convinced that the foreign press did not support their cause and viewed them as enemy agents. Browne, therefore, should not be surprised about being sent into a potential trap. "They love to report our reverses," the officer said of Western reporters. "Instead of helping us build up the fighting morale of the Vietnamese and American people, they break it down." Browne pointed out that the poor reputation of the South Vietnamese press did not help matters, as politicians had been known to bribe Vietnamese reporters to write glowing articles about them, and some Saigon newspapers made "large profits by extortion—threatening to print damaging articles about people unless they are paid not to." American media were seen as being no better, he added. "In any case," Browne wrote, "Vietnamese tend to regard American news organizations and the men and women representing them as arrogant and insensitive and interested only in the American point of view."[7]

In his articles for the *Times*, Browne had made sure to document the determined resistance offered by some ARVN units, especially the fire bases established near Pleiku that served to support the South Vietnamese Second Airborne Division. The bases repulsed attacks mirroring North

Vietnamese tactics that had devastated American facilities near the city in 1965. Visiting Fire Base 42A, Browne had to take cover in a sandbagged bunker with its commander, Captain Dang Trung Duc, as a half-dozen mortar shells fell nearby. "When incoming mortar shells are not casting a pall of gray smoke and spraying deadly steel splinters," Browne reported, "the infantrymen here, who are exposed as any in Vietnam, seem in good spirits and prepared to fight." He cited the professionalism of the crews manning two 105-mm howitzers at the fire base: "They do not seem unduly concerned by occasional heavy and extremely accurate enemy fire, although they expressed disappointment that they have not received more air support." When the firing finally died down, Captain Duc and his aide, Warrant Officer Bui Ngoc Thi, invited the reporter to join them inside the safety of a bunker for a meal of rice, noodle soup, cucumbers, and roast pork. While they ate, Duc spoke fondly about his experiences training at Fort Knox, Kentucky, and traveling by car to see the rest of the United States. "We've had good times," he told Browne as a pair of American-made Skyraider aircraft dropped napalm on a nearby forest. "Let's hope there will be good times again, if there is ever peace."[8]

Browne's decision to cite the press-military tensions apparent in the country during the Easter Offensive angered Thieu's government, which complicated the newsman's return three years later to report on South Vietnam's final agony. Government officials might also have been unhappy with a trip Browne and his wife, Le Lieu, by now a naturalized American citizen, made in March 1973. The Brownes were part of a delegation of twenty-eight American, British, and French reporters who traveled to Hanoi to witness the release of the last sixty-seven American prisoners of war held by the North Vietnamese. Browne watched at the Gia Lam Airport as Lieutenant Commander Alfred Howard Agnew became the last American to board one of the two US Air Force C-141 transports flying the prisoners to Clark Air Base in the Philippines. "None of the Vietnamese cheered the prisoners, but no insults were shouted," Browne recalls. "Some smiled and waved. Comments by Vietnamese chattering among themselves as they watched the prisoners file by included: 'He's fat,' 'He is very young, poor man,' and 'He looks so rosy.'" As for the returning Americans, the "general mien . . . bespoke a terrible ordeal." For Browne, the simple fact of being in Hanoi and "politely shaking hands with smiling officials wearing green pith helmets was the strangest experience of all."[9]

The person who drew the most attention from the North Vietnamese was Le Lieu, who became the first Vietnamese American to visit Hanoi since the war's beginning. At first, the people in Hanoi mistook Le Lieu as Chinese until they heard her speaking in Vietnamese. "By then, whenever we walked, I was surrounded by ordinary Vietnamese who were curious to know about the South," remembered Le Lieu, who was accredited for the assignment as a *Times* photographer. "They examined my clothing—a green pantsuit; my jewelry—my engagement diamond ring; and my cameras. I was conscious of being observed by guides, who prevented me from asking too many questions. I nevertheless was aware of the poverty around me through these conversations. Stores on the main street, such as they were, were scarce, and almost empty." Browne said those who talked to his wife included some with relatives fighting for the Viet Cong and others with the ARVN, but most were interested not in political or military matters, but "rather in the fate of welfare of their families." He discovered that while officials, soldiers, and ordinary citizens all expressed "strong patriotism," they showed little hesitation in "discussing food and clothing shortages, homesickness for families and friends in South Vietnam and even favorable impressions made on North Vietnamese troops by the South Vietnamese towns in which they had fought." Browne later compared his experience in Hanoi to being almost like a family reunion, with some of the North Vietnamese "almost in tears as they talked. It was the first real sense that by God, this is an artificial civil war. Why are these guys killing each other?"[10]

The visit sparked a diplomatic problem for the Brownes. Hanoi officials had stamped all US correspondents' passports. The simple action meant that the American journalists in the delegation had violated a US Immigration and Naturalization Service edict that its citizens could not travel to North Vietnam without State Department permission (other restricted countries included Cuba and North Korea). "Since all of us had less than eight hours' warning before making the trip from Vientiane [Laos], none of the correspondents had been able to obtain the required State Department clearance," he noted. The State Department decided to overlook the infraction for the newsmen, but Le Lieu could not enter South Vietnam to visit her family with a North Vietnamese visa stamped in her passport. When she tried to obtain a duplicate passport at the US consulate in Phnom Penh, officials there confiscated her passport, replacing it with "a temporary document" that only allowed her to travel to the United States, Browne said. Fortunately, under pressure from the *Times*, Le Lieu finally received a new passport.[11]

When Browne arrived in Saigon in March 1975 to report about the renewed North Vietnamese offensive, he initially breezed through police checks at the airport. His entry had been noticed, however, by the South Vietnamese government's Information Ministry, which issued an arrest warrant for him. These were dangerous times for foreign newsmen. On March 15 Saigon police shot and killed Paul Leandri, deputy bureau chief for the French news agency Agence France Presse, after questioning him about the source of one of his stories. Because of Leandri's death, "arrest warrants were being taken seriously," Browne noted. James Markham, the *Times*'s Saigon bureau chief, met Browne near the newspaper's office on Tu Do Street and drove him to hide out in the home of a US embassy official for a couple of days. "It was a ridiculous situation," Browne recalled. It did give him the time he needed to call in some favors with sympathetic officials in the South Vietnamese government, who squashed the arrest warrant. "Nothing came easy in that country," he noted. The help from the US embassy came despite the hostility Graham Martin, who had been the ambassador in South Vietnam since August 1973, felt for the *Times*. One of Browne's predecessors from the newspaper (probably David K. Shipler) had written some articles that had infuriated Martin—so much so that the ambassador refused to ever see Browne. At one point Martin had gone as far as to claim that the *Times*'s editorial page possessed "a deep emotional involvement in the success of North Viet Nam's attempt to take over South Viet Nam by force of arms."[12]

Unlike its response in 1972, when Nixon had authorized numerous bombing missions against the invaders, Thieu's government could not depend on such assistance three years later. Nixon was gone, forced to resign in disgrace because of the Watergate scandal. Congress had cut aid to South Vietnam and President Gerald Ford proved unwilling to risk

American airpower to save his erstwhile allies. ARVN soldiers faced severe supply shortages, with some units having only a few hand grenades per patrol and flying hours for helicopters slashed by 80 percent. One of the first stories Browne explored upon his return involved rumors he began to hear from sources that Thieu had decided to withdraw troops from most of the northern two-thirds of the country. "The area left to be defended would be the rich and populous southern part of the country, or everything south of a line running roughly from the Cambodian border at Tay Ninh in the west, to Phan Thiet on the South China sea," he reported. "In addition, the Government would try to hold a narrow coastal strip northward at least to Da Nang, and Hue if possible." Browne's dire report put him at odds with Markham, who had had a source in American intelligence telling him that although the situation seemed serious, ARVN soldiers could hold out against the North Vietnamese, at least for the short term. The two reporters argued but agreed to discuss the matter later. "That was the last I ever saw of Jim," Browne noted. Markham decided to take his family and leave Vietnam, taking a flight to Hong Kong. "He was leaving his furniture and everything else," recalled Browne. "I guess he had become convinced asking around himself that what I was saying was somewhere near the truth." Butterfield, who worked in the *Times*'s Saigon bureau and had gone to high school with Markham, never learned for sure what happened but conjectured that Markham had an emotional breakdown, resulting in his departure.[13]

As the North Vietnamese offensive rolled on, it became harder and harder for the *Times* bureau to cover the news, as there "were no telephone links to any of the places that we needed to be in touch with," Browne said. To travel around the country more easily, the *Times* bureau chartered its own plane, a twin-engine Beechcraft Baron, which came with a daredevil pilot named Rocky. Browne discovered that Rocky was willing to "fly almost anywhere, even inside territory occupied by the North Vietnamese." After South Vietnamese troops abandoned Hue on March 25, Browne traveled to Da Nang, located just south of Hue, and discovered that the panic had spread there. Picking up a Honda motorcycle at the airport, Browne gave a ride to an ARVN colonel, dropping him off at his home. "I've got to get them out," the officer told Browne. "That's all that matters. The

Americans have abandoned us and the war's over." Refugees fled south any way they could, including by land and sea. At Vung Tau, a beach resort about forty miles southeast of Saigon, where people were still swimming in the South China Sea and enjoying ice cream and beer, Browne came upon a navy barge, AN 2801, which had been at sea for nine days packed with soldiers and their families. "The sun had scorched them on the open deck all that time and they had been without food and water," Browne reported. "From the huge piles of debris on the deck—smashed bicycles, suitcases with the contents strewn about, dolls, pots—at least 50 bodies were pulled out by nightfall, most of them women and children." He could see flies droning over the corpses of children still holding their dolls and teddy bears.[14]

AN 2801 was one of hundreds of large and small boats that had moved down the coast to escape the North Vietnamese. Most of the boats had dead aboard, who had perished from "starvation, thirst and exposure, some from shooting by renegade soldiers turned bandit, some in disputes over fragments of bread," wrote Browne. Talking to a woman who had survived the ordeal, he learned that while at sea people had come out to the barge with water, offering to sell it to them for 1,500 dong (about two dollars) a glass. "Of course," she said, "most people could not afford a whole glass, so we tried to share it." When it rained, the refugees lay on deck, "trying to lick up what gathered, although the deck was so thick with human waste it was awful," she added. Another survivor, a student fleeing Da Nang, had been on another ship that received food dropped by an American helicopter. Talking to dozens of former soldiers, none showed any sign of being eager to return to fighting, Browne recalled. While government officials hoped to re-form retreating troops into new fighting units, he reported that, judging from what he had heard in Vung Tau and elsewhere, there seemed little hope of doing so.[15]

As North Vietnamese forces closed in on Saigon, Browne and Butterfield had to abandon using their chartered aircraft in favor of a car owned by the *Times*'s bureau for short trips to the front lines. "During some of these I came closer to getting killed than at any time during my Indochina combat experience," said Browne. On an excursion to a besieged government outpost at Xuan Lo with *Newsweek* reporter Ron Moreau, Browne became concerned that something seemed wrong. He pulled the car over, stopped, and he and Moreau walked to a nearby shady grove. There, they used binoculars to scan their surroundings. "Seconds later a barrage of well-aimed mortar shells began bursting all around us," Browne noted. "Flat on our bellies, we endured several minutes of bombardment as steel splinters from the shells whined past our bodies."[16]

With their country collapsing, the South Vietnamese turned some of their anger against Americans still in their country. They were particularly bitter about the evacuation of orphans, including one organized by Richard J. Daly, the owner of World Airways, an Oakland-based charter airline. The crusty Daly had little time for official approval, using one of his DC-8 transport planes to ferry fifty-eight orphans from Saigon on one flight. "We got an airplane. We got crew members, doctors, nurses and the old bastard himself," Daly told a reporter. "That's all the clearance we need." While there were 25,000 orphans in institutions in South Vietnam, only about 1,500 to 2,000 were eligible to immigrate to the United States, Browne noted. Children had to be younger than nine years old and sponsored by one of the seven American-licensed organizations—Holt's Children's Services, International Social Services, Friends for All Children, Friends of the Children of Vietnam, Catholic Relief Services, the Pearl Buck Foundation, and World Vision. Most of the correspondents, Browne said, disliked what came to be known as the orphan lift, considering it "a cruel public relations stunt, causing more grief than happiness." One US Air Force flight ended in tragedy when a giant C-5A aircraft carrying more than two hundred orphans crashed, killing most of those aboard. "It is nice to see you Americans taking home souvenirs of our country as you leave—China elephants and orphans," a Vietnamese air force lieutenant bitterly remarked to Browne after the crash. "Too bad some of them broke today, but we have plenty more." Another Vietnamese told the newsman about the catastrophe: "It is awful, but somehow that crash of the orphan plane is symbolic of America's experience in Vietnam. It is your last hurrah."[17]

As North Vietnam's forces continued their advance, Thieu's government prohibited its citizens from leaving. Browne remembered that an expert on such matters informed him that it was harder for a South Vietnamese to leave the country, even in normal times, than "for an East German to leave the Communist bloc." US news organizations in South Vietnam, however, worked in secret to evacuate those of its Vietnamese employees who wanted to flee; the *Times* alone, he noted, had thirty it wanted to evacuated. They were able to leave thanks in part because of a "black airlift" run by the Central Intelligence Agency, through its airline, Air America. "The news community was just one of many beneficiaries; thousands of others, including Vietnamese military, police and government officials and their families were also taken to safety," Browne said. He remembered seeing the French owner of a Saigon bordello seated on a helicopter alongside an ARVN general. Deciding who should stay and who should leave tore some families apart, he noted, with some people sacrificing themselves to save their loved ones, while others, in panicked fear, decided to leave without their wives and children. In one example, Browne pointed to a Vietnamese named Thanh, who worked as a senior mechanic for the Northrup Corporation, the US company that made F-5 jet fighters. Thanh had a wife, four young children, and an elderly mother under his care. When the Americans at Northrup decided to leave, they offered to help Thanh get out, but only him. "Not my wife. Not my children. Not my mother. So what choice have I but to stay?" asked Thanh.[18]

Browne relied on Le Lieu, who joined him in Saigon, to counsel the refugees about the problems they might confront in the United States. He also worked closely with another reporter, H. D. S. "David" Greenway of the *Washington Post*, which had a neighboring office to the *Times*'s bureau, on what Greenway described as a "Scarlet Pimpernel operation" to smuggle those Vietnamese employees eligible to escape. While the US embassy turned a blind eye to the operation, the news organizations still had to worry about having police arrest those trying to leave from Saigon's Tan Son Nhut Air Base. "Several times a day he and I would don ties and jackets with airline tickets protruding prominently from our jacket pockets," Browne remembered. "Using our two cars, we would load up as many refugees as we could carry, drive them to the airport, and explain to the cops at the gate that some of our Vietnamese friends were seeing us off as we departed for America." Once they made it past the police, most of whom, he noted, were so downhearted about what was going on that they "weren't really doing their job very well anyway," they would go to the passenger terminal and then to the cafeteria for a drink. "Finally, when we had made certain that the airport MPs and civilian police were not watching us," he said, "we would lead our little flocks outside and sprint the last hundred yards to the entrance of Air America's sprawling compound." Eventually, the police caught on to the scheme and on one trip turned back Browne and Greenway's attempt to get out two male employees whose families had already been evacuated. "We shamelessly decided to play the colonial card," Greenway recalled. "We went back, dressed up in suits and ties, and sat in the backseat while one of our Vietnamese drove the car. Seeing a Vietnamese driving two Americans, especially dressed in suits in the backseat, seemed right and proper to the guards so they waved us through, never suspecting that it was the chauffeur who was about to board a plane for Clark Field in the Philippines." It worked, and they did it again for the second employee.[19]

News about the undercover evacuation leaked out, and many ordinary Vietnamese desperate for escape beseeched any American they came across for help, some promising large cash bribes and others going as far as offering to marry their benefactors. "Only a handful of places were available," said Browne, "so the Americans involved dissembled, comforted and lied." While spending hours at Tan Son Nhut, he observed every emotion imaginable, including "misery, fury, sacrifice, corruption, betrayal and selfless nobility." Wealthy Vietnamese military men and government officials offered huge bribes to get them on any list that got them out of the country. "There were Americans who were fraudulently advertising themselves as purveyors of these golden passports, in effect," Browne said, "who would sort of haunt Saigon airport or some of the downtown bus stations spotting senior Vietnamese officers that they knew would probably be wanting to get out and say, 'I can probably arrange something for you, but it's going to cost you.' That went on. The wretchedness of human behavior really came to the fore." Some took a bribe only to fail to come through as they had promised. Abandoned Vietnamese filled the airport's passenger terminal with the sound of their weeping.[20]

There were, however, those who displayed decency among the madness. Some Vietnamese holding valid documents guaranteeing their freedom decided, at the final moment, to "trade places with people they considered more worthy, thereby sacrificing their own chance for freedom," Browne said. He remembered that there were also several Americans, called "big noses" by the Vietnamese, who had lived and worked in the country years ago who came back to do what they could to help, somewhat lessening their own guilt. These people, who were now private citizens, went into debt to buy airline tickets to give to Vietnamese friends or relatives. "At least during those final hours at the gate outside the airport, trying to get my own people in, I maybe helped one woman," a fellow American told the newsman. "She was Vietnamese, with an American passport, but of course without a big nose no one was getting through on their own. I had to leave my own behind, but at least I got her through."[21]

Given Browne's previous troubles with American officials in Saigon, it seemed fated that he would find a way to embroil himself in another controversy as the war came to its chaotic conclusion. Trying to keep abreast of the military and political situation, Browne made sure to maintain connections with CIA station chief Thomas Polgar, who had been born in Hungary, and North Vietnamese and VC officers stationed in a liaison office at Tan Son Nhut as part of the 1973 peace accord. The Communist officers' regular press conferences were halted as the North Vietnamese neared Saigon, but they still accepted calls from newsmen. "Such contacts were often more informative than the nightly news broadcasts from Radio Hanoi," said Browne, who kept in regular touch with both Polgar and a VC press officer named Phuong Nam. Polgar, who Browne believed was the "best informed American left in town," told the reporter that the United States had three objectives remaining in Vietnam: to stop Saigon from being bombed and shelled, to ensure Americans could safely evacuate, and to arrange the formation of a transition government "to permit an orderly transfer of power." Browne said the press and the spies had a "temporary truce" in their longtime rivalry, sharing, instead of hiding, information from one another. "I visited or telephoned the Viet Cong often—sometimes two or three times an hour in the last couple of days," he recalled. "And I was in touch about as often with Polgar or one of his people. As one side told me something I would report it to the other to get its reaction, sending the whole exchange back to the *Times* as a news dispatch whenever something significant seemed to have happened." He did this with the "full knowledge of all concerned, including my employer." Although he noted that what he did at the time was "highly irregular," Browne said he would "do it again under similar circumstances." He also pointed out that the articles he wrote were all based on "first hand reporting that had nothing to do with anything told me by either the Viet Cong or CIA."[22]

Polgar had also been in touch with Hungarian and Polish diplomats from the International Commission of Control and Supervision, established by the 1973 peace accords to supervise the cease fire. "And the Hungarian Chief of Staff comes to me one day and says he has had conversations with the North Vietnamese and he got the impression that if we would do certain things, the Vietnamese Communists would be prepared to arrange a political solution—a kind of fig leaf for Communist control," said Polgar, who reported the conversation to Ambassador Martin and officials in Washington, DC. According to Polgar, Martin talked with Secretary of State Henry Kissinger. "But in fact the American government could not get itself organized to say in effect, 'Okay, we surrender, what are the terms?'" said Polgar, who described it as a "wasted opportunity."[23]

According to Martin, Polgar had been "sucked in by his fellow Hungarian. I didn't even know he was doing that." When Martin, who had been concerned that an early evacuation might lead to widespread panic, learned about Polgar using Browne as a go-between with the North Vietnamese delegation at Tan Son Nhut, he was livid. "I called him in and I told him that if I had any more trouble I'd cut his balls [off] and stuff one in each ear," Martin remembered. Frank Snepp, the CIA's chief strategy analyst in Saigon, believed that Polgar and Browne had both been duped by the North Vietnamese in believing a coalition government might be possible. "Hanoi could not have put together a more effective team of disinformation specialists if it had tried," noted Snepp, who believed such false hopes delayed the evacuation of at-risk Vietnamese allies. A bitter US official later complained to Butterfield: "We were sold a line and we were so anxious to save face that we were taken in." Browne had believed that the Americans, at the end, recognized South Vietnam's inevitable defeat and sought only that an "orderly transfer of power take place, avoiding a tank assault and allowing the Americans and as many of their Vietnamese friends as possible to get out safely." The North Vietnamese delegation he had been talking to, "if not exactly friendly," he noted, had been "making it clear that his side understood American signals and had no major objection." Browne was stunned, however, by a Radio Hanoi broadcast denouncing everything the South Vietnamese and Americans were doing "as mere treachery and calling for a 'general uprising' in Saigon," he said.[24]

On April 28 Browne could hear artillery fire less than a mile from his office. He and Butterfield were close to exhaustion. They had been working twenty hours a day "like automata," Browne remembered, dodging bullets, writing articles, and "trying to act human, all of it more by inertia than any remaining act of will." Realizing what might happen to Le Lieu even though she was a naturalized American citizen, he encouraged her to leave; two of her brothers and their families had already left, while two of her older brothers and her widowed mother decided to stay. She was able to obtain a seat on an Air Viet Nam 727 aircraft leaving for Hong Kong. At around noon Browne received a telephone call at his office from Le Lieu telling him that her flight had been delayed due to mechanical problems. He advised her to grab a taxi and return "before it was too late, since North Vietnamese tanks, I knew, were already moving into a former GI recreation compound on the outskirts of the city." Le Lieu passed the information to the airliner's crew; five minutes later, the flight was in the air. "The Vietnamese flight crew never even had time to say goodbye to the families they were leaving, some of them forever," Browne said.[25]

Le Lieu had escaped from the chaos just in time. The next morning, Butterfield reported that Saigon underwent one of the heaviest rocket attacks of the war. By 6:00 a.m. he had counted approximately 150 rockets hitting Tan Son Nhut and the South Vietnamese Joint General Staff headquarters adjoining the air base, he recalled. The attack killed two US Marines, Corporals Charles McMahon Jr. and Darwin Lee Judge, who became the last American ground casualties of the war. From his downtown office, Butterfield could see the rockets' "bright red flashes," as well as "long streams of tracer bullets" fired by the government's helicopter gunships. He tried to use the bureau's car to travel to the zoo to grab pictures of Vietnamese selling provisions—steak, beer, frozen orange juice, and Sara Lee cakes—supposedly looted from an American commissary. Unfortunately, Butterfield could not get the car to start.[26]

Waking in his room at the Caravelle Hotel, Browne could see that large parts of the city were aflame. Days before, US correspondents had been warned by embassy officials to listen to the radio for a weather report with a forecast of "one hundred five degrees and rising," followed, remembered Greenway, by a Bing Crosby recording of "White Christmas." The newsmen were then supposed to report to designated assembly points scattered throughout the city. At about 11:00 a.m., a CBS employee informed Butterfield that the embassy was "pulling the plug" and the evacuation was on. Browne and Butterfield wanted to stay in Saigon to report on the North Vietnamese takeover and the beginning of a new era in the country. *Times* publisher Arthur Ochs Sulzberger, however, ordered them to get out. "There was no 'I'm Dreaming of a White Christmas,' but the word was getting around anyway," Browne remembered. Earlier that morning he called to check on members of the North Vietnamese delegation, who had survived a shelling by their own side. "I cannot tell you how grateful we are for you asking, especially considering the circumstances," a Communist representative told the reporter. "We hope you all get through this somehow."[27]

The next few hours were a whirlwind for the *Times* reporters, including gathering what belongings they could carry. Bowne only had time to stuff into his backpack a few shirts, a suit, a tie, twelve pairs of red socks, and a souvenir penguin tie clip he had picked up while on a trip to McMurdo Station in the Antarctic. For protection, he donned a vintage World War II–era German helmet he had purchased at a New York war-surplus store and a flak jacket. The outfit reminded Butterfield what an iconoclast his colleague could sometimes be, attracting the attention of a French photographer, who stopped his car to snap a photo of Browne. The two *Times* reporters hustled from the hotel to their designated evacuation point to wait for a seat on a US Army bus. "The first, near the Saigon navy base, was empty," Butterfield remembered. "A second one on Gia Long Street was jammed with other correspondents. The door to the building and embassy housing complex was locked, so the anxious evacuees had to wait outside, attracting a huge crowd of Vietnamese, some of whom joined the Americans." The bus ride proved to be an adventure. Normally a fifteen- to twenty-minute trip, it took more than an hour for the driver, a private contractor who did not know his way around Saigon, to arrive at their destination, the Defense Attaché Office at Tan Son Nhut, Butterfield noted.[28]

As the evacuees got off their bus, they saw a South Vietnamese C-119 gunship take off from the base to hit targets near the city. "Just after we had taken our eyes off it there had been a loud explosion," he remembered. "Only a cloud of black smoke remained." An enemy missile had struck the aircraft, and it crashed near Cholon, the Chinese section of Saigon. With rockets continuing to hit the base, marine guards armed with M-16 rifles and mortars exchanged small-arms fire with the North Vietnamese. Guards moved the evacuees into the large DAO building, which, fortunately, had a reinforced roof. Several thousand people jammed into the building's long and winding corridors, including "nervous looking Vietnamese men, women and children, Vietnamese generals and their families, and embassy secretaries," wrote Butterfield. "Everywhere there were suitcases that their owners had abandoned when told that there would be no room for them aboard the helicopters." The reporters kept their spirits up by using black humor, with some claiming America had finally turned the corner in Vietnam. The joke most often repeated had someone asking their colleagues to make sure that the last man out of the country should turn out the light at the end of the tunnel.[29]

Divided into groups of fifty, the evacuees had to run about seventy-five yards ("it sure seemed longer," noted Butterfield) to the waiting Sikorsky CH-53 helicopters, their rotors whirling as they awaited their passengers. "The evacuees would leave the bunker and, to avoid the shelling and firing, they would run in sort of serpentine pattern out to where the helicopter was standing, run up the ramp on the rear deck and the helicopter would take off immediately, in some cases with firing from the rear machine gun and climb as fast as possible," Browne wrote. Because the evacuation helicopter's rear loading ramp remained open to provide a good field of fire for its machine gun, Browne had an excellent view of the city below as the craft turned to the southeast. Although he often hated what he described as "the evils of the place," he discovered that his "roots were deeper in Indochina than any other place in the world, and I was crying like a school boy when I said my last goodbyes."[30]

At about 4:15 p.m. the helicopter carrying Browne and Butterfield touched down on the *Mobile*'s stern flight deck; they were two of the approximately one thousand Americans and six thousand Vietnamese evacuated as part of Operation Frequent Wind. Upon exiting the helicopter, the newsmen were confronted by gun-toting marines and sailors, who seemed surprised to see the bedraggled journalists; they had expected to be confronting "mutinous South Vietnamese soldiers," Butterfield remembered. All those who boarded the ship, whether American or Vietnamese, he added, had to submit to "a rigorous screening process—two searches, a medical check-up and registration." Navy and marine corpsmen provided aid to those who had been injured in the evacuation, including children, hundreds of whom, Butterfield reported, suffered from boils, fevers, and seasickness. "A few soldiers and civilians had lacerations from rocket wounds at Tan Son Nhut," he said. "Some elderly Vietnamese collapsed from nervous exhaustion." To Butterfield, those refugees seeking medical attention for themselves or their family members represented, to him, another example of the "unreasoning faith that many Vietnamese still have in America. Despite the hatred and contempt that some Vietnamese have displayed toward all foreigners . . . many others have never lost faith in America's power to save them."[31]

Looking out to sea as the sun set, Browne described what he saw stretched out before him as looking like a "version of hell." As far as the eye could see, the ocean was filled with burning fishing boats. Vietnamese living along the coast had begged, borrowed, or stolen any vessel they could get their hands on to sail out to the American fleet. They burned their boats for two reasons, said Browne, including denying their use by the North Vietnamese and "as a gesture of faith" that they would be rescued by the Americans. "These fine wooden junks had cost a fortune, in some cases the savings of poor fishing families, now destitute, their life savings going up in flames," he noted. Browne also remembered that helicopters flown by South Vietnam Air Force pilots were appearing over the fleet at the rate of about one every minute. Butterfield remembered that the choppers "appeared on the horizon flying in like a flock of fireflies." He observed more than a dozen land on the USS *Midway*, an aircraft carrier, while others looked for a spot on any ship they could find to land on. Three landed on the *Mobile*, with all eventually heaved overboard because of a lack of space. "Each time one of these machines landed, a few seconds would elapse while its crew and passengers got out, and then the American sailors would heave the Huey overboard to make room for the next one," Browne noted. "We watched hundreds of millions of dollars' worth of choppers thrown into the South China Sea that evening, but we refugees were thinking mostly of the people we had left behind."[32]

Navy and marine cooks in white aprons fed rice and noodles mixed with chicken to the eight hundred Americans and Vietnamese who took shelter on the transport. "Some Navy men carried Vietnamese children around the decks on their shoulders, and the children played with the sailors' beards," added Butterfield. Chief Maurice Ring, who stayed up for two days to cook for the refugees, told the reporter he did not mind having to do the extra work. "What makes us angry is when the United States stands by and does nothing to keep our word," Ring said. "After Vietnam, who is going to believe us any more. First Vietnam, then it will be Israel, then the United States itself." After almost four days on the *Mobile*, Browne and Butterfield were among the journalists to climb aboard another helicopter to be transferred to the USS *Blue Ridge*, the command ship for the evacuation. One evening on the *Blue Ridge* they heard over the ship's loudspeakers the daily prayer: "Dear Father, you have safely brought us through another trying and frustrating week. Forgive us when we complain about our troubles."[33]

Browne missed witnessing North Vietnamese tanks crashing through the gates of Saigon's Independence Palace on April 30. Walking down a Saigon Street that morning, Peter Arnett of the Associated Press came across a convoy of Russian-made Molotova trucks crammed with North Vietnamese soldiers. "A few local Vietnamese are standing near me," Arnett recalled. "They are staring, speechless." Arnett ran to his office, burst through the door, and shouted to bureau chief George Esper: "George. Saigon has fallen. Call New York." Checking his watch, Arnett marked the time as 11:43 a.m. As for Browne, he did not learn that the war had finally ended in a Communist victory until arriving with some other evacuees in Manila. It took him years, he admitted, to "come to terms with the trauma those last days of the war left me," and he preferred to forget what had happened during that "cruel April."[34]

Trying to make sense of South Vietnam's defeat, Browne sought answers from a variety of sources during the final days in 1975 as the North Vietnamese routed their opponents. It seemed as if everyone had a different opinion. Many Vietnamese, including former president Thieu, believed the blame should fall directly upon the United States and its failure to send critical military aid while the Russians and Chinese continued to supply North Vietnam. Browne noted that many believed the fatal flaw of Saigon's army was its dependence upon "military luxury—an appetite for which the United States must bear special responsibility." He recalled accompanying a government battalion raiding a Viet Cong stronghold in 1962 and stumbling upon an arms factory that made casings for grenades from "scrap aluminum, shotgun cartridges made of brass tubing and of French coins with holes in the centers accommodating percussion caps, and serviceable 60-mm. mortars designed to fire captured ammunition." Even then, the VC's crude weapons made life difficult for South Vietnamese soldiers equipped with "American rifles and carbines, howitzers, landing craft and communications equipment and had cover from fighter-bombers," Browne noted. Attitude also made a difference, as Browne learned from an ARVN officer, who asked him to consider what happened when an army had been given the means to travel into battle via helicopters or on roads with unlimited artillery and air support, and had gotten used to sleeping in their beds at night. "I will tell you what happens," the officer told the reporter. "At a certain point neither the troops nor the officers are willing any longer to walk to battle, hacking their way through jungles if necessary. So they stay in their helicopters and get shot down or cut off from American rescue, or they drive along the road, where they get shelled or ambushed, and cut to pieces. Every officer knows this, but our army has become flabby and lazy over the years, and we owe some of that to the kind of luxury aid you gave us."[35]

Although it became the fashion at the war's end to blame the United States for all that had gone wrong, Browne did point out that there were large numbers of Americans who had given their all for a country far from home with "dedication, courage and insight, to a degree most Americans at home will never fully realize." Before Saigon fell, a Vietnamese veteran of the fighting told an American he knew that both nationalities had known what had gone wrong but, considering everything that happened, "both our peoples remained blind, and even now we seem to have learned nothing. Well, it no longer matters."[36]

Browne believed that the main reason the United States eventually extricated itself from the conflict came from Americans becoming bored. "It seemed to be going on forever and ever. It was the longest war we ever fought," he said. "Nothing much was ever happening. There was no front line, no storming of San Juan Hill, no storming of Pork Chop Ridge, or any of the other battles in American history. It was just a grinding, grinding, grinding thing that killed a trickle, an appreciable trickle, of Americans every year without ever going anywhere." He also pointed out that taxes were rising, as was inflation, causing many to change their minds about the Vietnam War. "It had nothing to do with the work that I did or my colleagues did," Browne believed. If what they wrote was going to influence the war, it should have occurred during this country's early days of involvement, he reasoned, when there were still decisions to be made on just how deeply the United States should be involved, or whether, as some politicians advised, "to declare we've won and pull out." There were many critics who remembered the reporters who covered the war as "traitors to the United States, which we certainly were not," said Browne. Instead, he and other journalists were "believers with Tom Paine and other citizens that the truth was more important than being on the team. It's as simple as that."[37]

Epilogue

"MY GOD, WE'RE GOING to die and I must pray!"

The Saudi taxi driver floored the accelerator and started chanting in Arabic as air-raid sirens wailed to mark the appearance of Iraqi Scud-B missiles, looking like "fireballs from Roman candles," streaking over Dhahran, Saudi Arabia. The taxi careened past a half-dozen wrecked cars, including a police vehicle, on its way to deliver its passenger, Malcolm Browne of the *New York Times*, to an air-raid shelter at the Dhahran International Hotel. Arriving at the hotel, Browne discovered that its lobby, one of the few places open during such raids, was jammed with Saudis, "some wearing gas masks but most huddling in corners with their red and white head cloths tied over their noses and mouths" to ward off an expected poison-gas attack. The threat of Scuds armed with gas warheads alarmed everyone. "You can kill me with a knife or gun or bomb, and I won't care, but I don't want to die of gas," a Saudi soldier, his voice muted by a bulky respirator, told the reporter.[1]

Although Browne was close to turning sixty at the time, his employer had sent the veteran war correspondent to the Persian Gulf in the winter of 1991. President George H. W. Bush had assembled an international coalition of approximately forty countries to face off against Iraqi forces, who had invaded and taken over the oil-rich nation of Kuwait in August 1990. The rules imposed by US military authorities made the Gulf War "more difficult to cover" than anything Browne had experienced before, except for the Indian-Pakistan conflict in 1971. During the month he spent in Saudi Arabia, he could not escape the feeling that the military had learned all the wrong lessons from its 1983 invasion of Grenada, a smashing triumph for American troops, all without the bothersome presence of civilian journalists. "It was impossible to altogether bar the Persian Gulf to the thousands of correspondents from many countries who poured in," Browne noted, "but by confining newsmen to officially licensed tour groups called pools, the U.S. commanders achieved much the same thing." Defense Department officials also seemed fixated on avoiding the mistakes with the press they believed had contributed to the country's ignominious defeat in Vietnam. Browne believed that an "anti-press cant" had been prevalent in American military journals and pronouncements since the war in Southeast Asia ended. Influential military officials, he said, had "implied a causal relationship between two facts: that reporters were barred from on-the-ground coverage of the Grenada war in October 1983, and that Grenada has been America's only unequivocal military victory since World War II."[2]

Browne's return to the battlefield had come after some soul searching about his journalism career. He and his wife, Le Lieu, had returned to the United States in 1977 after their many years wandering the globe for the *Times*. During a home leave before returning from Eastern Europe, the couple bought a house in Ascutney, Vermont; they later moved to Thetford, Vermont. Browne decided to pursue a different kind of writing—one that consumed him for the next twenty-two years. "After a time, a news writer may begin to sense a kind of sameness in most of the events that pass as news," he observed. "When that happens a lucky few of us discover that in science, almost alone among human endeavors, there is always something new under the sun." The transition from his previous post to life as a *Times* science writer nearly overwhelmed him, as he had forgotten just how fast the discipline could change. As an example, Browne pointed out that over a twenty-five-year period the American Chemical Society "added more than 10 million chemical substances to its list of known molecules, most of them man-made." He also learned that the material he had to use for his stories about important discoveries often was based on cryptic news releases from universities, a brief telephone message from a scientist, or hard-to-decipher papers in professional journals. "It is up to the science writer to judge the significance of the findings and place them in context," Browne noted. "This means that a science writer must be a perpetual student. . . . Practice may not make perfect, but a science writer who stays in the game long enough is bound to get better."[3]

During the years he spent writing about science for the *Times*, Browne heard from readers who he thought shared his tastes for "a certain amount of quiet reflection." These readers included older people with the "time and freedom to wonder about things as they approach the ultimate reality of death," as well as students for whom the ideas of science were like "enchanted toys, sparkling like diamonds." He also had fans among American house-wives, weary of the "drab concerns of the economy and daily existence in a seemingly lusterless world offering no escape." All these people did not nec-essarily have the tools needed to comprehend such complicated scientific concepts as quantum mechanics and molecular biology, but they were, Browne was convinced, hungry for something much more important, what he called "the poetry of science." After all, he noted, science came as the result of acts of creation "as inspired in their way as a Picasso painting, a Blake sonnet, a Vivaldi concerto. The impulse behind science itself, as I think every scientist would agree, is essentially aesthetic." As important as the fruits of science are to doctors, soldiers, engineers, and other professions, they offered something even more imperative to humankind, Browne said. In a world in which religious faith had begun to erode, science could help people "come to terms with the terror of our own mortality. . . . We can come to understand that we are not alone in the universe but part of it, and that understanding can bring peace, inner reconciliation and even a subtle but intense satisfaction."[4]

Writing about science for the *Times* gave him "more satisfaction" than most of the work he had ever done, but Browne, in the spring of 1981, left the newspaper. He took a job as a senior editor for a new monthly science magazine, *Discover*, created by *Time* magazine's parent company. "We want to get readers interested in science and we want them to read the maga-zine from cover to cover," said *Discover*'s managing editor Leon Jaroff. He added that he strove to publish articles containing about four thousand words because "your average intelligent reader stops reading after a while if the articles are too long, if there is too much detail, or if they contain too much jargon." Browne thought long and hard about making the change, but Jaroff convinced him that he would play a key role in "shaping a trail-blazing magazine." Jaroff also initially seemed confident enough about their relationship to suggest that Browne had a good chance of succeeding him as the magazine's managing editor. Browne remembered that he took up his new position, with an office on the fifteenth floor of the Time-Life Building at Rockefeller Center in New York City, bursting with "ideas for stories, projects, covers and more."[5]

Over the next three years, Browne struggled in his new editorial role. After only a few months, he related to a friend that he had mixed feelings about his job. Editing the efforts of a staff of "semiliterate PhDs can be galling sometimes," Browne admitted, "and the long nights are often pure drudgery." He proved to be clear-eyed about some of his shortcomings as an editor, including alienating the magazine's writers by revising their copy too much, possessing too authoritarian a tone when interacting with them, and failing to "challenge unsupported assertions and . . . insist on sharpness of detail." Not surprisingly, he often rewrote passages in "short, choppy paragraphs or sentences, more suggestive of 'newspaper style' than magazines." He pointed out that he had a quarter-century of experience in a different publishing tradition in which there was "very little tolerance for unacceptable copy, and from which the majority of writers are swiftly forced out into public relations jobs or second- or third-rate news organizations."[6]

Browne spent more and more time at the office, sometimes working sixteen hours a day to mold a young staff into decent writers, a process he called "fun but demanding." Le Lieu recalled that one afternoon while working at her job at the International Rescue Committee helping refugees, she received a call from her husband from the emergency room, where he had been taken after experiencing heart palpitations. "I rushed to the hospital, but it was a false alarm," she noted. "He told me that he had felt faint, and the Discover manager had called the ambulance. He had never had a hint of any such symptom before." Le Lieu believed that during his time at the magazine her husband must have been "very unhappy and disappointed." He never shared with her, however, "all he had endured during his time there. I only caught some hints of disagreements with his superior. I naively took it as natural that such a job required a lot of responsibility and determination."[7]

Working at *Discover* finally became "more drudgery than fun" for Browne. Ideas that he thought were exciting were too often ignored in favor of those "perceived as safe, and in the process, something nasty was happening to the staff: survival was becoming more important than excellence." Office politics sapped his creative energy, something Browne believed had also been the case for many of the magazine's staff. He was appalled at *Discover's* dramatic attrition rate. When he compared a staff list with one from twelve months earlier, Browne noticed that *Discover* had lost nearly 50 percent of its people in just one year. Although starting to hunt for a new livelihood in his fifties scared him, in March 1984 he took a six-month leave of absence, after which he decided not to return to his job. Browne spent his leave at his Vermont house, where he worked on a novel. When Le Lieu joined him that summer, he "looked happy and healthy." As he pointed out to a friend, creating "Noble Fiction" proved to be a difficult task, and he was never sure "whether it will turn out as hoped, but what the hell, we're only middleaged once." Browne's attempt at a novel, however, failed to attract a publisher. He asked to return to the *Times*, which first offered him a job as its Pentagon correspondent but finally negotiated his return to the Science Department, rejoining the staff on March 28, 1985. As he later noted, being on the science beat allowed him the freedom to do more than just visit offices and laboratories. "Although science is chiefly about universal realities," Browne noted, "the handmaiden of science, applied to technology, encompasses poison gas, smart bombs, stealth fighters and germ warfare, so that there's always use for a science writer on the battlefield."[8]

The *Times* made sure to draw upon Browne's expertise when it came to reporting from a war zone. Shortly before the United Nations deadline of January 15, 1991, for Iraq's forces to withdraw from Kuwait, Browne arrived in Saudi Arabia to join the approximately 1,200 correspondents and technicians covering Operation Desert Shield, the buildup of Allied troops in the Persian Gulf. He described the newsmen working in Dhahran and

Riyadh, Saudi Arabia, as "by far the largest concentration of journalists assembled to cover any American conflict since World War II." Browne became one of the lucky few reporters (initially only 130; later raised to 192) to be part of the official pool system, whereby representatives from wire services, newspapers, magazines, television, and radio were assigned to ground, air, naval, and rapid-reaction units. All media members covering units in the field had to be escorted by a public affairs officer, who was present for all interviews. Reporters' dispatches, videos, and photographs were available to all the media organizations accredited by the military. "In effect, each pool member is an unpaid employee of the Department of Defense," reflected Browne, "on whose behalf he or she prepares the news of the war for the outer world." Some of the journalists began to "feel more like draftees than civilians," he recalled. Assistant Secretary of Defense Pete Williams announced that news media not part of the official pools would be banned from forward areas and US military commanders would "maintain extremely tight security throughout the operational area and will exclude from the area of operations all unauthorized individuals." Browne said he had never witnessed such an attempt at controlling the press. He pointed out that in Vietnam, military authorities often concealed information "for reasons other than security, but correspondents were free to move about Vietnam, Laos and Cambodia in private cars, commercial and chartered aircraft, and even by train. More than 40 correspondents were killed, but they succeeded in covering most of the major military developments fully."[9]

Browne had to fill out a detailed questionnaire asking for his blood type, religion ("important to the Saudis"), and his next of kin. He also had to sign a two-page agreement promising not to reveal military secrets and to submit everything he reported for a "security review." While the agreement tried to reassure reporters that any "material will be examined solely for its conformance to the attached ground rules, not for its potential to express criticism or cause embarrassment," Browne had his doubts. Officials photographed and fingerprinted him and issued "a Saudi press badge, a Geneva convention card identifying me as a noncombatant accompanying United States forces and a steel dog tag embossed with the kind of information . . . useful to medics and graves-registration teams." Unlike his early days in Vietnam, when he had to prowl the black market to outfit himself for combat, Browne noted that the US military provided him with everything he needed, including a field jacket and pants, a sleeping bag, a canteen with a chemical-warfare cap, a durable backpack, a gas mask with antidotes for nerve gas, and a chemical warfare suit with boots, goggles, and a helmet.[10]

Being outfitted for the coming fray caused Browne's blood to stir with the "heady prospect" of once again being near the front lines. "Recidivist war correspondents have difficulty explaining the thrill of anticipation of combat," he mused. "We scarcely understand the feeling ourselves, or why it is that we are so powerfully drawn to combat, even against the revulsion most of us feel for the sights, sounds and smells of death." His zeal lessened, however, when he and other journalists assigned to his pool were taken by bus to an auditorium. While there, a US Air Force "operational commander" gave a briefing. Before his talk, he informed the newsmen he wanted to let them know where they stood with each other. "Let me say up front that I don't like the press," the officer said. "Your presence here can't possibly do me any good, and it can hurt me and my people." Despite his unfriendly beginning, the commander went on to give what Browne, always a fan of aircraft, called "one of the most lucid and informative briefings on fighter tactics" he had ever heard. He wondered if the officer's frostiness might have been a way to establish his credentials as a "bluff but honest leader of men, rather than as a Pentagon publicity seeker."[11]

In the years since he had reported from Vietnam, Browne noticed numerous changes in the methods by which his profession communicated from the field. Once used to waiting for hours to use a staticky radio phone line or bribing an official to use a slow telex machine, he viewed the technology available to him in 1991 as "simply amazing." For example, reporters from the *Times* had in their hotel room in Dhahran a dish antenna a little larger than a toilet seat and a Honda generator in case the power went out. "It would have been just great," he remembered, "except that we all were under the thumb of US censors, so nifty communications were largely canceled out." He ended up writing his dispatches on a typewriter not much different than those used by reporters in World War II. It might have been for the best. As Browne noted, electronic emissions from a dish antenna could attract the deadly attention of air-to-surface high-speed antiradiation missiles, if any were in the area.[12]

On January 17, with Iraqi troops still in Kuwait, coalition forces launched Operation Desert Storm, an air campaign against targets in Iraq, including its capital, Baghdad. For the opening of the air war, Browne was assigned by the US Armed Forces Joint Information Bureau to a desert air base from which F-117A Nighthawk stealth fighters from the Thirty-Seventh Tactical Fighter Wing operated. Two squadrons from the unit flew thirty sorties against sixty Iraqi targets. The wing's commander, Colonel Alton C. Whitley, showed Browne and other reporters, including Frank Bruni of the *Detroit Free Press*, videotapes in which the F-117A's had hit underground bunkers, command stations, microwave communication links, and other "high-value" sites. "The opening shot of the war against Iraq was a 2,000-pound laser-guided bomb dropped into the AT&T Building in Baghdad near the bank of the Tigris River," Browne reported. "The tape showed the bomb hitting the building squarely in the center, probably demolishing its communications nerve centers." The Stealth fighters also attacked one of the "presidential facilities" supposed to be used by Saddam Hussein. "The video tape shows the bomb flying right into a rooftop skylight and demolishing the structure," Browne wrote. Returning from their missions, pilots at the base talked to the *Times* newsman about the stress they felt flying in combat: "Your heart beats faster, your mouth goes dry, and when you depart the target area you take a big gulp from your water bottle. Of course, you still have to find the refueling tanker on the way home, but the hardest part is over."[13]

As per regulations, a US Army public information officer had cleared articles from Browne and Bruni and sent them on for transmission to pool headquarters in Dhahran. Three hours later, however, Colonel Whitley had second thoughts about the stories, changing some words and deleting others. "None of them appear to have anything to do with security," Browne noted. "In Frank's copy, the adjective 'giddy' used to describe the pilots, has been changed to 'proud,' and in my story, the words 'fighter-bomber' have been changed to 'fighter.'" Browne guessed that the air force had changed his description to fighter because it had been waging a battle with Congressional critics about its B-2 Stealth Bomber and feared they might use such a description to scuttle the program. To meet their deadlines, both reporters agreed to the proposed changes if their copy was transmitted to pool headquarters via a fax machine. "This proves a forlorn hope," Browne noted. He learned the next day that their stories had instead been sent to the home base of the Stealth fighters, the Tonopah Test Range in Nevada, "where everything we wrote has been deemed a breach of security." The pieces were finally cleared by the military twenty-four hours after they were written, making their "perishable" news "hopelessly stale," he said. Browne considered it quite an irony because the dispatches portrayed the missions as brilliant successes.[14]

The F-117A pilots trusted Browne and the other journalists enough to let them know that they had destroyed Iraqi sites believed to have been involved in producing nuclear weapons—a matter of grave concern for the Bush administration. The excited newsmen sought permission to report on the successful missions, which Browne believed would be page-one news, but military authorities asked them to withhold from writing about it due to security concerns, as future attacks against the facilities might be needed. The correspondents reluctantly agreed, but, less than twelve hours later, were chagrined to learn that Agence France-Presse, the French press agency, had distributed a story about the raids based on a tip from the staff of a US senator, who also informed reporters in Washington, DC, about the mission. Later, General Norman Schwarzkopf Jr., commander of US Central Command, gave an official briefing to the newsmen in Saudi Arabia. "As members of the pool, we wondered why we have bothered even to visit the F-117A base," Browne recalled, as they could have saved both time and a great deal of trouble by simply attending the briefings. He did not blame the foul-up on Colonel Bill Mulvey, who commanded the Joint Information Bureau in Dhahran and did "a heroic job in an unenviable position, caught between a patently unworkable system and the daily complaints of the frustrated newsmen he tries to help."[15]

As a print journalist, Browne faced another frustration during the conflict. He had to deal, as he had never had before, with the "overwhelming prestige" television enjoyed, especially the powerful live coverage provided from Baghdad by CNN reporters Bernard Shaw, John Holliman, and Browne's former Associated Press colleague Peter Arnett. "These reports rivet the attention of American servicemen," Browne remembered. The ground crews at the airbase he visited eagerly watched the CNN reports. Field commanders appeared to be bending the rules for television crews, Browne noted, and treated print reporters "as also-rans." Censorship guidelines also worked against print journalists, who had to submit type-written texts of their dispatches to field information officers and commanders for a security review, while television and radio reporters "could broadcast live without prepared texts, permitting them greater latitude," said Browne.[16]

Upon his return to the United States in early February, Browne, invited by Senators John Glenn and Herb Kohl, was one of the journalists who testified at a February 20 hearing held by the Senate Governmental Affairs Committee on "Pentagon Rules Governing Press Access to the Persian Gulf War." Browne expressed his concerns about the pool system as well as the lack of direct access to American soldiers and to front-line areas. Newsmen, he pointed out, wanted to spend time with soldiers and marines, not to "spy on American military intentions, but to see how the troops are getting on in difficult circumstances. Today's correspondents identify ourselves with the soldiers of our generation as strongly as Ernie Pyle did with the soldiers of his." Browne's testimony, combined with articles he wrote and television appearances he made repeating his complaints, unleashed on him what he called "an avalanche of angry letters" that accused him and other journalists of undermining both the security and morale of soldiers in the field. One letter went as far as to describe the press as "not only anti-American but pro-Communist," and suggested that the "so-called Fourth Estate should more properly be called the Fifth Column." Browne believed it was probably futile for him to remind those who wrote such angry letters that democracy itself depended "on a free people informed by honest journalists." It dawned on him, Browne recalled, that honest reporting was "the last thing most people want when the subject is war." And while Benjamin Franklin had observed that "there never was a good war or a bad peace," his experience taught Browne that in the eyes of many people, "there may never have been a bad war. War is thundering good theater, in which cheering the home team is half the fun."[17]

Feeling that he might be nearing the end of his journalism career, and

perhaps his life, Browne decided it might be nice to capture "so much of
the contemporary history" he had been privileged to observe. With the
encouragement of a colleague, Peter Osnos, whom he had known since
meeting him in Saigon in 1972 (Osnos had moved on from journalism to an
editorship at Random House, serving as publisher of its Times Book
imprint), Browne set out to write his memoirs. "He [Osnos] encouraged me
to undertake it and suggested that when I wrote it that I keep my grandchildren in mind, which is exactly what I did." Osnos had published several
books about Vietnam and was delighted with his experience with Browne,
someone he described as always marching to the beat of his own, an attri-
bute that made him a "first-rate" correspondent. "He was a professional,
he wrote the book, we published it, no melodrama," recalled Osnos. Upon
receiving Browne's approximately six hundred–page manuscript—originally titled "Wandering Minstrel"—in October 1992, Osnos praised his
author for presenting his life "in an appealing, open voice that keeps the
reader engaged and provides a lot of information along the way."[18]

Published in 1993, *Muddy Boots and Red Socks: A Reporter's Life*, Browne's
book, which he dedicated "To the dear dead whose sparks lighted my life,"
had its title inspired by his time in Vietnam, where, he noted, there were
"two kinds of observers: Those who heard about the war from others and
those with muddy boots. I preferred the latter category." The title had also
been drawn from his life as a soldier in the 1950s, a period when he had
come to "loath olive drab" and had purchased at an army post exchange
several pairs of red socks. "I've worn red socks ever since," he recalled,
"which assures me of a match even when one disappears. And I still like
red." Browne found parts of the book hard to write, because he put on
paper things he had never told anyone before, especially his feelings about
the fall of Saigon. "It's like going to a father confessor or to a psychoana-
lyst, I suppose," he said.[19]

Although always aware of his profession's shortcomings, Browne
defended journalism from its detractors who often, throughout history,
viewed reporters as eager to damage good people's reputations. In his
experience, however, he discovered that the longer an honest reporter
plied his trade, he became more "adept at observation and shrewd judgment, if only in the sense that a mature burglar finds it second nature to

crack a safe as easily as a bread box." Browne conceded that if journalists seemed less willing than most people to revere such symbols as "flags, yellow ribbons, medals, hymns, wealth, motherhood, prizes, titles," it did not mean they respected nothing. "More than most people," Browne pointed out, "we admire honesty and courage, because we know how rare those qualities are." He called upon the public to give reporters some understanding, as their reflections, "however flawed and filtered, are the stuff of history: the archival mother lode that scholars mine when they cannot witness the show themselves—which, by the way, is usually the case." At its most basic, his profession would always be shaped by the perspective of the person doing the reporting. "At root, journalism is subjective—never objective—and the best we practitioners can do is to try to be fair," Browne reasoned.[20]

Muddy Boots and Red Socks received positive reviews from fellow journalists, including CBS anchor Dan Rather, who despite dinging Browne for taking some "heavy-handed shots at what he sees as the shortcomings of network television news," called the book "superb." The memoir also attracted a glowing review from Vietnam veteran Larry Heinemann, who after his service returned home and became an acclaimed novelist (his book *Paco's Story* received a National Book Award in 1987). An ordinary soldier with the Twenty-Fifth Infantry Division, Heinemann praised Browne and the other "young Turks of the Saigon press corps" for doing their jobs and telling the public honestly about what they observed in Vietnam. He admired Browne for spending his life in a "line of work that will always take a beating when the news is bad," wrote Heinemann. Describing the reporter as both "canny and candid," Heinemann noted that Browne did his "damnedest to tell us 'what the weather was.' And for all that, as one grunt to another, Mr. Browne, thanks."[21]

In early 1994 and accompanied by Le Lieu, Browne returned to a country for which he had shed many tears—Vietnam, now unified and under the control of the Communist Party of Vietnam. President Bill Clinton had recently lifted the US trade embargo and Browne visited the first American trade fair in Vietnam since the war ended in 1975, Vietnamerica Expo '94. "Among the exchanges at the four-day fair: Vietnamese visitors learned how to withdraw fake money from American cash machines, and

American entrepreneurs learned that Vietnamese are not fond of potato chips," Browne reported. While in the country, Browne also wrote about a US Army veteran of the war, Sergeant First Class John Foggin, who had decided to make his home and run a business among his former enemies in a remote hamlet in the Mekong Delta; uncovered how unexploded ordnance from an old battlefield, Khe Sanh, continued to claim Vietnamese victims; and reported on the efforts by Americans and Vietnamese to find those servicemen still listed as missing-in-action. "The campaign by American investigators to account for every missing American remains as determined as it was in September, 1988," wrote Browne, "when the Vietnamese government first allowed United States teams to look for Americans who disappeared in Vietnam during the war." In April 1994 alone, a task force that included ninety-one forensic anthropologists, medical technicians, graves-registration experts, and other technicians investigated sixty-two cases at seventeen sites in eighteen provinces. "They will use earth-moving equipment, jack hammers, aircraft and any other implements needed for the job, which they know will be difficult," he wrote.[22]

In both Hanoi and Ho Chi Minh City, the name the victors had given to the former Saigon, Browne saw Vietnamese who washed down their slices of pizza with sips of Coke, paid for their purchase with American dollars, and wore jackets with US flag patches. Behind the friendliness, however, he remembered that the country still raised triumphant banners proclaiming the Communist victory over the Americans. "Beneath an outwardly friendly curiosity many Vietnamese display toward Americans," Browne said, "a predatory undertone tinged with bitter resentment is often detectable." While some resented that it took the US government nineteen years to lift its trade embargo, Vietnamese leaders sought American investment and tourists and were reaching out to those who had fled the country, known as Viet Kieu, to "return to their native land and help rebuild it."[23]

To mark the anniversary of Saigon's surrender, Browne received an invitation to visit the home of General Vo Nguyen Giap, the successful commander of Communist forces against the French and the Americans. The eighty-three-year-old Giap proved to be magnanimous, refusing, Browne remembered, to gloat about his triumphs. "We certainly have no fight with the American people," said Giap, who conducted the interview in French, "and we welcome peaceful contacts with your country." Browne could not help but point out that while the Communists had erected a monument marking the 1964 Christmas Eve bombing by Viet Cong guerrillas of the Brink Hotel, a billet for US Army officers, there was no marker at the floating My Can Restaurant in Ho Chi Minh City, though "many Americans remember it as the place where Vietcong bombs set off in June 1965 killed 44 diners, including 12 Americans." Among the dead had been Sergeant Al Combs, a Special Forces soldier and Browne's friend, as well as Combs's wife and children.[24]

Despite the government's movement to a market-oriented economy, and its release of several political prisoners, Vietnamese, Browne pointed out, still feared midnight knocks on their doors from government agents. An unlucky suspect could face a year in jail before even going to trial. "Political trials, which are closed to foreign observers, still result in long prison sentences for such vaguely defined crimes as 'counterrevolutionary propaganda,'" Browne reported. "Prudent citizens choose their words carefully, even in casual conversation." The owner of a leather-goods store in the city, which many still referred to as Saigon, told him that two of his brothers had killed themselves rather than face being again sent to a "re-education camp" or a "new economic zone," the country's "equivalent of Siberian gulags." Responding to criticism from human-rights organizations, Le Mai, the deputy foreign minister for American affairs, told Browne in an interview that foreigners who came to his country to "press their ideas about human rights on Vietnam are not welcome."[25]

As they had when Browne reported from South Vietnam in 1963, the Buddhists challenged the government's authority with self-sacrifice and fire. In May 1993 a man entered Hue's Linh Mu Pagoda and set himself on fire, perishing from the flames. Police attempted to arrest the pagoda's chief monk, Thich Trii Tuu, but the move sparked large-scale antigovernment demonstrations, Browne noted. Visiting several monks he knew who had been active during the 1963 Buddhist uprising, he learned they still feared being arrested. "Because I have known you for three decades," one of the monks told Browne, "I couldn't turn you away, but please don't mention that you have seen me. The police watch this pagoda all the time. Monks from Hue and Vung Tau are in prison now, and many others could be arrested tomorrow, even though we have done nothing. You can't help any of us, except by remaining silent." One Vietnamese from the southern part of the country said the only way his nation could heal its wounds would be by time. "The old guard, both persecutors and their victims, are dying off or growing senile," he told the newsman. "Little by little, Vietnam is rejoining the world, and our children or grandchildren will know better times."[26]

Browne retired from the *Times* on February 28, 2000, already feeling the effects of the Parkinson's disease that would lead to his death twelve years later at age eighty-one on August 27, 2012. The disease proved to be a "morale buster," as it made it difficult for Browne to "keep track of my reality." It also confined him to a wheelchair during the last years of his life. Entire sentences, as well as words, he noted, were transposed, resulting in "gobbledy-gook. I'm conscious of getting myself into sentences with no exit." He could console himself, however, with the memories of the places he had visited during his long journalism career. Especially soothing were those of a region where he, never a religious person, could recharge his "spiritual batteries," Antarctica. He made five trips to a continent he described as "beautiful but unmerciful," all under the auspices of the National Science Foundation, including visits to McMurdo Station on the south tip of Ross Island and Palmer Station on Anvers Island. While some visitors could never get used to the region's strange environment of six months of daylight and six months of darkness, hurricane-strength winds, bitter-cold temperatures, and endless desolation, Browne came to appreciate Antarctica's unique attractions. "To me, Antarctica is a luminous cathedral—a special gift to all of us that deepens the perspective of its pilgrims even while threatening them with death," he said, calling his time there the high point of his travels as a foreign correspondent. Browne even began to judge a region based on the number of people and the number of penguins it possessed. "The fewer people and the more penguins, the better it is," he concluded.[27]

From his first visit in 1974, when he had been one of only seven reporters allowed to travel there from a hundred who had applied, Browne was entranced by the continent's towering blue, white, and green icebergs; its massive penguin rookeries; and, during the winter, when the continent was shrouded in perpetual darkness, its glittering aurora australis. "It's like living at the edge of outer space, at the fringes of human civilization, where the only things that seem to matter to most people are the science and the beauty of the place," he said. "I love it." Antarctica's attraction as an enchanted land for adventure and discovery had always been tempered for Browne by the real dangers involved trying to survive in its hostile environment. The subfreezing cold and dry air preserved snapshots of the continent's history, including the Ross Island huts used by such intrepid explorers as Captain Robert Falcon Scott of the Royal Navy and Ernest Shackleton. At Scott's Cape Evans hut, Browne remembered seeing "hay in the pony stable, frozen seal meat in the storage room, piles of clothing strewn around, letters and magazines showing no signs of age, and many shelves of canned food."[28]

Scott and his men reached the South Pole on January 17, 1912, only to find that Norwegian explorer Roald Amundsen had preceded their achievement by a month. All the expedition members died on their return journey. Browne, too, lost friends to the extreme elements. In 1991 he had spent time aboard the *Erebus*, a French ship ferrying supplies and scientists between Punta Arenas, Chile, and Palmer Station. He got to know the vessel's first mate, Mark Eichenberger, a thirty-eight-year-old American sailor and adventurer. Eichenberger had achieved some fame when he and some friends paddled a modified rowboat across the Drake Passage for six hundred miles. Shortly after Browne met Eichenberger, however, a sudden storm swept him off the *Erebus*. "His body was never found," Browne recalled. Six years later, the newsman lost another friend, Bruno Zehnder, a Swiss photographer known for "his eagerness to take on any danger for the sake of a good picture." Zehnder had arranged to spend a few months at Russia's Mirnyy Station, located on the Antarctica coast along the Indian Ocean. Zehnder had gone on a trek to photograph subjects near the station when a violent storm hit with so much force that visibility was severely limited. "Bruno did not return," remembered Browne, "and when the storm finally abated, the Russians started searching. They found his frozen body less than 100 yards from the station."[29]

Several ghosts haunted Antarctica. They were constant presences at McMurdo, as many of the buildings and sites near it were named to honor those killed in accidents, Browne noted. Visitors transgressed rules at their own peril. Hikers and cross-country skiers could follow a safe route to a landmark known as Castle Rock, a rocky peak about eight miles from the station. A group of skiers on one occasion disregarded the official trail route; two of them died at the bottom of a crevasse. Browne believed that most of those who perished in Antarctica would have "preferred to die as they did rather than, say, ill or in a nursing home. Even in death, some people are luckier than others."[30]

Acknowledgments

A ringing telephone woke Malcolm W. Browne at 2:30 in the morning on September 18, 1964. He stumbled across his apartment, located above his Associated Press office in Saigon, South Vietnam, to answer the call. A police source told the AP's bureau chief that there had been a fight at the docks involving Americans and he might want to visit the scene.

Browne quickly dressed and drove to the docks in the office's Land Rover, painted bright red with white signs in Vietnamese and English reading "Bao Chi," identifying it as belonging to a member of the press. Once there, he learned that four seamen from Guam had been in a fight with some South Vietnamese Rangers and police; a sailor had been wounded in the throat but had survived. Browne returned to his office, wrote his story, and took it to the telecommunications center to send it to the AP office in Tokyo, Japan, for distribution to member newspapers in the United States. He finally made it back to his bed at 3:50 a.m.

As the head of AP's operation in Saigon, Browne was used to having his schedule interrupted by the unexpected twists and turns of being in the middle of a war zone. As a biographer researching his time in Vietnam, including the day in 1963 when he caught on film one of the most dramatic images of the conflict, I had expected a quiet day of research in his papers, available in the Library of Congress's Manuscript Reading Room in the James Madison Memorial Building in Washington, DC. On the morning of August 19, 2021, however, a man from North Carolina decided to drive his truck onto the sidewalk in front of the Library of Congress's Thomas Jefferson Building, telling authorities he had a bomb in his vehicle—no explosives were eventually found—and it was time for "a revolution."

I had just read a March 3, 1965, letter to Browne from US Senate Majority Leader Mike Mansfield of Montana praising the journalist's new book about his Vietnam experiences, *The New Face of War*, when alarms sounded throughout the building. The department's staff quickly hustled those doing research out of the building, leaving me no time to grab my belongings locked safely away in a nearby locker, including my wallet. Luckily, I still had my iPhone, so I was able, once safely back at my hotel, to let my wife, Megan McKee, know I was OK. Fortunately, the would-be bomber surrendered to police, and I was back doing my work in Browne's papers the next day. Although only a small glitch in my effort to tell Browne's story, it did mark one of the most eventful days I have ever spent in an archive during my more than two decades of researching and writing books.

Luckily for me, there were several people who helped rather than hindered getting this project completed. Browne's widow, Le Lieu, kindly responded to my queries about the couple's time together in Vietnam and provided permission for the use of several photographs. Thomas D. Herman, director of the remarkable 2016 documentary *Dateline-Saigon*, went above and beyond the call of duty by allowing me to use transcripts of his interviews with Browne from the production. When the COVID-19 pandemic precluded travel, Valerie Komor, director of the Associated Press Corporate Archives in New York, provided online access to materials about AP's operation in Saigon, as well as important documents from Browne's papers in the archives. Komor and her staff were essential to getting this book done. AP account manager Tricia Gesner guided me through obtaining images, including Browne's famous photos of Thich Quang Duc's self-immolation, from the news agency.

For editorial support, I relied once again upon the staff at the University of New Mexico Press, especially senior acquisitions editor Michael Millman. The outside readers for my manuscript, Dr. Jim Willis and Dr. Mark Lawrence, were supportive and offered suggestions for revisions that greatly improved the finished work. From the initial proposal, my agent, Philip Turner, has been a godsend for making what could be a painful process as easy as possible. As she has done for all my previous books, stretching back to the first in 1998, my wife carefully reviewed the manuscript, pointing out errors and smoothing rough patches in the narrative. She is my everything.

Notes

Prologue

1. Malcolm W. Browne, "7-Cent Bullet Drops 'Geisha Girl' Helicopter," *Saint Petersburg* (FL) *Times*, January 26, 1964; Browne, *Muddy Boots and Red Socks*, 118; and Browne, "Geisha Girl," Malcolm Browne Papers, Manuscript Division (hereafter cited as Browne Papers).

2. Browne, *The New Face of War*, 53–54. The revised edition of *New Face of War*, published in 1968, has on its cover a photograph by Horst Faas of the Associated Press of an American soldier from the 101st Airborne Division holding aloft the severed head of a suspected Viet Cong insurgent in January 1966. The enemy guerrilla had thrown a grenade at the Americans, injuring four of them. See Browne, *New Face of War*, rev. ed., 1968, 336–37.

3. Browne, *New Face of War*, 41–42.

4. Browne, "Geisha Girl"; Browne, "7-Cent Bullet Drops 'Geisha Girl' Helicopter"; Browne, *New Face of War*, 49.

5. Browne, "Geisha Girl"; Browne, *New Face of War*, 50.

6. Browne, "7-Cent Bullet Drops 'Geisha Girl' Helicopter"; Browne, *New Face of War*, 50.

7. Browne, "7-Cent Bullet Drops 'Geisha Girl' Helicopter"; and Browne, *Muddy Boots and Red Socks*, 120.

8. Browne, "Geisha Girl."

9. Browne, *Muddy Boots and Red Socks*, 120.

10. Ibid., 121.

11. Ibid.

12. Malcolm W. Browne to Ann Kerrey, April 5, 1967, Browne Papers. See also Browne, *Muddy Boots and Red Socks*, 85–86.

13. Browne to Kerrey, Browne Papers.

Chapter 1

1.   Browne, *Muddy Boots and Red Socks*, 45–46.

2.   Ibid., 46.

3.   Malcolm Browne to Mlle. Khuong, February 5, 1966, Browne Papers; Malcolm Browne, interview by Harold "Hal" Buell, April 21, 1998, Associated Press Corporate Archives Oral History Program.

4.   Ferrari, comp., "Malcolm W. Browne," 93; Browne, *Muddy Boots and Red Socks*, 47, 49, 51, 56–57.

5.   Lamb, "Malcolm W. Browne."

6.   Malcolm Browne talk to Swarthmore College class, November 23, 1999, Browne Papers; Associated Press, "The Unquiet American"; Ferrari, comp., "Malcolm W. Browne," 33; Browne, *Muddy Boots and Red Socks*, 63–64.

7.   Browne, *Muddy Boots and Red Socks*, 7, 81–82; Malcolm W. Browne to William Prochnau, January 9, 1996, Browne Papers.

8.   Malcolm Browne speech, International Press Institute, London, May 25, 1965, Browne Papers; Lamb, "Malcolm W. Browne."

9.   Peter Arnett e-mail to author, June 6, 2020; Nolting, *From Trust to Tragedy*, 90; author interview with Fox Butterfield, July 27 and August 1, 2022.

10.   Malcolm Browne to Thomas H. Wolf, April 21, 1966, Malcolm Browne to Ann Kerrey, April 5, 1967, and Malcolm Browne to Sunday Book Review Editor, *New York Times*, November 24, 1995, Browne Papers.

11.   Browne, *Muddy Boots and Red Socks*, 40; "From Vietnam to Quantum Mechanics and Everything in Between," Malcolm Browne speech, Science Reporters' Workshop, American Chemical Society, August 22, 1992, in Browne Papers.

12.   Browne, *Muddy Boots and Red Socks*, 52; Browne interview, AP Corporate Archives; and Malcolm Browne to Joe Lelyveld, May 10, 1994, Browne Papers.

13.   David Halberstam, "Associated Press in Saigon in 1962," in David Halberstam Collection; Browne, *The New Face of War*, 256–58.

14.   Browne, *Muddy Boots and Red Socks*, 10–11; Witty, "Malcolm Browne"; and AP Explore, The Burning Monk 50th Anniversary, https://www.ap.org/explore/the-burning-monk. In addition to Browne, another person, Nguyen Van Thong, a South Vietnamese freelance reporter and photographer who died in 2019, snapped photographs of the monk's self-immolation. "My hands were shaking and tears began to roll from my eyes as I witnessed the whole thing," Thong remembered. See "Photographer Who Captured Iconic 'Burning Monk' Moment in Wartime Vietnam Dies at 94," *Tuoi Tre News*, September 9, 2019.

15.   Danielle Gibson, "The Saigon Execution," https://medium.com/history-through-the-lens/the-saigon-execution-da8f16c2366; Gendy Alimurung, "Nick Ut's Napalm Girl Helped End the Vietnam War," *LA Weekly*, July 17, 2014, https://www.laweekly.com/nick-uts-napalm-girl-helped-end-the-vietnam-war-today-in-l-a-hes-still-shooting; and Judith Coburn, "Image of Peace," *Chicago Tribune*, September 7, 1989.

16. Witty, "Malcolm Browne"; Browne, *Muddy Boots and Red Socks*, 3–4, 19; Ferrari, comp., *Reporting America at War*, 102.

17. Browne, *Muddy Boots and Red Socks*, 16–17; Ferrari, *Reporting America at War*, 104–5. The song Browne alludes to was Staff Sergeant Barry Sadler's 1966 hit "The Ballad of the Green Berets," which climbed to number one on the *Billboard* charts for five weeks. For more about Sadler and his song, see Marc Leepson, *Ballad of the Green Beret: The Life and Wars of Staff Sergeant Barry Sadler, From the Vietnam War and Pop Stardom to Murder and an Unsolved, Violent Death* (Guilford, CT: Stackpole Books, 2017).

18. Browne, *Muddy Boots and Red Socks*, 180; Malcolm Browne to Louis D. Boccardi, January 6, 2000, Browne Papers; Malcolm Browne draft of talk, April 22, 1963, AP annual meeting, New York, Browne Papers; Browne talk to Swarthmore College class, November 23, 1999, Browne Papers.

19. Browne, *New Face of War*, 275; Ula Ilnytzky and Richard Pyle, "Malcolm Browne; Shot Iconic Vietnam Image," *Hackensack* (NJ) *Record*, August 29, 2012; Browne, *Muddy Boots and Red Socks*, 85.

20. Malcolm Browne to Susan Malin, January 8, 1993, Browne Papers.

21. Malcolm Browne, "Life and Times: Death Benefits," *New York Times*, October 3, 1993.

Chapter 2

1. Browne, *Muddy Boots and Red Socks*, 37–38. See also Malcolm Browne speech, 1967, Browne Papers.

2. Browne, *Muddy Boots and Red Socks*, 20, 38; Malcolm Browne to Louis D. Boccardi, January 6, 2000, Browne Papers; Arnett, "A Long-Range View of the Associated Press in Vietnam," 3; Chris Farlekas, "Reporter with the Feel for Life," *Middletown* (NY) *Record*, November 21, 1993.

3. Malcolm Browne speech, 1967.

4. Malcolm Browne speech, 1967; Browne, *Muddy Boots and Red Socks*, 21–22.

5. Browne, *Muddy Boots and Red Socks*, 25–26; Lamb, "Malcolm W. Browne."

6. Browne, *Muddy Boots and Red Socks*, 23–24.

7. Ibid.

8. Ibid., 25, 26.

9. Ibid., 29; Farlekas, "Reporter with the Feel for Life."

10. Browne, *Muddy Boots and Red Socks*, 27, 29; Farlekas, "Reporter with the Feel for Life."

11. Browne, *Muddy Boots and Red Socks*, 26, 27, 29, 35.

12. L. Browne, *Bend the Willow*, 72, 98–99; Malcolm W. Browne to Ben, February 6, 1967, Browne Papers. See also Browne, *Muddy Boots and Red Socks*, 313–15.

13. Browne, *Muddy Boots and Red Socks*, 30–31. See also "Maxim Schur, Pianist, 67," obituary in *New York Times*, October 23, 1974; Fountain, "Danby Eden," 58–61.

14. Lamb, "Malcolm Browne"; Malcolm Browne to Susan Malin, January 8, 1993, Browne Papers; Farlekas, "A Reporter's Life"; Malcolm Browne talk, March 16, 1994,

Friends Seminary Meeting House, in Browne Papers. For more on Friends Seminary, see Gibbs, *Children of Light*.

15. Farlekas, "A Reporter's Life"; Browne, *Muddy Boots and Red Socks*, 35; Malcolm Browne, "A Goodbye to Adventures Gone By," *New York Times*, January 29, 1980.

16. Browne, *Muddy Boots and Red Socks*, 32–33; Lamb, "Malcolm Browne"; Browne, interview with Thomas D. Herman, p. 17.

17. Farlekas, "A Reporter's Life"; Browne, *Muddy Boots and Red Socks*, 31, 34.

18. Farlekas, "A Reporter's Life"; Browne, *Muddy Boots and Red Socks*, 32; Browne interview with Terry Gross, *Fresh Air*.

19. "Diana Kirchwey is Wed," *New York Times*, June 27, 1951; Malcolm Browne speech, 1967; Stephen Schlesinger, "Ghosts of Guatemala's Past," *New York Times*, June 4, 2011.

20. Browne, *Muddy Boots and Red Socks*, 36–37; Malcolm Browne speech, 1967.

21. Browne, *Muddy Boots and Red Socks*, 38–39.

22. Ibid., 39–41.

23. Ibid., 50.

24. Ibid., 50–51.

25. Browne, *Muddy Boots and Red Socks*, 57–59; Browne interview by Herman, p. 1. See also "Hevenor, Browne named Record bureau managers," *Middletown Daily Record*, December 22, 1958.

26. "The Press: Newcomer in Middletown," *Time*, August 13, 1956; Browne, *Muddy Boots and Red Socks*, 59–60; "The Will to Succeed," *Middletown (NY) Times Herald*, May 6, 1964; Paul Weissman, "Wire Service Man in Saigon," *New York Post*, June 14, 1964. In 1960 Ottaway Newspapers-Radio, which owned the *Middletown (NY) Times Herald*, bought the *Record*. See "Upstate Paper is Sold," *New York Times*, April 19, 1960.

27. Thompson, *The Proud Highway*, 152–53. Although Thompson got away with falsifying his experience to get the job on the *Record*, he lasted only a short time at the newspaper, often clashing with management. Editor Al Romm fired Thompson in February 1959 after an incident involving the office's candy machine. "I had put two nickels in the thing without getting anything out of it," Thompson recalled. "I then gave it a severe rattling which rendered the coin slot obsolete. Word got around in the back shop and a 'run' on the machine followed almost immediately." See Thompson, *The Proud Highway*, 156–57; and William McKeen, *Outlaw Journalist: The Life and Times of Hunter S. Thompson* (New York: W. W. Norton, 2008), 46–47.

28. Malcolm Browne, "5 Cows Strewn Along 15 miles Off 'Leaky Truck," *Middletown (NY) Daily Record*, July 30, 1959; "Fallsburgh Hotel Burns; 50 Flee, 1 is Hospitalized," *Middletown (NY) Daily Record*, August 28, 1959; "Ex-Nazi Pilot Teaching Wife to Glide Here," *Middletown (NY) Daily Record*, December 5, 1958; "Sheriffs on Duty at Chester Cable," *Middletown (NY) Daily Record*, November 12, 1958; "'I'll Have News About Dugan': White's Promise Came on Schedule," *Middletown (NY) Daily Record*, November 14, 1958; and "A Short Short Story . . . of Life in Monroe," *Middletown (NY) Daily Record*, June 11, 1959. See also Browne, *Muddy Boots and Red Socks*, 60–61.

29. Browne, *Muddy Boots and Red Socks*, 65–66, 69–70.

30.   Malcolm Browne, "Americans Leaving Cuban Army," *Middletown* (NY) *Daily Record*, July 15, 1959. See also Browne, *Muddy Boots and Red Socks*, 73–75; "Cuba: Chief Executioner," *Time*, April 13, 1959; "Herman Marks, Stateless American," *Milwaukee Journal*, January 31, 1961; and Michael D. Sallah, "Cuba's Yankee Comandante," *Toledo Blade*, March 3, 2002.

31.   Browne, "Americans Leaving Cuban Army"; Browne, *Muddy Boots and Red Socks*, 71–72; Francis I. McCarthy, "Young Marine Who Helped Castro Says He 'Wants To Go Home Now,'" *Mount Carmel* (IL) *Daily Republic-Register*, July 11, 1959; Shelia Webb, "Radical Portrayals: Dickey Chapelle on the Front Lines," *American Periodicals* 26, no. 2 (2016): 202–3; "Court Orders 24 Months For Holthaus," *Decatur* (IL) *Daily Review*, January 17, 1960.

32.   Malcolm Browne, "Now That The Revolution is Over . . . Will Castro's Cuba turn Red?," July 17, 1959, and "Cuba Word is 'Reform,'" *Middletown* (NY) *Daily Record*, July 20, 1959; Browne, *Muddy Boots and Red Socks*, 68–69.

33.   Browne, *Muddy Boots and Red Socks*, 78–79, 210; Loh, "I'm With AP . . .'," 6; and Bassett, "The AP Foreign Correspondents," 5. For the growth of AP's wirephoto technology, see Will Mari, *The American Newsroom: A History, 1920–1960* (Columbia: University of Missouri Press, 2021), 41.

34.   "A Busy Sunday in 1956," *AP World* 27 (Winter 1971): 42; and Associated Press, *Breaking News*, 261, 403–4.

35.   Browne, *Muddy Boots and Red Socks*, 79–80; Associated Press, *Breaking News*, 412; Mike Feinsilber, "Flashes! Bulletins! When Bells in the Newsroom Really Meant Something," About Editing and Writing Blog, https://jacklimpert.com/2016/04/flash-bulletin-when-ten-bells-or-five-bells-really-meant-something.

36.   Browne, *Muddy Boots and Red Socks*, 81–82; Browne interview by Herman, p. 25; and Nicola Smith, "Vietnam on His Mind, Then and Now," *West Lebanon* (NH) *Valley News*, November 7, 2009.

37.   Browne, *Muddy Boots and Red Socks*, 92; Malcolm Browne to Ann Kerrey, April 5, 1967, Browne Papers.

Chapter 3

1.   USS *Core*, https://www.history.navy.mil/research/histories/ship-histories/danfs/c/core.html; Jacques Nevard, "U.S. 'Copter Units Arrive in Saigon," *New York Times*, December 12, 1961; Browne, *Muddy Boots and Red Socks*, 106.

2.   Browne, *Muddy Boots and Red Socks*, 108.

3.   Malcolm Browne, "Viet Nam Gets U.S. Copters," *Wichita Falls* (TX) *Times*, December 11, 1961.

4.   Browne, *Muddy Boots and Red Socks*, 108; Prochnau, *Once Upon a Distant War*, 19–21; Ferrari, comp., *Reporting America at War*, 95; Aronson, *The Press and the Cold War*, 182. See also Malcom Browne dispatch, October 23, 1962, Associated Press Saigon Bureau.

5.   "Saigon Impeding Western Press," *New York Times*, March 24, 1962; Browne, *Muddy Boots and Red Socks*, 83; Malcolm W. Browne, "Vietnam Reporting: Three Years

of Crisis," 102; Malcolm W. Browne, "The Fighting Words of Homer Bigart: A War Correspondent is Never a Cheerleader," *New York Times*, April 11, 1993; and Malcolm Browne, "A Short Guide to News Coverage in Viet Nam," 1, Browne Papers.

6.   Browne, "Vietnam Reporting," 102–3, and Homer Bigart, "G.I.'s in Vietnam Lied as Ordered," *New York Times*, May 5, 1962.

7.   Browne, "Vietnam Reporting," 102–3; Mecklin, *Mission in Torment*, 112–13.

8.   Browne, "A Short Guide to News Coverage in Viet Nam," 1; Ferrari, comp., *Reporting America at War*, 92–93; Browne, *Muddy Boots and Red Socks*, 83. See also Aronson, *The Press and the Cold War*, 192; Arnett, "A Long-Range View of the Associated Press in Vietnam," 3.

9.   Bekey, "Dateline: Danger—Mal Browne in Viet Nam," 15; Browne, *Muddy Boots and Red Socks*, 4–5, 112, 127.

10.   "Malcolm Browne," in Appy, *Patriots*, 65; Browne, interview by Thomas D. Herman; Associated Press, "The Unquiet American."

11.   Browne, *Muddy Boots and Red Socks*, 7; "Under Guard," *AP Ticker*, no. 3, in Browne Papers.

12.   Browne, *Muddy Boots and Red Socks*, 4–5.

13.   Malcolm W. Browne, "Wars Come and Go—But Siesta Remains," *Louisville Courier-Journal*, January 22, 1962.

14.   Browne, *Muddy Boots and Red Socks*, 89–90, 112.

15.   Browne, "A Short Guide to News Coverage in Viet Nam," 15–16; Malcolm W. Browne, "Nolting Our Man in Viet Nam: U.S. Guide in a Minefield," *Detroit Free Press*, February 18, 1962; and Browne, *Muddy Boots and Red Socks*, 86–87.

16.   Browne, *Muddy Boots and Red Socks*, 124–26; Malcolm W. Browne, "Pessimism Shadows Viet Nam," *Pensacola* (FL) *News Journal*, November 27, 1961.

17.   Browne, "The Fascinating Life of AP Men in South Viet Nam," *AP World* 19 (Summer 1964): 28; Browne, "A Short Guide to News Coverage in Viet Nam," 14–15; Browne, *Muddy Boots and Red Socks*, 7.

18.   Browne, *Muddy Boots and Red Socks*, 98–99; Paul Weissman, "Wire Service Man in Saigon," *New York Post*, June 14, 1964. Neil Sheehan, who led the United Press International bureau in Saigon, recalled that getting material to a "pigeon" sometimes proved hairy, involving a correspondent getting to the airport at the last minute, jumping over a customs barrier, running to the aircraft, and climbing up its steps "as they were about to withdraw the ladder and close the door" to hand over the text or images to a passenger or stewardess. "The customs men knew this was going on," Sheehan noted. "They'd laugh and say did you get it out? . . . They hated the regime." See Moeller, *Shooting War*, 361.

19.   Browne, "A Short Guide to News Coverage in Viet Nam," 1–2.

20.   Peter Kross, "General Maxwell Taylor's Mission to Vietnam," HistoryNet, https://www.historynet.com/general-maxwell-taylors-mission-to-vietnam.htm; Wyatt, *Paper Soldiers*, 79–80; Miller, *Misalliance*, 228–29.

21.   Dallek, *Camelot's Court*, 240–41; Herring, *America's Longest War*, 83–85.

22.   Browne, *Muddy Boots and Red Socks*, 95.

23. Malcolm W. Browne, "U.S. Planes Crowd Field Near Saigon—Guerrilla War Flares Nightly Nearby," *Allentown* (PA) *Morning Call*, November 16, 1962; Browne, *Muddy Boots and Red Socks*, 95–96.

24. Browne, "U.S. Planes Crowd Field Near Saigon"; Browne, *Muddy Boots and Red Socks*, 96–97.

25. Browne, *Muddy Boots and Red Socks*, 97.

26. Browne, "U.S. Planes Crowd Field Near Saigon"; Browne, *Muddy Boots and Red Socks*, 98.

27. Malcolm W. Browne, "Viet Nam Paradise for Spies," *Allentown* (PA) *Morning Call*, February 15, 1962.

28. Browne, *Muddy Boots and Red Socks*, 99–101.

29. Le Lieu Browne e-mail to author, November 18, 2021; Appy, *Patriots*, 73.

30. L. Browne, *Bend the Willow*, 29, 42; Appy, *Patriots*, 73; Browne interview by Herman, p. 3.

31. Malcolm Browne to William Prochnau, August 15, 1990, and January 9, 1996, Browne Papers; Browne, *Muddy Boots and Red Socks*, 100–101; Appy, *Patriots*, 74; L. Browne, *Bend the Willow*, 74, 88, 96–98, 104–5, 123. The Ozzie and Harriet Browne referred to is Ozzie and Harriet Nelson, the couple featured in the long-running television sitcom *The Adventures of Ozzie and Harriet*, which appeared on the ABC network from 1952 to 1966.

32. Browne, *The New Face of War*, 1; Browne, *Muddy Boots and Red Socks*, 101–2.

33. Joseph Alsop, "A Day in the Life of Colonels Hung and Thao," *Louisville Courier-Journal*, April 15, 1961; "Matter of Fact," *Medford* (OR) *Tribune*, April 16, 1961. See also Browne, *Muddy Boots and Red Socks*, 102–3.

34. Browne, *New Face of War*, 2; Malcolm Browne, December 4, 1961, newscast to Tokyo, AP Saigon Bureau Collection; and Browne, *Muddy Boots and Red Socks*, 104.

35. Browne, *New Face of War*, 4, 6; Browne, December 4, 1961, newscast; and Browne, *Muddy Boots and Red Socks*, 105.

36. Browne, *New Face of War*, 6; Browne, *Muddy Boots and Red Socks*, 105.

37. Browne, December 4, 1961, newscast; Browne, *Muddy Boots and Red Socks*, 105–6.

38. Browne, *Muddy Boots and Red Socks*, 135; Demery, *Finding the Dragon Lady*, 125–26; Malcolm Browne, December 6, 1961, newscast to Tokyo; Malcolm W. Browne, "South Viet Nam's First Lady Arouses Very Strong Reactions in the Press," *Raleigh* (NC) *News and Observer*, December 17, 1961.

39. Browne, "South Viet Nam's First Lady Arouses Very Strong Reactions in the Press"; Browne, *Muddy Boots and Red Socks*, 135–36.

40. Browne, *Muddy Boots and Red Socks*, 109; Malcolm W. Browne, "15 U.S. Soldiers in Lonely Viet Nam Outpost Have Yule," *Ironwood* (MI) *Daily Globe*, December 25, 1961.

41. Browne, *Muddy Boots and Red Socks*, 110–11.

42. Browne, "15 U.S. Soldiers in Lonely Viet Nam Outpost Have Yule"; Browne, *Muddy Boots and Red Socks*, 111–12.

43. Browne, "15 U.S. Soldiers in Lonely Viet Nam Outpost Have Yule."

44. Ben Bassett to Malcolm Browne, December 27, 1961, Browne Papers; Browne, *Muddy Boots and Red Socks*, 112–13.

45. Browne, "There's Strong Feeling Tide Runs for US in S. Viet Nam," *Del Rio* (TX) *News Herald*, January 1, 1962.

Chapter 4

1. Browne, *Muddy Boots and Red Socks*, 126–27; Malcolm W. Browne, "A Saga of Death in the Jungles of Viet Nam," *Des Moines Tribune*, March 3, 1962; Malcolm W. Browne, "Here's One Example of Daily Viet Nam Battle," *Tacoma* (WA) *News Tribune*, March 3, 1962. See also Browne, *The New Face of War*, 88–91.

2. Browne, *Muddy Boots and Red Socks*, 127; Browne, *New Face of War*, 94–95; "More News and Work Per Square Foot," *Swarthmore College Bulletin* (December 1964): 23.

3. Browne, "A Saga of Death in the Jungles of Viet Nam"; Browne, *New Face of War*, 98–100.

4. Browne, *Muddy Boots and Red Socks*, 129–30; Homer Bigart, "Saigon Discounts Pilots' Raid on President," *New York Times*, February 28, 1962; "South Vietnam: Durable Diem," *Time*, March 9, 1962.

5. Browne, *Muddy Boots and Red Socks*, 130; Arnett, "1972: Reflections on Vietnam, the Press and America"; Arnett, "A Long-Range View of The Associated Press in Vietnam," 3.

6. Arnett, *Live from the Battlefield*, 73–74; Arnett, *Saigon Has Fallen*, 17–18.

7. Arnett, interview by Komor.

8. Browne, interview by Herman, pp. 4, 6; David Halberstam, "Foreword," *Breaking News*, 8; Arnett, *Saigon Has Fallen*, 17.

9. Arnett, "1972: Reflections on Vietnam, the Press and America"; Prochnau, *Once Upon a Distant War*, 109; Arnett, *Saigon Has Fallen*, 20; Browne, "A Short Guide to News Coverage in Viet Nam," 18, Browne Papers.

10. Arnett, *Live from the Battlefield*, 78; Browne to William Prochnau, January 9, 1996, Browne Papers. See also Prochnau, *Once Upon a Distant War*, 119.

11. Hamill, "Introduction," *Vietnam: The Real War*, 27–29; Herman, dir., *Dateline-Saigon*; and Halberstam, "Foreword," 7.

12. Arnett, *Live from the Battlefield*, 78–79; Browne interview by Herman, p. 6; Arnett, "A Long-Range View of the Associated Press in Vietnam," 4; Faas, interview by Komor, 34; and Faas, interview by Buell and Scott, 16.

13. Browne, interview by Herman, 7–8; and Halberstam, "Foreword," 9–10, 16.

14. Browne to Jess Zousmer, June 13, 1965, Browne Papers; Browne to Joe Lelyveld, May 10, 1994, Browne Papers; Faas, interview by Buell and Scott, 17; Arnett, "A Long-Range View of the Associated Press in Vietnam," 4.

15. Malcolm W. Browne speech, Sigma Delta Chi Fourth Annual Regional Conference, May 2, 1964, Phoenix, Arizona, Browne Papers; Browne, interview by Herman, 12–13.

16. David Halberstam, untitled essay about Associated Press's Saigon bureau, David Halberstam Papers (hereafter cited as Halberstam essay).

17. Browne, *Muddy Boots and Red Socks*, 179–80.

18. Arnett, *Saigon Has Fallen*, 27–28.

19. Malcolm Browne, "He Speaks for U.S. . . . And Guides Policy in South Viet Nam," *Durham* (NC) *Herald-Sun*, February 18, 1962; Browne, "The New Face of Censorship," 90–91; Nolting, *From Trust to Tragedy*, 90.

20. Malcolm W. Browne, "General Praises Viet Nam," *Arizona Republic*, April 8, 1962.

21. Malcolm W. Browne, "Meaning of Words Causes Argument," *Owensboro* (KY) *Messenger-Inquirer*, October 23, 1962.

22. Browne, *Muddy Boots and Red Socks*, 179–80; Wes Gallagher to Malcolm Browne, November 16, 1962, Browne Papers.

23. Salinger, *With Kennedy*, 324.

24. Nolting, *From Trust to Tragedy*, 86–87; Wyatt, *Paper Soldiers*, 91.

25. Nolting, *From Trust to Tragedy*, 87; Ferrari, comp., *Reporting America at War*, 86; Malcolm Browne, "The Fighting Words of Homer Bigart: A Correspondent is Never a Cheerleader," *New York Times*, April 11, 1993; Wade, comp. and ed., *Forward Positions*, 185.

26. Salinger, *With Kennedy*, 322. See also Hammond, *Public Affairs*, 15–16.

27. Telegram from the Department of State to the Embassy in Vietnam, Washington [DC], February 21, 1962, https://history.state.gov/historicaldocuments/frus1961-63v02/d75; Mecklin, *Mission in Torment*, 110–11; Homer Bigart, "Saigon Regime Rejects Pressure for Reforms," *New York Times*, June 3, 1962; Herman, dir., *Dateline-Saigon*. Rowan refuted claims from a House Subcommittee on Information, chaired by Congressman John E. Moss, a Democrat from California, that he had tried to restrict American newsmen in Vietnam during his time as deputy assistant secretary of state for public affairs. In a prepared statement, Rowan said: "I find it incredible that the Congressional subcommittee would issue such a report without having asked me for the facts as to my involvement. Had the committee bothered to get the whole truth, it would have only one valid reason for singling me out: In February, 1962, I was a government official campaigning most zealously to secure removal of restrictions on newsmen in Saigon." See "Rowan Denies He Curbed U.S. Newsmen in Vietnam," *New York Times*, October 4, 1963.

28. Mecklin, *Mission in Torment*, 100, 105, 124–25.

29. Ibid., 108–10; Jacobs, *Cold War Mandarin*, 131–32; Halberstam, interview by Ted Gittinger, p. 34.

30. Mecklin, *Mission in Torment*, 131–32.

31. Malcolm Browne, "Viet Nam Reporting: Three Years of Crisis," *Columbia Journalism Review*, Fall 1964, https://archives.cjr.org/fiftieth_anniversary/viet_nam_reporting_three_years.php?page=ala.

32. Malcolm Browne, "Stupid Americans Hurt Touchy Allies," *Kansas City Star*, August 19, 1962.

33. Wade, comp. and ed., *Forward Positions*, 198–201; Nolting, *From Trust to Tragedy*, 88; Prochnau, *Once Upon a Distant War*, 49–50. See also Mecklin, *Mission in Torment*,

129. Bigart joked in a letter in early 1962 that he had composed a song, sung to the tune of "I'm an Old Cowhand," that included the words: "We must sink or swim / With Ngo Din Diem / We will hear no phoo / About Madame Nhu / Yippee-i-aye, i-aye, etc." See Jacobs, *Cold War Mandarin*, 129.

34. Herman, dir., *Dateline-Saigon*; Prochnau, *Once Upon a Distant War*, 52–54; Rothmyer, "The Quiet Exit of Homer Bigart."

35. Browne, interview by Herman, pp. 16–17, 19, 23; Prochnau, *Once Upon a Distant War*, 66, 85; Herman, dir., *Dateline-Saigon*; Browne, *Muddy Boots and Red Socks*, 184.

36. "David Halberstam," interview in Ferrari, comp., *Reporting America at War*, 112; Halberstam, interview by Gittinger, 5, 19, 20; Halberstam, "Getting the Story in Vietnam," *Commentary Magazine*, https://www.commentarymagazine.com/articles/getting-the-story-in-vietnam; Halberstam, *The Making of a Quagmire*, 5–7.

37. Halberstam, interview by Gittinger, 5–6, 8; Neil Sheehan, "The Combatant," *New York Times*, December 30, 2007.

38. Ferrari, comp., *Reporting America at War*, 113; Nolting, *From Trust to Tragedy*, 88.

39. Halberstam, interview by Gittinger, 19–20; Halberstam untitled essay about Associated Press's Saigon bureau.

40. Browne, interview by Herman, 20; Malcolm Browne to Sunday Book Review Editor, *New York Times*, November 24, 1995, Browne Papers; Prochnau, *Once Upon a Distant War*, 150, 152–53.

41. Malcolm W. Browne to William Prochnau, January 9, 1996, Browne Papers. In a letter to an editor for *Newsday*, Browne said he believed that winning a Pulitzer Prize could be "more detrimental than beneficial," with those receiving one becoming "arrogant and unlikable, which in turn can wreck their careers." He compared it to scientists referring to the Nobel Prize as "that evil prize." See Malcolm W. Browne to David Kahn, April 21, 1993, Browne Papers.

42. Sheehan, *A Bright Shining Lie*, 319–20; Prochnau, "The Upside of Anger," 49.

43. Sheehan, "The Combatant," *New York Times*, December 30, 2007; Herman, dir., *Dateline-Saigon*; Browne, interview by Herman, 20–21.

44. Browne, interview by Herman, 23–24; Browne, *Muddy Boots and Red Socks*, 184–85.

Chapter 5

1. Malcolm W. Browne, "Death Robs U.S. of 'Future General,'" *Birmingham* (AL) *News*, January 7, 1963. In addition to Good, the two other Americans killed in action were Sergeant William Deal of Mays Landing, New Jersey, and Specialist 4 Donald Braman of Radcliff, Kentucky. See "South Viet Nam: The Helicopter War Runs into Trouble," *Time*, January 11, 1963.

2. Malcolm W. Browne, "14 U.S. Helicopters Shot Up By Viet Reds," *Troy* (NY) *Record*, January 3, 1963; Browne, *The New Face of War*, 12, 14–15; "South Viet Nam: The Helicopter War Runs into Trouble"; and Sheehan, *A Bright Shining Lie*, 274–75.

3. Yablonka, *Vietnam Bao Chi*, 22–23; Arnett, *Live from the Battlefield*, 96–97.

4. Peter Arnett, "Battle Casualties Moved in Bloody Ap Bac Area," January 3, 1963, *Lexington* (KY) *Herald Leader*; Tregaskis, *Vietnam Diary*, 375, 378; Neil Sheehan, "Vietnamese Ignored U.S. Battle Order," *Washington Post*, January 7, 1963; Hastings, *Vietnam: An Epic Tragedy, 1945–1975*, 162–64.

5. Halberstam, *The Making of a Quagmire*, 89–90; David Halberstam, "Harkins Praises Vietnam Troops," *New York Times*, January 11, 1963; Frederick Nolting, interview Ted Gittinger, November 11, 1982, pp. 11–12.

6. Wyatt, *Paper Soldiers*, 108–9.

7. Tregaskis, *Vietnam Diary*, 380–81; Browne, *New Face of War*, 15.

8. Malcolm W. Browne, "Viet Nam War Needs 'Understanding,'" *Corpus Christi* (TX) *Caller-Times*, January 20, 1963.

9. Malcolm W. Browne, "Viet Nam is 'Time in Hell,'" *Shreveport* (LA) *Times*, February 3, 1963; and AP Spotlight Advance, Browne Papers.

10. AP Spotlight Advance, Browne Papers. Browne received a letter praising his "beautifully done" story about Dickerson from Ben Bassett, AP's foreign news editor. In his letter, Bassett noted that the AP could use "more of this type of copy that brings the war down to terms of people." Ben Bassett to Malcolm Browne, January 30, 1963, Browne Papers.

11. Malcolm Browne, "U.S. Advisers at Odds with Viet Nam General," *Corpus Christi* (TX) *Caller*, May 28, 1963.

12. Ibid.

13. Browne, *Muddy Boots and Red Socks*, 112–13, and Browne, The *New Face of War*, 75.

14. Halberstam, "The Other Enemy," 62; "Richard Olsen" in Appy, ed., *Patriots*, 62; and Browne, *Muddy Boots and Red Socks*, 113.

15. Browne, *Muddy Boots and Red Socks*, 113; Malcolm W. Browne, "Helicopters Vital to War in South Vietnam," *Indianapolis Star*, April 4, 1963.

16. Browne, "Helicopters Vital to War in South Vietnam."

17. Ibid.; David Halberstam, "Army Copter Pilots in Vietnam Say H-21's Are Not Adequate," *New York Times*, January 19, 1963.

18. Malcolm W. Browne, "'Choppers' Proven as Weapon," *Cincinnati Enquirer*, January 1, 1963; Browne, *New Face of War*, 76.

19. "'More US Support for S. Viet Nam Chief Than From His People,'" *San Francisco Examiner*, April 23, 1963.

20. "Viet Nam War Could Drag on For 10 Years," *Mount Vernon* (IL) *Register-News*, April 23, 1963; Draft of Talk for April 22 by Malcolm W. Browne, Browne Papers.

21. Malcolm W. Browne, "Viet Cong Recruiting Easy," *Decatur* (AL) *Daily*, May 1, 1963.

22. Ibid.

23. Jones, *Death of a Generation*, 271; Malcolm Browne dispatch, May 21, 1963, AP Saigon Bureau.

24. Browne, *Muddy Boots and Red Socks*, 7–8; Malcolm W. Browne, "Eyewitness Describes Buddist [*sic*] Burning Alive," *Allentown* (PA) *Call-Chronicle*, October 27, 1963.

25. Arnett, *Live from the Battlefield*, 99–100.

26. Wyatt, *Paper Soldiers*, 110; Miller, *Misalliance* 266–67.

27. Halberstam, *The Making of a Quagmire*, 118; Browne, *Muddy Boots and Red Socks*, 6; Browne, *The New Face of War*, 269; and Malcolm Browne, May 13 dispatch, AP Saigon Bureau.

28. Nolting, *From Trust to Tragedy*, 107; Joseph E. O'Connor, interview with Frederick E. Nolting, p. 18; and Mecklin, *Mission in Torment*, 160. For the view that the Buddhist ranks were infiltrated by agents from Hanoi, see Moyar, *Triumph Forsaken*, 216–17. While Moyar believed that the Communists had "plenty of its own operatives working in the lower and middle echelons of the Buddhist opposition, Hanoi's influence at the top level is less certain." Moyar, *Triumph Forsaken*, 217–18.

29. William C. Trueheart, interview by Ted Gittinger, pp. 32–33; Nolting, *From Trust to Tragedy*, 108–9; Rust, *Kennedy in Vietnam*, 103; Prochnau, *Once Upon a Distant War*, 321; Mecklin, *Mission in Torment*, 169.

30. Malcolm W. Browne, "New Buddhist Frenzy Stirs South Viet Nam," *Tacoma (WA) News-Tribune*, June 26, 1962; Browne, *The New Face of War*, 186–87; Malcolm W. Browne, interview by Thomas D. Herman, p. 38; and Browne, *Muddy Boots and Red Socks*, 8.

31. Browne, *Muddy Boots and Red Socks*, 8–9.

32. Arnett, *Live from the Battlefield*, 102; Malcolm Browne, May 13 dispatch, AP Saigon Bureau.

33. "Danger Seen in Viet Nam Religious Drift," Associated Press report in *Spokane (WA) Chronicle*, May 17, 1963; Miller, *Misalliance*, 262, 270–72; Malcolm Browne, May 21 dispatch, AP Saigon Bureau. For a discussion of the Buddhists' aims during the crisis, especially its attempt to "restore Buddhism to its place of national primacy," see Miller, "Religious Revival and the Politics of Nation Building," 1903–62.

34. Browne, *The New Face of War*, 176–77; Malcolm W. Browne, "Buddhists Presenting Threat," *Daily Ardmoreite (OK)*, June 7, 1963.

35. Prochnau, *Once Upon a Distant War*, 255–56; Browne, "Viet Nam Reporting: Three Years of Crisis"; Mecklin, *Mission in Torment*, 163–65.

36. Mecklin, *Mission in Torment*, 165; Arnett, *Live from the Battlefield*, 102.

37. Malcolm W. Browne to Robert Eunson, June 10, 1963, Browne Papers.

38. Miller, *Misalliance*, 269; Browne, *The New Face of War*, 177; Browne, *Muddy Boots and Red Socks*, 101; Browne, "Viet Nam Reporting: Three Years of Crisis," 6; and Browne, "Eyewitness Describes Buddist [sic] Burning Alive."

39. Halberstam, *Making of a Quagmire*, 124; Browne, "Viet Nam Reporting: Three Years of Crisis," 6.

40. Miller, *Misalliance*, 270; Browne, *The New Face of War*, 175; Buell, "Capturing the Ultimate Protest," 42; Browne, "Viet Nam Reporting: Three Years of Crisis," 6; Browne, "Eyewitness Describes Buddist [sic] Burning Alive"; Witty, "Malcolm Browne." For the type of camera Browne used for the monk's self-immolation, see Malcolm Browne to B. Sandels, February 24, 1994, Browne Papers. See also "The News Challenge," *Santa Cruz (CA) Sentinel*, July 10, 1963.

Chapter 6

1. Browne, *The New Face of War*, 175, 178–79; Lamb, "Malcolm W. Browne."
2. Browne, *Muddy Boots and Red Socks*, 10; "'Burning Monk' Photo World Press Winner," *Editor & Publisher*, December 21, 1963, p. 13; Malcolm W. Browne, interview by Thomas D. Herman, p. 40; Browne, "Eyewitness Describes Buddist [sic] Burning Alive."
3. Browne, *The New Face of War*, 177–78; "Malcolm Browne" in Appy, ed., *Patriots*, 68; Buell, "Capturing the Ultimate Protest," 42.
4. Browne, *Muddy Boots and Red Socks*, 10; Malcolm W. Browne, interview by Harold "Hal" Buell, April 21, 1998, Associated Press Corporate Archives; Browne, *The New Face of War*, 178–79.
5. Browne, *Muddy Boots and Red Socks*, 11; Browne, *The New Face of War*, 179. For a complete timeline of the incident, see Associated Press, AP Explore, "The Burning Monk." In his memoirs, Browne reported that one of the Buddhist monks later told him they had experimented with the best way to burn a person, realizing after a few trials that gasoline alone, while it was easy to ignite and burned "with great heat, it is consumed too rapidly to complete the destruction of a human body and assure death." The monks discovered that "by mixing equal parts of gasoline and diesel fuel we could produce a fire that was both intense and sufficiently long-lasting." See Browne, *Muddy Boots and Red Socks*, 9.
6. Browne, *The New Face of War*, 179; Browne, "Eyewitness Describes Buddist [sic] Burning Alive"; Browne, *Muddy Boots and Red Socks*, 13.
7. Buell, "Capturing the Ultimate Protest," 44; Witty, "Malcolm Browne"; Browne, interview by Herman, p. 41; Browne, *Muddy Boots and Red Socks*, 11; Halberstam, *The Making of a Quagmire*, 128–29; Browne, "Eyewitness Describes Buddist [sic] Burning Alive."
8. Halberstam, *Making of a Quagmire*, 127–28; Prochnau, *Once Upon a Distant War*, 315–16.
9. Halberstam, *Making of a Quagmire*, 128; Browne, "Viet Nam Reporting: Three Years of Crisis," 7.
10. Browne, *The New Face of War*, 180–81; "Monk Burns Self; Diem Urges Calm," *Montgomery (AL) Advertiser*, June 12, 1963. See also "Viet Nam Crisis Wrap-Up," Browne Papers.
11. Browne, *The New Face of War*, 181; "Viet Nam Crisis Wrap-Up," Browne Papers.
12. Witty, "Malcolm Browne."
13. Le Lieu Browne e-mail to author, November 18, 2021. According to Browne, the South Vietnamese authorities, after his success in getting the raw film of Quang Duc's suicide out of the country, "insisted on developing all film before it left Saigon. They developed an informal, but effective, form of censorship." See "Malcolm Browne" in Appy, ed., *Patriots*, 69.
14. Ha Van Tran and Malcolm Browne dispatches, Associated Press Saigon Bureau, News Reports, 1963 June 11; Buell, "Capturing the Ultimate Protest," 44.

15. Witty, "Malcolm Browne"; David Halberstam, "Diem Asks Peace in Religion Crisis," *New York Times*, June 12, 1963; Morris, "This We Remember," 75. See also June 11, 1963, front pages of the following: "Sacrificial Death!" *Madisonville* (KY) *Messenger*; "Flaming Suicide Protests Curbs," *Decatur* (IL) *Daily Review*; "Viet Monk Turns Self Into Torch," *Capital Journal* (Salem, OR); and "Monk Turns Self Into Human Torch," *South Bend* (IN) *Tribune*.

16. See "Monk Sacrifices Self in Religious Protest," *Tucson* (AZ) *Citizen*, June 11, 1963; Letters to Editor, *Tucson* (AZ) *Citizen*, June 13 and June 18, 1963.

17. Reeves, *President Kennedy*, 517, 519; Rust, *Kennedy in Vietnam*, 98–99.

18. Henry Cabot Lodge, interview by Charles Bartlett, pp. 4–7; Browne, "Blood, Ink, and Tears," 7.

19. Nichter, *The Last Brahmin*, 199.

20. Witty, "Malcolm Browne"; Wes Gallagher to Malcolm Browne, June 18, 1963, Browne Papers; Earnest Hoberecht to Neil Sheehan, June 17, 1963, Frank Tremaine to Earnest Hoberecht, June 13, 1963, and Earnest Hoberecht to Neil Sheehan, June 26, 1963, Neil Sheehan Papers; and Prochnau, *Once Upon a Distant War*, 316–17.

21. Browne, "Viet Nam Reporting: Three Years of Crisis," 8; "We, Too, Protest" advertisement, *New York Times*, June 27, 1963.

22. Browne, "Viet Nam Reporting: Three Years of Crisis," 8; Browne, *The New Face of War*, 182; Malcolm W. Browne dispatch in Associated Press Saigon Bureau Records, Series II Message Wires.

23. Malcolm W. Browne, "The News Challenge," *Santa Cruz* (CA) *Sentinel*, July 10, 1963.

24. Browne, "The News Challenge."

25. David Halberstam, "20 of Diem's Police Maul U.S. Newsmen," *Atlanta Constitution*, July 8, 1963; Peter Arnett statement, July 7, 1963, Browne Papers. During the scuffle, Arnett lost a Sekonic light meter but learned that it had been returned to Browne by the police. See Arnett statement, Browne Papers.

26. Arnett, *Saigon Has Fallen*, 43; Browne, *Muddy Boots and Red Socks*, 12–13. See also Prochau, *Once Upon a Distant War*, 328–29.

27. Peter Arnett e-mail to author, June 6, 2020.

28. Horst Faas testimony, July 9, 1969, and testimony of Malcolm W. Browne, July 9, 1969, Browne Papers.

29. "Viet Nam Secret Police Assault U.S. Newsmen," *Valley Morning Star* (Harlingen, TX), July 8, 1963; "Reporting in Viet Nam," *Staunton* (VA) *Daily News Leader*, July 18, 1963; David Halberstam, "Police in Saigon Jostle Newsmen," *New York Times*, July 8, 1963; Prochnau, *Once Upon a Distant War*, 329; Associated Press, "The Unquiet American." See also Roy Essoyan AP dispatch, Associated Press Saigon Bureau Records, July 1–July 10, 1963.

30. Associated Press, "The Unquiet American."

31. Mecklin, *Mission in Torment*, 173–74.

32. "ASNE Probe into Vietnam News Block," *Editor & Publisher*, July 27, 1963, pp. 9, 49.

33. Prochnau, *Once Upon a Distant War*, 330; Wes Gallagher to General Executive Eunson, August 6, 1963, in Associated Press, "The Unquiet American."

34. Gallagher letter, Associated Press, "The Unquiet American."

35. Browne, *Muddy Boots and Red Socks*, 13–14; Bowles, *Promises to Keep*, 486–87.

36. Browne, interview by Herman, p. 43; Browne, *Muddy Boots and Red Socks*, 14–15; Manning, *The Swamp Root Chronicle*, 268; Prochnau, *Once Upon a Distant War*, 327.

37. Browne, *Muddy Boots and Red Socks*, 15.

38. Robert J. Manning, interview by Joseph E. O'Connor, p. 20.

39. Manning, interview by O'Connor, p. 19; Reeves, *President Kennedy*, 556.

40. Manning, interview by O'Connor, pp. 19–20; Manning, *Swamp Root Chronicle*, 269–70.

41. Manning, interview by O'Connor, 21; Manning, *Swamp Root Chronicle*, 271; Mecklin, *Mission in Torment*, 176–77. See also "Viet Nam Drops Charges Against US Newsmen," *Sacramento* (CA) *Bee*, July 25, 1963.

42. Manning, interview by O'Connor, 21–22; Manning, *Swamp Root Chronicle*, 273. Diplomat William Trueheart, who participated in several meetings with Diem, remembered that these interactions could last for hours and "were always a monologue by Diem, nobody else ever got a word in, and they were always almost the same thing: a long lecture on the history of Vietnam and the history of Ngo Dinh Diem." Trueheart pointed out that he could leave a long meeting with South Vietnam's chief of state and "have absolutely nothing to report, because nothing new had been said." See William Trueheart, interview by Ted Gittinger, March 2, 1982.

43. Higgins, *Our Vietnam Nightmare*, 172. See also Miller, *Misalliance*, 274–75.

Chapter 7

1. Browne, "Viet Nam Crisis Wrap Up," Browne Papers; Malcolm W. Browne, "Attempts to Crush Rebellious Buddhists," *Saint Joseph* (MO) *Gazette*, August 22, 1963; "1 Killed, 30 Wounded In S. Viet Nam Drive Against Buddhists," *Meriden* (CT) *Record-Journal*, August 22, 1963; Malcolm W. Browne, "Vietnam Pushes War on Buddhists," *Cincinnati Enquirer*, August 23, 1963.

2. Browne, "Viet Nam Crisis Wrap Up."

3. Browne, "Viet Nam Crisis Wrap Up"; Neil Sheehan, "Eyewitness Reports Assault on Pagodas," *Jackson* (MS) *Clarion-Ledger*, August 22, 1963; Browne, *Muddy Boots and Red Socks*, 211.

4. Browne, "Viet Nam Crisis Wrap Up"; Halberstam, *The Making of a Quagmire*, 143.

5. Browne, "Viet Nam Crisis Wrap Up"; Malcolm W. Browne, "Saigon Quiet After Martial Law Decree," *Gettysburg* (PA) *Times*, August 22, 1963; Browne, "Vietnam Pushes War on Buddhists."

6. Browne, "Viet Nam Crisis Wrap Up"; Karnow, "The Edge of Chaos," 27; Kalb, "The Uncontrollable Element," 93; "Viet Nam Crackdown Spurs Lodge Flight; Diem Envoy Resigns," *Tucson* (AZ) *Citizen*, August 22, 1963; Malcolm W. Browne, "Situation

in South Viet Name Confusing, to Say the Least," *Bloomington* (IL) *Pantagraph*, September 22, 1963.

7.   Malcolm W. Browne, "Vietnamese Army Gains Control of Ministries," *Paducah* (KY) *Sun*, August 23, 1963; David Halberstam, "Plan Said to Be Nhu's," *New York Times*, August 23, 1963; Mecklin, *Mission in Torment*, 181, 186; Wyatt, *Paper Soldiers*, 112; "Saigon's First Lady, Arch Foe of Reds, Powers Relentless War on Buddhists," *Hartford* (CT) *Courant*, August 19, 1963. Madame Nhu had become so incensed by President Diem's attempts to compromise with the Buddhists that she threw a bowl of soup they were sharing for lunch at her brother-in-law. See Wyatt, *Paper Soldiers*, 112.

8.   Mecklin, *Mission in Torment*, 177–78.

9.   Browne, "Viet Nam Crisis Wrap Up"; Arnett, *Live from the Battlefield*, 105.

10.   Malcolm W. Browne, "Buddhists See Fake Plot to Kill Lodge," *Akron* (OH) *Beacon Journal*, August 20, 1963. When Lodge arrived at his US embassy residence, an official took him aside to warn him of a supposed plot to kill the ambassador during a staged visit to a strategic hamlet, where the shooting could be blamed on the Viet Cong. "If these people intend to kill me," asked Lodge, "Why do we have to whisper and be so careful about keeping their secret for them?" See Miller, *Henry Cabot Lodge*, 340.

11.   Malcolm W. Browne, "Buddhists Admonish U.S. Envoy," *Hope* (AR) *Star*, August 1, 1963; "Tense Viet Nam Fears Clashes with Buddhists," *Hartford* (CT) *Courant*, August 20, 1963; Browne, "Viet Nam Crisis Wrap Up"; and Halberstam, *Making of a Quagmire*, 143–44.

12.   "Vietnam Pushes War on Buddhists"; Halberstam, *Making of a Quagmire*, 147; Peter Arnett, "Diem's Action Shocks U.S. Military Men," *Saint Joseph* (MO) *Gazette*, August 23, 1963; Arnett, *Live from the Battlefield*, 106.

13.   Arnett, "Diem's Action Shocks U.S. Military Men."

14.   Hilsman, *To Move a Nation*, 483; Nolting, *From Trust to Tragedy*, 118, 120–21.

15.   Blair, *Lodge in Vietnam*, 33–34; Lodge, interview by Charles Bartlett, p. 7; Karnow, "The Edge of Chaos," 36.

16.   "Lodge, Diem Confer in Wake of Student Revolt in Saigon," *Bridgewater* (NJ) *Courier-News*, August 26, 1963; Malcolm W. Browne, "Saigon Charges US Shows Unjust Doubt of Diem," *Sacramento Bee*, August 28, 1963; Peter Arnett, "The Schoolboy of South Vietnam," *York* (PA) *Gazette and Daily*, September 23, 1963.

17.   Mecklin, *Mission in Torment*, 197; Arnett, *Live from the Battlefield*, 113.

18.   Arnett, *Live from the Battlefield*, 106; Mecklin, *Mission in Torment*, 184–85.

19.   Arnett, *Live from the Battlefield*, 109; "Viet Bundles Via Couriers Elude Censor," *Editor & Publisher*, September 7, 1963, p. 10; Malcolm W. Browne, "Saigon Quiet After Martial Law Decree," *Gettysburg* (PA) *Times*, August 22, 1963.

20.   Arnett, *Live from the Battlefield*, 110; *AP Log*, August 28–September 3, 1963, and Malcolm W. Browne speech to Sigma Delta Chi Fourth Annual Conference, May 2, 1964, Phoenix Arizona, Browne Papers.

21.   Malcolm W. Browne, "3 Top Viet Officials Quit Posts," *Lima* (OH) *Citizen*, August 23, 1963; Browne, *Muddy Boots and Red Socks*, 211–12. See also Karnow, "The Edge of Chaos," 36.

22.   Browne, *Muddy Boots and Red Socks*, 212. Other newspapers also printed the photograph highlighting Browne's chicanery. See, for example, page 3, *Baltimore Evening-Sun*, August 24, 1963.

23.   Karnow, "The Quandary of Henry Cabot Lodge," 72; Frederick W. Flott, interview by Ted Gittinger, 13; Wyatt, *Paper Soldiers*, 125; "Lodge Arrives in Saigon as Buddhist Crisis Grows," *Boston Globe*, August 23, 1963; Mecklin, *Mission in Torment*, 189–90; Arnett, *Live from the Battlefield*, 107.

24.   Halberstam, *Making of a Quagmire*, 164; Nichter, *The Last Brahmin*, 205; "Military Takes Government Offices in South Viet Nam," *Burlington* (VT) *Free Press*, August 24, 1963; Malcolm W. Browne, "Buddhist Repression is Examined," *Asheville* (NC) *Citizen-Times*, September 27, 1963; and Malcolm W. Browne, "Fear Under Surface in Viet Nam Capital," *Green Bay Press-Gazette*, September 7, 1963.

25.   Browne, *Muddy Boots and Red Socks*, 152; Sheehan, *A Bright Shining Lie*, 359–60; W. D. Friedenberg, "In Viet Nam: U.S. Vs. One Family," *Memphis Press-Scimitar*, August 31, 1963.

26.   John Michael Dunn, interview by Ted Gittinger, pp. 9–10; Flott, interview with Gillette, 14.

27.   Mecklin, *Mission in Torment*, 224; Nichter, *The Last Brahmin*, 226.

28.   Sheehan, *A Bright Shining Lie*, 361; *Vietnam: A Television History*, "Interview with David Halberstam"; Halberstam, *The Making of a Quagmire*, 155; Browne, *The New Face of War*, x.

29.   Browne, *Muddy Boots and Red Socks*, 153–54; David Halberstam, interview by Ted Gittinger, p. 38; Karnow, *Vietnam: A History*, 305.

30.   Roger Hilsman, interview by Dennis J. O'Brien, pp. 30, 32. Hilsman later said he would revise his estimate to a "20 percent chance that Diem will pull up his socks, there's a 20 percent chance there'll be a coup, and there's a 60 percent chance that nothing will happen at all." See Hilsman interview, 31.

31.   Browne, *Muddy Boots and Red Socks*, 153; Malcolm W. Browne, "U.S. Using Economic Lever to Get Changes," *Spokane Spokesman-Review*, October 18, 1963.

32.   Malcolm W. Browne, "Viet 'Victory' May Have Cost Life of Town," *Tampa Times*, September 13, 1963.

33.   Ibid.

34.   David Halberstam, "Vietnamese Reds Gain in Key Area," *New York Times*, August 15, 1963.

35.   Sheehan, *A Bright Shining Lie*, 346; Reeves, *President Kennedy*, 587, 636–37; Wyatt, *Paper Soldiers*, 246–47; Halberstam, *Making of a Quagmire*, 168–69; Stacks, *Scotty*, 226; Prochnau, "The Upside of Anger," 48.

36.   Browne, *Muddy Boots and Red Socks*, 154–55; Sheehan, *A Bright Shining Lie*, 347.

37.   Higgins, *Our Vietnam Nightmare*, 122–23, 128; Joseph Alsop, "The 'Noble' Crusaders," *San Francisco Examiner*, September 23, 1963; Sheehan, *A Bright Shining Lie*, 348. See also Wyatt, *Paper Soldiers*, 120–21.

38.   Browne, *Muddy Boots and Red Socks*, 182–83; Prochnau, *Once Upon a Distant War*, 417.

39.   Browne, *Muddy Boots and Red Socks*, 182–84. At their dinner, Browne was surprised to learn that Higgins, who had spent many years in Asia, could not use chopsticks. "Since the restaurant had no Western tableware, she resorted to picking up her noodles with her fingers, to the evident surprise and embarrassed snickering of the other diners," Browne noted. Ibid., 183–84. Higgins died on January 3, 1966, at the age of forty-five from complications from a tropical parasite she had picked up during her travels in South Vietnam, Pakistan, and India. See "Marguerite Higgins Dies at 45; Reporter Won '51 Pulitzer Prize," *New York Times*, January 4, 1966.

40.   "Foreign Correspondents," 62; Browne, *Muddy Boots and Red Socks*, 93–94; Wyatt, *Paper Soldiers*, 121–22.

41.   Prochnau, *Once Upon a Distant War*, 408–10; Browne, *Muddy Boots and Red Socks*, 94, 189.

42.   "The Saigon Story," 55; "Returning Editor Praises U.S. Scribes in Viet Nam," *Battle Creek* (MI) *Enquirer*, October 12, 1963.

43.   Browne, *Muddy Boots and Red Socks*, 179–80; Prochnau, *Once Upon a Distant War*, 452–53, 456; Halberstam, *The Making of a Quagmire*, 185. Gallagher remembered that some conservative publishers he expected to cause trouble surprised him with their attitudes. When Eugene C. Pulliam, who owned newspapers in Indiana and Arizona, joined the AP board, Gallagher thought he might be a problem because of his right-wing views. "We never had a bit of trouble," Gallagher said. "Sometimes somebody would complain to him and we would tell him what the situation was and he'd say, 'Is it true?' And I said, 'Yes.' And he would say, 'Tell them to go to hell.' And he always had that attitude." See Berryhill, "An Oral History of Wes Gallagher," 269.

44.   Prochnau, *Once Upon a Distant War*, 465; Arnett, *Live from the Battlefield*, 120; Mecklin, *Mission in Torment*, 242–43, 245–46.

45.   Browne, *Muddy Boots and Red Socks*, 154; Faas, interview by Valerie Komor, 36.

46.   Keyes Beech, "Why U.S. Didn't Oust Diem," *Philadelphia Inquirer*, October 30, 1963.

47.   Nichter, *The Last Brahmin*, 240–42; Arnett, *Live from the Battlefield*, 121.

Chapter 8

1.   Malcolm W. Browne, November 7, 1963, dispatch to AP Saigon Bureau; Arnett, *Live from the Battlefield*, 121.

2.   Edwin Q. White, November 1, 1963, dispatch, and Browne, November 7, 1963, dispatch, AP Saigon Bureau.

3.   Browne, November 7, 1963, dispatch, AP Saigon Bureau; Browne, interview by Herman, 57–58. Newsmen had a hard time attempting to determine which South Vietnamese units were loyal to the Diem government and which ones had joined the anti-Diem forces. "It was quite a difficult job," David Halberstam observed, "because both sides wore the same uniform." See Halberstam, *The Making of a Quagmire*, 190.

4.   Browne, interview by Herman, 55; Karnow, "The Fall of the House of Ngo

Dinh," 76; Malcolm W. Browne, "Report Sun to Rotate Draws Saigon Crowds," *Shreveport Times*, October 29, 1963; Arnett, *Live from the Battlefield*, 120; Prochnau, *Once Upon a Distant War*, 411.

5. Halberstam, *Making of a Quagmire*, 180; Dunn, interview by Ted Gittinger, 22.

6. Karnow, *Vietnam: A History*, 307–8; Karnow, "The Fall of the House of Ngo Dinh," 75; Halberstam, *Making of a Quagmire*, 178; Shaplen, *The Lost Revolution*, 189; Nichter, *The Last Brahmin*, 224. See also Hastings, *Vietnam: An Epic Tragedy*, 171–72; Karnow, "Lost Chance in Vietnam," 18.

7. Kattenburg, *The Vietnam Trauma in American Foreign Policy, 1945–75*, 119–20; *Vietnam: A Television History*, interview with Paul M. Kattenburg. Kattenburg continued to dissent from official US policy regarding the country's involvement in South Vietnam but was eventually removed from direct involvement in planning for the region. He retired from the foreign service in 1972 at the age of fifty. See also Halberstam, *The Best and the Brightest*, 370–71.

8. Mendenhall, interview by Horace Torbert, p. 27.

9. Rust, *Kennedy in Vietnam*, 134–35; Jacobs, *Cold War Mandarin*, 136; Phillips, interview by Charles Stuart Kennedy, p. 28.

10. Jacobs, *Cold War Mandarin*, 167; Reeves, *President Kennedy*, 609, 615; Herring, *America's Longest War*, 102; Higgins, *Our Vietnam Nightmare*, 208. See also Kinnard, *The Certain Trumpet*, 125–26; Clarke, *JFK's Last Hundred Days*, 212–13.

11. Karnow, "The Fall of the House of Ngo Dinh," 77; Browne, November 6, 1963, dispatch to Tokyo, AP Saigon Bureau.

12. Jacobs, *Cold War Mandarin*, 174–76; Karnow, "The Fall of the House of Ngo Dinh," 78; Browne, November 4, 1963, dispatch, AP Saigon Bureau.

13. Browne, November 4, 1963, dispatch, AP Saigon Bureau.

14. Rust, *Kennedy in Vietnam*, 168–69.

15. Flott, interview by Michael L. Gillette, pp. 42–45; Moyar, *Triumph Forsaken*, 269–70.

16. Nichter, *The Last Brahmin*, 251, 245–46; Reeves, *President Kennedy*, 647.

17. Arnett, *Live from the Battlefield*, 121–22; Browne, November 7, 1963, dispatch, AP Saigon Bureau.

18. Arnett, *Live from the Battlefield*, 122–23; Browne, November 2, 1963, dispatch, AP Saigon Bureau; Browne, interview by Herman, p. 58.

19. Faas, interview by Valerie Komor, pp. 36–37, AP Corporate Archives; Prochnau, *Once Upon a Distant War*, 474–75.

20. Browne, November 4, 1963, dispatch, and White, November 2, 1963, dispatch, AP Saigon Bureau. See also Malcolm W. Browne, "Accounts Still Differ on Diem, Nhu Death," *Eugene* (OR) *Register-Guard*, November 5, 1963.

21. Mecklin, *Mission in Torment*, 268, 269–70.

22. Faas, interview by Komor, pp. 37–38; Peter Arnett, November 7, 1963, dispatch, AP Saigon Bureau; Hilsman, *To Move a Nation*, 521.

23. Halberstam, *Making of a Quagmire*, 191; David Halberstam, "Suicides Doubted: Deposed Chiefs Fled, Then Were Seized," *New York Times*, November 3, 1963; Browne,

November 7, 1963, dispatch, AP Saigon Bureau. See also Karnow, "The Fall of the House of Ngo Dinh," 79.

24. Mecklin, *Mission in Torment*, 271–72.

25. Prochnau, *Once Upon a Distant War*, 476–77.

26. Browne, November 4, 1963, dispatch, AP Saigon Bureau; Fox Butterfield, "Man Who Sheltered Diem Recounts '63 Episode," *New York Times*, November 4, 1971.

27. Browne, November 7, 1963, dispatch, AP Saigon Bureau; Jones, *Death of a Generation*, 429; Karnow, *Vietnam: A History*, 325–26.

28. Dallek, *Camelot's Court*, 417–18; Taylor, *Swords and Plowshares*, 301; Higgens, *Our Vietnam Nightmare*, 225.

29. Malcolm W. Browne, "Secret Police Torture Typist," *Corsicana* (TX) *Daily Sun*, November 8, 1963; Arnett, *Live from the Battlefield*, 126. For other accounts about the torture of Diem's political opponents, see Karnow, "The Fall of the House of Ngo Dinh," 79.

30. Browne, "Secret Police Torture Typist."

31. Ibid.

32. Jones, *Death of a Generation*, 444; "Confusing Picture," *Greenwood Index-Journal*, September 9, 1964.

33. Malcolm W. Browne, "GI's Phone Time Carries AP Story," *Editor & Publisher*, September 19, 1964, p. 13; Victor Heckler to William B. Dickinson, October 8, 1964, Browne Papers.

34. Browne, "GI's Phone Time Carries AP Story."

35. Browne, "GI's Phone Time Carries AP Story"; Heckler to Dickinson, October 8, 1964, Browne Papers.

36. Malcolm W. Browne to Ben Bassett, September 15, 1964, Browne Papers.

37. Wes Gallagher to Malcolm Browne, September 23, 1964, Browne Papers; Wes Gallagher obituary, Associated Press News, October 13, 1997, https://apnews.com/article/482f64e9ac5e6b7ddca337b59a1e32c1.

38. Browne, *Muddy Boots and Red Socks*, 180–81.

39. Arnett, *Live from the Battlefield*, 132–33; Peter Arnett and Horst Faas, "Anti-Red War of Viet Nam in New Phase of Violence," *Shreveport Times*, March 22, 1964.

40. Malcolm W. Browne, "Terror Joining War in Land of Viet Nam," *Centralia* (WA) *Daily Chronicle*, October 31, 1964.

41. "AP Chief Cites Viet Dangers," *Macon Telegraph*, May 11, 1964; Berryhill, "An Oral History of Wes Gallagher," 210, 221.

42. Berryhill, "An Oral History of Wes Gallagher," 224–25. See also Arnett, *Live from the Battlefield*, 170.

43. "'Burning Monk' Photo World Press Winner," *Editor & Publisher*, December 21, 1963; 1964 Pulitzer Prizes, https://www.pulitzer.org/winners/malcolm-w-browne-and-david-halberstam; "Two Reporters Tell of Their Pulitzers," *Arizona Daily Star*, May 5, 1964; Associated Press Pulitzer Prize dispatch, May 4, 1964, Browne Papers. While Mecklin suspected there was a "defensive factor" among journalism awards committees to "counter attacks on the correspondents," he did note that the prizes the

newsmen based in South Vietnam received for their work were "richly deserved" due to their "personal courage, doggedness and professional sense of duty." Mecklin also regretted that the UPI's Neil Sheehan had been ignored by the Pulitzer committee, believing that his "energy, ingenuity and personal integrity were outstanding." See Mecklin, *Mission in Torment*, 121–22.

44. Malcolm W. Browne to Wes Gallagher, June 21, 1965, Browne Papers; Browne, *Muddy Boots and Red Socks*, 213–14.

45. Malcolm W. Browne to Jesse Zousmer, June 13, 1965, Browne Papers; Browne, *Muddy Boots and Red Socks*, 214–15.

46. Browne to Gallagher, June 21, 1965, Browne Papers; Browne, *Muddy Boots and Red Socks*, 215; Arnett, *Live from the Battlefield*, 183. Browne recommended to Gallagher that to fill his post as bureau chief his first choice would be Edwin Q. White, someone he described as "one of the unsung heroes of this shop. Ed works 15 hours a day daily, he has a fine insight into the angles of this story, he is liked and respected by all members of the staff, and has mastered the art of infighting with the officials without really alienating them," Browne wrote. Gallagher agreed with Browne's assessment, and White remained in the job until the fall of Saigon in 1975. See Browne to Gallagher, June 21, 1965, Browne Papers.

47. Wes Gallagher to Malcolm W. Browne, June 29, 1965, Browne Papers.

48. Don Ridings, "Perk Up . . . Batman is Coming," *Charlotte Observer*, December 19, 1965; Browne, *Muddy Boots and Red Socks*, 213. See also Lucile Parish, "Malcolm Browne Joins ABC's Saigon Bureau," *Jackson (TN) Sun*, July 20, 1965.

Chapter 9

1. Safer, *Flashbacks*, 88–89; Wyatt, *Paper Soldiers*, 144–45; Morley Safer interview in Ferrari, comp., *Reporting America at War*, 138–39. Safer later learned from a fellow reporter that Cam Ne had been destroyed on the orders of a South Vietnamese province official upset by villagers' refusal to pay their taxes. See Halberstam, *The Powers That Be*, 488.

2. Ferrari, comp., *Reporting America at War*, 140; Halberstam, *The Powers That Be*, 490; Burning of Cam Ne, South Vietnam, August 4, 1965, CBS Evening News, YouTube, https://www.youtube.com/watch?v=Mxo-8p2zdQI; and Peter Brush, "What Really Happened at Cam Ne," History News Network, https://www.historynet.com/what-really-happened-at-cam-ne. Safer's cameraman, Ha Thuc Can, a South Vietnamese fluent in French and English, bravely stopped a marine officer from ordering one of his men to use a flamethrower to burn a hut from which voices could be heard. Can's action saved the lives of an old man, two children, and a young woman with a baby. See Safer, *Flashbacks*, 90–91; and Halberstam, *The Powers That Be*, 488.

3. Browne, *Muddy Boots and Red Socks*, 214; Browne, interview by Herman, p. 61.

4. Herring, *America's Longest War*, 128; Browne, *The New Face of War*, 88–90.

5. Safer, "Television Covers the War," 91–93. See also Hammond, *Reporting in Vietnam*, 57.

6.   Safer, "Television Covers the War," 94; Brown, *Muddy Boots and Red Socks*, 96.

7.   Browne, *Muddy Boots and Red Socks*, 215–16; Browne, interview by Herman, p. 62; Jesse Zousmer to Malcolm Browne, August 25, 1965, Browne Papers.

8.   Malcolm W. Brown to Sydney E. Byrnes, September 27, 1965, Browne Papers; Browne, interview by Herman, p. 63; Browne, *Muddy Boots and Red Socks*, 216, 218. For the Saigon black market and the items it provided for US troops, see Browne, *The New Face of War*, 111.

9.   Browne, *The New Face of War*, 119–20.

10.   Ibid., 120.

11.   Ibid., 121.

12.   Ibid., 122–23.

13.   Ibid., 123–24.

14.   Ibid., 125.

15.   Ibid., 125–26.

16.   Ibid., 126–28.

17.   Browne, *Muddy Boots and Red Socks*, 217; Browne, interview by Herman, pp. 65–66.

18.   Browne, *Muddy Boots and Red Socks*, 163, 218–19.

19.   Malcolm W. Browne to Elmer Lower, February 1, 1966, Browne Papers.

20.   Ibid.

21.   Malcolm W. Browne to Colleen Reubelt, July 1, 1967, Browne Papers.

22.   Browne, *Muddy Boots and Red Socks*, 220–21; Malcolm W. Browne to Miss Ehlers, March 29, 1966, Browne Papers.

23.   Malcolm W. Browne to Erika, February 15, 1966; Malcolm W. Browne to Pat, March 14, 1966; Malcolm W. Browne to Henry Cabot Lodge, July 27, 1964, Browne Papers. See also Browne, *The New Face of War*, xii, 274–75.

24.   John Hughes, "Two Reports from the Front," *Christian Science Monitor*, May 27, 1965; Richard Tregaskis, "One Man's View of the Terrible War," *Chicago Tribune*, May 16, 1965.

25.   Geoffrey C. Ryan to Malcolm W. Browne, February 10, 1965, Malcolm Browne to Howard Cohn, July 19, 1965, and Howard Cohn to Malcolm Browne, July 28, 1965, Browne Papers.

26.   Cohn to Browne, July 28, 1965, Browne Papers; Browne, *Muddy Boots and Red Socks*, 221–22.

27.   Browne, *Muddy Boots and Red Socks*, 222; Howard Cohn to Malcolm W. Browne, June 10, 1966, Browne Papers. See also Malcolm Browne to Howard Cohn, March 10, 1966, Browne Papers.

28.   Malcolm W. Browne to Howard Cohn, July 3, 1966, Browne Papers.

29.   Jonathan Randal, "We're Ready to Discuss Peace: Rusk," *Salt Lake Tribune*, May 25, 1966; Malcolm W. Browne to Wes Gallagher, May 24, 1966, Browne Papers; Browne, *Muddy Boots and Red Socks*, 224; and L. Browne, *Bend the Willow*, 136–37.

30.   Malcolm W. Browne to Rolland H. Bushner, February 26, 1969, Browne Papers.

31.   Malcolm W. Browne to Ben, February 6, 1967, Browne Papers; Browne, *Muddy Boots and Red Socks*, 224–25.

32. Malcolm W. Browne to Peter Arnett, November 20, 1966, Browne Papers.

33. Browne, *Muddy Boots and Red Socks*, 226, 227, 228.

34. Marshall, interview number 11 by Dale L. Walker, p. 7; S. L. A. Marshall, "Press Failure in Vietnam," *New Leader*, October 10, 1966, 4–5. See also "Keep Our Eyes on War Score Card," *Battle Creek Enquirer*, October 21, 1966.

35. Malcolm W. Browne, For *The New Leader*, Browne Papers. The tension between Marshall and Browne became so great that Marshall refused to ride in the same vehicle with the newsman after an April 8, 1967, Winds of Change seminar at Michigan State University. "At a party later he [Marshall] spilled a drink over me as he walked past, and that was the last I saw of him," Browne noted in a letter to Peter Arnett. Browne added that he had gotten along much better with Sylvester, "who has slightly mellowed since leaving public office." See Norris Ingells, "Writer Says Viet Stories Quality Good," *Lansing* (MI) *State Journal*, April 9, 1967; and Malcolm W. Browne to Peter Arnett, April 22, 1967, Browne Papers.

36. Malcolm W. Browne to Seymour Topping, April 15, 1967, and Wes Gallagher to Malcolm W. Browne, May 5, 1967, Browne Papers; Browne, *Muddy Boots and Red Socks*, 230. Browne wrote Gallagher apologizing for his decision to join the *Times* over the AP. "I hope, Wes, that you won't feel I'm an ungrateful bastard. You and the AP have given me most of the things I value most, and my basic allegiance is never likely to change," wrote Browne. See Malcolm W. Browne to Wes Gallagher, May 19, 1967, Browne Papers.

37. Browne, *Muddy Boots and Red Socks*, 264–65.

38. "Chile Bars Times Reporter, Charging Hostile Articles," *New York Times*, September 3, 1970; Malcolm W. Browne to *New York Times* Foreign Desk, September 2, 1970; Malcolm W. Browne to James L. Greenfield, September 4, 1970, Browne Papers; Browne, *Muddy Boots and Red Socks*, 260. See also James L. Greenfield to Honorable Clodomiro Alymedya Medina, December 7, 1970, Browne Papers.

39. Browne, *Muddy Boots and Red Socks*, 325, 343; Malcolm W. Browne, "Reporter's Notebook: Tenderness, Hatred and Grief Marks Saigon's Last Days," *New York Times*, May 6, 1975.

Chapter 10

1. Browne, *Muddy Boots and Red Socks*, 342; Browne to Mary Bray, May 25, 1975, Browne Papers.

2. Haulman, "Vietnam Evacuation: Operation Frequent Wind," 83–84; Malcolm W. Browne, "Vietnam Refugees Stream From Highlands To Coast," *New York Times*, March 19, 1975; Herring, *America's Longest War*, 264–65.

3. Malcolm Browne, "Saigon Reported Abandoning Two-Thirds of South Vietnam," *New York Times*, March 20, 1975; Malcolm W. Browne, "Greatest Agony for Vietnam Families: Deciding Who Flees and Who Stays," *New York Times*, April 13, 1975; Greenway, *Foreign Correspondent*, 87–88; Malcolm W. Browne to John and Diana, May 25, 1975, Browne Papers.

4. Farrell, *Richard Nixon*, 490; Lawrence, *The Vietnam War*, 154–55.

5. Author interview with Craig Whitney, November 19, 2021; Browne, *Muddy Boots and Red Socks*, 196–97.

6. Malcolm W. Browne, "Saigon Officers' Hostility to Foreign Newsmen at Peak," *New York Times*, July 13, 1972; Browne, *Muddy Boots and Red Socks*, 198–99. After his encounter with the artilleryman, Shimkin returned to the Quang Tri area, only to be killed after accidentally walking into enemy lines. Chad Huntley, a United Press International photographer who was with Shimkin, said he tried to let the North Vietnamese know he was a newsman. The last time Huntley saw the reporter "he was standing straight up with his arms stretched out with a grenade lying about two feet from his feet. He looked down once, looked back up and kept trying to explain. An explosion occurred, he startled to crumple and an AK rifle opened up on me," Huntley reported. See "American Correspondent is Wounded in Vietnam," *Spokane Spokesman-Review*, July 15, 1972.

7. Browne, "Saigon Officers' Hostility to Foreign Newsmen at Peak."

8. Malcolm W. Browne, "Fire Base 42 the Morning After," May 7, 1972, and "Highland Defenders Dig in by Day, Await Death by Night," May 9, 1972, *New York Times*.

9. Malcolm W. Browne, "Thousands Watch 67 Prisoners Depart," *New York Times*, March 30, 1973; Browne, *Muddy Boots and Red Socks*, 201. Weeks after almost being denied entry to South Vietnam, Browne said the same Information Ministry official who had tried to keep him out of the country came to the *Times*'s office "asking for forgiveness and help in getting out of Viet Nam," Browne recalled. "I may have made a wry face, but I did as he asked." See Browne, *Muddy Boots and Red Socks*, 326.

10. Malcolm W. Browne, "Hanoi's People Still Curious and Friendly," *New York Times*, March 31, 1973; L. Browne, *Bend the Willow*, 153–54; Browne, interview by Thomas D. Herman, p. 72.

11. Browne, *Muddy Boots and Red Socks*, 203–4.

12. "Saigon Police Kill Newsman," *Anderson (SC) Independent*, March 15, 1975; Browne, *Muddy Boots and Red Socks*, 325, 334; Browne, interview by Herman, p. 73; Wyatt, *Paper Soldiers*, 213.

13. Fox Butterfield, "How South Vietnam Died—By the Stab in the Front," *New York Times*, May 25, 1975; Malcolm W. Browne, "Saigon Reported Ready to Give Up 10 Provinces," *New York Times*, March 20, 1975; Browne, *Muddy Boots and Red Socks*, 326–27; Butterfield, interview with author. After Vietnam, Markham, who had been with the *Times* since 1971, served as the newspaper's Paris bureau chief. Before taking a position as *Times* deputy foreign editor, Markham killed himself in his Paris home. See Eric Pace, "James M. Markham Is Dead at 46," *New York Times*, August 10, 1989.

14. Browne, interview by Herman, pp. 74–75; Browne, *Muddy Boots and Red Socks*, 327–28; Malcolm W. Browne, "Hue Lost, Da Nang May Go," March 26, 1975, "A Refugee Barge Yields 50 Dead at Vietnam Pier," April 7, 1975, and "Saigon's Finale," October 13, 1999, *New York Times*.

15. Browne, "A Refugee Barge Yields 50 Dead at Vietnam Pier."

16. Browne, "A Reporter Looks Back: The CIA and the Fall of Viet Nam," 18–19; Browne, *Muddy Boots and Red Socks*, 338.

17. Browne, *Muddy Boots and Red Socks*, 329–30; "Daly: He Has His Own Way of Cutting Red Tape," *Boston Globe*, April 3, 1975; Malcolm W. Browne, "Orphans Called U.S. 'Souvenirs' By Bitter S. Viets Left Behind," *Salem (OR) Statesman-Journal*, April 5, 1975.

18. Browne, *Muddy Boots and Red Socks*, 331; Malcolm W. Browne, "Greatest Agony for Vietnam Families: Decided Who Flees and Who Stays," *New York Times*, April 13, 1975.

19. Browne, *Muddy Boots and Red Socks*, 336; Browne, interview with Herman, pp. 77–78; Greenway, *Foreign Correspondent*, 90–91.

20. Malcolm W. Browne, "U.S., Viet Relations a Mix of Tenderness, Hatred, Grief," *Lowell (MA) Sun*, May 6, 1975; Lamb, "Malcolm Browne."

21. Browne, *Muddy Boots and Red Socks*, 337–38.

22. Browne, "A Reporter Looks Back"; Browne, *Muddy Boots and Red Socks*, 334.

23. Willenson, ed., *The Bad War*, 313–14.

24. Willenson, ed., *The Bad War*, 314; Snepp, *Decent Interval*, 380–81; Fox Butterfield, "Reporter's Notebook: Six Days In the Evacuation From Saigon," *New York Times*, May 5, 1975; Browne to John and Diana, May 25, 1975, Browne Papers.

25. Browne, *Muddy Boots and Red Socks*, 335, 340; Malcolm W. Browne to John and Diana, May 25, 1975, Browne Papers.

26. Butterfield, "Reporter's Notebook: Six Days in the Evacuation of Saigon"; Butterfield, interview with author.

27. Browne, *Muddy Boots and Red Socks*, 342; "Handful of Newsmen Staying in Saigon," *Tampa Tribune*, April 30, 1975; Butterfield, interview with author; and Browne, "U.S., Viet Relations a Mix of Tenderness, Hatred, Grief." Those journalists who decided to stay behind in Saigon included members of the Associated Press bureau, including bureau chief George Esper and reporters Peter Arnett and Matt Franjola. "I was here at the beginning, and I think it's worth the risk to be here at the end," said Arnett. See Arnett, *Saigon Has Fallen*, 5–6.

28. Malcolm W. Browne to Jerry Stringer, June 30, 1975, Browne Papers; Butterfield, "Reporter's Notebook: Six Days in the Evacuation From Saigon"; and Butterfield, interview with author.

29. Butterfield, "Reporter's Notebook: Six Days in the Evacuation From Saigon"; and Butterfield, interview with author.

30. Browne, interview with Herman, 82; Butterfield, interview with author; Malcolm W. Browne to Vera Jean Graeter, May 24, 1975, Browne Papers; Browne, *Muddy Boots and Red Socks*, 342; William Yardley, "Thomas Polgar, C.I.A. Officer, Dies at 91," *New York Times*, April 7, 2014. See also Weiner, *Legacy of Ashes*, 343.

31. Butterfield, "Reporter's Notebook: Six Days in the Evacuation From Saigon."

32. Herman, interview with Browne, 82; Fox Butterfield, "Saigon Copters Found a Haven at Sea," *New York Times*, May 3, 1975; Browne, *Muddy Boots and Red Socks*, 342–43.

33. Brown to John and Diana, May 25, 1975, Browne Papers; Butterfield, "Reporter's Notebook: Six Days In the Evacuation From Saigon."

34.   Malcolm W. Browne, "Vietnam: Memorabilia of a War Best Forgotten," *New York Times*, April 24, 1994; Arnett, *Saigon Has Fallen*, 13; Browne, *Muddy Boots and Red Socks*, 343.

35.   Malcom W. Browne, "How Did It Happen? Some Replies," *New York Times*, April 24, 1975.

36.   Ibid.

37.   Browne, interview by Herman, pp. 86–87.

Epilogue

1.   Malcolm W. Browne, "Jitters" article draft, January 21, 1991, Browne Papers.

2.   Statement by Malcolm W. Browne before the Senate Governmental Affairs Committee, February 20, 1991, p. 1, in Browne Papers (hereafter cited as Browne statement); Browne, *Muddy Boots and Red Socks*, 346; Malcolm W. Browne, "The Military vs. the Press," *New York Times*, March 3, 1991.

3.   Malcolm W. Browne, "A Perpetual Student Charts a Course Through a Universe of Discoveries," *New York Times*, February 27, 2000.

4.   Malcolm W. Browne to Henry A. Grunwald, August 15, 1981, Browne Papers.

5.   Malcolm W. Browne to Henry A. Grunwald, March 26, 1984, Browne Papers; Eugene Garfield, "Introducing *Discover*, Time Inc.'s Monthly Newsmagazine of Science," *Essays of an Information Scientist* 5 (March 16, 1981): 52–56; L. Browne, *Bend the Willow*, 166.

6.   Malcolm W. Browne to August Howard, September 7, 1981, and Malcolm W. Browne to Leon Jaroff, September 16, 1981, Browne Papers.

7.   L. Browne, *Bend the Willow*, 166, 168; Browne to Howard, September 7, 1981, Browne Papers.

8.   Browne to Jaroff, September 16, 1981; Browne to Grunwald, March 26, 1984, Browne Papers; L. Browne, *Bend the Willow*, 167; Browne, *Muddy Boots and Red Socks*, 345.

9.   Browne, "The Military vs. the Press"; Malcolm W. Browne Press dispatch, January 20, 1991, Browne Papers; Sweeney, *The Military and the Press*, 165. See also Joint Information Bureau Dhahran Welcome Brief, January 17, 1991, Browne Papers.

10.   Browne, "The Military vs. the Press."

11.   Browne, "The Military vs. the Press"; Browne Press dispatch.

12.   Malcolm W. Browne to Mort Rosenblum, September 9, 1992, Browne Papers.

13.   Malcolm W. Browne, From Pool 9, Stealth dispatch, January 18, 1991, Browne Papers.

14.   Browne, "The Military vs. the Press"; Browne Press dispatch.

15.   Browne statement; Browne Press dispatch.

16.   Malcolm W. Browne memo to *New York Times*, January 22, 1991, Browne Papers; Browne statement.

17.   John Glenn and Herb Kohl to Malcolm W. Browne, February 6, 1991, and W. D.

Ferguson to Malcolm W. Browne, March 1, 1991, Browne Papers; Browne, *Muddy Boots and Red Socks*, 348–49.

18.   Lamb, "Malcolm W. Browne"; Osnos, interview with author; and Peter Osnos to Malcolm W. Browne, October 5, 1992, Browne Papers.

19.   Browne, "An Explanation," *Muddy Boots and Red Socks*, ix; Lamb, "Malcolm W. Browne."

20.   Browne, *Muddy Boots and Red Socks*, xii–xv.

21.   Dan Rather, "Dispatches From the Fronts," *New York Times Book Review*, September 12, 1993; Larry Heinemann, "The Road to Saigon and On: A Reporter's Story," *New York Times*, October 13, 1993.

22.   Malcolm W. Browne, "First U.S. Trade Exhibit is Held in Hanoi," April 24, 1994, "G.I. Settles in Vietnam, at Peace With Old Foes," May 16, 1994, "Battlefields of Khe Sanh: Still One Casualty a Day," May 13, 1994, and "Vietnamese Also Extending a Search for Their M.I.A.s," May 20, 1994, *New York Times*.

23.   Malcolm W. Browne, "Where Monuments Speak of a U.S. Defeat, the Talk is of 'Peaceful Contacts,'" *New York Times*, May 10, 1994.

24.   Ibid.

25.   Malcolm W. Browne, "Security Tactics in Vietnam Still Inspire Widespread Fear," *New York Times*, May 21, 1994.

26.   Ibid.

27.   Nicola Smith, "Vietnam on His Mind, Then and Now," *West Lebanon* (NH) *Valley News*, November 7, 2009; Browne, *Muddy Boots and Red Socks*, 350; Malcolm W. Browne to Jack Renirie, November 30, 1983, Browne Papers; Malcolm W. Browne, "Antarctica: As Gorgeous and Deadly Today as Ever," April 9, 1999, and "Reflections on a Cold Place," March 25, 1990, *New York Times*; Lamb, "Malcolm W. Browne."

28.   Malcolm W. Browne, "Dateline: Antarctica," *Times Talk: News About the New York Times*, March 1992, 4; Lamb, "Malcolm W. Browne"; and Malcolm W. Browne, "Classified Ads Providing Easy Shortcut to South Pole Work," *Greenwood* (SC) *Index-Journal*, January 9, 1975.

29.   Browne, "Antarctica: As Gorgeous and Deadly Today as Ever."

30.   Malcolm W. Browne, "Picking Up Litter in Scott's Footsteps," December 24, 1989, *New York Times*; Browne, "Dateline: Antarctica," 5.

Selected Bibliography

Manuscript Collections

Associated Press Saigon Bureau Collection. Associated Press Corporate Archives, New York.

Malcolm W. Browne Papers. Associated Press Corporate Archives, New York.

Malcolm W. Browne Papers. Manuscript Division, Library of Congress, Washington, DC.

David Halberstam Collection. Howard Gotlieb Archival Research Center, Boston University, Boston.

Interviews and Oral Histories

Arnett, Peter. Interview by Valerie S. Komor. January 30, 2006. Associated Press Corporate Archives, New York.

Browne, Malcolm. Interview with Terry Gross. *Fresh Air*, September 21, 1993. https://freshairarchive.org/segments/journalist-malcolm-browne.

Browne, Malcolm. Interview by Thomas D. Herman. June 30, 2001. (Interview courtesy of Thomas D. Herman.)

Butterfield, Fox. Interview with author. July 27, and August 1, 2022.

Dunn, John Michael. Interview by Ted Gittinger. July 25, 1984. Lyndon B. Johnson Library Oral Histories, LBJ Library and Museum, Austin, TX.

Faas, Horst. Interview by Harold "Hal" Buell and Kathryn A. Scott. September 29, 1997. Associated Press Corporate Archives, New York.

Faas, Horst. Interview by Valerie Komor. May 21, 2007. Associated Press Corporate Archives, New York.

Flott, Frederick W. Interview by Michael L. Gillette. July 22, 1984. Lyndon B. Johnson Library Oral Histories, LBJ Library and Museum, Austin, TX.

Halberstam, David. Interview by Ted Gittinger. November 1, 1982. Lyndon B. Johnson Library Oral Histories, LBJ Presidential Library, Austin, TX.

Hilsman, Roger. Interview by Dennis J. O'Brien. August 14, 1970. John F. Kennedy Library Oral History Program, JFK Library and Museum, Boston.

Lodge, Henry Cabot. Interview by Charles Bartlett. August 4, 1965. John F. Kennedy Library Oral History Program, JFK Library, Boston.

Manning, Robert J. Interview by Joseph E. O'Connor June 19, 1967. John F. Kennedy Library Oral History Program. JFK Library and Museum, Boston.

Marshall, S. L. A. Interview number 11 by Dale L. Walker. May 18, 1972. Institute of Oral History, University of Texas at El Paso, TX.

Mendenhall, Joseph A. Interview by Horace Torbert. February 11, 1991. Association for Diplomatic Studies and Training Foreign Affairs Oral History Project, https://adst.org/OH%20TOCs/Medanhall,%20Joseph%20A.toc.pdf.

Nolting, Frederick. Interview by Joseph E. O'Connor. May 14, 1966. John F. Kennedy Library Oral History Program, John F. Kennedy Library, Boston.

Nolting, Frederick. Interview by Ted Gittinger. November 11, 1982. Lyndon Baines Johnson Presidential Library, Austin, TX.

Osnos, Peter. Interview with author, November 5, 2021.

Phillips, Rufus, III. Interview by Charles Stuart Kennedy. July 19, 1995. Association for Diplomatic Studies and Training Foreign Affairs Oral History Project, https://adst.org/OH%20TOCs/Phillips,%20Rufus%20C.toc.pdf.

Trueheart, William C. Interview by Ted Gittinger. March 2, 1982. Lyndon B. Johnson Library Oral Histories, LBJ Presidential Library, Austin, TX.

Whitney, Craig. Interview with author. November 19, 2021.

Television and Film

Herman, Thomas D., dir. *Dateline-Saigon*. Documentary. 2016. Northern Lights Productions.

Lamb, Brian, host. "Malcolm W. Browne: Muddy Boots and Red Socks." C-SPAN Booknotes. Aired September 26, 1993. http://booknotes.org/FullPage.aspx?SID=50825-1.

Books, Articles, and Dissertations

Appy, Christian G., ed. *Patriots: The Vietnam War Remembered from All Sides*. New York: Viking, 2003.

Arnett, Peter. *Live from the Battlefield: From Vietnam to Baghdad: 35 Years in the World's War Zones*. New York: Simon and Schuster, 1994.

———. "A Long-Range View of the Associated Press in Vietnam." *AP World* (Spring 1968): 3.

———. "1972: Reflections on Vietnam, the Press and America." *Nieman Reports*, December 15, 1999. https://niemanreports.org/articles/1972-reflections-on-vietnam-the-press-and-america.

———. *Saigon Has Fallen*. 2015; New York: Associated Press, 2018.

Aronson, James. *The Press and the Cold War*. 1970; New York: Monthly Review Press, 1990.

Associated Press. AP Explore. "The Burning Monk: A Defining Moment Photographed by AP's Malcolm Browne." https://www.ap.org/explore/the-burning-monk.

———. *Breaking News: How the Associated Press Has Covered War, Peace, and Everything Else.* New York: Princeton Architectural Press, 2007.

———. "The Unquiet American: Malcolm Browne in Saigon, 1961–65." August 6, 2013. https://www.ap.org/assets/images/about/corporate-archives/brochures/201309_malcolm-browne_brochure.pdf.

Balk, Alfred, and James Boylan, eds. *Our Troubled Press: Ten Years of the* Columbia Journalism Review. Boston: Little, Brown, 1971.

Bassett, Ben. "The AP Foreign Correspondents." *AP World* (Spring 1965): 5.

Bekey, Erika V. "Dateline: Danger—Mal Browne in Viet Nam." *Editor & Publisher*, September 15, 1962, 15, 50.

Berryhill, Susan Burchmore. "An Oral History of Wes Gallagher." Master's thesis, California State University, Northridge, May 1984.

"A Busy Sunday in 1956." *AP World* 27 (Winter 1971): 42.

Blair, Anne. *Lodge in Vietnam: A Patriot Abroad.* New Haven, CT: Yale University Press, 1995.

Bowles, Chester. *Promises to Keep: My Years in Public Life, 1941–1969.* New York: Harper and Row, 1971.

Browne, Le Lieu. *Bend the Willow: A Story of Family, Friendship and Love.* Monee, IL: Tiny Diver Press, 2018.

Browne, Malcolm W. "Blood, Ink, and Tears." *Swarthmore College Bulletin*, May 1994.

———. "The Fascinating Life of AP Men in South Viet Nam." *AP World* 19 (Summer 1964): 28.

———. *Muddy Boots and Red Socks: A Reporter's Life.* New York: Times Books, 1993.

———. "The New Face of Censorship." *True*, April 1967, 39, 91–95.

———. *The New Face of War.* Indianapolis: Bobbs-Merrill, 1965.

———. "Report from Viet Nam: Daughters of the Dragon Lady." *True*, February 1966, 41–43, 96.

———. "Report from Viet Nam: Devil Weapons of the Viet Cong." *True*, October 1966, 47, 66, 70.

———. "Report from Viet Nam: Ghosts of Christmas Past." *True*, December 1965, 39, 123–24.

———. "Report from Viet Nam: Hell in the Highlands." *True*, January 1966, 54–56, 73.

———. "Report from Viet Nam: The Last Week is the Longest." *True*, August 1966, 35, 81–82.

———. "Report from Viet Nam: Our Toughest Foe Since Rommel." *True*, June 1966, 37, 96–98.

———. "Report from Viet Nam: . . . To Fly Again Another Day." *True*, March 1966, 39, 90–91.

———. "A Reporter Looks Back: The CIA and the Fall of Viet Nam." *Washington Journalism Review* (January–February 1978): 18–19.

———. "Viet Nam Reporting: Three Years of Crisis." *Columbia Journalism Review* (Fall

1964). https://archives.cjr.org/fiftieth_anniversary/viet_nam_reporting_three_years.php?page=ala.

Buell, Hal. "Capturing the Ultimate Protest." *Vietnam*, June 2013.

Clarke, Thurston. *Honorable Exit: How a Few Brave Americans Risked All to Save Our Vietnamese Allies at the End of the War*. New York: Doubleday, 2019.

——. *JFK's Last Hundred Days: The Transformation of a Man and the Emergence of a Great President*. New York: Penguin, 2013.

Dallek, Robert. *Camelot's Court: Inside the Kennedy White House*. New York: HarperCollins, 2013.

Demery, Monique Brinson. *Finding the Dragon Lady: The Mystery of Vietnam's Madame Nhu*. New York: Public Affairs, 2013.

Farrell, John A. *Richard Nixon: The Life*. New York: Doubleday, 2017.

Faulkner, Francis D. "Bao Chi: The American News Media in Vietnam, 1960–1975." PhD diss., University of Massachusetts, February 1981.

Ferrari, Michelle, comp. "Malcolm W. Browne." In *Reporting America at War*. New York: Hyperion, 2001.

"Foreign Correspondents: The View from Saigon." *Time* (September 20, 1963): 62.

Fountain, Joe H. "Danby Eden." *Vermont Life* 8 (Summer 1954): 58–61.

Freedman, Lawrence. *Kennedy's Wars: Berlin, Cuba, Laos, and Vietnam*. New York: Oxford University Press, 2000.

Garfield, Eugene. "Introducing *Discover*, Time Inc.'s Monthly Newsmagazine of Science." *Essays of an Information Scientist* 5 (March 16, 1981): 52–56.

Gibbs, Nancy Reid. *Children of Light: Friends Seminary, 1786–1986*. New York: Friends Seminary, 1986.

Giglio, James N. *The Presidency of John F. Kennedy*. Lawrence: University Press of Kansas, 1991.

Greenway, H. D. S. *Foreign Correspondent: A Memoir*. New York: Simon and Schuster, 2014.

Halberstam, David. *The Best and the Brightest*. 1969; New York: Modern Library, 2001.

——. Foreword to *Breaking News: How the Associated Press Has Covered War, Peace, and Everything Else*, 6–17. New York: Princeton Architectural Press, 2007.

——. "Getting the Story in Vietnam." *Commentary Magazine*. https://www.commentarymagazine.com/articles/getting-the-story-in-vietnam.

——. *The Making of a Quagmire: America and Vietnam during the Kennedy Era*. 1965; Lanham, MD: Rowman and Littlefield, 2008.

——. "The Other Enemy." In *The Vietnam Experience: Raising the Stakes*. By Terence Maitland, Stephen Weiss, et al., 62. Boston: Boston Publishing, 1982.

——. *The Powers That Be*. New York: Alfred A. Knopf, 1979.

Hallin, Daniel C. *The "Uncensored War": The Media and Vietnam*. New York: Oxford University Press, 1986.

Hamill, Pete. Introduction to *Vietnam: The Real War: A Photographic History of the Associated Press*, 21–35. New York: Abrams, 2013.

Hamilton, John Maxwell. *Journalism's Roving Eye: A History of American Foreign Reporting*. Baton Rouge: Louisiana State University Press, 2009.

Hammond, William M. *Public Affairs: The Military and the Media, 1962–1968*. Washington, DC: US Army Center of Military History, 1988.

———. *Reporting in Vietnam: Media and Military at War*. Lawrence: University Press of Kansas, 1998.

Hastings, Max. *Vietnam: An Epic Tragedy, 1945–1975*. New York: HarperCollins, 2008.

Haulman, Daniel C. "Vietnam Evacuation: Operation Frequent Wind." https://media.defense.gov/2012/Aug/23/2001330098/-1/-1/0/Oper%20Frequent%20Wind.pdf.

Herring, George C. *America's Longest War: The United States and Vietnam, 1950–1975*. 1979; New York: Alfred A. Knopf, 1986.

Higgins, Marguerite. *Our Vietnam Nightmare*. New York: Harper and Row, 1965.

Hilsman, Roger. *To Move a Nation: The Politics of Foreign Policy in the Administration of John F. Kennedy*. Garden City, NY: Doubleday, 1967.

Jacobs, Seth. *Cold War Mandarin: Ngo Din Diem and the Origins of America's War in Vietnam*. Lanham, MD: Rowman and Littlefield, 2006.

Jones, Howard. *Death of a Generation: How the Assassinations of Diem and JFK Prolonged the Vietnam War*. New York: Oxford University Press, 2003.

Kalb, Deborah Susan. "The Uncontrollable Element: American Reporters in South Vietnam, 1961–1963." PhD thesis, Harvard University, March 21, 1985.

Karnow, Stanley. "The Edge of Chaos." *Saturday Evening Post*, September 28, 1963, 27–36.

———. "The Fall of the House of Ngo Dinh." *Saturday Evening Post*, December 21, 1963, 75–79.

———. "Lost Chance in Vietnam." *New Republic*, February 2, 1974, 17–19.

———. "The Newsmen's War in Vietnam." *Nieman Reports*, December 1963, 3–8.

———. "The Quandary of Henry Cabot Lodge." *Saturday Evening Post*, February 8, 1964, 70–72.

———. *Vietnam: A History*. 1983; New York: Penguin Books, 1997.

Kattenburg, Paul M. *The Vietnam Trauma in American Foreign Policy, 1945–75*. 1980; New Brunswick, NJ: Transaction, 1992.

Kinnard, Douglas. *The Certain Trumpet: Maxwell Taylor and the American Experience in Vietnam*. McLean, VA: Brassey's, 1991.

Knightley, Phillip. *The First Casualty: From the Crimea to Vietnam: The War Correspondent as Hero, Propagandist, and Myth Maker*. New York: Harcourt Brace Jovanovich, 1975.

Lawrence, Mark Atwood. *The Vietnam War: A Concise International History*. New York: Oxford University Press, 2008.

Loh, Jules. "'I'm With AP . . .' Decades of Dedication." *AP World* (Winter 1998): 6.

Manning, Robert. *The Swamp Root Chronicle: Adventures in the World Trade*. New York: W. W. Norton, 1992.

Mecklin, John. *Mission in Torment: An Intimate Account of the U.S. Role in Vietnam*. Garden City, NY: Doubleday, 1965.

Miller, Edward. *Misalliance: Ngo Dinh Diem, the United States, and the Fate of South Vietnam*. Cambridge, MA: Harvard University Press, 2013.

———. "Religious Revival and the Politics of Nation Building: Reinterpreting the 1963 'Buddhist crisis' in South Vietnam." *Modern Asian Studies*. http://journals. cambridge.org/abstract_S0026749X12000935.

Miller, William I. *Henry Cabot Lodge*. New York: James H. Heineman, 1967.

Moeller, Susan D. *Shooting War: Photography and the American Experience of Combat*. New York: Basic Books, 1989.

Morris, John G. "This We Remember." *Harper's*, September 1972. https://harpers.org/ archive/1972/09/this-we-remember.

Moyar, Mark. *Triumph Forsaken: The Vietnam War, 1954–1965*. New York: Cambridge University Press, 2006.

Nichter, Luke A. *The Last Brahmin: Henry Cabot Lodge Jr. and the Making of the Cold War*. New Haven, CT: Yale University Press, 2020.

Nolting, Frederick. *From Trust to Tragedy: The Political Memoirs of Frederick Nolting, Kennedy's Ambassador to Diem's Vietnam*. New York: Praeger, 1988.

Pardos, John. *Vietnam: The History of an Unwinnable War, 1945–1975*. Lawrence: University Press of Kansas, 2009.

Prochnau, William. *Once upon a Distant War: Reporting from Vietnam*. New York: Times Books, 1995.

———. "The Upside of Anger." *American Journalism Review* 29 (June–July 2007): 48–49.

Reeves, Richard. *President Kennedy: Profile of Power*. New York: Simon and Schuster, 1993.

Rothmyer, Karen. "The Quiet Exit of Homer Bigart." *American Journalism Review* (November 1991). https://ajrarchive.org/Article.asp?id=1543.

Rust, William J. *Kennedy in Vietnam*. New York: Charles Scribner's Sons, 1985.

Safer, Morley. *Flashbacks: On Returning to Vietnam*. New York: Random House, 1990.

———. "Television Covers the War." In *News Policies in Vietnam: Hearings before the Committee on Foreign Relations, U.S. Senate, 98th Congress, Second Session on News Policies in Vietnam, August 17 and 31, 1966*. Washington, DC: US Government Printing Office, 1966, 91–93.

"The Saigon Story." *Time* (October 11, 1963): 55

Salinger, Pierre. *With Kennedy*. Garden City, NY: Doubleday, 1966.

Salisbury, Harrison E., ed. *Vietnam Reconsidered: Lessons from a War*. New York: Harper and Row, 1984.

Schecter, Jerrold. *The New Face of Buddha*. New York: Coward-McCann, 1967.

Shaplen, Robert. *The Lost Revolution: The U.S. in Vietnam, 1946–1966*. New York: Harper and Row, 1966.

Sheehan, Neil. *A Bright Shining Lie: John Paul Vann and America in Vietnam*. New York: Random House, 1988.

Snepp, Frank. *Decent Interval: An Insider's Account of Saigon's Indecent End Told by the CIA's Chief Strategy Analyst in Vietnam*. New York: Random House, 1977.

"South Vietnam: Durable Diem." *Time*, March 9, 1962. https://content.time.com/time/ subscriber/article/0,33009,939947-1,00.html.

"South Viet Nam: The Helicopter War Runs into Trouble." *Time*, January 11, 1963.

Stacks, John F. *Scotty: James B. Reston and the Rise and Fall of American Journalism*. Boston: Little, Brown, 2003.

Sweeney, Michael S. *The Military and the Press: An Uneasy Truce*. Evanston, IL: Northwestern University Press, 2006.

Taylor, Maxwell. *Swords and Plowshares*. New York: W. W. Norton, 1972.

Thompson, Hunter S. *The Proud Highway: Saga of a Desperate Southern Gentleman, 1955–1967*. New York: Ballantine Books, 1997.

Toczek, David M. *The Battle of Ap Bac: They Did Everything But Learn From It*. Annapolis, MD: Naval Institute Press, 2001.

Tregaskis, Richard. *Vietnam Diary*. New York: Holt, Rinehart and Winston, 1963.

VanDeMark, Brian. *Road to Disaster: A New History of America's Descent into Vietnam*. New York: HarperCollins, 2018.

Vietnam: A Television History. "Interview with David Halberstam." 1979 [part 4 of 5]. GBH Archives. http://openvault.wgbh.org/catalog/V_F16F9047D2AF4D-C6B58E05E8ADC18B0A.

Vietnam: A Television History. "Interview with Paul M. Kattenburg." 1981. GBH Archives, http://openvault.wgbh.org/catalog/V_9F88F3716D8243FA8B1919DDFA6454E6.

Wade, Betsy, comp. and ed. *Forward Positions: The War Correspondence of Homer Bigart*. Fayetteville: University of Arkansas Press, 1992.

Webb, Shelia. "Radical Portrayals: Dickey Chapelle on the Front Lines." *American Periodicals* 26, no. 2 (2016): 202–3.

Weiner, Tim. *Legacy of Ashes: the History of the CIA*. New York: Doubleday, 2007.

Willenson, Kim, ed. *The Bad War: An Oral History of the Vietnam War*. New York: NAL Books, 1987.

Witty, Patrick. "Malcolm Browne: The Story Behind the Burning Monk." *Time*, August 28, 2012. https://time.com/3791176/malcolm-browne-the-story-behind-the-burning-monk.

Wyatt, Clarence R. *Paper Soldiers: The American Press and the Vietnam War*. New York: W. W. Norton, 1993.

Yablonka, Marc Phillip. *Vietnam* Bao Chi: *Warriors of Word and Film*. Philadelphia: Casemate, 2018.

Index